SELF-DEALING　GIFTS　OUTSIDE ACTIVITIES　BREACH OF TRUST　HONORARIA　CONFLICT OF INTEREST　APPEARANCE OF BIASED BEHAVIOR　TRANSPARENCY　ETHICS TRAINING　PROTECTION AGAINST CORRUPTION　INDEPENDENT JUDGMENT　REVOLVING DOOR　INSPECTOR GENERAL
DISCLOSURE
PUBLIC CONFIDENCE　SUNSHINE
SUNSHINE

THIRD EDITION

ETHICAL STANDARDS
IN THE PUBLIC SECTOR
A GUIDE FOR GOVERNMENT LAWYERS, CLIENTS, AND PUBLIC OFFICIALS

SELF-DEALING　PROTECTION AGAINST CORRUPTION　CONFLICT OF INTEREST
APPEARANCE OF BIASED BEHAVIOR　INDEPENDENT JUDGMENT　OUTSIDE ACTIVITIES
PUBLIC CONFIDENCE　HONORARIA
DISCLOSURE
BREACH OF TRUST　　GIFTS
TRANSPARENCY　INSPECTOR GENERAL　ETHICS TRAINING　REVOLVING DOOR

JENNIFER G. RODGERS and EVAN A. DAVIS, EDITORS

Cover design by Sara Wadford/ABA Design

The materials contained herein represent the opinions of the authors and/or the editors and should not be construed to be the views or opinions of the law firms or companies with whom such persons are in partnership with, associated with, or employed by, nor of the American Bar Association or the State and Local Government Law Section, unless adopted pursuant to the bylaws of the Association.

Nothing contained in this book is to be considered as the rendering of legal advice for specific cases, and readers are responsible for obtaining such advice from their own legal counsel. This book is intended for educational and informational purposes only.

© 2022 American Bar Association. All rights reserved.

No part of this publication may be reproduced, stored in a retrieval system, or transmitted in any form or by any means, electronic, mechanical, photocopying, recording, or otherwise, without the prior written permission of the publisher. For permission, complete the request form at www.americanbar.org/reprint or email ABA Publishing at copyright@americanbar.org.

Printed in the United States of America.

26 25 24 23 22   5 4 3 2 1

A catalog record for this book is available from the Library of Congress.

Discounts are available for books ordered in bulk. Special consideration is given to state bars, CLE programs, and other bar-related organizations. Inquire at Book Publishing, ABA Publishing, American Bar Association, 321 N. Clark Street, Chicago, Illinois 60654-7598.

www.shopABA.org

Summary of Contents

About the Editors	xi
About the Contributors	xiii
Preface	xxi
Jennifer G. Rodgers, Evan A. Davis	

CHAPTER 1
The Nature and Purpose of Ethical Rules for Governmental Officials 1
Evan A. Davis

CHAPTER 2
Ethics, Lawyers, and the Public Sector: A Historical Overview 9
John D. Feerick

CHAPTER 3
Transparency 35
Ann Ravel

CHAPTER 4
Sunshine in the Statehouse: Financial Disclosure Requirements for Public Officials 47
Barry Ginsberg

CHAPTER 5
Who Is the Client of the Government Lawyer? 89
Jane T. Feldman

CHAPTER 6
The Government Attorney–Client Privilege 97
Ross Garber

CHAPTER 7
Safeguarding against Government for Purchase: Restrictions on Gifts and Honoraria 115
Martha Harrell Chumbler

CHAPTER 8
**Postemployment Restrictions on Government Employees:
Closing the "Revolving Door"**   131
Michael Donaldson, Benjamin Stearns

CHAPTER 9
Considering Ethics at the Local Government Level   149
Mark Davies

CHAPTER 10
The Federal Inspectors General   195
The Honorable Mark Lee Greenblatt

CHAPTER 11
Whistleblower Law and Ethics   217
Thomas Devine, Janet Arnott

CHAPTER 12
Lobbying Ethics   275
Heather Holt

CHAPTER 13
Conflicts of Interest   299
Rose Gill

Index   *305*

Contents

About the Editors — xi

About the Contributors — xiii

Preface — xxi
Jennifer G. Rodgers, Evan A. Davis

CHAPTER 1
The Nature and Purpose of Ethical Rules for Governmental Officials — 1
Evan A. Davis

    The Purpose of Ethics Regulation Depends in Part on the Role of the Regulated Persons — 1
    The Nature of Public Service — 3
    Purposes of Government Ethics and Prime Consequences of Those Purposes — 4
        Foster Public Confidence That Government Serves the Common Good — 4
        Prevent Breaches of the Public Trust — 4
        Be a First Line of Defense against Corruption and Abuse of Power — 5
        Play a Risk Management Role for Government and Public Officials — 6
    Summary of Key Points — 7
    Notes — 7

CHAPTER 2
Ethics, Lawyers, and the Public Sector: A Historical Overview — 9
John D. Feerick

    Early History — 10
    Federal Efforts — 11
        New York City Bar Association — 11
        The Ethics in Government Act of 1978 — 13
        Campaign Finance Reform — 14
        Issues Concerning the Emolument Clauses — 15
    State Efforts at Ethics Reforms — 17
        New York State — 18
        California — 20
        Texas — 21
        North Dakota — 21
        Iowa — 22
        Virginia — 22
        Electoral College Swing States — 23
    Municipal Ethics Reforms — 23

Greater Citizenry Interest in Ethics 24
The Future of Government Ethics Legislation 25
Notes 27

CHAPTER 3
Transparency 35
Ann Ravel

Introduction 35
What Is Public Sector Transparency and Why Is It So Important? 36
Federal and State Laws Governing Transparency 36
    The Federal Government 36
    California: Public Records Act and Open Meeting Laws 39
    New York: Freedom of Information Law and Open Meetings Law 40
Ways to Improve Government Transparency 41
    Practices That Should Be Adopted by Governments Wanting
    to Facilitate Genuine Transparency 42
    Making Disclosures Proactively 42
Summary of Key Points 43
Notes 43

CHAPTER 4
Sunshine in the Statehouse: Financial Disclosure Requirements for Public Officials 47
Barry Ginsberg

The Constitutionality of Financial Disclosure Requirements 48
Financial Disclosure: A Survey of the States 50
    Outside Interests 51
    Overview of Financial Disclosure Requirements 51
    Specific Financial Disclosure Issues 52
    Other Developments 54
Summary of Key Points 56
Notes 56
Appendix A: State Legislative Disclosure Requirements 61
Appendix B: State Executive Disclosure Requirements 71
Appendix C: State Financial Disclosure Statutes 81

CHAPTER 5
Who Is the Client of the Government Lawyer? 89
Jane T. Feldman

Private Sector Practice: Allegiance to a Client 90
Government Practice: To Whom Are Legal Responsibility and Allegiance Owed? 90
Identifying Hypothetical "Public Interest" or the "Public" as Clients 93
Summary of Key Points 95
Notes 95

CHAPTER 6
The Government Attorney–Client Privilege — 97
Ross Garber

Introduction	97
The Rules of Professional Conduct and Confidential Communications	98
State Statutes Governing Attorney–Client Privilege for Government Attorneys	99
Connecticut	99
New York	99
Ohio	100
Massachusetts	100
The Federal Attorney–Client Privilege	101
The Attorney-Client Privilege for Government Lawyers and Their Public-Sector Clients	101
The Freedom of Information Act	102
The Attorney–Client Privilege in Criminal Cases	103
Second Circuit	103
Eighth Circuit	104
District of Columbia Circuit	105
Seventh Circuit	105
Implementation Concerns for Government Lawyers	106
Practical Considerations for Government Attorneys	108
Advise Client of the Uncertainty of the Privilege	108
Determine Who the Client Is	108
Take Note of the Purpose of One's Communication	109
Advise Individual Government Officials to Obtain Independent Legal Counsel for Criminal Matters	109
Summary of Key Points	109
Notes	110

CHAPTER 7
Safeguarding against Government for Purchase: Restrictions on Gifts and Honoraria — 115
Martha Harrell Chumbler

Definition of "Gift"	116
Exceptions Based on the Nature of the Gift or Circumstances in Which Given	117
Gift Restrictions and Exceptions Based on the Identity of the Recipient	118
Restrictions and Exceptions Based on the Source of the Gift	119
Honoraria	122
Summary of Key Points	125
Notes	125

CHAPTER 8
Postemployment Restrictions on Government Employees: Closing the "Revolving Door" — 131
Michael Donaldson, Benjamin Stearns

The Ban on Appearances before a Former Employee's Agency (the "Agency Ban")	132
What Services Are Prohibited?	133
What Is Considered a Former Employee's Agency?	134

Applicability to Partners and Associates of Former Employees ... 136
Applicability of the Ban to Representation of, or Further Employment with, the Government ... 137
The Ban on Involvement in Matters Handled While in Government (the "Matter Ban") ... 138
How Involved Must the Employee Have Been in the Matter? ... 139
What Postemployment Activities Are Covered? ... 139
How Is "Matter" Defined? ... 140
Restricting the Use of Confidential Information ... 141
Using One's Public Position to Obtain Private Employment ... 142
The Limitations Imposed by ABA Model Rules of Professional Conduct ... 143
Conclusion ... 143
Notes ... 144

CHAPTER 9
Considering Ethics at the Local Government Level ... 149
Mark Davies

Introduction ... 149
Sources of Local Government Ethics Laws ... 151
    State Constitutions ... 152
    State Statutes ... 152
    Local Laws Other Than Ethics Laws ... 153
    Agency Regulations ... 153
    Common Law ... 153
A Note on Process ... 153
First Pillar: Code of Ethics ... 154
    Generally ... 154
    Prohibited Interests ... 156
    Use of Public Office for Private Gain ... 156
    Moonlighting ... 158
    Appearances, Representation, and Contingent Compensation ... 158
    Gifts ... 159
    Compensation by Private Entities for Municipal Work ... 160
    Confidential Information ... 160
    Political Activities ... 161
    Superior–Subordinate Relationships ... 162
    Pre-Employment Restrictions ... 162
    Payment for a Municipal Position ... 162
    Postemployment (Revolving Door) ... 163
    Inducement of Violations ... 164
    Avoidance of Conflicts of Interest ... 164
    Whistleblower Protection ... 164
Restrictions on Private Citizens and Companies ... 165
    Generally ... 165
    Inducement of Ethics Violations and Influencing Officials ... 165
    Appearances by Officials' Outside Employers ... 166
Second Pillar: Disclosure ... 166
    Transactional Disclosure ... 167
    Applicant Disclosure ... 167
    Annual Disclosure ... 168

Third Pillar: Administration	169
Generally	169
Enforcement	171
Stages of the Enforcement Process	171
Penalties	173
Confidentiality	174
Summary of Key Points	175
Notes	175
Appendix 9A: Municipal Ethics Boards and Enforcement Authority	183
Appendix 9B: Web Sites of Municipal Ethics Laws and Boards	191

CHAPTER 10
The Federal Inspectors General   195
The Honorable Mark Lee Greenblatt

Introduction	195
Overview of the Federal IG Community: Legal Framework and Structure	196
Ensuring OIG Independence: Dual-Reporting and Other Mechanisms	198
OIG Responsibilities and Related Powers	200
The Inspector General Empowerment Act of 2016 and Other Proposals for Change	207
Summary of Key Points	209
Notes	209

CHAPTER 11
Whistleblower Law and Ethics   217
Thomas Devine, Janet Arnott

The Controversial Nature of Whistleblowing	218
The At-Will Employment Doctrine	220
Statutory Protection for Public-Sector Whistleblowers—Why Is There a Need for Whistleblower Protection in the Public Sector?	222
Federal Statutory Protections for Whistleblowers	223
Federal Whistleblower and Anti-Retaliation Provisions outside the Merit System	228
Statutory Whistleblower Protection at the State Level	232
Generally	232
Protected Conduct	233
Communications	234
Retaliation and Remedies	235
Financial Incentives for Whistleblowing	237
Common-Law Protections for Whistleblowers	239
Professional Ethics Codes as Sources of Public Policy	242
Special Issues Encountered by Lawyers	243
The In-House Counsel's Dilemma	244
The Law Firm Corollary to the In-House Counsel Dilemma	252
Corporate Whistleblower Statutes and Lawyers	254
Whistleblowing and the Federal Government Lawyer	255
Summary of Key Points	260
Notes	260

CHAPTER 12
Lobbying Ethics   275
Heather Holt

Background	275
Definitions	278
Lobbying	278
Lobbyist	278
Client	280
Registration	280
Content	280
Timing	281
Identification	281
Fees	282
Disclosure	282
Content	282
Frequency	283
Identification	284
Prohibitions	284
Generally	284
Contingency Fees	285
Governmental Ethics	285
Campaign Finance	287
Public Officials	287
Enforcement	288
Debarment	289
Late Fees	290
Training	290
Summary of Key Points	291
Notes	292

CHAPTER 13
Conflicts of Interest   299
Rose Gill

Notes	303

Index   *305*

About the Editors

JENNIFER G. RODGERS

Jennifer G. Rodgers is a lecturer in law at Columbia Law School, an adjunct professor of clinical law at the NYU School of Law, and a legal analyst for CNN. She teaches, writes, and speaks all over the world about government ethics, public corruption, and sports corruption. Jennifer is a member of both the Task Force on the Rule of Law and the Federal Courts Committee at the New York City Bar Association, and is the former chair of the association's Government Ethics Committee. She also serves on the Independent Review Panel for Conviction Review for Kings County (Brooklyn) District Attorney Eric Gonzalez. From 2013 to 2018, Jennifer was the executive director of the Center for the Advancement of Public Integrity at Columbia Law School (CAPI), which works to improve the capacity of public offices to identify, deter, and combat corruption. Between 2000 and 2013, Jennifer worked at the U.S. Attorney's Office for the Southern District of New York, where she served in numerous capacities, including as a deputy chief appellate attorney, the chief of the Organized Crime Unit, and a chief of the General Crimes Unit. Jennifer also worked as an associate in the litigation department of Cravath, Swaine & Moore LLP, and as a law clerk to former U.S. District Judge Stanley A. Weigel in the Northern District of California. Jennifer graduated from the University of California, Berkeley School of Law, and the University of California, Los Angeles.

EVAN A. DAVIS

Evan A. Davis resides in New York City and is a senior counsel at Cleary Gottlieb Steen & Hamilton, LLP. He graduated from Columbia Law School in 1969 where he was editor in chief of the Columbia Law Review. He clerked for Harold Leventhal on the D.C. Circuit and Potter Stewart on the Supreme Court. Following his clerkships, he was appointed the first general counsel of the New York City budget division and later made the chief of the Consumer Protection Division in the city's Law Department. In 1974, he joined the Impeachment Inquiry staff of the U.S. House Judiciary Committee. He practiced law as a Cleary litigation associate and then partner from 1975 to 1985 when he was appointed counsel to Governor Mario Cuomo. He returned to Cleary in 1991 and later served as president of the

New York City Bar and vice chair of the Columbia University Trustees. He also chaired the American Bar Association's Standing Committee on Public Education and served on the New York State Bar's Committee on Standards of Attorney Conduct when it revised the ethics rules for lawyers. He currently serves as manager of the Committee to Reform the State Constitution, which was initially established as a committee to advocate for calling a state constitutional convention. Strengthening enforcement of the state's Code of Ethics has been a continuing priority for the group.

About the Contributors

JANET ARNOTT

Janet Arnott is an attorney based in Annapolis, Maryland. She focuses her practice in the area of taxation. Her background includes estates and trusts and veterans law.

Janet is the recipient of awards from the Maryland State Bar Association, the Kentucky Bar Association, and the Military Spouse JD Network. She has volunteered with and served in multiple positions at the Maryland State Bar Association Veterans Affairs and Military Law Section.

Janet received an LLM in taxation from Boston University School of Law and a JD from the University of the District of Columbia David A. Clarke School of Law, where she was the recipient of the Mason Civil Rights Award. She earned a BA in political science from the University of Kentucky. She is admitted to practice in Maryland, the Commonwealth of Kentucky, and the U.S. Court of Appeals for Veterans Claims.

Janet is an avid runner in her free time and has completed multiple marathons.

MARTHA (MARTI) HARRELL CHUMBLER

Martha (Marti) Harrell Chumbler has more than 40 years' experience in Florida government law and administrative practice. Over her career, she has advised government agencies and public contractors on issues relating to the applicability of, and their compliance with, Florida's public records and open meetings laws. Representative matters handled by Ms. Chumbler include advising clients in the protection of trade secret information from disclosure through public records and meetings, counseling clients regarding the applicability of Florida's Sunshine Laws to their operations as public contractors, and defense of government contractors against allegations of Sunshine Act violations. Ms. Chumbler has also trained the staff and officers of clients that are subject to Florida's government in the Sunshine Laws due to their roles as either government entities, public contractors, or semi-public entities. She developed a training manual for the Florida Association of District School Superintendents for use by superintendents and school district employees in responding to public records requests and has participated in annual school superintendent training relating to compliance with government in the Sunshine Laws and government ethics. She is also the editor and a chapter author of the book *Access to Government in the Computer Age: An Examination of State Public Records Laws*, published by the ABA Section of State & Local Government Law in 2007, and *Ensuring an Informed Public: State Open Records and Meetings Laws*, published by the ABA Section of State & Local Government Law in 2021.

Ms. Chumbler recently retired as of counsel with the Carlton Fields law firm, which she joined in 1984 after serving for four years as an attorney with the former Department of Environmental Regulation (DER). She is a past chair of the Section of State & Local Government Law and is certified by the Florida Bar as a specialist in the area of State and Federal Government and Administrative Practice. She received her law degree from Florida State University, with honors, and her BA from Vanderbilt University, magna cum laude.

MARK DAVIES

Mark Davies served as executive director of the New York City Conflicts of Interest Board, the ethics board for the City of New York, from 1994 through 2015. He previously served as executive director of the New York State Temporary State Commission on Local Government Ethics and as a Deputy Counsel to the New York State Commission on Government Integrity. Prior to that, he was a full-time law professor and a private practitioner, specializing in municipal law and litigation. A graduate of Columbia College and Columbia Law School, he is the former chair of the Municipal Law Section of the New York State Bar Association, co-chair of the Section's Government Ethics and Professional Responsibility Committee, and an adviser to the American Law Institute's Project on Public Integrity. He also served as president of Global Integrity and from 1990 to 2019 was an adjunct professor of law at Fordham Law School, where he taught New York Practice. He has lectured extensively on government ethics, both nationally and internationally, including in Brasilia at the IV Global Forum on Fighting Corruption, at the United Nations Experts Group Meeting and Capacity-Development Workshop on Preventing Corruption in Public Administration: Citizen Engagement for Improved Transparency and Accountability, and at the U.S. Office of Government Ethics' 17th National Government Ethics Conference. He has authored numerous publications, including chapters for *Municipal Ethics in New York: A Primer for Attorneys and Public Officials* (NYSBA 2016), *Ethics and Law Enforcement: Toward Global Guidelines* (Praeger 2000), and *Ethics in Government—The Public Trust: A Two-Way Street* (NYSBA 2002). He is also the lead author of *New York Civil Appellate Practice* (West 3d ed. 2020). Currently, he is studying for a master of divinity degree at Union Theological Seminary in New York City.

TOM DEVINE

Tom Devine has served since 1979 as legal director of the Government Accountability Project, where he has assisted more than 8,000 whistleblowers and not lost a case since 2006. He also has been on the front lines for passage and oversight of 38 whistleblower laws, including nearly all U.S. federal laws and internationally from Serbia to the UN and World Bank, most recently the EU Whistleblower Directive and Ukraine. He is an adjunct professor at the DC Law School, has been recognized annually since 2012 by the Metropolitan Washington Lawyer's Association as one of Washington DC's top employment lawyers, appears regularly as a media expert, has authored numerous books and law journals, spoken in over a dozen nations as the State Department's informal "Ambassador of Whistleblowing," and co-founded Whistleblowing International Network where he serves on the board.

MICHAEL DONALDSON

Michael Donaldson is a primary member of the Carlton Fields (Tallahassee Office) Government Law and Consulting Practice Group, serving as chair of the Practice Group's Affordable Housing and Licensure Subcommittees. His practice is concentrated in the areas of land use and environmental law, with a particular focus in assisting or representing developers of affordable housing in obtaining funding for projects including Low Income Housing Tax Credits (LIHTC). Michael's practice also includes assisting utilities, building contractors, and other licensed professionals with licensure issues, including initial licensure and any subsequent disciplinary issues. Michael also assists clients in competitive bid protests and other contract procurement matters. He also assists clients with comprehensive planning and permitting issues before state and local agencies. In addition to his administrative practice, Michael also has a general litigation practice including construction litigation.

Michael has given numerous presentations on a range of issues, including the following: "The Nuts and Bolts of Open Meeting Law," FOIA and Ethics; "Metadata and Its Ethical Implications for the Government Lawyer"; "Land Use Ethics—Advocating for Your Client Without Getting Disbarred or Hauled before the Ethics Commission"; and "The Good, the Bad, and the Ugly, Part II: Ethical Dilemmas in Government Representations."

JOHN D. FEERICK

John D. Feerick served as the dean of Fordham University School of Law till 2002 after being a partner at Skadden, Arps, Slate, Meagher & Flom, developing its labor and employment law practice. He is currently the Sidney C. Norris Professor of

Public Service at Fordham University School of Law. He is also the founder and senior counsel of Fordham Law School's Feerick Center for Social Justice.

He has served in a number of public positions, including as a member of the New York State Law Revision Commission, as chair of the New York State Commission on Government Integrity from 1987 to 1990, and as president of the Association of the Bar of the City of New York. He has been a mediator and arbitrator of many disputes. He previously chaired the Ethics Committee of the Dispute Resolution Section of the American Bar Association.

During his career, Professor Feerick served as a member of a task force that helped develop the Twenty-Fifth Amendment to the U.S. Constitution, and he was a draftsman of the proposed constitutional amendment on Electoral College reform that passed the U.S. House of Representatives in 1969.

Professor Feerick is a graduate of Fordham College '58 and Fordham Law School '61, where he served as editor in chief of its Law Review. He has received a number of recognitions, including a special award from the American Bar Association for his work in the development of the Twenty-Fifth Amendment to the Constitution; honorary degrees from the College of New Rochelle, St. Francis College and Hamilton College; the Fordham Law School and Fordham College Medal of Achievement; the Cardinal's Committee on the Laity Thomas More Award; the Ellis Island Medal of Honor; the distinguished lawyer's award of the New York State Bar Association, its Gold Medal; and in 2017, the American Bar Association's ABA Medal.

JANE T. FELDMAN

Jane T. Feldman was the executive director of the Colorado Independent Ethics Commission for nearly six years. Prior to that, she was a first assistant attorney general in the Natural Resources Section of the Colorado Attorney General's Office, and an assistant attorney general in the Criminal Enforcement Section. She began her legal career in the New York County District Attorney's Office in New York City, and was in that office for more than eight years, the last two as a bureau chief in the Office of the Special Narcotics Prosecutor. She is a magna cum laude graduate of the Benjamin N. Cardozo School of Law, and a cum laude graduate of Wesleyan University with honors in history.

She served on the Steering Committee and as president of the Council on Government Ethics Laws (COGEL). She previously served on the Denver Board of Ethics in 2015, but resigned in December of 2015, because she moved to New York state to serve as the executive director of the Office of Ethics and Compliance for the New York State Assembly. She served for a year and a half in that position before returning to Colorado in 2017. She currently is the principal of Rocky Mountain Ethics Consulting, which advises local governments on ethics issues, and has acted as pro bono counsel in several immigration cases. She has been reappointed to the Denver Board of Ethics by the City Council for a term that will expire in 2025.

ROSS GARBER

Ross Garber represents clients in government investigations and prosecutions, administrative processes, and congressional inquiries. He has also represented several U.S. governors and a state attorney general in impeachment proceedings. Ross also teaches political investigations and impeachment law at Tulane Law School.

ROSE GILL

Rose Gill is the principal of the Municipal Integrity, Efficiency and Transparency Practice at Bloomberg Associates. She served as commissioner of the New York City Department of Investigation (DOI) from 2002 through 2013 and was the longest-serving commissioner in its 140-year history. In 2013, Rose also helped create the Center for the Advancement of Public Integrity at Columbia Law School, which focuses on accountability in government and municipal jurisdictions throughout the world, and chairs its advisory board. Prior to her appointment at DOI, Rose was a federal prosecutor for ten years in the U.S. Attorney's Office for the Southern District of New York, where she served as deputy chief of the Criminal Division and chief of the Crime Control Strategies Unit. She has taught as an adjunct professor of law at Fordham University School of Law and worked as a litigator in the private sector. Rose is the former chair of the New York City Campaign Finance Board (2014–2017), a national model for nonpartisan regulation of public financing of campaigns and for voters' assistance.

BARRY GINSBERG

Barry Ginsberg has served as a leader of multiple New York state and local government entities, as follows: executive director and general counsel of the Commission on Public Integrity, which enforced the state's code of ethics and lobbying law and provided guidance regarding them to approximately 200,000 Executive Branch officers and employees, lobbyists, and their clients; deputy commissioner of the Department of Taxation and Finance, where he served as the Department's first chief risk officer, acting director of the Criminal Investigations Division and special counsel to the commissioner; and assistant district attorney in New York County, where he served as chief of the Labor Racketeering Unit and Senior Investigative Counsel, and in Bronx County, where he served as senior investigative assistant district attorney. Mr. Ginsberg began his legal career as a law clerk for the U.S. Court of Appeals for the Seventh Circuit. He also was a litigator in one of Chicago's premier law firms, a partner in one of the world's largest accounting and consulting firms, and a senior executive at several international investigation and consulting firms where, among other accomplishments, he started and led a practice that conducted fraud investigations and provided anti-fraud and compliance consulting services to global corporations and governments worldwide.

THE HONORABLE MARK LEE GREENBLATT

Mark Lee Greenblatt is the seventh inspector general for the U.S. Department of the Interior. As the inspector general, Mr. Greenblatt leads a nationwide workforce of investigators, auditors, evaluators, attorneys, and support staff whose mission is to provide independent oversight and promote excellence, integrity, and accountability within the programs and operations of the Department of the Interior. Mr. Greenblatt is the senior official responsible for providing oversight of more than 60,000 Department employees and assessing the Department's diverse programs, which includes millions of acres of public lands throughout the country, billions of dollars in acquisitions and royalty collection, and energy production, in addition to its important obligations to American Indians and Alaska Natives.

In January 2021, Mr. Greenblatt was appointed as the vice chair of the Council of the Inspectors General on Integrity and Efficiency (CIGIE), leading the inspector general community's mission to combat fraud, waste, and mismanagement.

Mr. Greenblatt has been in the federal oversight community since 2003 as part of the legislative and executive branches. Prior to becoming the DOI inspector general, he served as CIGIE's executive director. He previously served in leadership roles at the U.S. Department of Commerce Office of Inspector General (OIG) and the U.S. Senate Permanent Subcommittee on Investigations. Mr. Greenblatt also served as an investigative counsel at the U.S. Department of Justice OIG. Over the course of his federal career, he has received several awards, including a CIGIE award for excellence, Department of Commerce gold medal and bronze medals, and a Department of Justice OIG distinguished service award.

Mr. Greenblatt graduated from Columbia University School of Law, where he was a Harlan Fiske Stone Scholar, and received his undergraduate degree from Duke University. He also completed a Senior Manager in Government Fellowship at the Harvard University Kennedy School of Government.

HEATHER HOLT

Heather Holt has been in public service for more than 30 years. She has been in leadership with the Los Angeles City Ethics Commission since 2006, serving as its policy director, deputy executive director, and executive director. She began her work in governmental ethics at the Los Angeles County Metropolitan Transportation Authority and, before that, served as Deputy City Attorney for several cities in San Diego County. A Southern California native, Ms. Holt thoroughly enjoyed a number of years on the East Coast. While there, she had the opportunity to provide legal and policy analysis to the Maine State Legislature, the U.S. Environmental

Protection Agency, and the U.S. House of Representatives' Committee on Government Reform. She also purchased snow boots. Ms. Holt graduated from the Honors College at Washington State University and holds a juris doctor from Pepperdine Caruso School of Law.

ANN RAVEL

Ann Ravel served as the county counsel in Santa Clara County from 1988 until 2009, deputy assistant attorney general in U.S. DOJ Civil Division overseeing consumer litigation and torts, then chair of the California Fair Political Practices Commission from 2011 to 2013, and in 2013 was appointed by President Obama, and Senate confirmed, as commissioner and chair of the Federal Election Commission. She has served as a member of the Board of Governors of the State Bar of California and was appointed to the Judicial Council in California. Additionally, she has served on the Committee on Responsibility and Professionalism of the State Bar, writing ethics opinions.

As a member of the State County Counsel's Association, she often spoke and wrote about ethics and professionalism. As an adjunct professor at UC Berkeley Law School, she teaches ethics and professional responsibility.

BENJAMIN STEARNS

Benjamin Stearns counsels insurance industry clients on regulatory, compliance, transactional, international, and cross-border matters and defends insurers in coverage litigation. His practice extends to other regulated industries as well, providing licensing and compliance counsel to professional services, cannabis, and alcohol industry clients. He also lobbies the Florida executive branch and legislature.

Benjamin's notable prior engagements include representing the state of Florida in an original action against Georgia in the U.S. Supreme Court over the apportionment of the waters in the Chattahoochee-Flint-Apalachicola river system. His work has led to presentations on the SAFETY Act, a government program designed to promote the development of anti-terrorism technologies, and statutory and municipal diversity and social equity programs in the marijuana industry, among others. He has written extensively on insurance coverage matters, alternative dispute resolution, and cannabis law.

Preface

Jennifer G. Rodgers, Evan A. Davis

This book is intended to educate and assist government employees, particularly lawyers (and those private persons who face government ethics issues such as lobbyists, journalists, good government groups, and vendors), who may encounter some of the many ethical issues that tend to arise in public sector work. While the book cannot address every possible ethical quandary, and in many cases will not address the laws of every jurisdiction, we hope to provide a meaningful overview of frequently recurring ethics issues, and to give practical guidance and insights to help readers determine their most ethical course of conduct.

Government ethics issues can be challenging, because providing sound advice on such matters may require knowledge of any or all of the following: ethics codes and rules; laws at the federal, state, and local levels; binding opinions of ethics commissions and other relevant bodies; and rules promulgated by government agencies. In addition, a government ethics practice encompasses much more than just conflicts of interest; government ethics advisers may need to be familiar with laws and regulations about transparency measures, whistleblowers and their legal protections, and lobbying rules and their enforcement mechanisms, among other topics. Finally, a foundational concern of government lawyers everywhere is determining whether an attorney–client relationship is in place, and the applicability of any resulting privilege to their work.

This publication builds on the work of editor Patricia Salkin and many expert contributing authors in two prior editions. The first edition of *Ethical Standards in the Public Sector* came out in 1997; the second edition was published in 2008. It has been 14 years since then. In part to better address some of the issues identified in the preceding paragraph, we made some changes to the third edition in addition to ensuring that each chapter was thoroughly updated to account for recent developments in law and practice. For one thing, we wanted to expand the scope of the book to make it more useful to practitioners nationwide by recruiting new authors from all over the country and asking many of our authors—both new and returning—to broaden the scope of their chapters to account for a wider range of laws and practices than had been addressed previously. The third edition also adds several new chapters in an effort to explore relevant laws and ethical standards in a greater variety of government contexts.

Chapter 1, *The Nature and Purpose of Ethical Rules for Government Officials*, is a new chapter that introduces the concept of ethics rules and emphasizes the importance of ethical standards in societies that seek effectiveness in government.

Chapter 2, *Ethics, Lawyers, and the Public Sector: A Historic Overview*, is an updated discussion of the history of government ethics. It explores early statutory efforts, campaign finance reform, issues related to the emoluments clause of the Constitution, ethics reform efforts in selected states, and municipal ethics reforms; and it provides thoughts on the future of government ethics legislation.

Chapter 3, *Transparency*, is a new chapter that discusses what government transparency means and why it is important, and describes the most prominent transparency mechanisms like FOIA, Open Meetings Laws, and the Digital Accountability and Transparency Act, as well as their corollaries in two of the largest states. The chapter concludes with best practices suggestions for how to improve transparency.

Chapter 4, *Sunshine in the Statehouse: Financial Disclosure Requirements for Public Officials*, concerns the purpose of and constitutionality issues around financial disclosure laws, a key tool in government attempts to avoid conflicts of interest. The chapter also describes current federal financial disclosure requirements and includes an appendix surveying financial disclosure requirements in all 50 states.

Chapter 5, *Who Is the Client of the Government Lawyer?*, focuses on the thorny topic of exactly whom a government lawyer represents, including the potentially dueling obligations some lawyers face when, for example, a client government agency's interests may diverge from those of other government actor clients or the "public interest."

Chapter 6, *The Government Attorney Client Privilege*, looks at how the attorney–client privilege applies to government lawyers' communications with their clients in both civil and criminal contexts, and provides guidance for lawyers navigating this uncertain area of law.

Chapter 7, *Safeguarding Against Government for Purchase: Restrictions on Gifts and Honoraria*, discusses what kinds of remuneration are restricted for government employees and the nature of those restrictions, in both federal and state law.

Chapter 8, *Postemployment Restrictions on Government Employees: Closing the "Revolving Door,"* considers restrictions that apply pursuant to federal, state, and local law, as well as case law, when public sector lawyers leave their jobs for non-public employment opportunities.

Chapter 9, *Considering Ethics at the Local Government Level*, contains a practical guide to drafting local ethics rules, including detailed references to ethics guidance promulgated by many different jurisdictions.

Chapter 10, *The Role of Inspectors General*, is a new chapter that informs the reader of the statutory authorities, duties, responsibilities, and powers of federal Inspectors General, the anti-corruption watchdogs keeping a close eye on our federal agencies.

Chapter 11, *Whistleblower Law and Ethics*, gives a thorough lesson on the statutory framework and constitutional protections available for whistleblowers under both federal and state law.

Chapter 12, *Lobbying Ethics*, is a new chapter that explores questions around defining lobbying and determining who is a lobbyist and describes common requirements found in lobbying laws at the federal and state levels, such as registration and disclosure requirements.

Finally, Chapter 13, *Conflicts of Interest*, is a new chapter that provides an overview of how conflicts of interest can arise and discusses the importance of regulating such conflicts and potential conflicts to ensure that government leaders are working on behalf of the people instead of in their own personal interests.

Ethics issues are wide-ranging and can be challenging, but there are some places in addition to this book where government employees working through such matters can seek assistance. We particularly recommend the American Bar Association's Section on State and Local Government Law, as well as the Division for Government and Public Sector Lawyers, which both have resource materials that are accessible online. The Council on Government Ethics Laws is a national umbrella organization for federal, state, and local ethics agencies, along with elections, campaign finance, and lobbying regulators. Finally, the Center for the Advancement of Public Integrity at Columbia Law School provides training and assistance on government ethics issues to public sector offices and has an extensive online library of recorded events and written resources.

The authors of this third edition of *Ethical Standards in the Public Sector* collectively have hundreds of years of relevant experience and unquestionably represent some of the very best minds in the government ethics field. We hope that you will find their chapters informative, useful, and thought-provoking as you continue your crucial work to ensure the integrity of our government systems. Thank you for your service.

CHAPTER 1

The Nature and Purpose of Ethical Rules for Governmental Officials

Evan A. Davis

> This chapter explores the different purposes of ethics rules for various types of activities and discusses in greater depth various purposes of ethics rules in the public sector.

Clarity about the nature and purpose of the ethical rules for government officials is important for several reasons. Understanding this topic helps the drafters to craft rules adequate to their purpose. Agencies and judges applying such rules can be guided by their purpose in resolving ambiguities or fleshing out the specifics of rules stated in general terms. Training public servants about their ethical obligations is more effective when the instructor conveys a clear understanding of purpose. And convincing politicians of the need for government ethics is easier when the important purposes that ethics rules serve are evident.

Ethics rules for government officials also serve different purposes than the ethical rules applicable to those who are not government officials. Thus reference to the ethical rules that govern lawyers, doctors, journalists, or directors of businesses or nonprofit organizations may or may not be apt to describe the ethical duties of a public servant.

Finally, the topic addressed here is important because it advances understanding of the multiple reasons for rules governing government ethics. This multiplicity of purpose shapes the nature of ethical regulation of government. For example, to carry out some of these purposes it is necessary that ethical regulation extend beyond decision makers to every government employee as well as those who serve in governmental capacities without compensation.

THE PURPOSE OF ETHICS REGULATION DEPENDS IN PART ON THE ROLE OF THE REGULATED PERSONS

Because ethics rules serve to bar wrongful behavior, the specific purpose of an ethical regulation must be related to wrongful conduct for the particular group to which the rule applies.

Take for example ethical rules about conflicts of interest. Such rules exist for judges, lawyers, journalists, doctors, and boards of directors, but their goals are different in each case. For lawyers, conflict rules are designed to secure the undivided loyalty of the lawyer to the client. Thus, without client consent, lawyers may not ethically simultaneously represent clients with adverse interests.[1]

With judges, on the other hand, conflict of interest rules have the goal of something quite the opposite of loyalty; they exist to secure impartiality and freedom from perceived or real bias. A judge cannot ethically hear a case in which a party or the lawyer for the party is a relative.[2] It matters not that the judge may not have any personal reason to favor the particular relative in question; recusal is required because an objective observer could reasonably question the fairness of the proceeding.

Journalists, too, have conflict of interest rules. In their case, the rules are designed to make reporting accurate, without fear or favor, by securing the independence of the reporter.[3] Reporters may not ethically accept gifts, whether or not the gift comes as a quid pro quo for favorable coverage.[4] They must disclose unavoidable conflicts. They are to resist internal or external pressure to influence coverage or to give favored treatment to advertisers, donors, or any other special interests.[5]

Doctors have conflict of interest rules that are designed to prevent unnecessary risks to their patients' health, to protect the objectivity of medical research, and to address the issue of doctors with a financial interest in either the treatment or the service provider they may use or recommend. For example, a doctor who is both treating a patient and using that patient in a clinical trial must avoid having the needs of the trial take precedence over the best interests of the patient.[6]

Directors of for-profit and nonprofit corporations also have conflicts rules. These rules are designed to bring about the sound management of the corporation by securing a director's loyalty to the best interests of the corporation. New York has recently adopted the Non-Profit Revitalization Act, which requires nonprofit boards to adopt a conflict of interest policy for board members and key employees under which those with an interest in a transaction may not participate in the debate or vote on that transaction.[7] It also bars the hiring of relatives of board members or key employees unless the disinterested members of the board consider alternatives and document that consideration.[8] The model Code of Conduct of the National Council of Non-profits bars board members from deriving any profit or gain, directly or indirectly, from service as a board member.[9]

Consider also the various ethical requirements of confidentiality that govern members of various professions. Lawyers famously are required to refrain from revealing information relating to the representation of a client unless a specific exception applies, such as when the revelation is necessary to avoid death or serious injury or to prevent or rectify a crime or fraud involving substantial injury in which a lawyer's services were used.[10] A lawyer must take remedial action, including, if necessary, disclosure, when the duty of confidentiality conflicts with the duty of candor to a tribunal.[11]

Journalists, on the other hand, are not required to keep confidences unless they have agreed to keep the identity of a source confidential.[12] They are told to be circumspect in making such a pledge, both because they must at all costs defend it and because the existence of such a pledge may bear on the credibility of the source or the identity of the source may itself be newsworthy.

A doctor is ethically required to protect a patient's privacy.[13] By contrast, board members of corporations generally do not disclose board deliberations beyond what is recorded in the minutes, but because a board member has a fiduciary duty to the corporation, that duty may require a board member to report misconduct to the appropriate governmental authorities.

This is by no means a comprehensive survey of ethical rules governing persons engaged in various professional activities, but it is sufficient to show that ethical standards do depend in part on the nature of the activity to which they apply. What then is the nature of the activity of government officials that shapes the purposes of the ethical rules applicable to them?

THE NATURE OF PUBLIC SERVICE

The power of government is substantial, and public officials with a decision-making role exercise that power when adopting, administering, and enforcing laws, rules, and regulations having the force of law. All government employment differs from private employment in that government employees are paid from public revenue, most particularly taxes. As a result, waste, bribery, fraud, and favoritism in the course of government employment is of public financial concern.

It is essential that the great power of government be exercised for the common good. If that power is subverted to reap private gain or serve the interests of only a portion of society, then we lose the liberty that is the essential benefit of the republican form of government guaranteed by our federal and state constitutions.

Determining the public good in the political process of representative democracy is a matter of both lawyer-like advocacy for and loyalty to the best interests of both the elected official's constituents and the people as a whole. For government officials who enforce the law, their role requires impartiality when exercising discretion and loyalty to the public interest. In our federal constitution, this duty is called the faithful execution of the laws.

The fact that elected officials are chosen by the voters also potentially impacts officials' ethical obligations. Election of legislators makes conflict disclosure a theoretically reasonable way to address conflicts since the voters can weigh the conflict when casting their vote. However, since conflicts can arise at a time when voting does not provide implied consent, barring outside activities or requiring divestment is often a better way to manage conflicts for public officials.

Public service is famously subject to a relatively high risk of corruption and abuse of power. Bribery and extortion, in particular, have always been risks for those in power, and our federal constitution specifically mentions bribery as an impeachable offense for federal officials. The risk of bribery is heightened when relatively low-paid public servants participate in making decisions of great importance, financial or otherwise. The federal Foreign Corrupt Practices Act[14] exists because bribery and extortion are part of the governmental landscape in many parts of the world. That this is not generally not the case in the United States depends in part on maintaining a culture that rejects official corruption and abuse of power for personal benefit.

With this understanding of the nature of public service in mind, we can more readily assess the purposes of ethical rules for government officers and employees.

PURPOSES OF GOVERNMENT ETHICS AND PRIME CONSEQUENCES OF THOSE PURPOSES

Foster Public Confidence That Government Serves the Common Good

This is probably the most commonly stated purpose of rules of government ethics.[15] In a democracy, public confidence is evidence of the consent of the governed. Public confidence also facilitates voluntary compliance with the law, which both conserves public resources and avoids the hostile environment that a police state entails. Public confidence also encourages collective action, which furthers the common good.

The purpose of promoting public confidence is the reason for the "appearance" standard in government (and other) ethical rules. Ethics rules do not only prohibit the intentional use of an official position to further a conflicting interest. Ethics rules are also designed to avoid conduct that creates an appearance that official action is tainted by conflict. Put another way, it is not a defense that a public official had the strength of character and will to pay no regard to the conflicting interest. The public is not required to have trust that the public official will do the right thing, but rather is entitled to expect that the public official will remain free of conflicting interests that a reasonable person would see as impairing his or her independent judgment in loyal service to his or her constituents (if any) and to the public.

Sometimes people mistakenly refer to the appearance of a conflict as a "potential" conflict. A potential conflict is an interest that is not currently likely materially to impair independent judgment, but which might grow strong enough to be such an impairment. The appearance of a conflict of interest, by contrast, is an actual conflict of interest, because of its corrosive effect on the public trust.

Prevent Breaches of the Public Trust

A fiduciary duty arises from a relationship of trust and confidence where one party is under a duty to act for the benefit of another.[16] Public officials have a relationship of trust and confidence with the public and a duty to act for their benefit and are therefore fiduciaries. This relationship is often referred to as a public trust and breaches of the public trust are ethical violations.[17]

A comprehensive definition of what constitutes a breach of the public trust is elusive, but the general standards that the law imposes on a fiduciary provide helpful guidance. The duties of a fiduciary include loyalty, candor, and diligence. Each of these has relevance for a public official.

Loyalty is the duty to avoid conflicts of interest so that the government official can serve the public with undivided loyalty. Loyalty to the public also requires the reporting of official misconduct to enforcement authorities, and bars public servants from using their official positions for private gain through self-dealing or otherwise exchanging official action for personal benefit.

Candor is reflected in the ethical concept of transparency. Ethics agencies often enforce disclosure requirements in connection with their conflict of interest programs. But transparency extends beyond financial disclosure. Transparency should extend to the process by which laws are made, official communications with the public, and transparency about public spending. Indeed, lying to the public is a clear breach of the public trust, excusable only in the case of dire public necessity.[18] Open meeting and freedom of information laws also help to fulfill the government's duty of candor to the public.

The nature of government service, however, does place some limits on the duty of candor. Many kinds of investigatory proceedings are confidential during their pendency, and planned governmental actions may be kept confidential pending an orderly release of information to avoid insider and tipee trading and the like. Moreover, government officials enjoy the legal protection of a deliberative or executive privilege that is not generally available to the private sector. Important decisions in the lawmaking process are often taken behind closed doors in political party caucuses. This exception to candor is justified by the idea that the public interest is not served when half-formed thoughts are exposed to public view in a way that would discourage real deliberation.

The third fiduciary duty is the duty of diligence. In the private sector context, this duty requires a showing of real deliberation before a court will defer to a board of directors' determination of the best interests of the corporation, be it for profit or nonprofit. Various procedural steps have been proposed and implemented to encourage real deliberation in the lawmaking process, but perhaps the most effective would be an ethical requirement that a lawmaker become reasonably informed of the substance of legislation before voting on it. In the executive branch, the duty to take care that the laws be faithfully executed carries with it a duty of diligence.

Be a First Line of Defense against Corruption and Abuse of Power

Official corruption is often difficult to prove. Giving something of value in return for the vote of a legislator or action by an executive official is bribery, but proof of bribery typically requires proof of a quid pro quo exchange and criminal intent. Few participants in the political process are so knavish as to make it clear that the vote or official action is in return for the thing of value provided. Rather, if discovered, the benefit may be characterized as a gift.

Ethics rules help address this problem by prohibiting gifts to public officials. Because a gift will result in an ethical violation, if adequately enforced a gift ban serves as a first line of defense against bribery.

This is also true of ethical rules against self-dealing. Misappropriation of public resources is a crime, but criminal enforcement is resource-intensive, and catches a mere fraction of the problematic conduct at issue. When self-dealing is barred by ethics rules, misappropriation becomes more difficult for would-be corrupt officials. For example, it would be a crime for a public official to cause public funds to go to a controlled nonprofit corporation to pay his spouse for a no-show job. But if it is unethical for a legislator to vote on a matter involving an entity employing his spouse, then that corrupt criminal conduct will be less likely.

This is also true of ethical rules that bar the appearance of a conflict of interest. Serving a personal interest at the expense of the public interest is an abuse of power. But ethics rules do not draw the line at such actual abuse, let alone actual criminal conduct. Ethics rules prohibit conduct that creates an appearance that a conflicting interest will impair an official's independent judgment. These rules are, therefore, the first line of defense. A government official necessarily will cross the ethical line well before crossing the line of actual corruption.

Campaign finance law is a species of ethical regulation designed to prevent the conflicts of interest that arises from large contributions. But here, too, the ethics line is not drawn at taking a contribution explicitly in return for a vote or other official action, which would be a crime. Rather, contribution limits are set using an appearance of corruption standard, so that such limits function as a first line of defense against actual corruption.

The other side of the coin is that enforcement of ethics rules, which typically have light sanctions as compared to those imposed by criminal law, should not be a substitute for vigorous prosecution of official corruption cases. That is why ethics agencies need to refer cases that have the potential for criminal prosecution to the prosecuting authorities. Federal prosecution of state and local official corruption is part and parcel of the federal obligation under our Constitution to secure a republican form of government to each state, and where there is doubt as to the efficacy of referral of such matters to state prosecutors, referral might be made to federal prosecutors if that route provides greater likelihood of due consideration.

Play a Risk Management Role for Government and Public Officials

Seemingly overlooked is the role that ethics rules can play in minimizing the risk of government scandal. Scandals harm government as an institution because they call into question its soundness. They harm officials not directly involved in the scandals because they may be seen by the public as responsible for things happening on their watch. Scandals can easily become part of a public official's legacy, even without the official's personal involvement.

In the private sector, scandals affect the financial fortunes of businesses. For example, conflicts of interest that become scandals are a frequent cause of malpractice liability. In the public sector, government has substantial protection from lawsuits, but conflicts of interest still pose the risk of substantial waste of public resources and a resulting scandal. Even though political leaders are often fearful of ethical regulations, these regulations actually benefit them—provided that the enforcement mechanism is independent, nonpartisan, and fair—by clamping down on behavior that could result in career-ending scandal.

SUMMARY OF KEY POINTS

- The overarching goal of government ethics rules is to develop an ethical culture that promotes the good behavior the public expects.
- Maintaining an ethical culture requires fair and independent enforcement, an easy way to obtain ethics advice, and the government's continuous promotion of ethics.

NOTES

1. MODEL RULES OF PRO. CONDUCT r 1.7.
2. 28 U.S.C. § 455(b)(5).
3. *ASNE Statement of Principles*, AM. SOC'Y OF NEWS EDITORS, https://www.asne.org/asne-principles (last visited Mar. 10, 2022).
4. *SPJ Code of Ethics*, SOC'Y OF PRO. JOURNALISTS, https://www.spj.org/ethicscode.asp (last visited Mar. 10, 2022).
5. *Id.*
6. *Conflicts of Interest Research*, AM. MED. ASS'N, https://www.ama-assn.org/delivering-care/ethics/conflicts-interest-research (last visited Mar. 10, 2022).
7. N.Y. NOT-FOR-PROFIT CORPORATION LAW § 715-a.
8. *Id.* § 715.
9. NAT'L COUNS. OF NONPROFITS, SAMPLE CODE OF CONDUCT § 1(a) (2010).
10. MODEL RULES OF PRO. CONDUCT r 1.6.
11. *Id.*
12. *ASNE Statement of Principles*, *supra* note 3; *SPJ Code of Ethics*, *supra* note 4.
13. *Code of Medical Ethics Overview*, AM. MED. ASS'N, https://www.ama-assn.org/delivering-care/ethics/code-medical-ethics-overview (last visited Mar. 10, 2022).
14. 15 U.S.C. §§ 7dd-1 *et seq.*
15. *About the Ohio Ethics Commission*, OHIO ETHICS COMM'N, https://ethics.ohio.gov/about/index.html (last visited July 22, 2019). ("The Ohio Ethics Commission promotes ethics in public service to strengthen the public's confidence that Government business is conducted with impartiality and integrity."); *Guide to the Sunshine Amendment and Code of Ethics for Public Officers and Employees*, FLORIDA COMM'N ON ETHICS (2019), http://www.ethics.state.fl.us/Documents/Publications/GuideBookletInternet.pdf ("foremost among the goals of the

Code is to promote the public interest and maintain the respect of the people for their government"); N.Y. STATE CODE OF ETHICS PUBLIC OFFICERS LAW § 74(3)(f) ("An officer or employee of a state agency, member of the legislature or legislative employee should not by his conduct give reasonable basis for the impression that any person can improperly influence him or unduly enjoy his favor in the performance of his official duties, or that he is affected by the kinship, rank, position or influence of any party or person.").

16. RESTATEMENT (SECOND) OF TORTS § 874.

17. 65 PA. STAT. AND CONS. STAT. ANN. § 1101.1(a) ("The Legislature hereby declares that public office is a public trust...."); *Ct. State Legislators Guide to the Code of Ethics*, CT. OFFICE OF STATE ETHICS (2016), http://www.ct.gov/ethics/lib/ethics/guides/2016/legislators_guide_to_the_code_of_ethics_rev_2016.pdf ("... the Code's conflict-of-interest rules ... are grounded on a single rationale: that public service is a public trust"); *see also* N.Y. PUBLIC OFFICERS LAW § 74(3)(h).

18. For example, a wartime decision by Allied leaders to deceive the Germans about the place of the D-Day invasion necessarily required deceiving the public.

CHAPTER 2

Ethics, Lawyers, and the Public Sector: A Historical Overview[1]

John D. Feerick[2]

Government is a trust, and the officers of the government are trustees; and both the trust and the trustees are created for the benefit of the people.
—Henry Clay, Speech at Ashland, Kentucky, March 1829

> This chapter provides background on the historical developments in government ethics from the debates at the Constitutional Convention of 1787 through federal and state efforts at the beginning of the 21st century.

Representing one's fellow citizens in our form of democratic government is a formidable challenge. Our society demands much of those who accept the role of public servant. Beyond the sacrifice of private sector luxuries and opportunities and the time commitment that must be pledged, the men and women who serve the public are held to a higher degree of scrutiny in their public and, perhaps too often, their private lives. Theodore Roosevelt noted in "Manly Virtues and Practical Politics" that "[t]he first requisite on the citizen who wishes to share the work of our public life . . . is that he shall act disinterestedly and with a sincere purpose to serve the whole commonwealth." The dedication of public servants to serve the public good is a tribute not only to them but to our system of representative democracy.

The use of law as a means of assuring that public officials meet high ethical standards is rooted in the Constitution of the United States.[3] One cannot read the debates at the Constitutional Convention of 1787 and the state ratifying conventions without concluding that the Framers were concerned about the potential for the abuse of power. In addition to constituting a civil government, the Constitution treats very carefully the exercise of governmental power through a system of self-government, separation of powers, and checks and balances. Indeed, in a few instances, the Constitution specifically deals with subjects of conflicts of interest. For example, article I, section 6, provides:

> No Senator or Representative shall, during the Time for which he was elected, be appointed to any civil Office under the Authority of the United States, which shall

have been created, or the Emoluments whereof shall have been increased during such time; and no Person holding any office under the United States, shall be a Member of either House during his Continuance in Office.

Article I, section 9, provides that "no Person holding any Office of Profit or Trust under them, shall, without the Consent of the Congress, accept of any present, Emolument, Office, or Title, of any kind whatever, from any King, Prince, or foreign state." Plainly, these clauses illustrate that the Framers recognized the potential for conflicts of interest in a democratic government and the necessity for provisions to protect government integrity. As James Madison pointedly stated in the Federalist Papers:

> If men were angels, no government would be necessary. If angels were to govern men, neither external nor internal controls on government would be necessary. In framing a government which is to be administered by men over men, the great difficulty lies in this; you must first enable the government to control the governed; and in the next place oblige it to control itself. A dependence on the people is, no doubt, the primary control on the government; but experience has taught mankind the necessity of auxiliary precautions.[4]

EARLY HISTORY

The "experience" to which Madison referred in the Federalist Papers certainly included the first great city-states, when individuals began to consider their relationship with others in an organized society. For example, Aristotle said in one of his lectures on ethics, "Justice can only exist between those whose mutual relations are regulated by law. This is why we do not permit man to rule, but the law."[5] Similarly, the public servants of Athens took an oath in which they pledged to promote respect for the laws and to make their city greater, better, and more beautiful than it was when they received it:

> We will never bring disgrace to this our city by any act of dishonesty or cowardice, nor ever desert our suffering comrades in the ranks; We fight for the ideals and the sacred things of the city, both alone and with many; We will revere and obey the city's laws and do our best to incite to a like respect and reverence those who are prone to annul or set them at naught; We will strive unceasingly to quicken the public sense of public duty; That thus, in all these ways, we will transmit this city not only less, but greater, better and more beautiful than it was transmitted to us.[6]

In many ways, the Athenian Oath captured all of the ideals of public office as a public trust. It spoke of public servants as trustees in three significant ways: as fiduciaries of those whom they serve; as proxies of delegated political power; and as holders of the common interest to be preserved for the generations to come. Through such roles, public servants serve the common good, and for these reasons the integrity of public servants must be assured. In our country, various mechanisms have been implemented to safeguard the integrity of public servants.

One distinguished student of the subject has noted that "ethics laws in this country have proceeded not from a comprehensive view of the rights and duties of public officials but largely in reaction to specific scandals, and until recently on a piecemeal basis."[7]

Threshold requirements for integrity in public office were adopted by the First Congress in the creation of the United States Treasury. The act provided:

> And be it further enacted, That no person appointed to any office instituted by this act, shall directly or indirectly be concerned or interested in carrying on the business of trade or commerce, or be owner in whole or in part of any sea-vessel, or purchase by himself, or another in trust for him, any public land or other public property, or be concerned in the purchase or disposal of any public securities of any State, or of the United States, or take or apply to his own use, any emolument or gain for negotiating or transacting any business in the said department, other than what shall be allowed by law; and if any person shall offend against any of the prohibitions of this act, he shall be deemed guilty of a high misdemeanor, and forfeit to the United States the penalty of three thousand dollars, and shall upon conviction be removed from office, and forever thereafter incapable of holding any office under the United States.[8]

This provision, pervasive in its approach to preventing conflicts of interest, revealed the concern of our initial representatives that public officials left unchecked could, even unwittingly, fall prey to unscrupulous practice. Unfortunately, as government has grown in size and complexity to meet the needs of an expanding society, so too have concerns over governmental integrity.

FEDERAL EFFORTS

During the 20th century, various organizations and bodies attempted to evaluate the status of government ethics laws and develop safeguards to ensure the integrity of our public officials.

New York City Bar Association

In 1960, the Association of the Bar of the City of New York made public the results of a two-year study by its Special Committee on the Federal Conflict of Interest Laws, chaired by Roswell B. Perkins. The committee's judgment was severe. It concluded that existing restraints were "obsolete, inadequate for the protection of the Government, and a deterrent to the recruitment and retention of executive talent and some kinds of needed consultative talent."[9] The committee found that the statutory law at that time, most of which was at least a century old, was incapable of dealing with the modern, complex problems of government. The committee pointed to several areas that the antiquated laws had failed to address, including the expansion of civil service positions, the blending of the public and private sectors in American society, and the modernization of economic life. It said that government had "failed to provide a rational, centralized, continuing and effective administrative machinery to deal with the [aforementioned] problem."[10] It found that there was a hodgepodge of uncoordinated and uninterpretable statutes and regulations that made conformance impractical. Accordingly, it recommended that Congress take 13 steps to ameliorate the state of conflict of interest regulation.

The first group of suggestions related to the structure of conflict of interest laws. The committee called for Congress to recognize conflict of interest problems and treat them as important, complex, and independent subjects of attention and concern in the management of government. It suggested that "[t]he present scattered and uncoordinated statutes relating to conflicts of interest . . . be consolidated into a single unified Act, with a common set of definitions and a consistent approach" and that "[a]rchaic provisions should be repealed."[11] It said that only if Congress identified and isolated potential problems could the status of government ethics be improved and that only a unified act could provide the general law of conflict of interest an enforceable and more rational format. The committee also recommended that Congress expand the scope of existing restraints to include all matters in which the public deals with federal government. It defined a "transaction involving the government" as "'any proceeding, application, submission, request for a ruling or other determination, contract, claim, case or other such particular matter' which will be the subject of Government action."[12]

The committee's second group of recommendations focused on the need to recruit effective public officials. It proposed that in order to encourage participation in public office, "the statutes should permit the retention by Government employees of certain security-owned economic interests, such as continued participation in private pension plans."[13] It also stated that "it is safe, proper and essential from the viewpoint of recruitment, [that] the statutes should differentiate in treatment between regular employees and citizens who serve the Government only intermittently, for short periods, as advisors and consultants."[14] By doing so, the committee felt, more knowledgeable and skilled private citizens would participate in the management of the government.

A third group of recommendations addressed the structure and enforcement of a modern conflict of interest act. The committee said that violations should be addressed by administrative remedies rather than by criminal penalties. This approach was designed to combat the reluctance of government officials to pursue expensive, time-consuming, and often overly harsh criminal sanctions and to restore the deterrent power of conflict of interest laws. Furthermore, in order to centralize and simplify the current regulatory scheme, the committee proposed that an administrator be appointed by the president to oversee the implementation and enforcement of the act. Through this mechanism, the committee believed that clear overall responsibility for ethical conduct would be placed on the president and that appropriate attention would be given to the critical importance of the act. The committee also suggested that the president be given the power to create a second and third tier of regulations in administrative agencies so that the responsibility for the day-to-day enforcement of the statutes and regulations would rest upon the agency heads.

The fourth group of committee recommendations focused on the need to perceive and take proactive steps to combat conflicts of interest in government. The committee suggested that preventative measures, such as an orientation program for new government employees, be undertaken; that there be more effective prohibitions on the conduct of persons outside the government; and that Congress initiate a study of conflicts of interest of members and employees of the legislative branch.

The work of the Perkins committee contributed significantly to a growing perception that the government was in dire need of ethics reform. As suggested by the committee, the Kennedy administration took steps to broaden the administrative scope of the rules of ethics[15] by ordering all administrative agencies to issue regulations on conflicts of interest. Moreover, by executive order, President Kennedy set standards for the heads and assistant heads of departments and agencies, full-time members of boards and commissions, and members of the White House staff.[16] President Johnson took similar steps during his presidency, signing Executive Order 11222, which dictated rules governing the acceptance of gifts, outside employment, the safeguarding of confidential information, and the avoidance of financial conflicts.[17]

The Ethics in Government Act of 1978

The absence of a federal statute coupled with increased public concern over the integrity of public officials in the wake of the Watergate scandal led, in the late 1970s, to major legislative ethics initiatives and laws at both the federal and state levels.

In 1977, the House and Senate Judiciary Committees began debate on a comprehensive plan to assure governmental integrity. The Senate Judiciary Committee explained in its report:

> During the extensive hearings this committee held . . . [after the Watergate scandal], there was little if any dispute about two crucial facts: (1) The Department of Justice has not in the past allocated sufficient Departmental resources to handle official corruption cases and cases arising out of the federal election laws; and (2) That the Department of Justice has difficulty investigating and prosecuting crimes allegedly committed by high-ranking Executive Branch officials because the department as an institution is poorly equipped to handle cases involving senior Executive Branch officials.[18]

The committee went on to say:

> The solution to these problems is not merely the enactment of more criminal laws. It is essential that the President, the Attorney General and other top officials in the Department of Justice be men of unquestioned integrity. However, it is also

essential that we have a system of controls and institutions which makes the misuse and abuse of power difficult, if not impossible.[19]

The result of these congressional efforts was the adoption of the Ethics in Government Act of 1978, a thorough and comprehensive system of conflict of interest prevention. The act proceeded along a number of lines. It contained detailed conflict of interest provisions, including regulation of the postemployment area. It set forth wide-ranging financial disclosure requirements for members and employees of the legislative, executive, and judicial branches of government.[20] It created an Office of Government Ethics (OGE) and authorized the president to appoint an administrator to oversee the new regulatory system. The OGE would guide the agencies and departments of the executive branch in administering the financial disclosure system, issue regulations on standards of conduct and advisory opinions on questions of ethics, and provide for the education of employees about the rules.[21]

In 1979, Congress made several clarifying changes to the act. These included a definition of "executive branch" to include independent regulatory commissions; an amendment to open to public scrutiny reports made by the three branches with relation to the act; and a change to make clear that the act preempted state and local disclosure laws. In 1983, the act was reevaluated by Congress, which resulted in several changes relating to the reauthorization of the OGE. However, as the Senate Judiciary Committee indicated: "The OGE has, in its almost five-year history, performed its statutory duties thoroughly and responsibly, and thus should be reauthorized for five more years."[22]

Federal ethics in government regulations underwent a total reorganization in 1989 under the Ethics Reform Act of 1989.[23] As described by the House Judiciary Committee, the act

> consolidated the ethics laws applicable to all three branches of government; expanded the post-employment restrictions for employees of the Executive Branch and extended such restrictions to the legislative branch; revised the financial disclosure rules for senior government officials; authorized "certificates of divestiture" for incoming political appointees who sell assets in order to avoid conflicts of interest; changed certain aspects of the laws pertaining to the acceptance of gifts, outside earned income, and outside employment; banned the receipt of honoraria by federal employees; and added civil penalties to the arsenal of political sanctions for violations of the criminal ethics laws.[24]

Thus, essentially, the 1989 act reflected the original goal of the Ethics in Government Act of 1978: a cohesive, thorough, and workable set of ethics regulations for public employees. The Ethics in Government Act remains in force today.

Campaign Finance Reform

In 2002, two fundamental developments in federal ethics legislation took place. In March 2002, Congress passed the Bipartisan Campaign Reform Act (BCRA),[25] known to many as the McCain-Feingold law. This has been referred to as "the most comprehensive change in federal campaign finance law in more than two decades."[26] The BCRA set new standards that restricted ways to donate soft money to political campaigns and strengthened regulations pertaining to advertisements.[27] The McCain-Feingold law was followed by the Help America Vote Act of 2002 (HAVA).[28] By passing this act, Congress created many federal obligations for state and local election administrations, and in exchange pledged $3.97 billion in federal funding for them.[29]

In 2008, Citizens United, a nonprofit corporation, released a film entitled *Hillary: The Movie*, and sought to promote it using short broadcast and cable television advertisements.[30] The Court found that the film and its advertisements, which negatively portrayed Hillary Clinton, were "electioneering communications" within the meaning of the BCRA, and would therefore be subject to an outright ban under section 441(b) of the BCRA.[31] In perhaps the most controversial decision of the term, the Court invalidated BCRA's ban on corporate spending in political campaigns, holding that corporations have a First Amendment right to spend unlimited amounts of money to support or oppose candidates for elected office.[32] Criticisms of this holding in *Citizens United* have been fierce. President Obama referred to the decision as a "huge victory for special interests,"[33] federal legislation was quickly proposed to restrict a corporation's spending in campaign advertisements,[34] and multiple members of Congress have proposed constitutional amendments that would overturn the decision.[35] Many still support overturning the decision, and this remains a common topic among academics, nongovernmental organizations (NGOs), and politicians.[36]

There have been no major updates to ethics legislation on the federal level since 2008. Many bills related to anti-corruption efforts have been introduced in both houses of Congress but very few have made it past the introductory stage to be turned into law, and none that have far-reaching effects.

Issues Concerning the Emolument Clauses

Issues related to anti-corruption have been at the forefront of political discussions since the 2016 election of President Donald Trump. One running theme has been a potential conflict of interest between his duties as president and the running of his corporate businesses, which include managing properties around the world.[37] During his campaign, President Trump stated that he would arrange to put his holdings in a blind trust, but acknowledged that such a strategy may be complicated by the fact that his three adult children would have access to the trust.[38]

Detangling public and private interests is a complicated question. The 1997 case *Clinton v. Jones* established the precedent that a sitting president of the United States does not have immunity from civil litigation for actions unrelated to the office of the president.[39] In 2017, as a sitting president, Trump faced a lawsuit brought by former students of "Trump University" real estate seminars.[40] Since this issue concerned the actions of the president before he took office, the litigation moved forward and resulted in a settlement.[41]

Turning to the Emoluments Clauses, they were included in the Constitution because the framers were wary that a president may be susceptible to undue influence.[42] The Foreign Emoluments Clause prohibits officers of the United States from receiving any "present, Emolument, Office, or Title" from foreign governments.[43] Similarly, the Domestic Emoluments Clause forbids the president from accepting gifts from the U.S. government or from individual states.[44] Several lawsuits have alleged that President Trump's private businesses violated the Emoluments Clauses during his time in office.[45] One case describes how his International Hotel, located close to the White House, hosted officials from foreign countries such as Georgia, Kuwait, and Saudi Arabia.[46] The lawsuit states that foreign and domestic officials' patronage of the hotel could be seen as a way to curry favor with the president, yet the president's lawyers have argued for a narrow interpretation of the Emoluments Clauses in which their oversight would not reach such commercial transactions.[47]

Emoluments violations have been discussed by the Office of Legal Counsel (OLC) in the context of previous administrations where decisions seemed to be made on a case-by-case basis.[48] In the 1980s, the OLC determined that there was no violation of the Domestic Emoluments Clause when President Ronald Reagan received retirement benefits from California as the state's former governor. The OLC adopted a narrow interpretation, explaining that "retirement benefits are not emoluments within the meaning of the Constitution because interests of this kind were not contemplated by the members of the Constitutional Convention."[49] Similarly, the OLC found no Foreign Emoluments Clause violation when President Barrack Obama accepted the Nobel Peace Prize in 2009 because the prize was awarded by the Nobel Committee, which was not considered a foreign state.[50] However, some scholarship has advocated for a broader understanding of "emoluments" that would bar the president from receiving any profit or benefit from state or foreign governments, aside from a salary.[51] It has been argued that a broader understanding of emoluments would more closely align with the spirit of the Emoluments Clauses as contemplated by the founders, who understood that "undue influence" could take the form of action beyond traditional bribery.[52] In 2017 and 2019 congressional bills such as the Presidential Conflicts of Interest Act were introduced, which would compel a president, vice president, and members of their families to divest from any conflicted business interest, as determined by the Office of Government Ethics. These bills have yet to become law.[53]

Though not specifically tied to the Emoluments Clauses, the question of inappropriate benefits and quid pro quo was at the center of President Trump's first impeachment. The House of Representatives, finding the evidence before it substantial, voted to impeach the president for using his position to solicit Ukraine's assistance in the investigation to discredit a political rival in the Democratic Party.[54] The House of Representatives passed two articles of impeachment: the first article concerned abuse of power and the second article charged obstruction of Congress.[55] In early 2020, the Senate found the president not guilty on these charges. On the first charge, 52 senators voted for an acquittal against 48 votes for conviction. Similarly, there were 53 votes to acquit the president on the second charge against 47 votes to convict.[56] It is notable that Congress members appeared to vote along party lines in both the House and the Senate.

I believe it can be said objectively and nonjudgmentally that over the course of the Trump presidency government lawyers' ethics was a subject frequently addressed by commentators. For example, during the Mueller investigation, the hearings of the House of Representatives leading to the president's first impeachment, and the resulting Senate trial, commentators raised questions about the conduct of lawyers in various settings, including, in particular, the conduct of Mueller and his staff, of lawyers who were members of Congress, of Attorney General Bill Barr, and of lawyers in the White House counsel's office. Ultimately, the focus of the House investigation and Senate trial related to the president's first impeachment was on the conduct of the president, who was not a lawyer. Questions about the surrounding lawyers' conduct were never adjudicated. But no one can doubt the importance of the lawyers who served as public officials in the Department of Justice, the White House, Congress, and elsewhere in government, or of the importance of holding these lawyers to high professional standards.

STATE EFFORTS AT ETHICS REFORMS

As the federal government undertook to deal comprehensively with the subject of government ethics, so did the states. In 1976, the National Municipal League undertook to give leadership to this effort by creating an ethics project to provide information and to evaluate existing state statutes. In 1979, it proposed a model state Conflict of Interest and Financial Disclosure Law to provide guidance, noting in the introduction:

> The committee began its work with one basic premise, which was that the only conflicts of interest which could be regulated under this law were those which concerned finances. Having a conflict of interest is not, in and of itself, evil, wrong or even unusual. Conflicts may be ethnic, cultural, emotional, nostalgic, regional, financial or philosophical. Conflict of interest laws are concerned with financial conflicts which set apart an individual office holder from most of the general public.[57]

It added:

> Conflict of interest provisions are designed to prevent public officials and employees from gaining financial profit from their official actions (other than government salaries), or from helping family or friends to profit unfairly because of inside information or preferential treatment. At the same time, the provisions can take some outside pressure off by making certain practices illegal instead of merely unethical. This is particularly true when the provisions are combined with those for financial disclosure and when the existence of conflicts or potential conflicts becomes a matter of public record.[58]

Unfortunately, the history of ethics legislation at the state level mirrors that of the federal level in terms of its slow and long evolution, spurred usually by scandal. Each state can point to some scandal that focused the issue and led to a governmental response. A representative review of the states follows.

New York State

In New York, Charles Evans Hughes was an early champion of ethics reform. He received his start in public life in 1905 when he investigated—on behalf of the legislature—corruption in both the public utilities industry and the insurance industry. At that time, several political bosses ran New York State politics and divided the patronage spoils among themselves and their allies. Hughes faced a difficult challenge; the bosses did everything they could to stymie his efforts. Nevertheless, he proved to be an extremely talented investigator. In order to remove his influence from the investigation, the bosses arranged for him to receive the Republican nomination for mayor of New York City.

As soon as Hughes came to know about the nomination, he recognized that he faced an ethical dilemma: Should he accept the mayoral nomination with its possibilities of personal advancement and service to the community, or should he reject it because it would destroy his investigative committee's credibility? The decision was not an easy one, but, in the end, he placed the public trust above his personal ambitions for public office. In turning down the offer, Hughes said: "In this dilemma I simply have to do my duty as I see it. In my judgment, I have no right to accept the nomination. A paramount public duty forbids it."[59]

As it turned out, choosing the ethical path did nothing to keep Hughes out of public office. He was elected governor of New York in 1907, and later he would be a presidential candidate and Chief Justice of the U.S. Supreme Court. As governor, Hughes provided persistent, vigorous leadership in the area of ethics reform. One success he had was in establishing a pair of independent public service commissions to free government from the earlier regulatory commissions controlled by old guard politicians and business interests. His idea became a blueprint for the modern public service commission in this country.

A second success in promoting ethical government was a statute to authorize the governor to carry on investigations or to appoint a commissioner to conduct investigations of the administration of various departments and institutions of government. The statute became known as the Moreland Act.

Difficulty in securing effective ethics legislation was highlighted by the work of the New York State Commission on Government Integrity. In 1987, the Moreland Act Commission was created by an executive order of Governor Mario Cuomo in response to widespread scandals in New York. The commission's mandate was exceedingly broad: to investigate laws and practices in the state and municipal governments of New York that fostered corruption and the appearance of impropriety, and to make recommendations for needed reforms. During its several-year tenure, the commission conducted investigations, held public hearings, and laid out an ethical framework worthy of emulation throughout the country. It published its agenda in reports, in a volume,[60] and in the form of a booklet entitled "Restoring the Public Trust: A Blueprint for Government Integrity."[61]

Among the subjects identified by the commission as important for any modern-day framework of government ethics were the following: conflicts of interest regulation, campaign finance reform, ballot access laws, open meetings, patronage prohibitions, whistleblower protections, procurement reform, and training and educational programs. Throughout its many reports, the commission emphasized the importance of legislating ethical standards for governmental employees in order to promote public confidence in government, protect the public sector from pressures by the private sector, provide guidance to public officials, reduce the temptation of some to abuse their trust, and to articulate a moral standard for the entire community. As Justice Brandeis wrote, "our Government is the potent, the omnipresent teacher. For good or for ill, it teaches the whole people by its example. . . . If the Government becomes a law breaker, it breeds contempt for law; it invites every man to become a law unto himself; it invites anarchy."[62]

One issue of paramount concern to the commission was municipal ethics. Although in 1987 New York passed an Ethics in Government Act covering statewide employees, the act had little application to local government. More than 95 percent of the municipalities of the state were left completely unaffected by the act, continuing to be controlled by vague regulations passed 25 years earlier. As the commission wrote in its report, "the result [of these laws] has been a confusing and often contradictory patchwork of unenforced and unenforceable ethics codes. New York needs a set of minimum ethical standards for all public officials, a statement that certain behavior is simply not acceptable for a government servant, no matter where he or she works and lives."[63] The logic of having one uniform and coherent set of standards is simple: not only does a uniform set of ethical regulations make it easier for the vast majority of dedicated and well-intentioned public actors to understand the ethical minimums, but it makes the regulations uniformly enforceable statewide.

The commission sought to provide leadership by proposing a Municipal Ethics Act that would set uniform ethical standards for municipal officials. The commission wrote that "the standards are intended only as a minimum; localities can adopt more stringent legislation where they feel it is appropriate to do so." Unfortunately, the commission's recommendations, and that of the subsequent Miller Commission,[64] have not been acted upon, with New York remaining rooted in a pre-Watergate view of municipal ethics.

Both the Commission on Government Integrity and the Miller Commission found that, in addition to ethical regulations, there was a clear need for disclosure requirements for local officials. Similar to statewide officials, local officials should be required to disclose meaningful information about their finances. With this in mind, the integrity commission proposed three solutions: first, that there be a requirement of applicant disclosure for individuals making bids for municipal businesses; second, that municipal officials be required to disclose annually all personal financial interests; and third, that transactional disclosure be required for situations where an official's actions may be personally profitable, in which case the official would take no action. These three disclosure requirements, the commission noted, would provide the public with much-needed information about municipal candidates and serve to discourage conflicted or self-interested action by officials. In January 2006, Governor George Pataki signed the Public Authorities Accountability Act of 2005 into law.[65] The act applied certain aspects of the federal Sarbanes-Oxley Act of 2002 to the public authority sector and established "comprehensive reporting, auditing, governance, and property disposition requirements for a multitude of" state and local public authorities.[66]

Similarly, the Public Employees Ethics Reform Act of 2007 and the Public Integrity Reform Act of 2011 significantly changed ethics regulations in New York state by reorganizing various watchdog agencies to ultimately create the Joint Commission on Public Ethics. This commission, known as JCOPE, is empowered to monitor the conduct of executive and legislative employees, oversee financial disclosures from public officials, as well as oversee the registration and conduct of lobbyists.[67] In 2015, JCOPE was assessed by the New York Ethics Review Commission and certain recommendations were made to increase transparency in how JCOPE functions and to better integrate technology to make disclosures more accessible to the public.[68]

In addition to change and reform in New York, many states have implemented significant legislation to promote ethics among their public servants.[69] Many states have felt an increased push for ethics reforms from various NGOs and associations of ethics professionals.[70] Technology has made mountains of data more readily available to the public and has allowed NGOs to manage and analyze information from all 50 states to identify trends and evaluate progress of ethics legislation. For example, the Center for Public Integrity, a nonpartisan and nonprofit investigative news organization,[71] completed a data-driven report to assess government transparency and accountability in each state.[72] The center's report, called the State Integrity Investigation, examined a number of factors in each state, including campaign finance, ethics, and lobbying regulations, and graded each state from "A" to "F."[73] The results of the State Integrity Investigation have motivated states to adopt ethics reforms.[74] For example, in her 2013 state of the state address, South Carolina Governor Nikki Haley addressed the State Integrity Investigation's report on her state.[75] Noting South Carolina's poor performance in the report, Governor Haley explained her decision to create the independent South Carolina Ethics Commission, which she hoped would help the state navigate through the ethical reform process.[76]

California

Though California is the country's largest state, it has experienced considerable success in maintaining a strong oversight system. After the state saw several notable ethics scandals,[77] ethical reform became a legislative priority, and the state saw new laws take effect in 2014 that would oversee protections for whistleblowers and restrict political campaign fundraising.[78] Like many other states, California has adopted a multipronged approach to stopping corruption among public officials. For example, to help prospective candidates recognize and prevent potential ethical pitfalls, California's Fair Political Practices Commission (FPPC) has implemented an online toolkit that gives candidates "step-by-step instructions . . . on how to comply with various rules and laws involved in running for office."[79] Conversely, the FPPC is also charged with investigating possible violations of the Political Reform Act and randomly auditing 25 percent of lobbying reports submitted by lobbyists and lobbying firms.[80] Upon finding a violation of the Political Reform Act, the FPPC's Enforcement Division may impose fines, issue warning letters, or pursue a civil action to seek a penalty.[81] Most results of enforcement actions are not kept confidential, and violators are regularly named in monthly press releases.[82] Similar to most states, California has faced corruption at the state and local level. In 2015, state senator Leland Yee was found to have accepted thousands of dollars in bribes and helped an undercover FBI agent buy automatic weapons from the Philippines.[83] As a result of such a shocking political scandal, in 2016 the Federal Bureau of Investigation and the district attorney of San Francisco created the public corruption task force.[84]

Texas

In Texas, a decades-old scandal led to efforts to create government transparency that is still present today. In the early 1970s, Frank Sharp was a Houston-based developer who hoped to bribe state government officials to pass favorable banking bills. This fraudulent activity was discovered by the U.S. Securities and Exchange Commission the following year and resulted in a large-scale political scandal such that, in 1972, every incumbent statewide elected official and half of the state legislature were voted out of office.[85] As a result of the Sharpstown scandal, the Texas Public Information Act was adopted to ensure that the public has access to information held by the state government, making Texas a national leader in such transparency efforts.[86] Despite its great strides in open access to the public, Texas is still plagued by public corruption-related setbacks. In 2015, the state legislature disbanded the Public Integrity Unit of the Travis County district attorney's office in Austin, which had investigated several state politicians.[87] This was the only unit of its kind in Texas, and its dissolution was viewed as a great loss to efforts to hold elected officials accountable.[88]

North Dakota

Size and population of a state may also affect its ethics culture. North Dakota, with its historically small population, has a particularly weak system of oversight. The state's sparsely scattered communities are characterized by an overwhelming sense of familiarity that overrides any perceived need for stronger ethical protections in law.[89] Further, North Dakota is only one of seven states to lack an ethics watchdog agency such as an inspector general or an ethics commission.[90] There have been efforts to establish a system of oversight, but the North Dakota legislature rejected proposals for such an entity in 2011, 2013, and 2015, reasoning that low civic engagement would make any type of ethics commission unnecessary in a state with a "culture of openness and accessibility."[91] Though corruption has not been a significant issue in North Dakotan state government, there has been an influx of capital and labor due to the state's oil industry, which increases the risk of corruption.[92]

Iowa

Similar to Texas, Iowa has also passed significant transparency reforms. After Iowa received an "F" grade for "Public Access to Information" in the State Integrity Investigation report, lawmakers took action.[93] Until the reforms spurred by this report, citizens lacked powerful options to force officials to turn over public records laws.[94] In 2012, Iowa Governor Terry Branstad signed a bill into law creating an entirely new state entity charged with enhancing access to Iowa's public records.[95] The Iowa Public Information Board is comprised of nine members from diverse backgrounds, including media professionals and local government officials, serving staggered terms.[96] The board's stated focus is to increase understanding of open government by providing outreach and mediation.[97] The board also has the power to review and resolve alleged violations of Iowa's open information laws.[98] Most requests for information are routine and result in production within ten days.[99] If a party feels that information has been wrongfully withheld, the board's statutory mandate is to resolve complaints informally and expeditiously; however, it retains the power to assess fines if necessary.[100]

Virginia

States have had to cope with issues surrounding gifts from lobbyists to government officials. In the wake of the scandal surrounding former Virginia Governor Bob McDonnell's federal trial for exchanging money and gifts for official favors, the Virginia Conflict of Interest and Advisory Council was created in 2014.[101] However, it is notable that the Supreme Court ultimately decided to overturn McDonnell's corruption conviction, believing that federal prosecutors' definition of political corruption was too broad.[102] Under the same bill that created the Virginia Conflict of Interest and Advisory Council, Virginia strengthened regulations on gifts to state or local government employees, legislators, and candidates to the General Assembly.[103] Now, Virginia officials must provide a description and report the source and approximate value of all gifts that exceed $250 in value given to them or an immediate family member by a lobbyist or certain parties seeking to conduct business with state or local government agencies.[104] This new advisory council is tasked with reviewing disclosure forms from lobbyists and government employees, creating and maintaining a publicly accessible and searchable database of all submitted disclosure forms, training lobbyists and state and local government officials in ethics and conflict of interest issues, and advising the Virginia state legislature on compliance with the new law.[105]

Electoral College Swing States

Public corruption has occurred in states important in the electoral college system, leading to reform efforts. States such as Pennsylvania, Michigan, and Florida have experienced significant political scandal. Pennsylvania created an independent State Ethics Commission to adopt and enforce ethics legislation after a large-scale scandal involving the state attorney general and state lawmakers.[106] Florida is another state that has a long history of political corruption but has created an ambitious program of anti-corruption oversight by allowing for the most number of independent inspectors general of any state.[107] Florida also has strong "sunshine laws" that open government records to public access.[108] In the Midwest, Michigan struggles with public corruption in state government. Unlike Florida's many inspectors general, Michigan has a weak oversight structure and any existing oversight has limited enforcement powers to execute effective ethics legislation.[109] The reason for lack of enforcement may be similar to the situation in North Dakota where political and societal norms preempt any effective ethics protections.[110] "It appears we are living with an honor system in an environment where there isn't much honor," said Rich Robinson, executive director of the Michigan Campaign Finance Network.[111] Indeed, Michigan's campaign finance disclosure laws are among the weakest in the country, making its state officials particularly vulnerable to corruption.[112]

MUNICIPAL ETHICS REFORMS

In 1989, New York City adopted what has become the largest local public financing of an elections system in the country with the passage of the Campaign Finance Act of 1989.[113] One of the cornerstones of the act was the creation of the Campaign Finance Board, an independent, nonpartisan city agency tasked with managing New York City's landmark Campaign Finance Program.[114] When the Campaign Finance Board was created, its architects recognized that it could not function as an effective watchdog unless it was insulated from politics.[115] This independence has allowed the board to function as a nonpartisan group of professionals committed to ethics reform.[116] To that end, the board administers New York City's Campaign Finance Program, which offers matching funds to participating candidates' small money campaign contributions.[117] To participate in the program, a candidate must agree to strict limits on campaign expenditures and submit to additional reporting requirements and audits on their spending.[118]

The program has raised the standard of government ethics in New York City over the last 30 years, and "gives a stronger, clearer voice to the everyday concerns of the vast majority of New Yorkers who can't afford to make large contributions to politicians. It encourages candidates to lend those concerns real weight and consideration, and to spend more time with their neighbors raising small-dollar contributions and less time chasing special-interest checks."[119] Indeed, by giving candidates an incentive to seek support from all their constituents, instead of the few with the deepest pockets, the program has helped to engage the electorate, and an engaged electorate is perhaps the way to ensure that all public servants act ethically in advancing the public good.[120] The program encourages more good candidates to run for office, and requires incumbents to actively campaign for reelection against challengers.[121] Further, participating candidates need to spend less time fundraising during a campaign and can instead focus on meeting with constituents and thoughtfully debating the issues with opponents.[122] The popularity of the program has also grown; in the 2017 elections, nearly three-quarters of all campaign contributions from New York City residents were small money contributions, totaling less than $175.[123] And participation among candidates is high as well; in 2017 it was more than 80 percent.[124]

This innovation was followed by the adoption of procurement reform in New York City and the establishment of a Conflicts of Interest Board. The mission of the Conflicts of Interest Board is based on the principle that employees of the city of New York have a "special public trust" and should therefore be held to a higher standard of ethical conduct than the private sector.[125] The board interprets and enforces the Conflicts of Interest Laws and educates city employees to stop violations before they occur.[126] The Conflicts of Interest Board does not work alone, however.[127] The New York City Department of Investigation,[128] under the pioneering leadership of then-commissioner Rose Gill, not only undertook many significant corruption investigations but also took the unique step of convening conferences in New York to share its work with various counterparts from around the world and to learn from them as to their approaches, challenges, and accomplishments.[129] In 2008 and 2013, the Department of Investigation hosted the National Watchdog Conference, where the anti-corruption officials representing various cities, federal agencies, and countries convened to exchange ideas relating to the promotion of integrity in government.[130]

GREATER CITIZENRY INTEREST IN ETHICS

As noted, there has been a growth in efforts by citizen groups, bar associations, and the academic community in areas of government ethics and integrity. Some examples include the Center for the Advancement of Public Integrity at Columbia University Law School, the Brennan Center for Justice at New York University School of Law, the Government Law Center at Albany Law School, the establishment of government ethics committees by bar associations, and the innovations of programs on corruption in America and abroad such as the one held at Fordham Law School in March 2015.[131] Civil society groups also have increased in number, activity, and visibility in the last few years, with groups like the Center for Public Integrity[132] and Citizens for Responsibility and Ethics in Washington[133] conducting investigations, issuing reports, and filing lawsuits to confront unethical conduct in government. This increased interested has resulted in some movement toward governmental reform. For example, the resignation of New York's state assembly speaker following corruption charges from the U.S. Attorney for the Southern District of New York[134] led Governor Andrew Cuomo to propose a slate of major ethics reforms and to refuse to sign any budget proposed by the state legislature that did not make significant strides toward transparency.[135] Referring to public corruption as a decades-old problem for the state, Governor Cuomo said that New Yorkers will never trust the "government's authenticity" until they are truly informed about the outside employment of lawmakers.[136] "Either end it entirely or thoroughly disclose. There is no middle ground."[137] Similarly, the New York City Bar Association, noting the tendency for ethical reforms to occur in "fits and starts" in the wake of various scandals, urged that 2015 should be the year for a meaningful resolution to decades of piecemeal ethics reforms.[138] Despite many efforts in this direction, however, New York has not yet managed to ban or limit outside income for its legislators.[139] Moreover, in August 2021, Governor Cuomo resigned from office and transferred power to his lieutenant governor, Kathy Hochul. Governor Hochul has since established a "State and Local Ethics Working Group."

THE FUTURE OF GOVERNMENT ETHICS LEGISLATION

It is of paramount importance that government ethics be constantly evaluated and reexamined as long as we view public office as a public trust. Indeed, the restrictions on the right to vote that occurred in 2021 and 2022 in 18 states, while not a subject of study in this chapter, call for close scrutiny in the years to come. A memorandum by Fordham Law School student Zackary Eckstein dated May 10, 2022, placed in the Fordham Law Library, provides a useful overview of these laws.

Public servants must enact strong laws governing official conduct and enforce those laws with vigorous prosecution and stiff penalties. In addition, they must find ways to establish clear, internal codes of conduct and police themselves for violations of such codes in advance of and not simply in reaction to scandal. A major role for existing government ethics commissions and agencies is to define strong ethical codes for present societal needs, monitor existing law on a continuing basis, close loopholes, and give force to sanctions.

Here professional associations and educational institutions have significant roles to play. In addition to promoting values, they can foster dialogue and provide the disinterested judgment necessary for a proper exploration of the subject of government ethics. It is far too great a burden to place on public servants alone to develop appropriate standards.

In government today, we need to renew the hope of young people that one does not have to be unethical to succeed in politics. There is a constant need to reaffirm and give meaning to the concept that public office is a public trust. Opportunities and incentives that pit self-interest against integrity must be reduced or eliminated. Leaders in all walks of life have a responsibility to help in this endeavor. Honest government officials labor under constraints unparalleled by those imposed upon the rest of us. When the burdens become too great, and there is no visible moral support from the communities at large, officials may fall prey to pressures that not infrequently come from the private sector. In the areas of campaign financing and procurement particularly, the potential for corruption of the public sector by private interests is great. If business leaders insist upon institutional codes and continued dialogue about the ethical implications of various kinds of contact between businesspeople and government officials, they will contribute to an atmosphere that will diminish the likelihood of both government and private unethical behavior. Hopefully, we can clarify gray areas so the process is not full of traps. It is a sad state of affairs when distinguished public servants can describe the present political system as a "dangerous business," but that is not the fault of politicians alone.

In addition to its examination of so many critical areas of government ethics, this volume provides useful guidance and practical tips for identifying and avoiding ethical conflicts. It will be a valuable resource for lawyers, government officials, and members of the public alike for a long time to come. I salute the organizers of the first edition, especially Dean Patricia Salkin, for the contribution the book has made to the process of civilization. I am also grateful to editors Jennifer Rodgers and Evan Davis, and to the Center for the Advancement of Public Integrity at Columbia Law School, whose extensive work in tracking the progress of state ethics institutions and legislation has been necessary to understanding the country's anti-corruption efforts. As Elihu Root observed in 1926:

> There are no worse enemies of all attempts at improving the machinery of government, in any field, state, municipal, national, international, than the people who are always in a hurry, who are dissatisfied if results are not reached today or tomorrow, who think that if they cannot on the instant see a result accomplished, nothing has been done. The process of civilization is always a process of building up brick by brick, stone by stone, a structure which is unnoted for years but finally, in the fruition of time, is the basis for greater progress. I think it makes but little difference what part of that process a man contributes his life to. I think it makes but little difference whether a man gives his life and his service to laying the foundation and building up the structure, or whether he is the man that floats a flag on the battlements and cries, Victory![140]

NOTES

1. I wish to acknowledge the enormous assistance I received from Debleena Mitra (Fordham '20) in connection with the revision and updating of this chapter. Her research, editing, and drafting met a standard of excellence for which I am deeply grateful. As this chapter builds on its earlier versions, I also wish to acknowledge again those who helped me greatly in the past. These include Evan King, Esq., Leigh Tuccio, Esq., Joseph Sponholz, and the late Michele Falkow of the Fordham Law School Library staff. As noted earlier, this introduction reflects views I expressed in speeches and writings either on behalf or in connection with New York State commissions on ethics and integrity, beginning in 1987 and ending in 2009. I discuss these commissions in chapters of a book of mine, *That Further Shore: A Memoir of Irish Roots and American Promise*, published by the Fordham University Press in 2020.

2. In revising this chapter, with the assistance of Debleena Mitra, I have attempted to broaden its focus by examining the development of new laws and ethics agencies in states across the country. Public ethics are of course essential to good governance in any state, but several states provide clear examples of governmental responses to common ethics concerns. *See* notes 57 to 112 *infra*, and accompanying text (discussing various state ethics reforms including the proposed reforms in South Carolina, California's Fair Political Practices Commission, transparency laws in Texas, oversight structure in North Dakota, the Iowa Public Information Board, and the Virginia Conflict of Interest and Advisory Council).

3. *See generally* Daniel Koffsky, *Coming to Terms with Bureaucratic Ethics*, 11 J.L. & Pol. 235 (1995).

4. The Federalist No. 51 (James Madison).

5. Aristotle, Nicomachean Ethics, Book V (J.A.K. Thompson, ed., Penguin Books, 1959).

6. The Athenian Oath, *reprinted in* The Ethics Factor Handbook (International City Management Association 1988).

7. Mark Davies, *The Public Administrative Law Context of Ethics Requirements for West German and American Public Officials: A Comparative Analysis*, 18 Ga. J. Int'l & Comp. L. 319, 324 (1988).

8. An Act to Establish the Treasury Department, 1 Stat. 65, 67 (1789).

9. Report of the Association of the Bar of the City of New York Committee on the Federal Conflict of Interest Laws (Roswell B. Perkins, Chairman, Feb. 23, 1960). *See also* Association of the Bar of the City of New York, *Congress and the Public Trust, in* Report of the Association of the Bar of the City of New York Special Committee on Congressional Ethics (1970).

10. Report of the Association of the Bar of the City of New York Committee on the Federal Conflict of Interest Laws (Roswell B. Perkins, Chairman, Feb. 23, 1960).

11. *Id.*

12. *Id.*

13. *Id.*

14. *Id.*

15. Koffsky, *supra* note 3, at 245.

16. *Id.* (describing Exec. Order No. 10939, 26 Fed. Reg. 3951 (1961)).

17. *Id.*

18. S. Rep. No. 170, 95th Cong., 1st Sess. (1977), *reprinted in* 1978 U.S.C.C.A.N. 4216, 1977 WL 9629.

19. *Id.*

20. 18 U.S.C. § 207 (1977).

21. Koffsky, *supra* note 3, at 250 (quoting 1978 U.S.C.C.A.N. 4246–47).

22. S. Rep. No. 98-59 (1983), *reprinted in* 1983 U.S.C.C.A.N. 1313.

23. Pub. L. No. 101-94 (1989).

24. H.R. Rep. No. 104-595(I), at 3, *reprinted in* 1996 U.S.C.C.A.N. 1356, 1358.

25. Bipartisan Campaign Reform Act of 2002, Pub. L. No. 107-155.

26. Trevor Potter, David Ortiz & Anthony Corrado, The Campaign Legal Center, *The Campaign Finance Guide: Introduction* (2006), http://www.campaignfinanceguide.org/guide-17.html.

27. Bipartisan Campaign Reform Act of 2002, Pub. L. No. 107-155.

28. Help America Vote Act of 2002, Pub. L. No. 107-252.

29. COMMISSION ON FEDERAL ELECTION REFORM, REPORT OF THE COMMISSION ON FEDERAL ELECTION REFORM: BUILDING CONFIDENCE IN U.S. ELECTIONS 2 (2005), http://www.american.edu/ia/cfer/report/full_report.pdf [hereinafter COMMISSION ON FEDERAL ELECTION REFORM].

30. *See* Citizens United v. Federal Election Comm'n, 558 U.S. 310, 319–20 (2010).

31. *See id.* at 329.

32. *See id.* at 341 (noting that the First Amendment protects political speech from corporations); Susanna Kim Ripken, *Corporate First Amendment Rights After* Citizens United*: An Analysis of the Popular Movement to End the Constitutional Personhood of Corporations*, 14 U. PA J. BUS. L. 209, 211–12 (discussing negative reaction to the decision).

33. Sheryl Gay Stolberg, *Obama Turns Up Heat over Ruling on Campaign Spending*, N.Y. TIMES (Jan. 23, 2010), https://www.nytimes.com/2010/01/24/us/politics/24address.html.

34. *See* H.R.J. Res. 68, 111th Cong. (2010); Ripken, *supra* note 32, at 227–28.

35. *See, e.g.*, H.R.J. Res. 74, 111th Cong. (2010) ("Proposing an Amendment to the Constitution of the United States Permitting Congress and the States to Regulate the Expenditure of Funds by Corporations Engaging in Political Speech," introduced by Congresswoman Donna Edwards, D-MD); S. Res. 525, 113th Cong. (2013) (proposing a constitutional amendment to "restore the rights of American people that were taken away by the Supreme Court's decision in the *Citizen's United* case," introduced by Senator Bernie Sanders, I-VT). *See generally* CONGRESSIONAL RESEARCH SEARCH SERVICE, LEGISLATIVE OPTION AFTER *CITIZENS UNITED V. FEC:* CONSTITUTIONAL AND LEGAL ISSUES 1–3 (2010) (summarizing the reaction to *Citizen United*).

36. *See, e.g.*, Jed Handelsman Shugerman, *Fighting Corruption in America and Abroad*, 84 FORDHAM L. REV. 407 (2015); *Citizens United*, COMMON CAUSE, http://www.commoncause.org/issues/money-in-politics/fighting-big-money/citizens-united/ (last visited Mar. 10, 2022); Press Release, Bernie Sanders, Constitutional Amendment Sponsors Renew Push to Undo *Citizens United* (Mar. 12, 2013), https://www.sanders.senate.gov/press-releases/constitutional-amendment-sponsors-renew-push-to-undo-citizens-united-2/ (noting that 11 states and more than 300 cities and towns have passed resolutions seeking to overturn *Citizens United*).

37. *See, e.g.*, Merrit Kennedy, *District of Columbia Sues Inaugural Committee for "Grossly Overpaying" At Trump Hotel*, NPR.com (Jan. 22, 2020), https://www.npr.org/2020/01/22/798500880/district-of-columbia-sues-inaugural-committee-for-grossly-overpaying-at-trump-ho.

38. *Citizens United*, COMMON CAUSE, http://www.commoncause.org/issues/money-in-politics/fighting-big-money/citizens-united/ (last visited Mar. 18, 2015).

39. Clinton v. Jones, 520 U.S. 681 (1997).

40. Camila Domonoske, *Judge Approves $25 Million Settlement of Trump University Lawsuit*, NPR (Mar. 31, 2017), https://www.npr.org/sections/thetwo-way/2017/03/31/522199535/judge-approves-25-million-settlement-of-trump-university-lawsuit.

41. *Id.*

42. For a detailed discussion of the subject of emoluments, see the 2020 report of the Fordham Law School Democracy and Constitution Clinic. James Auchincloss, Megha Dharia & Krysia Lenzon, *Enforcing the Intent of the Constitution's Foreign and Domestic Emoluments Clauses*, DEMOCRACY AND THE CONSTITUTION CLINIC, FORDHAM LAW SCHOOL (Jan. 2020), https://www.fordham.edu/download/downloads/id/14400/Enforcing_the_Intent_of_the_Emoluments_Clauses___Democracy_Clinic.pdf.

43. *Id.*, U.S. CONST. art. I, § 9, cl. 8.

44. *Id.*

45. Steve Eder, *How Federal Ethics Laws Will Apply to a Trump Presidency*, N.Y. TIMES (Nov. 11, 2016), https://www.nytimes.com/2016/11/12/us/politics/how-federal-ethics-laws-will-apply-to-a-trump-presidency.html.

46. Bobby Allyn, *Trump Still Faces 3 Lawsuits Over His Business Empire*, NATIONAL PUBLIC RADIO (Dec. 12, 2019), https://www.npr.org/2019/12/12/787167408/trump-still-faces-3-lawsuits-over-his-business-empire. See the three lawsuits against Trump: *CREW v. Trump*, *Blumenthal v. Trump* (suit brought by Congress), and *In re Trump*; *see also* Ciara Torres-Spelliscy, *Supreme Court Ducks an Opportunity on Trump Emoluments Cases*, BRENNEN CTR. FOR JUSTICE (Feb. 19, 2021), https://www.brennancenter.org/our-work/analysis-opinion/supreme-court-ducks-opportunity-trump-emoluments-cases: "In the suit brought by Congress, the justices simply declined to review the case in October, thus upholding the ruling by the DC Circuit Court of Appeals that members of Congress lacked the legal standing to sue under the Foreign Emoluments Clause. And on January 25, the Supreme Court dismissed the other two cases as moot since Trump was no longer in office." *See also* Josh Gerstein, *Supreme Court Shuts Down 2 Trump Emoluments Cases*, POLITICO (Jan. 25, 2021), https://www.politico.com/news/2021/01/25/supreme-court-trump-emolument-cases-462134.

47. *Id.*

48. Auchincloss, Dharia & Lenzon, *supra* note 42.

49. *See* Application of the Emoluments Clause and the Foreign Gifts and Decorations Act to the President's Receipt of the Nobel Peace Prize, 33 Op. O.L.C. 1 (2009); President Reagan's Ability to Receive Retirement Benefits from the State of California, 5 Op. O.L.C. 187 (1981), 192.

50. Auchincloss, Dharia & Lenzon, *supra* note 42.

51. *Id.* at 7.

52. *Id.*

53. *Id.* at 9.

54. Nicholas Fandos & Michael D. Shear, *Trump Impeached for Abuse of Power and Obstruction of Congress*, N.Y. TIMES (Dec. 18, 2019), https://www.nytimes.com/2019/12/18/us/politics/trump-impeached.html. In the House of Representatives, 230 members voted to pass the first article of impeachment ("Abuse of power") and 229 members voted to pass the second article of impeachment ("Obstruction of Congress").

55. *How Senators Voted on Trump's Impeachment*, POLITICO.COM (Feb. 5, 2020), https://www.politico.com/interactives/2019/trump-impeachment-vote-count-senate-results/.

56. *Id.*

57. NATIONAL MUNICIPAL LEAGUE, MODEL STATE CONFLICT OF INTEREST AND FINANCIAL DISCLOSURE LAW (1979).

58. *Id.*

59. MERLON J. PUSEY, CHARLES EVANS HUGHES 148 (1951).

60. *See* GOVERNMENT ETHICS REFORM FOR THE 1990S: THE COLLECTED REPORTS OF THE NEW YORK STATE COMMISSION ON GOVERNMENT INTEGRITY (Fordham University Press, 1991).

61. New York State Commission on Government Integrity, *Restoring the Public Trust: A Blue Print for Government Integrity,* 18 FORDHAM URB. L. J. 173, 180 (1990–91) [hereinafter New York State Commission on Government Integrity].

62. Olmstead v. United States, 277 U.S. 438, 485 (1928) (Justice Holmes, dissenting).

63. New York State Commission on Government Integrity, *supra* note 61, at 205.

64. *State of New York Temporary State Commission on Local Government Ethics Final Report*, 21 FORDHAM URB. L.J. 1 (1993).

65. S.B. 5927, 229th Ann. Leg. Sess., 2005 N.Y. ALS ch. 766 (N.Y. 2005); *see* Douglas Goodfriend & Thomas Myers, *Public Authorities Accountability Act of 2005: Dramatic New Rules—Applicability to Local Agencies, Organizations and Governmental Units*, NYSBA MUNICIPAL LAWYER (Spring 2006).

66. Goodfriend & Myers, *supra* note 65.

67. *See* Public Employees Ethics Reform Act of 2007, Assem. B. 3736, 230th Ann. Leg. Sess., 2007 N.Y. ALS ch. 14 (N.Y. 2007); Public Integrity Reform Act of 2011, Assem. B. A08301, 234th Reg. Leg. Sess. (N.Y. 2011); *see also* Karl Sleight & Thomas DeSimon, *Ethics, Lobbying and Public Integrity in New York Government,* 237 N.Y.L.J. 93 (May 15, 2007); *New*

York State Public Integrity Reform Act: An Overview for Public Officials, N.Y. JOINT COMMISSION ON PUBLIC ETHICS.

68. *New York*, Center for the Advancement of Public Integrity, COLUM. L. SCH. 4 (May 2018), https://web.law.columbia.edu/capi-map#capi-mapinfo (last visited Jan. 15, 2021).

69. More specific information about the states' government ethics regulations is available at the National Conference of State Legislators' website, https://www.ncsl.org/research/ethics/state-ethics-oversight-agencies.aspx (last visited Jan. 15, 2021) (listing all ethics oversight agencies in each state).

70. *See, e.g.*, COUNSEL ON GOVERNMENT ETHICS REFORM, http://www.cogel.org (last visited Jan. 15, 2021). The Counsel on Government Ethics Reform is a professional organization of ethics professionals from the public and private sector that disseminates ideas and best practices relating to campaign finance, access to public information, lobbying, and ethics. *See History*, COUNSEL ON GOVERNMENT ETHICS REFORM, http://www.cogel.org/page/History (last visited Jan. 15, 2021).

71. *See* CENTER FOR PUBLIC INTEGRITY, *About Us*, https:/publicintegrity.org/inside-publici/aboutus/ (last visited Jan. 15, 2021).

72. *See* STATE INTEGRITY INVESTIGATION, *About the State Integrity Investigation*, http://www.stateintegrity.org/about (last visited Jan. 15, 2021).

73. *See id.*

74. *See, e.g.*, Cuthbert Langley, *South Carolina Graded "F" for Ethics Laws as Debate Rages On*, WBTW 13, CBS (Florence, S.C.), (Apr. 12, 2014), https://plus.lexis.com/api/permalink/d3d1a3d4-f359-43cb-a6ce-0d70b646680d/?context=1530671.

75. Gov. Nikki Haley, S.C. State of the State Address (Jan. 16, 2013) (transcript available at https://www.thestate.com/news/politics-government/article14419142.html); South Carolina Corruption Risk Report Card, STATE INTEGRITY INVESTIGATION, http://www.stateintegrity.org/south_carolina (last visited Mar. 17, 2015) (reporting that South Carolina received grade "F," ranking 45th out of 50 states in the nation).

76. *See* Gov. Nikki Haley, S.C. State of the State Address (Jan. 16, 2013) (transcript available at https://www.thestate.com/news/politics-government/article14419142.html) (proclaiming that "[o]ur citizens must have confidence in how we [public officials] do our jobs").

77. *See, e.g.*, Norimitsu Onishi, *California Democrats Await Fallout after 3 Are Caught Up in Scandals*, N.Y. TIMES (Apr. 3, 2014), https://www.nytimes.com/2014/04/04/us/california-democrats-await-fallout-after-3-are-caught-up-in-scandals.html.

78. Jeremy B. White & Christopher Cadelago, *California Lawmakers Took Less Free Travel in 2014* (Mar. 3, 2015, 11:32 PM), https://www.sacbee.com/news/politics-government/capitol-alert/article12332504.html (reporting on a new state-wide prohibition on lobbyists holding fundraisers in their homes).

79. Press Release, California Fair Political Practices Commission, FPPC Launches Online Toolkit for New Candidates (Feb. 26, 2015), http://www.fppc.ca.gov/media/press-releases/2015-news-releases/fppc-launches-online-toolkit-for-new-candidates.html. The FPPC also provides an overview of the steps lobbyists must take to lawfully engage in lobbying activity, including registering with the Secretary of State and applicable reporting deadlines. *See Lobbyist Forms, Rules, & Manual*, CALIFORNIA FAIR POLITICAL PRACTICES COMM'N, http://www.fppc.ca.gov/learn/lobbyist-rules/lobbying-manual-and-forms.html.

80. CAL. GOV'T CODE § 83115 (West 2014) (providing investigative authority); CAL. GOV'T CODE § 90001 (West 2014) (requiring random audits).

81. *See* FPPC ENFORCEMENT DIVISION, 2013 YEAR END REPORT 16, https://www.fppc.ca.gov/content/dam/fppc/NS-Documents/Annual-Report/2013-Annual-Report.pdf.

82. *See, e.g.*, Press Release, California Fair Political Practices Commission, FPPC Enforcement Division Decisions: February 19, 2015 (Feb. 19, 2015), https://web.archive.org/web/20150918182319/http://www.fppc.ca.gov/press_release.php?pr_id=802.

83. Associated Press in San Francisco, *Former California State Senator Leland Yee Sentenced to Five Years in Prison*, THE GUARDIAN (Feb. 2016), https://www.theguardian.com/us-news/2016/feb/24/california-leland-yee-five-years-prison-bribes-weapons-philippines.

84. *California*, Center for the Advancement of Public Integrity, COLUM. L. SCH. 2 (May 2018).

85. Dianna Wray, *How the Sharpstown State Bank Brought Down Texas's Top Politicians*, HOUSTONIA MAG (Nov. 26, 2018), https://www.houstoniamag.com/news-and-city-life/2018/11/sharpstown-bank.

86. *Id.* In 2017 the state legislature successfully passed a package of reforms which included provisions taking away pensions from elected officials who had been convicted of felony public corruption charges, instituting a waiting period before retiring lawmakers can engage in lobbying services, and required more rigorous disclosure from elected officials.

87. *Texas*, Center for the Advancement of Public Integrity, COLUM. L. SCH. 2 (May 2018), https://web.law.columbia.edu/capi-map#capi-mapinfo.

88. Jim Malewitz, *Years after Perry Veto, Travis County Seeks Revival of Statewide Prosecuting Unit*, TEXAS TRIBUNE (Mar. 30, 2017), https://www.kut.org/post/years-after-perry-veto-travis-county-seeks-revival-statewide-prosecuting-unit.

89. *Id.*; *North Dakota*, Center for the Advancement of Public Integrity, COLUM. L. SCH. 1 (May 2018), https://web.law.columbia.edu/capi-map#capi-mapinfo (last visited Jan. 15, 2021).

90. *Id.* at 1.

91. Mike Nowatzki, *Lawmakers Say "No" to Letting Voters Decide on State Ethics Commission*, DICKINSON PRESS (Mar. 16, 2015), http://www.thedickinsonpress.com/news/government-and-politics/3701254-lawmakers-say-no-letting-voters-decide-state-ethics-commission.

92. *North Dakota*, Center for the Advancement of Public Integrity, COLUM. L. SCH. 1 (May 2018), https://web.law.columbia.edu/capi-map#capi-mapinfo.

93. *Iowa Corruption Risk Report Card*, STATE INTEGRITY INVESTIGATION, http://www.stateintegrity.org/iowa (last visited Mar. 17, 2015) (reporting that Iowa's only grade of "F" was in the category of "Public Access to Information"); Editorial, *Teaching Iowans to Hold Officials Accountable*, IOWA CITY PRESS CITIZEN, Aug. 30, 2012, https://plus.lexis.com/api/permalink/bee8e22e-c553-4504-87a0-172c489cab61/?context=1530671 (discussing the creation of the Iowa Public Information Board in the wake of the state's poor performance in the State Integrity Investigation's report on "Public Access to Information").

94. *See* IOWA CODE ANN. § 22.10 (West 2015) (providing for civil enforcement mechanisms); IOWA CODE ANN. § 23 (West 2015) (establishing the Iowa Public Information Board); Editorial, *Ensuring the Public's Business Is Done in Public*, IOWA CITY PRESS CITIZEN (May 5, 2012), http://advance.lexis.com/api/permalink/1053d23e-c4a2-4a46-a10f-57364a024b7b/?context=1000516; *Branstad Will Sign Open Creating Information Panel*, GLOBE GAZETTE (Mason City, IA), (May 3, 2012, 6:37AM), http://globegazette.com/news/iowa/branstad-will-sign-bill-creating-information-panel/article_34ba6492-9510-11e1-95b5-001a4bcf887a.html.

95. *Ensuring the Public's Business Is Done in Public, supra* note 94.

96. *See IPBB Powers, Duties, and Hot Topics*, IOWA PUBLIC INFORMATION BOARD (Oct. 10, 2014), https://ipib.iowa.gov/sites/default/files/WebsitePresentation_10-15-14.pdf.

97. *See id.* at 1.

98. *See id. at* 2–3, IOWA CODE ANN. § 23.10(b) (West 2015) (providing potential resolutions upon finding that a violation occurred).

99. *See Chapter 22 Frequently Asked Questions*, IOWA PUBLIC INFORMATION BOARD, https://www.ipib.iowa.gov/faqs/chapter-22 (last visited Mar. 16, 2015).

100. *See IPIB Powers, Duties, and Hot Topics, supra* note 96, at 2–3.

101. *See* Jenna Portnoy, *Va. Names Head of New Ethics Council Formed in Wake of McDonnell Case*, WASH. POST (Aug. 7, 2014), https://www.washingtonpost.com/local/virginia-politics/va-names-head-of-new-ethics-council-formed-in-wake-of-mcdonnell-case/2014/08/07/c46de39e-1e56-11e4-ae54-0cfe1f974f8a_story.html.

102. *See* Josh Gerstein, *Supreme Court Overturns Bob McDonnell's Corruption Convictions*, Politico.com (June 27, 2016, 10:33 AM), https://www.politico.com/story/2016/06/supreme-court-overturns-bob-mcdonnells-corruption-convictions-224833.

103. *See* S.B. 649 (2014), 2014 Va. Legis. Serv. 804 (West); *Virginia Adopts New Gift Law*, Insights: Skadden, Arps, Slate, Meagher, Flom (Apr. 28. 2014), https://www.skadden.com/insights/publications/2014/04/virginia-adopts-new-gift-law.

104. *See* Va. S.B. 649; *Virginia Adopts New Gift Law*, *supra* note 103.

105. *See* Va. S.B. 649 ch. 55.

106. *Id.* The Pennsylvania State Ethics Commission was created by the Pennsylvania Public Official and Employees Ethics Act, Act 170 of 1978.

107. *Id.*

108. *Florida*, Center for the Advancement of Public Integrity, Colum. L. Sch. 1 (May 2018), https://web.law.columbia.edu/capi-map#capi-mapinfo.

109. *Michigan*, Center for the Advancement of Public Integrity, Colum. L. Sch. 1 (May 2018), https://web.law.columbia.edu/capi-map#capi-mapinfo.

110. *Id.*

111. *Id.*

112. *Id.*

113. *See New York City Campaign Finance Act*, N.Y.C. Campaign Finance Board, https://www.nyccfb.info/law/act/campaign-finance-board/ (last visited May 17, 2022) (compiling relevant provisions of the New York City Charter and Administrative Code).

114. *See About Us*, N.Y.C. Campaign Finance BD., https://www.nyccfb.info/about (last visited May 17, 2022). The Campaign Finance Board is also tasked with educating the City's electorate by running the various political debates and publishing a comprehensive Voter Guide. *See id. See also NYC Campaign Finance Board Teams Up with Fordham to Celebrate 20 Years*, Inside Fordham Online (Mar. 17, 2008), https://news.fordham.edu/inside-fordham/nyc-campaign-finance-board-teams-up-with-fordham-to-celebrate-20-years/.

115. *See* Telephone Interview by Evan King with Eric Friedman, Assistant Executive Director for Public Affairs, New York Campaign Finance Board (Mar. 25, 2015) [hereinafter Eric Friedman Interview].

116. *See* Eric Friedman Interview, *supra* note 115.

117. *See* New York City Campaign Finance Board, *By the People: The New York City Campaign Finance Program in the 2013 Elections I* (2014) [hereinafter *By the People*], http://www.nyccfb.info/PDF/per/2013_PER/2013_PER.pdf.; Eric Friedman Interview, *supra* note 115.

118. *See By the People*, *supra* note 117, at 1.

119. *See* New York City Campaign Finance Board, *Keeping Democracy Strong: New York City's* Campaign Finance Program in the 2017 Citywide Elections (2018), https://www.nyccfb.info/pdf/2017_Post-Election_Report_2.pdf [hereinafter *Keeping Democracy Strong*], at 1.

120. *Id.*

121. *Id.* at 2.

122. *Id.*

123. *Id.* at 48.

124. *Id.* at 45.

125. *See About COIB*, NYC Conflicts of Interests Board, https://www1.nyc.gov/site/coib/about/about-coib.page (last visited May 17, 2022).

126. *See id.*

127. *See id.*

128. The Department of Investigation (DOI) is one of the nation's oldest law enforcement agencies, having been formed in the 1870s, with jurisdiction over all New York City agencies, elected and appointed officials, employees, contractors, and beneficiaries. DOI conducts investigations into fraud, waste, and abuse, engages in comprehensive training and education programs, and works with the agencies it oversees to instigate operational reforms to improve the way city government functions. See About DOI, NYC Department of Investigation, https://www1.nyc.gov/site/doi/about/about.page (last visited Jan. 27, 2021).

129. *See* Rose Gill Hearn, *The New York City Integrity System*, in Local Integrity Systems: World Cities Fighting Corruption and Safeguarding Integrity (Leo Huberts, Frank Anechiarico & Frédérique Six eds. 2008) (publishing a paper presented by Rose Gill Hearn at a February, 2007 conference in Amsterdam, The Netherlands, hosted by the City of Amsterdam and VU University); Rose Gill Hearn & Frank Anechiarico, *Who Is the Inspector General*, 12 Pub. Integrity 289 (providing additional information on the 2008 conference, Watchdog I, including details of the keynote address from the former Mayor of New York City, Edward I. Koch); Anti-Corruption Strategies, Economic Development and Good Governance, New York City Global Partners, http://www.nyc.gov/html/unccp/scp/html/summit/integrity_summit.shtml (providing an overview of the tenth New York City Global Partners Summit, held in June 2012, at Fordham University School of Law).

130. *See* Rose Gill Hearn & Frank Anechiarico, *supra* note 129 (Watchdog I); Press Release, New York City Department of Investigation, DOI Hosts Watchdog II Anti-Corruption Summit (July 21, 2013), http://www.nyc.gov/html/doi/downloads/pdf/2013/jul13/pr25watch dogII_73113.pdf (summarizing the 2013 conference, Watchdog II, which brought together scholars and officials from multiple states and countries, including Australia, Canada, and Tanzania).

131. Symposium, *Fighting Corruption in American and Abroad*, 83 Fordham L. Rev. (Nov. 2015).

132. *See About Us*, https://publicintegrity.org/inside-publici/aboutus/ (last visited Jan. 31, 2021).

133. *See About CREW*, https://www.citizensforethics.org/about/ (last visited Jan. 31, 2021).

134. Silver was ultimately convicted and exhausted his appeals, and is serving a 78-month sentence. *See* Benjamin Weiser & Jesse McKinley, *Sheldon Silver, Former N.Y. Assembly Speaker, Will Finally Go To Prison*, N.Y. Times (July 20, 2020), https://www.nytimes.com/2020/07/20/nyregion/sheldon-silver-sentencing-prison.html.

135. *See* Alexander Burns & Susanne Craig, *Pushing Ethics Reform, Cuomo Wants Lawmakers to Reveal Income or Lost It*, N.Y. Times (Feb. 2, 2015), https://www.nytimes.com/2015/02/03/nyregion/cuomo-seeks-ethics-reform-after-sheldon-silver-arrest.html. Several weeks after his office indicted Assemblyman Silver, Preet Bharara, the United States Attorney for the Southern District of New York, gave the keynote at Fordham Law Review's March 6, 2015, symposium entitled *Fighting Corruption in America and Abroad*. For video of the entire keynote address, see Fordham Law School, *U.S. Attorney Preet Bharara at Fordham Law Review Symposium on Fighting Corruption*, Vimeo (Mar. 6, 2015), https://Ivimeo.comI121502921. *See also* Benjamin Weiser, *U.S. Attorney Keeps Talking, but Leaves out Sheldon Silver*, N.Y. Times (Mar. 6, 2015), https://www.nytimes.com/2015/03/07/nyregion/us-attorney-keeps-talking-but-omits-sheldon-silver.html (discussing United States Attorney Bharara's address).

136. *Id.* One of the pillars of Governor Cuomo's proposed reforms was a complete overhaul of income disclosure requirements. *Id.* He demanded that the legislature ban all outside income for lawmakers or enact sweeping reforms on income disclosure requirements. *Id.*

137. *Id.*

138. *Albany Reform Tops City Bar's 2015 Legislative Agenda*, 44th Street Notes 8 (N.Y.C. Ass'n Winter 2015).

139. *See* Ethan Geringer-Sameth, *After Court Rulings, Unclear Future for Push to Restrict State Legislators Outside Income*, Gotham Gazette (Jan. 21, 2020), https://www.gothamgazette.com/state/9061-after-court-rulings-unclear-future-for-push-to-restrict-state-legislators-outside-income.

140. T. Schick, The New York State Constitutional Convention of 1915 and the Modern State Governor 133 (1978).

CHAPTER 3

Transparency
Ann Ravel

> This chapter provides an overview of federal and state transparency laws and discusses ways in which transparency might be improved.

INTRODUCTION

"Transparency and accountability are not only pie-in-the-sky ideals in building better, more democratic governments, they are also tools for improving civic participation and community well-being."[1] Transparency in government is also closely related to ethics in government. Most Americans generally accept that transparency within federal and state governments is essential and that citizens have a right to know what their government officials are up to.[2] In particular, transparency in government engenders trust in government and government institutions, but also provides an opportunity for the public and the press to ensure that government resources are being used to benefit the public. But just because transparency has become an expectation does not mean that it is being provided in a manner that makes it meaningful and accessible.[3]

The federal government has attempted to encourage transparency through the Freedom of Information Act (FOIA) and Open Meeting Laws, while many states such as California and New York have enacted their own statutes modeled after the FOIA to encourage the access of governmental records to the public.[4] In California, access to public records is governed by the California Public Records Act, while in New York it is governed by the Freedom of Information Law.[5]

Though public access to governmental records is now expected and encouraged, there remain major issues surrounding the openness, timeliness, and accessibility of these records.[6] Furthermore, when it comes to transparency and privacy within federal and state governments, there remains a great elephant in the room: where do governments draw the line when it comes to granting public access to information that may present a risk to the government?[7]

WHAT IS PUBLIC SECTOR TRANSPARENCY AND WHY IS IT SO IMPORTANT?

Transparency in the public sector has generally been equated with the simple "ability to access information about government via 'freedom of information' laws."[8] FOIA and its state equivalents allow citizens to request government-held information by paying a minimal cost.[9] As a matter of principle, public officials and civil servants have a duty to act "visibly, predictably, and understandably to promote participation and accountability."[10] While transparency is often touted as a key to democracy, most citizens accept this principle at face-value—without asking why transparency is so sought after. The Sunlight Foundation—a national, nonpartisan, nonprofit devoted to promoting open government—has conducted extensive research on the benefits of making government information public in cities.[11] Most significantly, its investigations have found that when cities make data regarding budgets, traffic collisions, or even potholes public ("open data"), residents are given the opportunity to participate in solving issues that directly impact a city's direction.[12]

Open data itself can build public trust in government, while also encouraging good governance by facilitating accountability, openness, and creativity between governments and community members.[13] But simply making vast amounts of information available is not enough to foster true transparency.[14] Information must be managed in a way that makes it accurate, timely, and accessible.[15]

FEDERAL AND STATE LAWS GOVERNING TRANSPARENCY

The Federal Government

Freedom of Information Act

The FOIA was originally enacted by the federal government in 1966 and took effect one year later.[16] The act established the process that citizens can use to request access to records from any federal agency, unless a portion of the records requested are subject to one of nine exemptions or three exclusions.[17] The Supreme Court of the United States has recognized that the basic purpose of FOIA is to create "an informed citizenry, vital to the functioning of a democratic society, needed to check against corruption and to hold the governors accountable to the governed."[18] However, the Court has also supported the provisions allowing for certain records to remain exempt from disclosure due to "the need of the Government 'to protect certain information.'"[19]

The FOIA contains 13 main subsections.[20] Subsections (a)(1) and (a)(2) describe in detail which information every federal agency must make available as generally posted public information.[21] Subsection (a)(3) is the mechanism that enables citizens to make public records requests of any federal agency.[22] This subsection provides that those records that are "not made available under subsections (a)(1) or (a)(2) can be requested by the public" and describes the procedures to be followed in making a FOIA request.[23] The two requirements for making such a request are that it must reasonably describe the record being requested, and the request must be made in accordance with the specific agency's published rules regarding time, place, fees, and procedures.[24] Pursuant to subsection (a)(6)(a), each agency must determine within 20 days of the receipt of the request whether to deny the request, grant the request, or grant the request in part.[25] If there is a need to extend the response period due to "unusual circumstances," the agency must notify the requester in writing of the extension.[26]

When an agency receives a request that is in accordance with the guidelines set out in subsection (a)(3), it is obligated to make the records "promptly available" in the format requested,[27] unless the records or a portion of the records fall under an exemption listed in subsection (b) or an exclusion listed in subsection (c).[28] Subsection (b) governs the nine exemptions to the FOIA.[29] These exemptions "authorize agencies to withhold information when they reasonably foresee that disclosure would harm an interest protected by [them]."[30] The nine exemptions are as follows: (1) information that is classified to protect national security; (2) information related solely to the internal personnel rules and practices of an agency; (3) information that is prohibited from disclosure by another federal law; (4) trade secrets or commercial or financial information that is confidential or privileged; (5) privileged communications within or between agencies, including those protected by the deliberative process privilege (provided the records were created less than 25 years before the date on which they were requested), attorney–work product privilege, attorney–client privilege; (6) information that, if disclosed, would invade another individual's personal privacy; (7) information compiled for law enforcement purposes that (a) could reasonably be expected to interfere with enforcement proceedings, (b) would deprive a person of a right to a fair trial or an impartial adjudication, (c) could reasonably be expected to constitute an unwarranted invasion of personal privacy, (d) could reasonably be expected to disclose the identity of a confidential source, (e) would disclose techniques and procedures for law enforcement investigations or prosecutions, or would disclose guidelines for law enforcement investigations or prosecutions if such disclosure could reasonably be expected to risk circumvention of the law, or (f) could reasonably be expected to endanger the life or physical safety of any individual; (8) information that concerns the supervision of financial institutions; and (9) geological information on wells.[31] The nine exemptions are discretionary in nature however, not mandatory.[32] The FOIA provides for an administrative appeals process in subsection (a)(6) and allows requesters to seek remedies in U.S. district courts—where the agency carries the burden of proof of defending its reasons for nondisclosure and the court determines whether the agency has the right to withhold information de novo.[33]

Congress has also provided for three categories of records that are exclusions to the FOIA.[34] This means that they are not subject to the act, and when responding to a request for a public record that falls into the "excluded" category, an agency can deny the request without even revealing the existence of such records.[35] The first exclusion protects an ongoing criminal investigation when the subject of the investigation is unaware it is pending and disclosure could interfere with enforcement proceedings.[36] The second exclusion applies only to criminal law enforcement agencies and protects the existence of informant records when the informant's status has not officially been confirmed.[37] The third exclusion is limited to the Federal Bureau of Investigation and protects the existence of classified records regarding foreign intelligence, counterintelligence, or international terrorism.[38]

FOIA also has provisions to provide reasonable attorneys' fees and litigation costs to a FOIA plaintiff who has substantially prevailed in litigation against the government. This requires a two-step substantive inquiry:

1. If the plaintiff is eligible for an award (generally, if the plaintiff has a representational relationship with an attorney), and
2. If the plaintiff is entitled to an award by having substantially prevailed in the litigation.[39]

However, any fees and costs award is entirely within the discretion of the court.

Over the years, the FOIA has been amended many times.[40] Most of the changes have been to narrow the FOIA exemptions.[41] Furthermore, given the inherent political nature of public sector transparency, the government's disclosure obligations under FOIA have varied based on the Office of the President.[42] For instance, on October 12, 2001, the attorney general, under the directive of President Bush, issued a FOIA Memorandum stating that the Department of Justice (DOJ) would "defend decisions to withhold records 'unless they lack a sound legal basis or present an unwarranted risk of adverse impact on the ability of other agencies to protect other important records.'"[43] In contrast, in a January 21, 2009, FOIA Memorandum, President Obama asserted that his administration would administer FOIA with a presumption of openness.[44] President Obama went on to articulate that agencies should post information online proactively before citizens made public requests, and when a request is made, agencies should "make it a priority to respond in a timely manner."[45] The Office of the Attorney General under President Obama elaborated in a March 19, 2009, Memorandum, stating that the DOJ would "defend a denial of a FOIA request only if (1) the agency reasonably foresees that disclosure would harm an interest protected by one of the statutory exemptions, or (2) disclosure is prohibited by law."[46]

Open Meeting Laws

The FOIA operates in conjunction with various federal open meeting laws such as the Government in the Sunshine Act and the Federal Advisory Committee Act

(FACA).[47] FACA provides that a committee must provide public notice in the Federal Register 15 days prior to every meeting.[48] It also states that the public notice must provide all information regarding the meeting, including the committee's name; the time, place, and purpose of the meeting; and a summary of the agenda.[49] If the meeting, or any part of the meeting, is closed to the public, the notice must include the committee's name; the time, place, and purpose of the meeting; a summary of the agenda; and the exemption from the Government in the Sunshine Act that applies to allow the meeting to be closed to the public.[50]

Digital Accountability and Transparency Act

The Digital Accountability and Transparency Act (DATA Act), enacted into law in 2014, has been one of the most significant developments in transparency at the federal level.[51] The DATA Act requires that the federal government transform information regarding its spending into open data.[52] It does so by requiring the Treasury Department and the White House Office of Management and Budget (OMB) to establish government-wide data standards for the spending information reported by federal agencies.[53] It also requires the Treasury and OMB to publish the standardized spending data for free access and download on the USASpending.gov website.[54]

California: Public Records Act and Open Meeting Laws

The California Public Records Act (PRA) was enacted in 1968 and modeled after the FOIA.[55] The California Supreme Court has explained that the PRA was enacted to "safeguard the accountability of government to the public, for secrecy is antithetical to a democratic system of 'government of the people, by the people [and] for the people.'"[56] The PRA provides for two different ways to access public records: (1) the right to inspect public records at the state or local agency during the agency's office hours or (2) the right to request a copy of public record documents from the state or local agency.[57] "Public records" are defined as "any writing containing information relating to the conduct of the public's business prepared, owned, used, or retained by any state or local agency regardless of physical form or characteristics."[58] Similar to the FOIA, unless a public record has been made exempt from disclosure through the express provision of law, upon the receipt of a request for disclosure of a record, a state or local agency must make the records promptly available as soon as appropriate fees have been paid.[59]

However, the PRA contains approximately 76 express exemptions and includes a balancing test, known as a "public interest" or "catchall" provision.[60] Some of the more frequently raised exemptions include attorney–client communications and attorney work product, voter registration information, law enforcement records, medical records, pending litigation or claims, taxpayer information, and utility customer information.[61] When an agency claims an exemption and does not grant a request for disclosure of information, it must state the specific exemption that applies in its response.[62] The catchall provision of the PRA is essentially a balancing test that enables local and state agencies to withhold records if the agency can demonstrate that the public interest served by nondisclosure of the record outweighs the public interest served by disclosure.[63] This analysis must be done on a case-by-case basis.[64]

The PRA provides strict guidelines in regard to the timeliness of responses to public records requests. Generally, the assumption provided in the PRA is that "nothing in this chapter shall be construed to permit an agency to delay or obstruct the inspection or copying of public records."[65] Local and state agencies are required to respond to requests within ten calendar days from receipt of the request and to notify the requester if records will be disclosed or not.[66] If an agency needs time to search for records, compile data, or confer with another agency, it may notify the requester in writing that it needs a 14-day extension maximum.[67]

Another similarity that the PRA shares with the FOIA is that it is largely enforced through the judicial process.[68] Any person whose request for disclosure of public records is denied can use an expedited civil judicial process to ask a judge to enforce their right to inspect or receive a copy of a public record.[69] And, a prevailing party can obtain court costs and reasonable attorneys' fees if he or she succeeded on any issue in the litigation, and achieved some of the public benefits sought in the lawsuit. The amount of the fees that can be obtained is left to the discretion of the trial court.[70]

In California, the PRA works in conjunction with the Open Meeting Acts—a combination of statutes regulating public access to local and state meetings.[71] The Ralph M. Brown Act (the Brown Act), guarantees the public's right to "attend and participate in meetings of [county and] local legislative bodies,"[72] while the Bagley-Keene Opening Meeting Act requires all state boards and commissions to "publicly notice their meetings, prepare agendas, accept public testimony and conduct their meetings in public unless specifically authorized by the Act to meet in closed session."[73]

These laws are generally not applicable to the legislatures. However, California does have a California Legislative Open Records Act (LORA), which is applicable to the State Senate and Assembly. LORA provides access to inspect and reproduce certain records, but many records are exempt from mandatory public inspection.[74]

New York: Freedom of Information Law and Open Meetings Law

New York's Freedom of Information Law (FOIL), originally enacted in 1974, provides citizens of New York with the right to access records reflective of government decisions and policies.[75] The FOIL is similar to the most recent enactment of the FOIA in that it is based on a presumption of access but allows disclosure of public records to be denied by a state agency if the records fall within one of the

11 "categories of deniable records."[76] The 11 categories are essentially the same as the FOIA exemptions, with a bit more specificity.[77]

The FOIL is distinct from both the FOIA and the PRA in that it requires state agencies to respond to public records requests within five business days of the receipt of a written request for a record reasonably described.[78] An agency's response must provide a written acknowledgment of receipt of the request and either provide a reasonably approximate date of when the request will be granted or denied, or state the reasons why the request cannot be granted in writing.[79] The approximate date cannot exceed 20 business days from the date of acknowledgment of the receipt of the request, and, if additional time is needed, the agency must explain the reason and provide a specific date for its grant of the request in whole or in part.[80] Similar to both the FOIA and the PRA, citizens can seek to enforce the FOIL through judicial review of an agency's decision to deny a public records request.[81] A prevailing party can receive from the agency reasonable attorney's fees and other litigation costs reasonably incurred when the party substantially prevailed and the agency failed to respond to a request of the appeal within the statutory time, or had no reasonable basis for denying access.[82]

New York has also adopted its own Open Meetings Law (OML), which operates in conjunction with the FOIL.[83] The OML grants the public the right to attend meetings of "public bodies" and "watch the decision-making process in action."[84] It does so by requiring public bodies to provide notice of the time and place of all meetings and keep minutes of all action taken at meetings.[85] If a meeting has not been scheduled at least a week in advance, then notice must be given to the public and the media at least 72 hours prior to the meeting.[86] Notice to the public must be given by posting in designated public locations and, if possible, online.[87] The OML allows exceptions for eight areas of the law during which members of the public may be excluded.[88] Examples include matters relating to public safety or ongoing law enforcement actions.[89]

WAYS TO IMPROVE GOVERNMENT TRANSPARENCY

Facilitating true government transparency through disclosures that are not only meaningful but also timely is a constant battle.[90] Though President Obama called for greater transparency in government and began his presidency promising vast improvements in transparency, the federal government has not managed to increase its transparency tremendously in most areas.[91]

What makes government transparency so difficult to accomplish? According to the CATO Institute, a public policy think-tank based in Washington, D.C., this is largely due to the fact that "the practices that produce transparency are not well understood and . . . because transparency is not in the interest of some parts of government [because it] shifts power from government agencies to their overseers in legislatures and the public."[92]

Practices That Should Be Adopted by Governments Wanting to Facilitate Genuine Transparency

After utilizing this policy for decades, many local governments have realized that just publishing open data is not enough to "build public trust and [inspire] local community action."[93] Extensive studies conducted by the Sunlight Foundation find that two things need to happen: "the quality of most open data need[s] to improve . . . and cities need to proactively find ways to engage hard-to-reach populations and disenfranchised residents."[94] When best practices are adopted to establish transparency in government, citizens become invested in problem-solving and community-driven action.[95] In order for this phenomenon to occur, however, governments must be intentional about their release of open data to the public.[96]

Making Disclosures Proactively

Though the most recent enactment of the FOIA states that public records disclosures will be made proactively, before citizens are required to make a request, this remains to be seen. Thus far, there has not been much meaningful proactive disclosure on the part of federal or state agencies.[97] Proactive disclosure of public records is important because it diminishes the number of individual requests made, thus reducing the backlog of public records requests for both the federal and state governments and allowing for more timely and efficient disclosure when individual requests are necessary.[98]

Another agency, the State of New York Attorney General, has an online "New York Open Government Portal," nyopengovernment.com, which provides many kinds of documents to the public in one place. This is a particularly efficient way for the public to be able to access public records, including, among other things, information about campaign contributions, state payments, state spending, state corporations, charities, and elected officials.

Ensuring the Meaningfulness and Accessibility of Public Records

"Government agencies risk burying value if published open data resources are large and unorganized; the point of open government data is significantly diminished, and thus so is public opinion."[99] Data should represent outcomes—both good and bad.[100] Selecting and highlighting relevant data sets to turn into open data is essential to increasing public trust in government.[101]

This is one of the reasons why the DATA Act is so revolutionary. If the act is implemented in the manner intended, the public could gain access to statistics about government spending and this could lead to vast improvements in public oversight.[102] Citizens may be able to draw connections between "bills introduced in Congress, the votes on them, and actual outcomes, whether those outcomes are beneficial infrastructure developments, such as a repaved highway, or damaging and counterproductive excess in overseas military operation. And they will be able to tie those outcomes to specific legislators' specific actions."[103]

Public Interest Override

Some experts argue that Congress must make changes to FOIA in order to make it a more effective statute.[104] Jameel Jaffer, director of the Knight First Amendment Institute, argues that Congress should amend FOIA to include a "public interest override."[105] Jaffer acknowledges that there are times where governments have a legitimate interest in maintaining secrecy, but pushes back on this concept by asserting that "the public interest in disclosure is greater than the sort of narrowly construed government interest in keeping the thing secret."[106] As FOIA currently stands, there is no mechanism to force disclosure in those instances.[107] However, many other countries with statutes similar to FOIA have added public interest overrides of this nature.[108] Jaffer also puts the onus on Congress to "reaffirm the government's obligation to disclose [its working] law."[109]

SUMMARY OF KEY POINTS

- Transparency leads to trust in the government and its institutions, and provides opportunities for the public and the press to ensure the appropriate use of government resources.
- Meaningful transparency requires more than the public release of large amounts of information; relevant information must be managed so that it is accurate, timely, and accessible.
- Governments committed to true transparency should improve the quality of their open data, and must find ways to engage hard-to-reach and disenfranchised populations.
- Proactive disclosure—without a triggering request—is important because it leads to more timely and efficient disclosures, but it is not yet common. Open government portals are one promising way to accomplish this.
- Governments should organize data and highlight relevant data sets to ensure accessibility, as intended by the revolutionary DATA Act.

NOTES

1. Katya Abazajian, *Government Transparency Is Key to Valuable Community Partnerships*, MEETING OF THE MINDS (Aug. 23, 2018), https://meetingoftheminds.org/government-transparency-is-key-to-valuable-community-partnerships-28058.

2. CATO HANDBOOK FOR POLICYMAKERS 302 (2017), https://object.cato.org/sites/cato.org/files/serials/files/cato-handbook-policymakers/2017/2/cato-handbook-for-policymakers-8th-edition.pdf.

3. *Id.*

4. 5 U.S.C. § 552; Cal. Gov't Code §§ 6250 *et seq.*; N.Y. C.L.S. Pub. O. §§ 84–90.
5. Cal. Gov't Code §§ 6250 *et seq.*; N.Y. C.L.S. Pub. O. §§ 84-90.
6. Cato Handbook, *supra* note 2, at 302.
7. Jameel Jaffer, *On Government Transparency under Bush, Obama, and Trump*, Colum. Journalism Rev. (May 23, 2017), https://www.cjr.org/analysis/government-transparency-trump-obama-bush.php.
8. Cato Handbook , *supra* note 2, at 302.
9. *Id.*
10. *How Do We Define Key Terms? Transparency and Accountability Glossary*, Transparency Accountability Initiative (Apr. 12, 2017), https://www.transparency-initiative.org/blog/1179/tai-definitions/ [hereinafter *Definitions*].
11. Abazajian, *supra* note 1.
12. *Id.*
13. *Id.*
14. *Definitions*, *supra* note 10.
15. *Id.*
16. *What Is FOIA?*, Foia.gov, https://www.foia.gov/about.html (last visited June 22, 2019).
17. 5 U.S.C. § 552(a)(3), (a)(4)(B), (b), (c).
18. NLRB v. Robbins Tire & Rubber Co., 437 U.S. 214, 242 (1978).
19. U.S. Dep't of Justice, Department of Justice Guide to the Freedom of Information Act, https://www.justice.gov/oip/doj-guide-freedom-information-act-0#:~:text=The%20United%20States%20Department%20of%20Justice%20Guide%20to,the%20key%20judicial%20opinions%20issued%20on%20the%20FOIA (citing John Doe Agency v. John Doe Corp., 493 U.S. 146, 152 (1989)).
20. 5 U.S.C. § 552.
21. *Id.* §§ 552(a)(1), 552(a)(2).
22. *Id.* § 552(a)(3).
23. Department of Justice Guide, *supra* note 19, at 3.
24. 5 U.S.C. § 552(a)(3).
25. *Id.* § 552(a)(6)(a).
26. *Id.*
27. *Id.*
28. *Id.* § 552(b), (c).
29. *Id.* § 552(b).
30. *What Is the FOIA?* Foia.gov, https://www.foia.gov/faq.html (last visited June 24, 2019).
31. *Id.*
32. Department of Justice Guide, *supra* note 19, at 6.
33. *Id.*
34. 5 U.S.C. § 552(c).
35. *OIP Guidance*, U.S. Dep't of Justice, https://www.justice.gov/oip/blog/foia-guidance-6 (last visited June 24, 2019).
36. *What Is the FOIA?*, *supra* note 30.
37. *Id.*
38. *Id.*
39. 5 U.S.C. § 552(a)(4)(E)(i) (2006), as amended by OPEN Government Act of 2007, Pub. L. No. 110-175, 121 Stat. 2524, and 5 U.S.C. § 552(a)(4)(E)(ii).
40. Department of Justice Guide, *supra* note 19, at 7.
41. *Id.*
42. Memorandum from Eric Holder, Att'y Gen., U.S. Dep't of Justice, to heads of executive departments and agencies (Mar. 19, 2009).
43. *Id.* (citing Memorandum from John Ashcroft, Att'y Gen., U.S. Dep't of Justice, to heads of all federal departments and agencies (Oct. 12, 2001)).
44. *Id.* (citing Memorandum from Barack Obama, U.S. President, White House, to heads of executive departments and agencies (Jan. 21, 2009)).

45. *Id.*
46. *Id.*
47. 5 U.S.C. § 552(b); 92 P.L. 463, 86 Stat. 770.
48. 92 P.L. 463, 86 Stat. 770, § 10.
49. *Id.*
50. 5 U.S.C. § 552(b).
51. Digital Accountability and Transparency Act of 2014, Pub. L. No. 113-101 (May 9, 2014).
52. Cato Handbook, *supra* note 2, at 304.
53. *Id.*
54. *Id.*
55. Cal. Gov't Code §§ 6250 *et seq.*; San Gabriel Tribune v. Super. Ct., 143 Cal. App. 3d 762, 771–72 (1983).
56. *San Gabriel Tribune*, 143 Cal. App. 3d at 772.
57. Cal. Gov't Code § 6253(a), (b), & (f).
58. *Id.* § 6252(e).
59. *Id.* § 6253(b).
60. League of Cal. Cities, The People's Business: A Guide to the California Public Records Act 27 (2017), https://www.calcities.org/detail-pages/resource/the-people's-business-a-guide-to-the-california-public-records-act?; Cal. Gov't Code § 6254(k).
61. The People's Business, *supra* note 60, at 28–54.
62. Cal. Gov't Code § 6255(a).
63. *Id.* § 6255.
64. *Id.*
65. *Id.* § 6253(d).
66. *Id.* § 6253(c).
67. *Id.*
68. The People's Business, *supra* note 60, at 57.
69. Cal. Gov't Code §§ 6258, 6259.
70. *Id.* § 6259(d).
71. *Open Meetings*, Rob Bonta, Att'y Gen., https://oag.ca.gov/open-meetings (last visited June 26, 2019).
72. Cal. Gov't Code § 54950; *The Brown Act: Open Meetings for Local Legislative Bodies* (2003), https://oag.ca.gov/sites/all/files/agweb/pdfs/publications/2003_Intro_BrownAct.pdf.
73. Cal. Gov't Code §§ 11120–11132; *A Handy Guide to the Bagley-Keene Open Meeting Act* (2004), https://oag.ca.gov/sites/all/files/agweb/pdfs/publications/bagleykeene2004_ada.pdf.
74. *See* Cal. Gov't Code §§ 9072, 9075.
75. N.Y. C.L.S. Pub. O. §§ 84–90; *Your Right to Know: New York State Open Government Laws*, https://eric.ed.gov/?id=ED301204.
76. *Your Right to Know, supra* note 75, at 3; N.Y. C.L.S. Pub. O. § 87(2).
77. *Id.*
78. *Your Right to Know, supra* note 75, at 5.
79. N.Y. C.L.S. Pub. O. § 89(3)(a).
80. *Your Right to Know, supra* note 75, at 5.
81. N.Y. C.L.S. Pub. O. § 89(4)(b).
82. *See* N.Y. C.L.S. Pub. O. § 89.4(c).
83. N.Y. C.L.S. Pub. O. §§ 100–111; *Your Right to Know, supra* note 75, at 11.
84. *Your Right to Know, supra* note 75, at 11.
85. N.Y. C.L.S. Pub. O. § 104.
86. *Id.*
87. *Id.*
88. N.Y. C.L.S. Pub. O. § 105.
89. *Id.*
90. Cato Handbook, *supra* note 2, at 301.

91. *Id.*
92. *Id.*
93. Abazajian, *supra* note 1.
94. *Id.*
95. *Id.*
96. *Id.*
97. Jaffer, *supra* note 7.
98. Memorandum from Eric Holder, *supra* note 42, at 3.
99. *A New Era of Transparency: 5 Best Practices for Sharing Government Data* 6, https://ccato.org/DocumentCenter/View/166/a_new_era_of_transparency-government-data-analysis?bidId=.
100. *Id.*
101. *Id.*
102. Cato Handbook, *supra* note 2, at 304.
103. *Id.* at 304–05.
104. Jaffer, *supra* note 7.
105. *Id.*
106. *Id.*
107. *Id.*
108. *Id.*
109. *Id.*

CHAPTER 4

Sunshine in the Statehouse: Financial Disclosure Requirements for Public Officials

Barry Ginsberg

This is a revision of a chapter originally prepared by Amy Levine and Leah Rush.

> The first part of this chapter includes a discussion of the constitutional issues relating to financial disclosure. The second part of the chapter explores current financial disclosure requirements. The Appendix features a survey of state financial disclosure laws.

Financial disclosure requirements for legislators, executive officials, candidates, and other government employees have been common for about 50 years.[1] These laws require elected and unelected public officials to disclose information such as outside employment and sources of income, investment interests, and property holdings. In some cases, financial disclosure laws may require similar disclosures of spouses' and dependents' financial interests, and they may require public officials to identify their clients.

Financial disclosure laws have several purposes. They provide information that can help to identify and resolve public officials' and candidates' conflicts of interest. By making completed financial disclosure forms available to the public and the news media, citizens can be better informed about the potential biases of their representatives and other public officials as well as candidates for public office. They are, accordingly, better positioned to play active roles in holding current and potential leaders accountable. And, knowing that the public will have access to their disclosure forms, public officials and candidates may be more likely to avoid activities that present actual or perceived conflicts of interest. Financial disclosure increases public confidence in government, numerous commentators have suggested.[2]

Financial disclosure laws are not without their critics. Private citizens are not expected to give up all of their personal financial interests upon seeking or assuming office. It is often contended that citizen-government better serves the public than does a government made up of self-financed elites and political professionals.[3] It can be expected that in a government comprised of "ordinary citizens," instead of elites or professional politicians, conflicts, real and apparent, will arise. Critics of fulsome financial disclosure requirements sometimes claim that existing ethics laws are sufficient to deal with conflicts that do arise, and that public disclosures often generate inappropriate public (i.e., news media) scrutiny akin to gossip that detracts from officials' ability to carry out their obligations.[4] It is sometimes claimed that the type of public scrutiny fostered by financial disclosure deters the most qualified people from running for office or accepting appointments, especially for positions that require either specialized expertise or experience in a particular field.[5] Other public officials (often those who do not hold high-ranking positions) argue that their personal financial dealings are simply not relevant to preventing conflicts of interest.[6] They thus see the reporting requirements as undue intrusions into their privacy that are not balanced by the public interest the requirements ostensibly serve.

THE CONSTITUTIONALITY OF FINANCIAL DISCLOSURE REQUIREMENTS

A number of early challenges brought against financial disclosure laws centered on the argument that disclosure rules deter qualified individuals from seeking or retaining public employment.[7] Characterizing this deterrence as an interference with either the right to run for office or the right to vote, courts have not considered it to rise to the level of constitutional impairment. In one of the earlier decisions, in 1978, the Fifth Circuit explained in *Plante v. Gonzales* that the right to run for office is not a fundamental right but a corollary of the right to vote, which, itself, is limited. The court noted that, while laws requiring candidates to pay large fees have been struck down because they limit the ability of less-affluent candidates to be presented to the voters, financial disclosure laws have no such effect on the pool of candidates—financial disclosure requirements do not, according to that court, "deny a cognizable group a meaningful right to representation."[8] Other courts have simply found that disclosure laws do not present a barrier to obtaining public employment. As the Supreme Court of Maryland explained, "[t]hat an employee may choose to resign rather than make a public disclosure of his finances does not mean that he is being unconstitutionally excluded from public employment."[9]

Objections based on privacy rights have tended to be more successful than those based on the right to run for or hold public office. The "right to privacy" in these cases is drawn from various provisions of the Bill of Rights, as has been explained in a strand of Supreme Court jurisprudence dealing with familial and sexual privacy.[10] The case law involving financial disclosures is replete with contentions that financial privacy is encompassed within the right to privacy, and that it therefore warrants strict judicial scrutiny. Following this line of thinking, one of the earliest financial disclosure cases, *City of Carmel-by-the-Sea v. Young*, struck down the reporting requirements as violative of privacy rights. As the court explained,

> the right of privacy concerns one's feelings and one's own peace of mind, and certainly one's personal financial affairs are an essential element of such peace of mind. . . . [W]e are satisfied that the protection of one's personal financial affairs and those of his (or her) spouse and children against compulsory public disclosure is an aspect of the zone of privacy which . . . falls within that penumbra of constitutional rights into which the government may not intrude absent a showing of compelling need and that the intrusion is not overly broad.[11]

Since the law at issue was directed to low-level government employees as well as those of the highest ranks, the court found the statute to be overbroad.

Most other courts, however, have not come to the same conclusion. *Plante v. Gonzales*, a case in which several Florida state senators threatened to resign if they were forced to file disclosures, presents a thorough explanations of privacy law in this area. The Fifth Circuit explained in *Plante* that the privacy interests protected by the Supreme Court have generally fallen into two categories: autonomy and confidentiality. The autonomy branch involves familial matters such as contraception, child rearing, and marriage. The court refused to include financial privacy within this group, noting that although "[t]here is no doubt that financial disclosure may affect a family . . . the same can be said of any government action."[12] As to the confidentiality aspect of privacy law, the court adopted a balancing test[13] and found that the public's interest in disclosure outweighed officials' interests in keeping their financial matters private.[14]

Most courts have followed this or similar balancing approaches and found that financial disclosures do not impermissibly interfere with privacy rights.[15] A number of courts have also drawn support from defamation jurisprudence, which assumes that public figures have different expectations of privacy than do most people.[16]

A separate consideration, however, is the effect that disclosure requirements may have on the privacy rights of persons other than the public officials required to make disclosures. The courts have generally agreed that public officials may be required to disclose financial information concerning their spouses and dependent children.[17] As the New Jersey Superior Court noted in *Kenny v. Byrne*,

> the financial holdings of a spouse are as significant in determining conflict of interest as those of the officeholder. The relationship between spouses is normally such that one who must decide as an officeholder is potentially subject to the same influences and pressures, whether that officeholder or his or her spouse is financially involved in the transaction. Furthermore, the absence of a provision inclusive of a spouse would obviously open the door to possible evasion of the requirements of the order by intrafamily transfers.[18]

A more complicated question arises when disclosure laws require the identification of a public official's clients. *Falcon v. Alaska Public Offices Commission* involved a doctor who refused to disclose the names of his patients after accepting a school board position. The Supreme Court of Alaska, while finding that the doctor-patient privilege would not always preclude disclosure, explained that disclosing the names of certain patients (such as those seeking treatment for psychiatric or sexual disorders) would constitute an impermissible infringement of those patients' privacy rights.[19] In *Hays v. Wood*, however, the Supreme Court of California came to a different conclusion regarding the disclosure of possibly privileged client identities. In that case, the court held that attorneys could be required to disclose the names of their clients.[20]

Although the U.S. Supreme Court has never directly addressed the constitutionality of financial disclosure requirements, support for disclosure laws was greatly strengthened by the Supreme Court's holding in *Buckley v. Valeo*. In that case, the Court determined that campaign finance disclosures are justified by the public's interest in information concerning candidates, the interest in deterring corruption, and by the government's need for transparency in order to police related campaign finance regulations.[21] *Buckley* made clear that the public's interests in the disclosure of campaign contributions will almost always outweigh public officials' interests in keeping this information private.[22] *Buckley* also enshrined the now famous observation of Louis Brandeis that "[s]unlight is said to be the best of disinfectants; electric light the most efficient policeman."[23] Financial disclosure cases have indeed cited *Buckley* as supporting broad financial disclosure requirements.[24]

FINANCIAL DISCLOSURE: A SURVEY OF THE STATES

The legality of financial disclosure rules has been fairly well established. After passing constitutional muster, it seems that public disclosure has become accepted as an effective way to foster transparency and accountability in government. When it is considered that about 7,400 lawmakers in state capitals across the country passed more than 33,000 laws[25] and spent an estimated $1.3 trillion in fiscal year 2006,[26] the most recent year for which such data is readily available, the need for financial disclosure becomes clear: government officials directly influence the way that public money is spent,[27] and there must be a way for the public to ensure that their decisions are made in the public interest, not to serve the interests of public officials or those having a relationship with the officials. Financial disclosures, which can alert us to when a public official stands to reap private benefits from his or her decisions,[28] are essential.

The Center for Public Integrity, a nonpartisan Washington, D.C.–based nonprofit journalism organization that tracks state government ethics laws, most recently studied the financial disclosure statements filed by 6,516 legislators during 2002 (which covered legislators' financial interests in 2001) in the states that require them.[29] The study considered outside employers, business interests, stock holdings, and directorships, and it was complemented by a survey of state financial disclosure laws.[30] Some of the results are presented here to clarify the importance of financial disclosure requirements and to illustrate the ways in which these laws function to identify conflicts. For more detailed and current information, the results of a nationwide survey concerning financial disclosure laws are presented in Appendices A and B, and a current list of state financial disclosure statutes is provided in Appendix C.

Outside Interests

The center's research found that a significant portion of state officials have outside economic ties that could present conflicts issues. The center found that at least 76 percent of state lawmakers nationwide reported outside income or employment for 2015.[31] That analysis, published in 2017, also showed that "State legislators work all kinds of jobs and sometimes more than one. Lawyers and those with ties to real estate tend to dominate, but some legislators also drive taxis, wait tables, own cemeteries, judge boxing matches, play guitar in rock bands or deal in rare coins."[32] According to the National Conference of State Legislatures (NCSL), in the ten legislatures that are full time or nearly full time in terms of pay and staff, legislators work on average 84 percent of a full-time job, whereas in the 15 part-time legislatures where, compensation averaged $18,477, legislators on average work 57 percent of a full-time job. For those in between, where the compensation averaged $41,110, legislators average 74 percent of a full-time job.[33] Because these numbers are only averages, legislators in particular cases can work a lower percentage of a full-time job. They can also do outside work in addition to the time requirements of a full-time job. Even in New York, which NCSL considers a quintessential full-time state, in 2015 income from outside ranged as high as $455,000, with ten legislators having outside income of more than $100,000.[34]

The prevalence of secondary, private-sector employment among state officials underscores the need for thorough financial disclosures. Government may often benefit from the employment of persons who have personal experience in and knowledge of businesses or industries, but the financial ties between state officials and industry may also affect government decision making. Disclosure ensures that government action will be transparent.

Overview of Financial Disclosure Requirements

Appendices A and B are comprised of state-by-state charts detailing state disclosure requirements for legislative and executive branch officials and candidates. Appendix C identifies all states' financial disclosure statutes, including the state agencies that either administer or enforce such laws.

The appendices show that almost all states require their state legislators, governors, and state high court judges to file personal financial disclosure reports. Only one state—Idaho—does not require these reports from officials in any branch of its government. Two states do not require financial interests to be reported by their governors or legislators but do require filings from their Supreme Court justices: Michigan and Vermont. Meanwhile, Utah requires disclosure only from its legislators and not from its governor or high court judges, and Montana requires disclosure from its legislators and governor but not from its high court judges.

In the executive branch, for elected positions other than the governor, five states do not require filings: Idaho, Louisiana, Michigan, Utah, and Vermont. For appointed executive branch positions, four additional states—Arizona, Colorado, New Mexico, and Wyoming—do not require filings, bringing the total number of states without comprehensive financial disclosure requirements for executive officials to nine.

Most states' disclosure laws apply to both state legislators and governors, although the respective disclosure forms may vary in appearance, or the oversight agency that collects the filings might be different. In these cases, the states require executive and legislative branch elected officials to disclose essentially the same information. Some states, however, require their governors to disclose much more information about their personal finances than they require their legislators to disclose. Louisiana is one such state. The governor files under a different law that requires reporting of entire categories of information not mentioned in the legislative disclosure law, including officer/director positions, real property holdings, and names of professional clients. The governor of Indiana also must disclose more than senators and representatives. The Indiana disclosure requirements differ in three respects: the governor must report real property holdings, names of professional clients, and names of all non-state employers; the agency exacts penalties for forms filed late or with intentionally incorrect information; and, finally, unlike the state Senate, the agency makes governors' filings accessible online. In Rhode Island, a 2006 provision for statewide officials requires the governor and other executive branch officials, but not legislators, to disclose information on the value, within certain ranges, of income and investments.

As for judicial financial disclosure requirements, judges file disclosure forms similar to those required for governors and legislators in 14 states.[35] In 21 states, they use different filing forms.[36] In another 12 states, judges must file more than one financial disclosure form: one required by state law and another by the state's adopted version of the American Bar Association's Model Code of Judicial Conduct.[37]

Specific Financial Disclosure Issues

The specifics of state financial disclosure laws vary significantly.

Thirty-five states do not require legislators to report the value of outside income, either as a precise number or a dollar range, and 33 states do not require such values to be disclosed by governors. Similarly, 35 states do not have value or income amounts for investments, and governors do not report investment values in 31 states. In other states, such as New York, legislators and the governor are required to report value amounts, and that information is made available to the public on the website of the Joint Commission on Public Ethics, which, among other responsibilities, administers New York's financial disclosure requirements.[38] Whether the public should have access to the value of outside income and investment interests is a difficult question. Such information is undoubtedly useful in determining whether an interest might present a material conflict for an official but requiring the disclosure of values may be considered a greater intrusion upon officials' privacy.

Twenty-nine states do not require descriptions of the services provided by the companies from which legislators receive outside income, and 28 do not require such information for governors. Thirty-seven states do not require descriptions of the organizations for which legislators and executive officials serve as advisers and directors. Lacking this type of information, the public may not be able to accurately judge whether their representatives' outside interests present conflicts. In one example of this type of confusion, news media reports in 2007 suggested that a New Jersey assemblyman had conflicts of interest due to his employment with an information technology consulting firm. The assemblyman responded by publicly disclosing additional information about the company and his duties there.[39] Better reporting requirements may have precluded the situation, saving the media, the public, and the assemblyman time and energy.

Many state financial disclosure laws require public officials who engage in the practice of law to disclose client identities and varying degrees and kinds of information about their client engagements. As of August 5, 2020, 35 of the 51 states and the District of Columbia have such requirements.[40] New York added such a requirement to Public Officers Law § 73-a, for example, when it enacted the broad Public Integrity Reform Act of 2011 (PIRA).[41] According to publicly available information regarding enforcement actions on the websites of the New York State Joint Commission on Public Ethics (JCOPE)[42] and the New York State Legislative Ethics Commission,[43] which have jurisdiction to investigate and enforce violations of this disclosure requirement, among other duties and responsibilities, since PIRA became effective, there have been a total 42 enforcement actions arising under Public Officers Law § 73-a. Of those, five have been for a failure to disclose required information. No such matter involved a member of the legislature and only two involved a lawyer subject to the Public Officers Law § 73-a client disclosure requirement. Both such lawyers worked for the New York Liquidation Bureau, which "carries out the responsibilities of the Superintendent of Financial Services as Receiver, in the discharging of the Superintendent's statutorily defined duties to protect the interests of the policyholders and creditors of insurance companies that have been declared impaired or insolvent."[44] The remaining 37 publicly reported enforcement actions arising under Public Officers Law § 73-a involved a required official's failure to file the required disclosure form, rather than having omitted required disclosure information from forms that were filed. Such failure-to-file violations were generally settled with the offending official agreeing to pay a civil penalty of $200 for each year in which he or she failed to file the required disclosure form.

Enforcement and auditing powers also present difficulties in relation to financial disclosure. Authorities in several states do not have the power to audit financial disclosure statements filed by legislators or governors for completeness and accuracy. Many states do not conduct even informal reviews on filings to ensure that disclosure statements are complete. Seven states (Indiana, Iowa, Maine, Mississippi, New Hampshire, Utah, and Virginia) make no provisions for penalizing legislators who fail to file disclosure statements on time, whereas for governors it is only two states: Mississippi and Virginia. The other states have filing fines or other penalties in place, but those penalties may not necessarily be effective.[45] Perhaps more useful at ensuring compliance, eight states reported naming late filers in a list made public on the web or in print, while nine states reported doing so in the executive branch survey.[46]

The public's access to financial disclosure filings varies widely across states. As shown in Appendices A and B, for both executive branch officials and legislators, Maryland is the only state that requires copies of forms to be picked up in person. Massachusetts and Wisconsin send governors the name and address of anyone who has inspected their financial disclosures, and an additional two states, New York and Virginia, do the same for legislators. This type of regulation may discourage people from seeking access to disclosure forms.

The internet is changing accessibility to financial disclosure filings. Twenty-two states have made gubernatorial disclosure statements available to anyone electronically via e-mail or the web, and 21 states did so as of 2006 for legislators' filings. State agencies are also making it easier for the public to access information on their public officials' private interests by creating systems that allow officials to file forms electronically. This trend has the potential to provide citizens with more timely access to information. The practice was too uncommon to be included in the legislative surveys, but by 2007 governors in 12 states had the ability to file reports electronically. Electronic filing systems for personal financial disclosure information are lagging far behind those set up for campaign finance disclosure[47] and lobbying disclosure.[48]

Other Developments

After ten years of examining financial disclosure laws, the Center for Public Integrity learned that the laws do not often change. But a renewed focus on ethics in government nationwide moved some legislatures to provide more information to the public relating to legislators' personal financial interests, either by revising their disclosure laws or by improving access to information.

Until 2007, for example, New York would not provide copies of the filings of governors or other executive branch officials; anyone wanting a New York disclosure filing had to appear at the ethics commission in person and copy the information on the disclosure reports by hand.[49] The state now allows for electronic filing of financial disclosure forms and makes elected officials' financial disclosure forms publicly available online through the website of the Joint Commission on Public Ethics. Financial disclosure forms of other public officials are available upon request submitted to the Joint Commission on Public Ethics. New York also requires lobbyists and lobby clients to disclose to the Joint Commission on Public Ethics certain business relations with certain state persons and the commission makes such disclosures publicly available on its website. See www.jcope.gov.

Michigan, one of the states that does not require its legislators or governor to make any details of private interests available to the public, has not made the same progress.[50] Some legislators have been proposing to start the practice, but have not been able to get a bill enacted into law since at least 2004.[51] Financial disclosure and other ethics reforms were a priority, however, for Louisiana's governor.[52,53]

The campaign, election, and conduct of President Donald Trump, a wealthy businessman who maintained worldwide business interests while serving in office, has resulted in sometimes contentious disputes regarding the federal financial disclosure requirements, and has spawned legal disputes centered on distinctions among public, political, and private financial interests arising under pertinent constitutional provisions and ethics provisions. In the only required financial disclosure form he was required to file, and has filed since taking office, released in May 2019, President Trump reported income of at least $434 million in 2018, including $40.8 million in revenue from his Trump International Hotel in Washington, DC, just blocks from the White House.[54] Bucking decades of modern practice as well as subpoenas, President Trump steadfastly refused to release his personal income tax returns and vigorously resisted efforts to require such disclosure that were initiated by the U.S. House of Representatives, a New York state grand jury, and private litigants.[55] There have also been challenges to the adequacy of the required financial disclosures President Trump made as a candidate. In *Lovitky v. Trump*, for example, the District of Columbia Court of Appeals rejected a claim under the Ethics in Government Act of 1978, 5 U.S.C. App. 4, made in pro se action brought by a lawyer who maintained that "President Trump has obscured . . . required disclosures by commingling his personal liabilities with debts owed by entities he controls, thereby depriving [plaintiff] of information to which he is entitled and needs to make informed voting decisions in the 2020 presidential primary and general elections."[56] *Forbes* reported on February 19, 2020, that "[President] Trump's private companies are continuing to charge the campaign for expenses like rent and consulting, according to the latest federal filings. That means that since January 20, 2017, the day Trump officially declared his intent to run for reelection, his campaign has put $1.9 million of donor money into the president's private business."[57]

In several civil actions, 29 senators and 186 members of the House of Representatives and other plaintiffs have maintained that President Trump violated the Emoluments Clause, U.S. Constitution, article I, section 9, clause 8, which provides that "[N]o Person holding any Office of Profit or Trust under [the United States], shall, without the Consent of the Congress, accept of any present, Emolument, Office, or Title, of any kind whatever, from any King, Prince, or foreign State." Plaintiffs have based their claims on, among other things, bookings at hotels in which President Trump maintained a financial interest by foreign government officials and regulation approvals that benefited President Trump's business interests abroad.

SUMMARY OF KEY POINTS

- Financial disclosure is commonplace, though some criticize it as an unnecessary invasion of privacy and a deterrent to public service.
- The constitutionality of disclosure is generally sustained under a privacy rights balancing test.
- Courts have upheld applying financial disclosure requirements to spouses and dependent children, but disclosure of clients or patients of an official presents a more complex question.
- Many public officials and their immediate families have non-job activities that create opportunities for benefit from official decision making or present other conflict issues.
- States differ on whether they require disclosure of the amount of investment and outside income, the substance of outside activities, the disclosure of clients by lawyers, the requirement to audit, and the ease of public access to disclosure information.
- The general lack of disclosure by former President Donald Trump has increased interest in disclosure requirements.

NOTES

1. *See* Note, *Fighting Conflicts of Interest in Officialdom: Constitutional and Practical Guidelines for State Financial Disclosure Laws*, 73 Mich. L. Rev. 758 (1975); Case Comment, *Barry v. City of New York*, 62 Wash. U. Law Q. 337, 344 (1984). Financial disclosure requirements were enacted at the federal level in the Ethics in Government Act of 1978, Pub. L. No. 95-521. The disclosure provisions are today codified at §§ 5 U.S.C. Appx. 101 *et seq. See* http://uscode.hous e.gov/view.xhtml?req=(title:5a%20section:101%20edition:prelim (current through 5/5/2019).

2. Note, *supra* note 1, at 761; Note, *The Constitutionality of Financial Disclosure Laws*, 59 Cornell L. Rev. 345, 346 (1974).

3. *See* Beth Nolan, *Public Interest, Private Income: Conflicts and Control Limits on the Outside Income of Government Officials*, 87 Nw. U. L. Rev. 57, 58–60 (1992); Rapp v. Carey, 44 N.Y.2d 157, 164–65 (1978). Indeed, Hélène Landemore, a Yale University Professor of Political Science, has suggested that, instead of electing representatives, ordinary citizens should serve in legislative positions for a fixed period. Citizen-legislators would be designated "by a method roughly akin to jury duty (not jury selection): every now and then, your number

comes up, and you're obliged to do your civic duty—in this case, to take a seat on a legislative body." "Politics Without Politicians," Nathan Heller, THE NEW YORKER, Feb. 19, 2020.

4. *See* James Fallows, *Why Americans Hate the Media*, THE ATLANTIC MONTHLY, Feb. 1996, https://www.theatlantic.com/magazine/archive/1996/02/why-americans-hate-the-media/305060/; Abner J. Mikva, Lecture delivered upon receiving the 1998 Paul H. Douglas Ethics in Government Award at the University of Illinois: ETHICS IN GOVERNMENT: NOT AN OXYMORON, https://igpa.uillinois.edu/page/douglas-honorees#section-20.

5. *See* Eric Lichtblau, *Panel's Finances Will Stay Private*, N.Y. TIMES (Feb. 15, 2004) (describing President Bush's reasons for not requiring disclosures from commissioners appointed to investigate American intelligence failures).

6. *See, e.g.*, O'Brien v. DiGrazia, 544 F.2d 543 (1st Cir. 1976); Gideon v. Alabama State Ethics Commission, 379 So. 2d 570 (1980); Barry v. City of New York, 712 F.2d 1554 (2d Cir. 1983).

7. *See, e.g.*, City of Carmel-by-the-Sea v. Young, 2 Cal. 3d 259 (1970); Stein v. Howlett, 52 Ill. 2d 570 (1972); Montgomery Cnty. v. Walsh, 274 Md. 502 (1975); Plante v. Gonzales, 575 F.2d 1119 (1978).

8. *Plante* at 1126 (internal citations omitted).

9. *Montgomery Cnty.* at 520.

10. *See, e.g.*, Griswold v. Connecticut, 381 U.S. 479 (1965); Eisenstadt v. Baird, 405 U.S. 438 (1972); Roe v. Wade, 410 U.S. 113 (1973); Lawrence v. Texas, 539 U.S. 558 (2003).

11. City of Carmel-by-the-Sea v. Young, 2 Cal. 3d 259, 268 (1970).

12. Plante v. Gonzales, 575 F.2d 1119, 1131 (1978).

13. The court analogized the balancing test that it adopted to the test used in equal protection cases, noting that it believed this standard of review to be appropriate given the Supreme Court's warning against recognizing new "fundamental rights" meriting strict scrutiny. *Id.* at 1134.

14. *Id.* at 1136. *Plante* drew on *Nixon v. Administrator of General Services*, 433 U.S. 425 (1977), for part of its discussion concerning the confidentiality prong of the privacy test. *Nixon* involved the screening of President Nixon's papers and recordings under the Presidential Recordings and Materials Preservation Act in order to separate his private papers from those to be archived. The Court determined that Nixon's legitimate privacy interests were outweighed by the necessity of the screening process, Nixon's status as a public figure, and the public interest in preserving the documents and recordings. *Id.* at 465. Although *Nixon* differs substantially from financial disclosure cases in that Nixon's effects were not to be made public, courts have looked to the case as support for the weighing of public informational interests against the privacy claims of public officials.

15. *See, e.g.*, Stein v. Howlett, 52 Ill. 2d 570, 578 (1972); Fritz v. Gorton, 83 Wn. 2d 275, 294–95 (1974); Ill. State Empls.' Ass'n v. Walker, 57 Ill. 2d 512, 523–24 (1974); *In re Kading*, 70 Wis. 2d 508, 526 (1975); Lehrhaupt v. Flynn, 140 N.J. Super. 250, 261–64 (1976); Goldtrap v. Askew, 334 So. 2d 20, 23 (1976); Evans v. Carey, 53 A.D.2d 109, 118 (1976); Klaus v. Minn. State Ethics Comm'n, 309 Minn. 430, 437 (1976); Kenny v. Byrne, 144 N.J. Super. 243, 254–55 (1976); Opinion of Justices to Senate, 375 Mass. 795 (1978); Duplantier v. United States, 606 F.2d 654, 670 (5th Cir. 1979); Gideon v. Ala. State Ethics Comm'n, 379 So. 2d 570 (1980); Barry v. New York, 712 F.2d 1554 (1993); Eisenbud v. Suffolk Cnty., 841 F.2d 42 (2d Cir. 1988); Igneri v. Moore, 898 F.2d 870 (2d Cir. 1990). Just four years after California's Supreme Court struck down the financial disclosure requirements in *City of Carmel-by-the-Sea v. Young*, the court upheld narrowed requirements in *County of Nevada v. MacMillen*, 11 Cal. 3d 662 (1974). The only other case to have invalidated financial disclosure requirements on privacy grounds is Advisory Opinion on Constitutionality of 1975 PA 227, 396 Mich. 465 (1976). Unlike California, the Michigan courts have not had a chance to revise their stance on the constitutionality of financial disclosure laws, as Michigan remains one of the few states not to require disclosure.

16. A few of the Supreme Court's most influential defamation cases in this area are N.Y. Times Co. v. Sullivan, 376 U.S. 254 (1964); St. Amant v. Thompson, 390 U.S. 727 (1968); and

Ocala Star-Banner Co. v. Damron, 401 U.S. 295 (1971). For financial disclosure cases drawing on this reasoning, *see* Ill. State Empls.' Ass'n v. Walker, 57 Ill. 2d 512, 524–25 (1974); Lehrhaupt v. Flynn, 140 N.J. Super. 250, 261 (1976); and *In re* Kading, 70 Wis. 2d 508, 526 (1975). *But, cf.* Advisory Opinion on Constitutionality of 1975 PA 227, 396 Mich. 465, 505 (stating that "[p]ublic officials must recognize their official capacities often expose their private lives to public scrutiny. However, we see a great difference between 'unavoidable exposure' and 'compelled disclosure.' We reject any notion that [*New York Times v. Sullivan*] can be read to require public officials to fuel the fires of those who seek to roast them.").

17. *See, e.g.*, Cnty. of Nev. v. MacMillen, 11 Cal. 3d 662, 675–76 (1974); Ill. State Empls.' Ass'n v. Walker, 57 Ill. 2d 512, 528 (1974); Montgomery Cnty. v. Walsh, 274 Md. 502, 517 (1975); *In re* Kading, 70 Wis. 2d 508, 528 (1975).

18. Kenny v. Byrne, 144 N.J. Super. 243, 256 (1976).

19. Falcon v. Alaska Public Offices Comm'n, 570 P.2d 469, 479–80 (1977).

20. Hays v. Wood, 25 Cal. 3d 772 (1979).

21. Buckley v. Valeo, 424 U.S. 1, 66–69 (1976).

22. *Buckley* left open the possibility that campaign finance disclosures might have unconstitutional applications, such as where they might deter people from making contributions to unfavorable political parties for fear of their names being publicly associated with them. However, the Court made clear that these cases would be dealt with on an as applied basis. *Id.* at 71–72.

23. *Id.* at 67.

24. *See, e.g.*, Igneri v. Moore, 898 F.2d 870, 877 (2d Cir. 1990); Barry v. New York, 712 F.2d 1554, 1564 (2d Cir. 1983); Eisenbud v. Suffolk Cty., 841 F.2d 42, 45 (2d Cir. 1988); Plante v. Gonzales, 575 F.2d 1119, 1132, 1135 (5th Cir. 1978); Gideon v. Ala. State Ethics Comm'n, 379 So. 2d 570, 574 (1980); Hays v. Wood, 25 Cal. 3d 772, 783 (1979).

25. *See* StateNet, *In The Hopper*, STATE NET CAPITOL J., Mar. 5, 2007, Vol. XV, No. 7 (counting the number of enacted/adopted bills in 2006 to be 33,333); *see also* Reid Wilson, *State Legislatures Are Very, Very Busy*, WASH. POST (Sept. 29, 2014), https://www.washingtonpost.com/blogs/govbeat/wp/2014/09/29/state-legislatures-are-very-very-busy/ (24,000 new state laws in 2014).

26. NATIONAL GOVERNORS ASSOCIATION & NATIONAL ASSOCIATION OF STATE BUDGET OFFICERS, THE FISCAL SURVEY OF STATES 2 (2007).

27. State representatives are often uniquely positioned to influence their personal financial fortunes or those of their employers while in office. In fact, more than 20 percent of state legislators who reported their finances sat on a committee with authority over at least one of their personal interests in 2001, according to a 2004 Center for Public Integrity report. *See* Daniel Lathrop, Susan Schaab & Leah Rush, *Personal Politics: All Too Often, Legislators' Private Interests Are Hidden from Public View*, Sept. 24, 2004. Eighteen percent disclosed ties to organizations registered to lobby state government, and 10 percent were employed by other government agencies, including public schools and universities.

28. For examples of instances in which financial disclosure filings have been used to identify possible misconduct or less than stellar behavior on the part of politicians, *see* Jodi Rudoren, *Congressman's Special Projects Bring Complaints*, N.Y. TIMES, Apr. 8, 2006; Manu Raju, *Catching Fish, Netting Earmarks up in Alaska*, THE HILL, Sept. 6, 2007, at 1; and Adam Lisberg & Kirsten Danis, *Council Takes Raise as Some Double-Dip*, THE DAILY NEWS (New York), Oct. 16, 2007, at 4.

29. The survey was made possible by the funding of the Ford Foundation and the Joyce Foundation. *See also* http://www.ncsl.org/research/ethics/financial-disclosure-for-legislators-income.aspx.

30. The center evaluated each state's financial disclosure laws for legislators and governors with a 43-question survey. The survey assessed the basic information that was made available, including outside employment or income, officer or director positions, investments, clients, real property ownership, family income and interests, public access to disclosure records, and whether the state imposed penalties for violations of these laws. Many

states required reporting of other details not included in the center's survey, including gifts and government contracts. The 5.4 percent of legislators in the 47 states with mandatory financial disclosure who did not file statements were excluded when the center calculated percentages of legislators with each type of connection.

31. Liz Essley Whyte & Ryan J. Foley, *Conflicted Interests: State Lawmakers Often Blur the Line between the Public's Business and Their Own*, CTR. FOR PUB. INTEGRITY (Dec. 6, 2017), https://publicintegrity.org/politics/state-politics/conflicted-interests-state-lawmakers-often-blur-the-line-between-the-publics-business-and-their-own/.

32. *Id.*

33. *Full- and Part-Time Legislatures*, NAT'L CONF. OF STATE LEGISLATURES (June 14, 2017), https://www.ncsl.org/research/about-state-legislatures/full-and-part-time-legislatures.aspx.

34. Prudence Katze & Susan Lerner, *Common Cause/NY Compiles a Major Review of Outside Income for NYS Lawmakers*, COMMON CAUSE (Dec. 2015), http://nyscommissiononcompensation.org/pdf/CCNY_OutsideIncome_Dec2015.pdf.

35. States where judges file disclosure forms similar to governors and legislators include Arizona, California, Delaware, Florida, Maryland, Massachusetts, Mississippi, Ohio, Oklahoma, Oregon, Texas, Virginia, Washington, and Wisconsin.

36. States where judges file disclosure forms different from governors and legislators include Connecticut, Hawaii, Indiana, Iowa, Kansas, Kentucky, Louisiana, Maine, Michigan, Minnesota, Missouri, Nebraska, Nevada, New Hampshire, New Jersey, New Mexico, New York, Pennsylvania, South Carolina, Vermont, and Wyoming.

37. States where judges file more than one form of disclosure include Alabama, Alaska, Arkansas, Colorado, Georgia, Illinois, North Carolina, North Dakota, Rhode Island, South Dakota, Tennessee, and West Virginia. For more information about judicial financial disclosure requirements, *see* Reity O'Brien, Kytja Weir & Chris Young, *State Supreme Court Judges Reveal Scant Financial Information*, CTR. FOR PUB. INTEGRITY (Dec. 4, 2013), https://publicintegrity.org/federal-politics/state-supreme-court-judges-reveal-scant-financial-information/.

38. *See* New York State Ethics Commission [Ethics Commission was replaced by Commission on Public Integrity in 2007 and CPI was replaced by Joint Commission on Public Ethics in 2011], *Guide to Filing the 2017 New York State Annual Statement of Financial Disclosure*, https://jcope.ny.gov/system/files/documents/2018/05/2017-fds-guide-final-rev-may-2018.pdf.

39. *See* Upendra Chivukula, *Lawmaker Denies Conflict of Interest*, COURIER POST (Cherry Hill, NJ), Oct. 13, 2007.

40. *Financial Disclosures: Client Identification*, NAT'L CONF. OF STATE LEGISLATURES (Aug. 5, 2020), https://www.ncsl.org/research/ethics/50-state-chart-financial-disclosure-client-names.aspx.

41. L. 2011, ch. 399.

42. *Enforcement Actions*, N.Y. STATE JOINT COMM'N ON PUB. ETHICS, https://jcope.ny.gov/enforcement-actions.

43. *Public Documents*, NYS LEGISLATIVE ETHICS COMM'N, https://legethics.ny.gov/public-documents.

44. New York Liquidation Bureau, http://www.nylb.org/home.htm. In settling the matter with JCOPE, the lawyer admitted to failing to disclose fees he received as compensation for appearances in immigration court and agreed to pay a civil penalty in the amount of $3,000. *See* https://jcope.ny.gov/michael-pisapia. The other lawyer agreed to pay a civil penalty in the amount of $1,000 for failing to report his uncompensated position with a start-up business incorporated in Delaware, https://jcope.ny.gov/kenneth-marvet.

45. *See, e.g.*, James Salzer, *Legislators Flout Filing Deadlines; Many Fail to Turn in Financial Disclosure Forms on Time; $75 Late Fee Not a Big Threat*, ATLANTA JOURNAL-CONSTITUTION, Aug. 10, 2007; Jane Prendergast, *Conflicts of Interest Can Nab Politicians*, CINCINNATI ENQUIRER, Sept. 8, 2007, at 1A.

46. The states that report tardy legislative filers are Alaska, Georgia, Hawaii, Minnesota, Oklahoma, Texas, Washington, and Wisconsin. Except for Wisconsin, those states, plus Florida and Iowa, publish the names of late-filing executives.

47. *See* The Campaign Disclosure Project, *Grading State Disclosure 2007: Evaluating States' Efforts to Bring Sunlight to Political Money* (Oct. 16, 2007), http://www.campaigndisclosure.org/gradingstate/efilefindings.html (noting that 40 states offer some type of electronic filing).

48. *See* Leah Rush & David Jimenez, *States Outpace Congress in Upgrading Lobbying Laws: 24 States Have Made Disclosure Strides since 2003* (Mar. 1, 2006).

49. *See* Lathrop, Schaab & Rush, *supra* note 27.

50. *See generally* Mark Hornbeck & Charlie Cain, *As Nation Embraces Ethics Reform, Michigan Shrugs*, Detroit News, Aug. 3, 2007, at 1A.

51. *See* Susan Schaab, *Posted: State Legislators' 2004 Personal Disclosures* (Jan. 24, 2005), https://publicintegrity.org/state-politics/our-private-legislatures/posted-state-legislators-2004-personal-disclosures/.

52. *See* Bobby Jindal, *Ethics Reform: Ending Corruption: Fresh Start for Louisiana*, http://www.legis.state.la.us/archive/08os/Jindal_Ethics_Plan.pdf (last visited Mar. 28, 2022).

53. *See* Linda Stein, *Assembly Hopefuls Outline Their Priorities*, Times of Trenton, Oct. 29, 2007, at A03.

54. Anna Bahney & Maegan Vazquez, *Trump Reports Making at Least $434 Million in 2018*, CNN.com, (May 16, 2019, 8:02 PM), https://www.cnn.com/2019/05/16/politics/donald-trump-financial-disclosure/index.html.

55. Trump v. Vance, No. 19-635 (S. Ct.); Trump v. Mazars, No. 19-715 (S. Ct.); and Trump v. Deusche Bank, No. 19-760 (S. Ct.).

56. Lovitky v. Trump, Civil Action No. 17-450 (CKK) (U.S. Dist. Ct. D.C. Apr. 18, 2017) (Memorandum Opinion at 4).

57. Dan Alexander, *Trump Has Now Shifted $1.9 Million from Campaign Donors to His Business*, Forbes (Feb. 19, 2020), https://www.forbes.com/sites/danalexander/2020/02/19/trump-has-now-shifted-19-million-from-campaign-donors-to-his-business/?sh=5592280267c3.

APPENDIX A

State Legislative Disclosure Requirements

	AL	AK	AZ	AR	CA	CO	CT	DE	FL	GA	HI	ID	IL
Requires financial disclosure filing?	Y	Y	Y	Y	Y	Y	Y	Y	Y	Y	Y	N	Y
Requires complete financial disclosure filing (no update)?	Y	Y	Y	Y	Y	N	Y	Y	Y	Y	N	N/A	Y
Requires financial disclosure filing annually?	Y	Y	Y	Y	Y	Y	Y	Y	Y	Y	Y	N/A	Y
Requires complete financial disclosure filing for candidates?	Y	Y	Y	Y	Y	Y	N	Y	Y	Y	Y	N/A	Y
Employment information required?	Y	Y	Y	Y	Y	Y	Y	Y	Y	Y	Y	N/A	Y
Employment information not narrowly defined?	Y	Y	Y	Y	N	Y	Y	Y	Y	Y	Y	N/A	Y
Employer/business name required?	Y	Y	Y	Y	Y	Y	Y	Y	Y	Y	Y	N/A	Y
Employment job title required?	Y	Y	Y	Y	Y	N	N	Y	N	Y	Y	N/A	Y
Employer description required?	N	N	Y	N	Y	N	Y	Y	N	Y	N	N/A	N
Value range/income amount required?	Y	Y	N	Y	Y	N	N	N	Y	N	Y	N/A	N
Spouse employment information required?	Y	Y	Y	Y	Y	Y	Y	N	N	Y	Y	N/A	N
Officer/director information required?	Y	Y	Y	Y	Y	Y	Y	Y	Y	Y	Y	N/A	Y
Officer/director information not narrowly defined?	N	Y	Y	Y	Y	Y	Y	N	N	Y	Y	N/A	N
Officer/director entity name required?	Y	Y	Y	Y	Y	Y	Y	Y	Y	Y	Y	N/A	Y
Officer/director entity description required?	N	Y	N	N	Y	N	Y	Y	N	Y	N	N/A	N
Spouse officer/director information required?	N	Y	Y	Y	N	Y	Y	Y	N	Y	Y	N/A	N
Investment information required?	Y	Y	Y	Y	Y	Y	Y	Y	Y	Y	Y	N/A	Y
Investment information not narrowly defined?	Y	Y	Y	Y	Y	Y	Y	Y	Y	N	Y	N/A	Y
Investment entity name required?	Y	Y	Y	Y	Y	Y	Y	Y	Y	Y	Y	N/A	Y
Investment entity description required?	N	Y	Y	N	Y	N	N	N	Y	Y	Y	N/A	N
Investment value range/holding amount required?	Y	N	Y	Y	Y	N	N	N	Y	N	Y	N/A	N
Spouse investment information required and clear?	N	Y	Y	Y	N	Y	Y	Y	N	Y	Y	N/A	N
Any client information required?	Y	Y	Y	N	Y	N	N	N	Y	N	Y	N/A	N
Client name required?	N	Y	N	N	Y	N	N	N	Y	N	Y	N/A	N

State Legislative Disclosure Requirements

	IN	IA	KS	KY	LA	ME	MD	MA	MI	MN	MS	MO	MT
Requires financial disclosure filing?	Y	Y	Y	Y	Y	Y	Y	Y	N	Y	Y	Y	Y
Requires complete financial disclosure filing (no update)?	Y	Y	Y	Y	Y	Y	Y	Y	N/A	N	Y	Y	Y
Requires financial disclosure filing annually?	Y	Y	Y	Y	Y	Y	Y	Y	N/A	Y	Y	Y	N
Requires complete financial disclosure filing for candidates?	Y	Y	Y	Y	N	Y	Y	Y	N/A	Y	Y	Y	Y
Employment information required?	Y	Y	Y	Y	Y	Y	Y	Y	N/A	Y	Y	Y	Y
Employment information not narrowly defined?	N	Y	Y	Y	N	Y	Y	Y	N/A	Y	Y	Y	Y
Employer/business name required?	Y	Y[1]	Y	Y	Y	Y	Y	Y	N/A	Y	Y	Y	Y
Employment job title required?	N	Y	N	Y	N	N	Y	Y	N/A	Y	Y	N	N
Employer description required?	Y	Y	Y	N	N	Y	N	N	N/A	N	N	Y	N
Value range/income amount required?	N	N	N	N	Y	N	N	Y	N/A	N	N	N	N
Spouse employment information required?	Y	N	Y	Y	Y	N	Y	Y	N/A	N	N	Y	N
Officer/director information required?	Y	Y[2]	Y	Y	N	N	Y	Y	N/A	Y	Y	Y	Y
Officer/director information not narrowly defined?	Y	Y[2]	Y	Y	N	N	N	Y	N/A	N	N	Y	Y
Officer/director entity name required?	Y	Y[2]	Y	Y	N	N	Y	Y	N/A	Y	Y	Y	Y
Officer/director entity description required?	Y	Y[1]	N	N	N	N	N	N	N/A	N	N	Y	N
Spouse officer/director information required?	Y	N	Y	N	N	N	Y	Y	N/A	N	N	Y	N
Investment information required?	Y	Y	Y	Y	Y	Y	Y	Y	N/A	Y	Y	Y	Y
Investment information not narrowly defined?	N	Y	Y	N	N	Y	Y	Y	N/A	Y	Y	Y	Y
Investment entity name required?	Y	Y[2]	Y	Y	Y	Y	Y	Y	N/A	Y	Y	Y	Y
Investment entity description required?	Y	Y	Y	N	N	N	N	N	N/A	N	Y	Y	Y
Investment value range/holding amount required?	N	N	N	N	N	N	Y	N	N/A	N	N	N	N
Spouse investment information required and clear	Y	N	Y	N	Y	N	N	Y	N/A	N	N	N	N
Any client information required?	Y	N	Y	Y	N	Y	Y	N	N/A	N	Y	N	N
Client name required?	Y	N	Y	Y	N	Y	Y	N	N/A	N	Y	N	N

1 This information is required to be reported by Iowa House representatives but not by state senators.

2 House filers are not required to report the name of stock holdings, but they are required to report the names of personal business interests. Senate filers are not required to identify any investment entities.

64 • Ethical Standards in the Public Sector

	NE	NV	NH	NJ	NM	NY	NC	ND	OH	OK	OR	PA
Requires financial disclosure filing?	Y	Y	Y	Y	Y	Y	Y	Y	Y	Y	Y	Y
Requires complete financial disclosure filing (no update)?	N	Y	Y	Y	Y	Y	N	Y	Y	N	Y	Y
Requires financial disclosure filing annually?	Y	Y	Y	Y	Y	Y	Y	N	Y	Y	Y	Y
Requires complete financial disclosure filing for candidates?	Y	Y	Y	Y	Y	Y	Y	Y	Y	Y	Y	Y
Employment information required?	Y	Y	Y	Y	Y	Y	Y	Y	Y	Y	Y	Y
Employment information not narrowly defined?	Y	Y	N	Y	Y	Y	Y	N	Y	Y	Y	Y
Employer/business name required?	Y	Y	Y	Y	Y	Y	Y	Y	Y	Y	Y	Y
Employment job title required?	N	N	N	N	Y	Y	Y	Y	Y	N	N	Y
Employer description required?	Y	N	Y	N	Y	Y	Y	N	N	Y	Y	N
Value range/income amount required?	N	N	N	Y	N	N	N	N	Y	N	N	N
Spouse employment information required?	N	Y	N	Y	Y	Y	Y	Y	N	Y	Y	N
Officer/director information required?	Y	N	N	Y	Y	Y	Y	Y	Y	Y	Y	Y
Officer/director information not narrowly defined?	Y	N	N	N	N	Y	Y	Y	N	N	Y	Y
Officer/director entity name required?	Y	N	N	N	Y	Y	Y	Y	Y	Y	Y	Y
Officer/director entity description required?	N	N	N	N	N	N	Y	N	N	N	Y	N
Spouse officer/director information required?	N	N	N	N	Y	Y	Y	Y	N	N	Y	N
Investment information required?	Y	Y	N	Y	Y	Y	Y	Y	Y	Y	Y	Y
Investment information not narrowly defined?	Y	Y	N	Y	Y	Y	Y	Y	Y	Y	Y	Y
Investment entity name required?	Y	Y	N	Y	Y	Y	Y	Y	Y	Y	Y	Y
Investment entity description required?	N	N	N	N	Y	Y	Y	N	N	Y	Y	N
Investment value range/holding amount required?	N	N	N	N	N	Y	N	N	N	N	N	N
Spouse investment information required and clear?	N	Y	N	Y	N	Y	Y	Y	N	N	N	N
Any client information required?	N	N	N	N	Y	Y	Y	N	Y	Y	Y	N
Client name required?	N	N	N	N	Y	Y	N	N	Y	Y	Y	N

State Legislative Disclosure Requirements

	RI	SC	SD	TN	TX	UT	VT	VA	WA	WV	WI	WY
Requires financial disclosure filing?	Y	Y	Y	Y	Y	Y	Y	Y	Y	Y	Y	Y
Requires complete financial disclosure filing (no update)?	Y	Y	Y	N	Y	Y	Y	Y	N	Y	Y	Y
Requires financial disclosure filing annually?	Y	Y	N	Y	Y	Y	N	Y	Y	Y	Y	Y
Requires complete financial disclosure filing for candidates?	Y	Y	Y	Y	Y	Y	Y	Y	Y	Y	Y	N
Employment information required?	Y	Y	Y	Y	Y	Y	Y	Y	Y	Y	Y	Y
Employment information not narrowly defined?	Y	N	Y	Y	Y	Y	Y	N	Y	Y	Y	Y
Employer/business name required?	Y	Y	Y	Y	Y	Y	Y	Y	Y	Y	Y	Y
Employment job title required?	Y	N	Y	N	Y	Y	N	N	Y	Y	N	Y
Employer description required?	N	N	N	N	N	Y	N	N	N	Y	Y	N
Value range/income amount required?	N	Y	N	N	N	N	N	N	Y	N	N	N
Spouse employment information required?	Y	Y	Y	Y	Y	Y	Y	Y	Y	Y	Y	N
Officer/director information required?	Y	Y	Y	Y	Y	Y	Y	Y	Y	Y	Y	Y
Officer/director information not narrowly defined?	Y	N	N	Y	Y	Y	Y	N	Y	Y	N	N
Officer/director entity name required?	Y	Y	Y	Y	Y	Y	Y	Y	Y	Y	Y	Y
Officer/director entity description required?	N	N	N	N	N	Y	Y	N	Y	Y	N	N
Spouse officer/director information required?	Y	N	Y	Y[3]	Y	Y	N	Y	Y	Y	Y	N
Investment information required?	Y	Y	Y	Y	Y	Y	Y	Y	Y	Y	Y	Y
Investment information not narrowly defined?	Y	N	Y	Y	Y	N	N	N	Y	Y	N	N
Investment entity name required?	Y	Y	Y	Y	Y	Y	N	Y	Y	Y	Y	Y
Investment entity description required?	N	N	N	N	N	Y	N	N	Y	N	N	N
Investment value range/holding amount required?	N	N	N	N	Y	N	N	Y	Y	N	Y	N
Spouse investment information required and clear?	Y	N	Y	Y	Y	Y	Y	N	N	Y	N	N
Any client information required?	N	Y	N	Y	Y	N	N	Y	Y	Y	Y	N
Client name required?	N	Y	N	N	Y	N/A	N	Y	Y	N	Y	N/A

	AL	AK	AZ	AR	CA	CO	CT	DE	FL	GA	HI	ID	IL
Client value range/income amount required?	Y	Y	N	N	N	N	N	N	N	N	N	N/A	N
Spouse client information required and clear?	N	Y	Y	N	N	N	N	N	N	N	N	N/A	N
Real-property information required?	Y	Y	Y	N	Y	Y	Y	Y	Y	Y	Y	N/A	Y
Real-property information not narrowly defined?	Y	Y	Y	N	Y	Y	Y	Y	Y	Y	Y	N/A	Y
Real-property value range/amount required?	Y	N	Y	N	Y	N	N	N	Y	Y	Y	N/A	N
Spouse real-property information required?	N	Y	Y	N	N	Y	Y	Y	N	Y	Y	N/A	N
Spouse name required?	Y	Y	Y	Y	N	N	Y	N	N	Y	Y	N/A	N
Dependent name required?	Y	Y	Y	N	N	N	Y	N	N	Y	Y	N/A	N
Financial disclosure filings in central office?	Y	Y	Y	Y	Y	Y	Y	Y	Y	Y	Y	N/A	Y
Lawmakers not forwarded reviewer information?	Y	Y	Y	Y	Y	Y	Y	Y	Y	Y	Y	N/A	Y
In-person appearance not required to obtain filings?	Y	Y	Y	Y	Y	Y	Y	Y	Y	Y	Y	N/A	Y
Copy fees less than 50 cents per page?	N	Y	Y	Y	Y	N	Y	N	Y	Y	Y	N/A	N
Blank disclosure form available on the web?	Y	Y	Y	Y	Y	Y	N	Y	Y	Y	Y	N/A	Y
Disclosure filings available electronically or online?	N	N	N	Y	N	N	N	Y	N	Y	Y	N/A	Y
Late-filing penalties on the books?	Y	Y	Y	Y	Y	Y	Y	Y	Y	Y	Y	N/A	Y
Misfiling penalties on the books?	Y	Y	Y	Y	Y	Y	Y	Y	Y	Y	Y	N/A	Y
State has auditing authority?	Y	Y	N	Y	Y	N	Y	N	Y	Y	Y	N/A	Y
State routinely reviews filings for accuracy and completeness?	Y	Y	N	N	Y	N	Y	Y	N	Y	Y	N/A	N
State published list of delinquent filers?	N	Y	N	N	N	N	N	N	N	Y	Y	N/A	N

State Legislative Disclosure Requirements

	IN	IA	KS	KY	LA	ME	MD	MA	MI	MN	MS	MO	MT
Client value range/income amount required?	N	N	N	N	N	N	Y	N	N/A	N	N	N	N
Spouse client information required and clear	N	N	Y	N	N	N	N	N	N/A	N	N	N	N
Real-property information required?	N	Y	Y	Y	N	N	Y	Y	N/A	Y	N	Y	Y
Real-property information not narrowly defined?	N	N	N	Y	N	N	Y	Y	N/A	Y	N	Y	Y
Real-property value range/amount required?	N	N	Y	N	N	N	Y	Y	N/A	N	N	N	N
Spouse real-property information required?	N	N	Y	Y	N	N	N	Y	N/A	N	N	N	N
Spouse name required?	N	N	Y	N	N	N	N	Y	N/A	N	N	Y	N
Dependent name required?	N	N	N	N	N	N	N	Y	N/A	N	N	Y	N
Financial disclosure filings in central office?	Y	Y	Y	Y	Y	Y	Y	Y	N/A	Y	Y	Y	Y
Lawmakers not forwarded reviewer information?	Y	Y	Y	Y	Y	Y	Y	N	N/A	Y	Y	Y	Y
In-person appearance not required to obtain filings?	Y	Y	Y	Y	Y	Y	N	Y	N/A	Y	Y	Y	Y
Copy fees less than 50 cents per page?	Y	Y	N	Y	Y	Y	Y	Y	N/A	Y	Y	Y	Y
Blank disclosure form available on the web?	N	Y[3]	Y	Y	N	N	Y	N	N/A	Y	Y	Y	Y
Disclosure filings available electronically or online?	Y	Y	N	Y	Y	N	N	N	N/A	Y	N	N	N
Late-filing penalties on the books?	N	N	Y	Y	Y	N	Y	Y	N/A	Y	N	Y	Y
Misfiling penalties on the books?	N	N	Y	Y	Y	Y	Y	Y	N/A	Y	Y	Y	Y
State has auditing authority?	Y	Y	Y	Y	Y	Y	Y	Y	N/A	Y	Y	Y	Y
State routinely reviews filings for accuracy and completeness?	N	Y	Y	Y	Y	Y	Y	Y	N/A	Y	Y	Y	Y
State published list of delinquent filers?	N	N	N	N	N	N	N	N	N/A	Y	N	N	N

3 Blank disclosure forms are not available online, but exact outlines of the forms are recorded in each chamber's code of ethics, which are available online.

68 • Ethical Standards in the Public Sector

	NE	NV	NH	NJ	NM	NY	NC	ND	OH	OK	OR	PA
Client value range/income amount required?	N	N	N	N	N	Y	N	N	Y	N	N	N
Spouse client information required and clear?	N	N	N	N	N	N	N	N	N	Y	N	N
Real-property information required?	Y	Y	N	Y	Y	Y	Y	N	Y	N	Y	Y
Real-property information not narrowly defined?	Y	Y	N	N	Y	Y	Y	N	Y	N	Y	N
Real-property value range/amount required?	N	N	N	N	N	Y	N	N	N	N	N	N
Spouse real-property information required?	N	N	N	Y	Y	Y	Y	N	N	N	Y	N
Spouse name required?	N	N	N	N	Y	Y	Y	Y	N	N	N	N
Dependent name required?	N	N	N	N	N	Y	Y	N	Y	N	N	N
Financial disclosure filings in central office?	Y	Y	Y	Y	Y	Y	Y	Y	N	Y	Y	Y
Lawmakers not forwarded reviewer information?	Y	Y	Y	N	Y	Y	Y	Y	Y	Y	Y	Y
In-person appearance not required to obtain filings?	Y	Y	Y	Y	Y	Y	Y	Y	Y	Y	Y	Y
Copy fees less than 50 cents per page?	Y	Y	Y	N	Y	Y	Y	Y	Y	Y	Y	Y
Blank disclosure form available on the web?	Y	Y	Y	Y	Y	Y	Y	Y	Y	Y	N	Y
Disclosure filings available electronically or online?	N	Y	N	Y	Y	Y	Y	Y	Y	Y	Y	Y
Late-filing penalties on the books?	Y	Y	N	Y	Y	Y	Y	Y	Y	Y	Y	Y
Misfiling penalties on the books?	Y	Y	Y	Y	Y	Y	Y	Y	Y	Y	Y	Y
State has auditing authority?	Y	N	Y	Y	Y	Y	N	Y	Y	Y	Y	Y
State routinely reviews filings for accuracy and completeness?	Y	N	Y	N	Y	Y	N	N	Y	Y	Y	Y
State published list of delinquent filers?	N	N	N	N	N	Y	N	N	N	Y	Y	N

State Legislative Disclosure Requirements

	RI	SC	SD	TN	TX	UT	VT	VA	WA	WV	WI	WY
Client value range/income amount required?	N	Y	N	N	Y	N/A	N	Y	Y		N	N/A
Spouse client information required and clear?	N	Y	N	Y	N	N/A	N	N	Y	Y	N	N/A
Real-property information required?	Y	Y	N	N	Y	N	N	Y	Y	Y	Y	Y
Real-property information not narrowly defined?	Y	N	N	N	Y	Y	N/A	Y	Y	N	Y	N
Real-property value range/amount required?	N	Y	N	N	N	N/A	N/A	N	Y	N	N	N
Spouse real-property information required?	Y	N	N	N	Y	N/A	N	Y	Y	Y	Y	N
Spouse name required?	Y	N	N	N	Y	Y	N	Y	Y	Y	N	N
Dependent name required?	Y	N	N	N	Y	N	N	Y	Y	N	N	N
Financial disclosure filings in central office?	Y	Y	Y	Y	Y	N/A	Y	Y	Y	Y	Y	Y
Lawmakers not forwarded reviewer information?	Y	Y	Y	Y	Y	Y	N	N	Y	Y	Y	Y
In-person appearance not required to obtain filings?	Y	Y	Y	Y	Y	Y	Y	Y	Y	Y	Y	Y
Copy fees less than 50 cents per page?	Y	Y	N	Y	Y	Y	Y	N	Y	Y	Y	N
Blank disclosure form available on the web?	Y	N	Y	Y	Y	Y	Y	Y	Y	Y	Y	Y
Disclosure filings available electronically or online?	Y	Y	Y	Y	N	Y	Y	N	Y	Y	Y	Y
Late-filing penalties on the books?	Y	Y	Y	Y	Y	Y	N	N	Y	Y	Y	Y
Misfiling penalties on the books?	Y	Y	Y	Y	Y	Y	N	Y	Y	Y	Y	Y
State has auditing authority?	Y	Y	Y	Y	Y	Y	N	Y	Y	Y	Y	N
State routinely reviews filings for accuracy and completeness?	Y	Y	Y	Y	Y	Y	N	Y	N	Y	Y	N
State published list of delinquent filers?	N	N	N	Y	Y	N	N	N	Y	Y	Y	N

APPENDIX B

State Executive Disclosure Requirements

72 • Ethical Standards in the Public Sector

	AL	AK	AZ	AR	CA	CO	CT	DE	FL	GA	HI	ID	IL
Requires financial disclosure filing?	Y	Y	Y	Y	Y	Y	Y	Y	Y	Y	Y	N	Y
Requires complete financial disclosure filing (no update)?	Y	Y	Y	Y	Y	N	Y	Y	Y	Y	N	N/A	Y
Requires financial disclosure filing annually?	Y	Y	Y	Y	Y	Y	Y	Y	Y	Y	Y	N/A	Y
Requires complete financial disclosure filing for candidates?	Y	Y	Y	Y	Y	Y	N	Y	Y	Y	Y	N/A	Y
Employment information required?	Y	Y	Y	Y	Y	Y	Y	Y	Y	Y	Y	N/A	Y
Employment information not narrowly defined?	Y	Y	Y	Y	N	Y	Y	Y	Y	Y	Y	N/A	Y
Employer/business name required?	Y	Y	Y	Y	Y	Y	Y	Y	Y	Y	Y	N/A	Y
Employment job title required?	Y	Y	Y	Y	Y	N	N	Y	N	Y	Y	N/A	N
Employer description required?	N	N	Y	Y	Y	N	Y	Y	Y	Y	N	N/A	Y
Value range/income amount required?	Y	Y	Y	Y	Y	N	N	N	Y	N	Y	N/A	N
Spouse employment information required?	Y	Y	Y	Y	N	Y	Y	N	N	Y	Y	N/A	N
Officer/director information required?	Y	Y	Y	Y	Y	Y	Y	Y	Y	Y	Y	N/A	Y
Officer/director information not narrowly defined?	N	Y	Y	Y	Y	Y	Y	N	N	Y	Y	N/A	N
Officer/director entity name required?	Y	Y	Y	Y	Y	Y	Y	Y	Y	Y	Y	N/A	Y
Officer/director entity description required?	N	N	N	N	Y	N	Y	Y	N	Y	N	N/A	Y
Spouse officer/director information required?	Y	Y	Y	Y	Y	Y	Y	Y	N	Y	Y	N/A	N
Investment information required?	Y	Y	Y	Y	Y	Y	Y	Y	Y	Y	Y	N/A	Y
Investment information not narrowly defined?	Y	Y	Y	Y	Y	Y	Y	Y	Y	N	Y	N/A	Y
Investment entity name required?	Y	Y	Y	Y	Y	Y	Y	Y	Y	Y	Y	N/A	Y
Investment entity description required?	N	N	Y	N	Y	N	N	N	Y	Y	N	N/A	N
Investment value range/holding amount required?	Y	N	Y	Y	Y	N	N	N	Y	N	Y	N/A	N
Spouse investment information required and clear?	Y	Y	Y	Y	Y	Y	Y	Y	N	Y	Y	N/A	Y
Client information required?	Y	Y	N	N	Y	Y	Y	N	Y	N	Y	N/A	N
Client name required?	N	Y	N	N	Y	Y	N	N	Y	N	Y	N/A	N
Client value range/income amount required?	Y	N	N	N	N	N	N	N	N	N	N	N/A	N

State Executive Disclosure Requirements • 73

	IN	IA	KS	KY	LA	ME	MD	MA	MI	MN	MS	MO	MT
Requires financial disclosure filing?	Y	Y	Y	Y	Y	Y	Y	Y	N	Y	Y	Y	Y
Requires complete financial disclosure filing (no update)?	Y	Y	Y	Y	Y	Y	Y	Y	N/A	N	Y	Y	Y
Requires financial disclosure filing annually?	Y	Y	Y	Y	Y	Y	Y	Y	N/A	Y	Y	Y	N
Requires complete financial disclosure filing for candidates?	Y	Y	Y	Y	Y	N	Y	Y	N/A	Y	Y	Y	Y
Employment information required?	Y	Y	Y	Y	Y	Y	Y	Y	N/A	Y	Y	Y	Y
Employment information not narrowly defined?	Y	Y	Y	Y	Y	Y	Y	Y	N/A	Y	Y	Y	Y
Employer/business name required?	Y	Y	Y	Y	Y	Y	Y	Y	N/A	Y	Y	Y	Y
Employment job title required?	N	Y	N	N	Y	Y	Y	Y	N/A	Y	Y	N	N
Employer description required?	Y	Y	Y	N	N	Y	Y	N	N/A	N	N	N	N
Value range/income amount required?	N	N	N	N	Y	N	N	Y	N/A	N	N	N	N
Spouse employment information required?	Y	N	Y	Y	Y	Y	Y	Y	N/A	N	Y	Y	N
Officer/director information required?	Y	N	Y	Y	Y	Y	Y	Y	N/A	Y	Y	Y	Y
Officer/director information not narrowly defined?	N	N	Y	Y	Y	Y	N	Y	N/A	N	N	Y	Y
Officer/director entity name required?	Y	N	Y	Y	Y	Y	Y	Y	N/A	Y	Y	Y	Y
Officer/director entity description required?	Y	N	N	N	Y	N	Y	N	N/A	N	N	Y	N
Spouse officer/director information required?	Y	N	Y	Y	Y	Y	Y	Y	N/A	N	Y	Y	N
Investment information required?	Y	Y	Y	Y	Y	Y	Y	Y	N/A	Y	Y	Y	Y
Investment information not narrowly defined?	N	N	Y	N	Y	Y	Y	Y	N/A	Y	Y	Y	Y
Investment entity name required?	Y	Y	Y	Y	Y	Y	Y	Y	N/A	Y	Y	Y	Y
Investment entity description required?	N	N	Y	N	N	Y	N	N	N/A	N	N	Y	Y
Investment value range/holding amount required?	N	N	Y	N	Y	N	Y	N	N/A	N	N	N	N
Spouse investment information required and clear?	Y	N	Y	N	Y	N	N	Y	N/A	N	Y	Y	N
Client information required?	Y	N	Y	Y	Y	Y	N	N	N/A	N	Y	N	N
Client name required?	Y	N	Y	Y	Y	Y	N/A	N/A	N/A	N/A	Y	N	N
Client value range/income amount required?	N	N	N	N	Y	N	N/A	N/A	N/A	N/A	N	N	N

74 • Ethical Standards in the Public Sector

	NE	NV	NH	NJ	NM	NY	NC	ND	OH	OK	OR	PA
Requires financial disclosure filing?	Y	Y	Y	Y	Y	Y	Y	Y	Y	Y	Y	Y
Requires complete financial disclosure filing (no update)?	N	Y	Y	Y	Y	Y	N	Y	Y	N	Y	Y
Requires financial disclosure filing annually?	Y	Y	Y	Y	Y	Y	Y	N	Y	Y	Y	Y
Requires complete financial disclosure filing for candidates?	Y	Y	Y	Y	Y	Y	Y	Y	Y	Y	Y	Y
Employment information required?	Y	Y	Y	Y	Y	Y	Y	Y	Y	Y	Y	Y
Employment information not narrowly defined?	Y	Y	N	Y	Y	Y	Y	N	Y	Y	Y	Y
Employer/business name required?	Y	Y	Y	Y	Y	Y	Y	Y	Y	Y	Y	Y
Employment job title required?	N	N	N	N	Y	Y	Y	Y	Y	N	N	Y
Employer description required?	Y	N	Y	N	Y	Y	Y	N	N	Y	Y	N
Value range/income amount required?	N	N	N	N	N	N	N	N	Y	N	N	N
Spouse employment information required?	N	Y	Y	Y	Y	Y	Y	Y	N	Y	Y	N
Officer/director information required?	Y	Y	Y	Y	Y	Y	Y	Y	Y	Y	Y	Y
Officer/director information not narrowly defined?	Y	N	Y	Y	N	Y	Y	Y	N	N	Y	Y
Officer/director entity name required?	Y	Y	Y	Y	Y	Y	Y	Y	Y	Y	Y	Y
Officer/director entity description required?	N	N	Y	N	N	N	Y	N	N	N	Y	N
Spouse officer/director information required?	N	Y	Y	Y	Y	Y	Y	Y	N	N	Y	N
Investment information required?	Y	Y	N	Y	Y	Y	Y	Y	Y	Y	Y	Y
Investment information not narrowly defined?	Y	Y	N/A	Y	Y	Y	Y	Y	Y	Y	Y	Y
Investment entity name required?	Y	Y	N/A	Y	Y	Y	Y	Y	Y	Y	Y	Y
Investment entity description required?	N	N	N/A	N	Y	Y	Y	N	N	Y	Y	N
Investment value range/holding amount required?	N	N	N/A	N	N	Y	N	N	N	N	N	N
Spouse investment information required and clear?	N	Y	N/A	Y	N	Y	Y	Y	N	N	N	N
Client information required?	N	N	N	Y	Y	Y	Y	N	Y	Y	Y	N
Client name required?	N	N	N/A	N	Y	Y	N	N	Y	Y	Y	N
Client value range/income amount required?	N	N	N/A	N	N	Y	N	N	Y	N	N	N

State Executive Disclosure Requirements • 75

	RI	SC	SD	TN	TX	UT	VT	VA	WA	WV	WI	WY
Requires financial disclosure filing?	Y	Y	Y	Y	Y	Y	N	Y	Y	Y	Y	Y
Requires complete financial disclosure filing (no update)?	Y	Y	Y	N	Y	Y	N/A	Y	N	Y	Y	Y
Requires financial disclosure filing annually?	Y	Y	N	Y	Y	Y	N/A	Y	Y	Y	Y	Y
Requires complete financial disclosure filing for candidates?	Y	Y	Y	Y	Y	Y	N/A	Y	Y	Y	Y	N
Employment information required?	Y	Y	Y	Y	Y	Y	N/A	Y	Y	Y	Y	Y
Employment information not narrowly defined?	Y	N	Y	Y	Y	Y	N/A	N	Y	Y	Y	Y
Employer/business name required?	Y	Y	Y	Y	Y	Y	N/A	Y	Y	Y	Y	Y
Employment job title required?	Y	N	Y	N	Y	Y	N/A	N	Y	Y	N	Y
Employer description required?	N	N	N	N	N	N	N/A	N	N	Y	Y	N
Value range/income amount required?	Y	Y	N	N	N	Y	N/A	N	Y	N	N	N
Spouse employment information required?	Y	Y	Y	Y	Y	Y	N/A	Y	Y	Y	Y	N
Officer/director information required?	Y	Y	Y	Y	Y	Y	N/A	Y	Y	Y	Y	Y
Officer/director information not narrowly defined?	Y	N	N	Y	Y	Y	N/A	N	Y	Y	N	N
Officer/director entity name required?	Y	Y	Y	Y	Y	Y	N/A	Y	Y	Y	Y	Y
Officer/director entity description required?	N	N	N	N	N	Y	N/A	N	Y	Y	N	N
Spouse officer/director information required?	Y	N	Y	Y[1]	Y	Y	N/A	Y	Y	Y	Y	N
Investment information required?	Y	Y	Y	Y	Y	Y	N/A	Y	Y	Y	Y	Y
Investment information not narrowly defined?	Y	N	Y	Y	Y	N	N/A	N	Y	Y	Y	N
Investment entity name required?	Y	Y	Y	Y	Y	Y	N/A	Y	Y	Y	Y	Y
Investment entity description required?	N	N	N	N	N	Y	N/A	N	Y	N	N	N
Investment value range/holding amount required?	N	N	N	N	Y	Y	N/A	Y	Y	N	Y	N
Spouse investment information required and clear?	Y	N	Y	Y	Y	Y	N/A	N	N	Y	N	N
Client information required?	N	Y	N	Y	Y	N	N/A	Y	Y	Y	Y	N
Client name required?	N	Y	N	N	Y	N/A	N/A	Y	Y	N	Y	N/A
Client value range/income amount required?	N	Y	N	N	Y	N/A	N/A	Y	Y	N	N	N/A

76 • Ethical Standards in the Public Sector

	AL	AK	AZ	AR	CA	CO	CT	DE	FL	GA	HI	ID	IL
Spouse client information required and clear?	Y	Y	N	N	N	Y	Y	N	N	N	Y	N/A	N
Real-property information required?	Y	Y	Y	N	Y	Y	Y	N	Y	Y	Y	N/A	Y
Real-property information not narrowly defined?	Y	Y	Y	N	Y	Y	Y	Y	Y	Y	Y	N/A	Y
Real-property value range/amount required?	Y	N	Y	N	Y	N	N	N	Y	Y	Y	N/A	N
Spouse real-property information required?	N	Y	Y	N	N	Y	Y	Y	N	Y	Y	N/A	N
Spouse name required?	Y	Y	Y	Y	N	N	Y	N	N	Y	Y	N/A	N
Dependent name required?	Y	Y	Y	N	N	N	Y	N	N	Y	Y	N/A	N
Electronic filing available?	Y	Y	N	N	Y	N	Y	Y	N	Y	Y	N/A	N
Governor not forwarded reviewer information?	Y	Y	Y	Y	Y	Y	Y	Y	Y	Y	Y	N/A	Y
In-person appearance not required to obtain filings?	Y	Y	Y	Y	Y	Y	Y	Y	Y	Y	Y	N/A	Y
Copy fees less than 50 cents per page?	N	Y	Y	Y	Y	N	Y	N	Y	Y	Y	N/A	N
Blank disclosure form available online?	Y	N	Y	Y	Y	Y	Y	Y	Y	Y	Y	N/A	Y
Disclosure filings available electronically or online?	Y	Y	N	Y	Y	N	N	Y	Y	Y	Y	N/A	Y
Late-filing penalties on the books?	Y	Y	Y	Y	Y	Y	Y	Y	Y	Y	N	N/A	Y
Misfiling penalties on the books?	Y	Y	Y	Y	Y	Y	Y	Y	Y	Y	Y	N/A	Y
State has auditing authority?	Y	Y	N	Y	Y	N	Y	N	Y	Y	Y	N/A	Y
State routinely reviews filings for accuracy and completeness?	Y	Y	N	N	Y	Y	Y	Y	N	Y	Y	N/A	N
State published list of delinquent filers?	N	Y	N	N	N	N	N	N	Y	Y	Y	N/A	N
Do elected executive branch officials other than governor file?	Y	Y	Y	Y	Y	Y	Y	Y	Y	Y	Y	N/A	Y
Do non-elected executive branch officials file?	Y	Y	N	Y	Y	Y	N	Y	Y	Y	Y	N/A	Y

State Executive Disclosure Requirements

	IN	IA	KS	KY	LA	ME	MD	MA	MI	MN	MS	MO	MT
Spouse client information required and clear?	N	N	Y	N	Y	N	N/A	N/A	N/A	N/A	N	N	N
Real-property information required?	Y	Y	Y	Y	Y	N	Y	Y	N/A	Y	N	Y	Y
Real-property information not narrowly defined?	Y	N	N	Y	Y	N/A	Y	Y	N/A	Y	N/A	Y	Y
Real-property value range/amount required?	N	N	Y	N	Y	N/A	Y	Y	N/A	N	N/A	N	N
Spouse real-property information required?	Y	N	Y	Y	Y	N/A	N	Y	N/A	N	N/A	Y	N
Spouse name required?	Y	N	Y	Y	Y	Y	N	Y	N/A	N	N	Y	N
Dependent name required?	N	N	N	Y	N	N	N	Y	N/A	N	N	Y	N
Electronic filing available?	Y	Y	Y	N	Y	Y	Y	Y	N/A	Y	Y	N	N
Governor not forwarded reviewer information?	Y	Y	Y	Y	Y	Y	Y	N	N/A	Y	Y	Y	Y
In-person appearance not required to obtain filings?	Y	Y	Y	Y	Y	Y	N	Y	N/A	Y	Y	Y	Y
Copy fees less than 50 cents per page?	Y	Y	N	Y	Y	N	Y	Y	N/A	Y	N	Y	Y
Blank disclosure form available online?	Y	N	Y	Y	Y	Y	Y	Y	N/A	Y	Y	Y	Y
Disclosure filings available electronically or online?	Y	Y	N	N	Y	Y	N	N	N/A	Y	Y	N	N
Late-filing penalties on the books?	Y	Y	Y	Y	Y	Y	Y	Y	N/A	Y	Y	Y	Y
Misfiling penalties on the books?	Y	Y	Y	N	Y	Y	Y	Y	N/A	Y	Y	Y	Y
State has auditing authority?	Y	Y	Y	Y	Y	N	Y	Y	N/A	Y	Y	Y	Y
State routinely reviews filings for accuracy and completeness?	Y	Y	Y	Y	Y	Y	Y	Y	N/A	Y	Y	N	Y
State published list of delinquent filers?	N	Y	N	N	Y	N	N	N	N/A	Y	N	N	N
Do elected executive branch officials other than governor file?	Y	Y	Y	Y	Y	Y	Y	Y	N/A	Y	Y	Y	Y
Do non-elected executive branch officials file?	Y	Y	Y	Y	Y	Y	Y	Y	N/A	Y	Y	Y	Y

78 • Ethical Standards in the Public Sector

	NE	NV	NH	NJ	NM	NY	NC	ND	OH	OK	OR	PA
Spouse client information required and clear?	N	N	N/A	N	N	N	N	N	N	Y	N	N
Real-property information required?	Y	Y	N	Y	Y	Y	Y	N	Y	N	Y	Y
Real-property information not narrowly defined?	Y	Y	N/A	Y	Y	Y	Y	N	Y	N	Y	N
Real-property value range/amount required?	N	N	N/A	N	N	Y	N	N	N	N	N	N
Spouse real-property information required?	N	Y	N/A	Y	Y	Y	Y	N	N	N	Y	N
Spouse name required?	N	N	N	N	Y	Y	Y	Y	Y	N	N	N
Dependent name required?	N	N	N	N	N	Y	Y	N	Y	N	N	N
Electronic filing available?	N	Y	Y	Y	N	Y	Y	Y	Y	Y	Y	Y
Governor not forwarded reviewer information?	Y	Y	Y	Y	Y	Y	Y	Y	Y	Y	Y	Y
In-person appearance not required to obtain filings?	Y	Y	Y	Y	Y	Y	Y	Y	Y	Y	Y	Y
Copy fees less than 50 cents per page?	Y	Y	Y	N	Y	Y	Y	Y	Y	Y	Y	Y
Blank disclosure form available online?	Y	Y	Y	Y	Y	Y	Y	Y	Y	Y	N	Y
Disclosure filings available electronically or online?	N	Y	Y	Y	Y	Y	Y	Y	Y	Y	Y	Y
Late-filing penalties on the books?	Y	Y	Y	Y	Y	Y	Y	Y	Y	Y	Y	Y
Misfiling penalties on the books?	Y	Y	Y	Y	Y	Y	Y	Y	Y	Y	Y	Y
State has auditing authority?	Y	N	Y	Y	Y	Y	Y	Y	Y	Y	Y	Y
State routinely reviews filings for accuracy and completeness?	N	N	N	Y	Y	Y	Y	N	Y	Y	Y	Y
State published list of delinquent filers?	N	N	N	N	N	Y	N	N	N	Y	Y	N
Do elected executive branch officials other than governor file?	Y	Y	Y	Y	Y	Y	Y	Y	Y	Y	Y	Y
Do non-elected executive branch officials file?	Y	Y	Y	Y	Y	Y	Y	Y	Y	Y	Y	Y

State Executive Disclosure Requirements

	RI	SC	SD	TN	TX	UT	VT	VA	WA	WV	WI	WY
Spouse client information required and clear?	N	Y	N	Y	Y	N/A	N/A	N	Y	Y	N	N/A
Real-property information required?	Y	Y	N	N	Y	N	N/A	Y	Y	Y	Y	Y
Real-property information not narrowly defined?	Y	N	N	N	Y	Y	N/A	Y	Y	N	Y	N
Real-property value range/amount required?	N	Y	N	N	N	N/A	N/A	N	Y	N	N	N
Spouse real-property information required?	Y	Y	N	N	Y	N/A	N/A	Y	Y	Y	Y	N
Spouse name required?	Y	N	N	N	Y	Y	N/A	Y	Y	Y	N	N
Dependent name required?	Y	N	N	N	Y	N	N/A	Y	Y	N	N	N
Electronic filing available?	Y	Y	N	Y	Y	N	N/A	Y	Y	Y	Y	Y
Governor not forwarded reviewer information?	Y	Y	Y	Y	Y	N	N/A	Y	Y	Y	N	Y
In-person appearance not required to obtain filings?	Y	Y	Y	Y	Y	Y	N/A	Y	Y	Y	Y	Y
Copy fees less than 50 cents per page?	Y	N	N	Y	Y	N	N/A	Y	Y	Y	Y	N
Blank disclosure form available online?	Y	N	Y	Y	Y	Y	N/A	Y	Y	Y	Y	Y
Disclosure filings available electronically or online?	Y	Y	Y	Y	N	Y	N/A	N	Y	Y	Y	Y
Late-filing penalties on the books?	Y	Y	Y	Y	Y	Y	N/A	N	Y	Y	Y	Y
Misfiling penalties on the books?	Y	Y	Y	Y	Y	Y	N/A	Y	Y	Y	Y	Y
State has auditing authority?	Y	Y	Y	Y	Y	N/A	N/A	Y	Y	Y	Y	N
State routinely reviews filings for accuracy and completeness?	Y	Y	Y	Y	Y	Y	N/A	Y	Y	Y	Y	N
State published list of delinquent filers?	N	N	N	Y	Y	N	N/A	N	Y	Y	N	N
Do elected executive branch officials other than governor file?	Y	Y	Y	Y	Y	Y	N/A	Y	Y	Y	Y	Y
Do non-elected executive branch officials file?	Y	Y	Y	Y	Y	Y	N/A	Y	Y	Y	Y	N

APPENDIX C

State Financial Disclosure Statutes

State	Executive Agency Name	Executive Statute	Legislative Agency Name
Alabama	Ethics Commission	Code of Ala. § 36-25-14	Ethics Commission
Alaska	Public Offices Commission	Alaska Stat. §§ 39.50.010 et seq.	Public Offices Commission
Arizona	Elections Division	Ariz. Rev. Stat. §§ 38-541 et seq.	Elections Division
Arkansas	Ethics Commission	Ark. Code Ann. §§ 21-8-701 et seq.	Ethics Commission
California	Fair Political Practices Commission	Cal. Gov't Code §§ 87200 et seq.	Fair Political Practices Commission
Colorado	Secretary of State	Colo. Rev. Stat. §§ 24-6-201 et seq.	Secretary of State
Connecticut	Office of State Ethics	Conn. Gen. Stat. § 1-83	Office of State Ethics
Delaware	Public Integrity Commission	29 Del. Code §§ 5811 et seq.	Public Integrity Commission
Florida	Commission on Ethics	Fla. Const. Art. II, § 8(a); Fla. Stat. § 112.3144	Commission on Ethics
Georgia	State Ethics Commission	Ga. Code Ann. §§ 21-5-50 et seq.	State Ethics Commission
Hawaii	State Ethics Commission	Haw. Rev. Stat. § 84-17	State Ethics Commission
Idaho		No executive disclosure required	
Illinois	Secretary of State Index Department	5 Ill. Comp. Stat. §§ 420/4A-101 et seq.	Secretary of State Index Department
Indiana	State Ethics Commission	Ind. Code § 4-2-6-8	Principal Clerk of the House/Principal Clerk of the Senate
Iowa	Iowa Ethics & Campaign Disclosure Board	Iowa Code § 68B.35	Chief Clerk of House and Secretary of the Senate
Kansas	Secretary of State, Elections Division; Governmental Ethics Commission	Kan. Stat. Ann. § 46-249	Secretary of State, Elections Division; Governmental Ethics Commission
Kentucky	Executive Branch Ethics Commission	Ky. Rev. Stat. § 11A.050	Legislative Ethics Commission
Louisiana	Board of Ethics	La. Rev. Stat. §§ 42:1114, 42:1124, 42:1124.2, 42:1124.2.1	Board of Ethics
Maine	Commission on Governmental Ethics and Election Practices	5 Me. Rev. Stat. § 19	Commission on Governmental Ethics and Election Practices
Maryland	State Ethics Commission	Md. Code Ann., Gen. Provisions §§ 5-601 et seq.	State Ethics Commission; Joint Ethics Committee
Massachusetts	State Ethics Commission	Ann. Laws Mass. Gen. Law ch. 268B, § 5	State Ethics Commission

State Financial Disclosure Statutes • 83

Legislative Statute	Judicial Agency Name	Judicial Statute	Judicial Filings under Code or Statute?
Code of Ala. § 36-25-14	Ethics Commission	Code of Ala. § 36-25-14	Two separate judicial filings required
Alaska Stat. §§ 24.60.200 et seq.	Public Offices Commission	Alaska Stat. §§ 39.50.010 et seq.	Two separate judicial filings required
Ariz. Rev. Stat. §§ 38-541 et seq.	Elections Division	Ariz. Rev. Stat. §§ 38-541 et seq.	Judicial filing only under the statute
Ark. Code Ann. §§ 21-8-701 et seq.	Ethics Commission	Ark. Code Ann. §§ 21-8-701 et seq.	Two separate judicial filings required
Cal. Gov't Code §§ 87200 et seq.	Fair Political Practices Commission	Cal. Gov't Code §§ 87200 et seq.	Judicial filing only under the statute
Colo. Rev. Stat. §§ 24-6-201 et seq.	Secretary of State	Colo. Rev. Stat. §§ 24-6-201 et seq.	Two separate judicial filings required
Conn. Gen. Stat. §1-83	Office of the Chief Court Administrator	Conn. Gen. Stat. § 51-46a	Judicial filing only under the statute (but different than executive/legislative filing requirements)
29 Del. Code §§ 5811 et seq.	Public Integrity Commission	29 Del. Code §§ 5811 et seq.	Judicial filing only under the statute
Fla. Const. Art. II, § 8(a); Fla. Stat. § 112.3144	Commission on Ethics	Fla. Const. Art. II, § 8(a); Fla. Stat. § 112.3144	Two separate judicial filings required
Ga. Code Ann. §§ 21-5-50 et seq.	State Ethics Commission	Ga. Code Ann. §§ 21-5-50 et seq.	Two separate judicial filings required
Haw. Rev. Stat. § 84-17		No statutory requirement	Judicial filing only under the code of judicial conduct
No legislative disclosure required		No statutory requirement	No judicial filing required
5 Ill. Comp. Stat. §§ 420/4A-101 et seq.	Secretary of State Index Department	5 Ill. Comp. Stat. §§ 420/4A-101 et seq.	Two separate judicial filings required
Ind. Code § 2-2.2-2-3		No statutory requirement	Judicial filing only under the code of judicial conduct
Iowa Code § 68B.35		No statutory requirement	Judicial filing only under the state court rules
Kan. Stat. Ann. § 46-249		No statutory requirement	Judicial filing only under the code of judicial conduct
Ky. Rev. Stat. §§ 6.781 et seq.	Registry of Election Finance	Ky. Rev. Stat. §§ 61.710 et seq.	Judicial filing only under the statute (but different than executive/legislative filing requirements)
La. Rev. Stat. §§ 42:1114, 42:1124.2		No statutory requirement	Judicial filing only under the code of judicial conduct
1 Me. Rev. Stat. §§ 1016-A et seq.		No statutory requirement	Judicial filing only under the code of judicial conduct
Md. Code Ann., Gen. Provisions §§ 5-514, 5-601 et seq.	Administrative Office of the Courts	Md. Code Ann., Gen. Provisions §§ 5-610 et seq.	Judicial filing only under the statute (but different than executive/legislative filing requirements)
Ann. Laws Mass. Gen. Law ch. 268B, § 5	State Ethics Commission	Ann. Laws Mass. Gen. Law ch. 268B, § 5	Judicial filing only under the statute

State	Executive Agency Name	Executive Statute	Legislative Agency Name
Michigan		No executive disclosure required	
Minnesota	Campaign Finance and Public Disclosure Board	Minn. Stat. § 10A.09	Campaign Finance and Public Disclosure Board
Mississippi	Ethics Commission	Miss. Code Ann. §§ 25-4-25 et seq.	Ethics Commission
Missouri	Ethics Commission	Rev. Stat. Mo. §§ 105.483 et seq.	Ethics Commission
Montana	Commissioner of Political Practices	Mont. Code Ann. § 2-2-106	Commissioner of Political Practices
Nebraska	Accountability and Disclosure Commission	Rev. Stat. Neb. §§ 49-1493 et seq.	Accountability and Disclosure Commission
Nevada	Secretary of State, Elections Division	Nev. Rev. Stat. §§ 281.559 et seq.	Secretary of State, Elections Division
New Hampshire	Secretary of State	N.H. Rev. Stat. §§ 15-A:1 et seq.	Legislative Ethics Committee
New Jersey	State Ethics Commission; Individual Agencies	Exec. Order No. 24 (2010)	Joint Legislative Committee on Ethical Standards
New Mexico	Secretary of State, Bureau of Elections & Ethics Administration	N.M. Stat. Ann. §§ 10-16A-1 et seq.	Secretary of State, Bureau of Elections & Ethics Administration
New York	Joint Commission on Public Ethics	N.Y. Pub. O. Law § 73-a	Legislative Ethics Commission & Joint Commission on Public Ethics
North Carolina	State Ethics Commission	N.C. Gen. Stat. §§ 138A-21 et seq.	State Ethics Commission
North Dakota	Secretary of State Elections Unit	N.D. Cent. Code §§ 16.1-09-01 et seq.	Secretary of State Elections Unit
Ohio	Ethics Commission	Ohio Rev. Code Ann. § 102.02	Joint Legislative Ethics Committee
Oklahoma	Ethics Commission	Okla. Ethics R. 3, codified at Okla. Stat. tit. 74, app. 1	Ethics Commission
Oregon	Government Ethics Commission	Or. Rev. Stat. §§ 244.050 et seq.	Government Ethics Commission
Pennsylvania	State Ethics Commission	65 Pa. Cons. Stat. §§ 1104 et seq.	State Ethics Commission
Rhode Island	Ethics Commission	R.I. Gen. Laws §§ 36-14-16 et seq.	Ethics Commission
South Carolina	State Ethics Commission	S.C. Code Ann. §§ 8-13-1110 et seq.	House and Senate Ethics Committees
South Dakota	Secretary of State, Elections Division	S.D. Codified Laws §§ 3-1A-1 et seq.	Secretary of State, Elections Division
Tennessee	Ethics Commission	Tenn. Code Ann. §§ 8-50-501 et seq.	Ethics Commission
Texas	Ethics Commission	Tex. Gov't Code §§ 572.021 et seq.	Ethics Commission

State Financial Disclosure Statutes

Legislative Statute	Judicial Agency Name	Judicial Statute	Judicial Filings under Code or Statute?
No legislative disclosure required		No statutory requirement	Judicial filing only under the code of judicial conduct
Minn. Stat. § 10A.09	Campaign Finance and Public Disclosure Board	Minn. Stat. § 10A.09	Two separate judicial filings required
Miss. Code Ann. §§ 25-4-25 et seq.	Ethics Commission	Miss. Code Ann. §§ 25-4-25 et seq.	Judicial filing only under the statute
Rev. Stat. Mo. §§ 105.483 et seq.	Ethics Commission	Rev. Stat. Mo. §§ 105.483 et seq.	Judicial filing only under the statute
Mont. Code Ann. § 2-2-106	Commissioner of Political Practices	Mont. Code Ann. § 2-2-106	Judicial filing only under the statute
Rev. Stat. Neb. §§ 49-1493 et seq.		No statutory requirement	Judicial filing only under the code of judicial conduct
Nev. Rev. Stat. §§ 281.559 et seq.	Secretary of State, Elections Division	Nev. Rev. Stat. §§ 281.559 et seq.	Two separate judicial filings required
N.H. Rev. Stat. §§ 14-B:8 et seq.		No statutory requirement	Judicial filing only under the code of judicial conduct
N.J. Legis. Code of Ethics r. 2.14		No statutory requirement	Judicial filing only under the code of judicial conduct
N.M. Stat. Ann. §§ 10-16A-1 et seq.		No statutory requirement	Judicial filing only under the code of judicial conduct
N.Y. Pub. O. Law § 73-a	Ethics Commission for the Unified Court System	N.Y. Jud. Law § 211(4)	Judicial filing only under the code of judicial conduct
N.C. Gen. Stat. §§ 138A-21 et seq.	State Ethics Commission	N.C. Gen. Stat. §§ 138A-21 et seq.	Two separate judicial filings required
N.D. Cent. Code §§ 16.1-09-01 et seq.	Secretary of State Elections Unit	N.D. Cent. Code §§ 16.1-09-01 et seq.	Two separate judicial filings required
Ohio Rev. Code Ann. § 102.02	Ohio Supreme Court—Board of Commissioners on Grievances & Discipline	Ohio Rev. Code Ann. § 102.02	Judicial filing only under the statute
Okla. Ethics R. 3, codified at Okla. Stat. tit. 74, app. 1	Ethics Commission	Okla. Ethics R. 3, codified at Okla. Stat. tit. 74, app. 1	Judicial filing only under the statute
Or. Rev. Stat. §§ 244.050 et seq.	Government Ethics Commission	Or. Rev. Stat. §§ 244.050 et seq.	Judicial filing only under the statute
65 Pa. Cons. Stat. §§ 1104 et seq.		No statutory requirement	Disclosure is mandated by court order
R.I. Gen. Laws §§ 36-14-16 et seq.	Ethics Commission	R.I. Gen. Laws §§ 36-14-16 et seq.	Two separate judicial filings required
S.C. Code Ann. §§ 8-13-1110 et seq.		No statutory requirement	Judicial filing only under the code of judicial conduct
S.D. Codified Laws §§ 3-1A-1 et seq.	Secretary of State, Elections Division	S.D. Codified Laws §§ 3-1A-1 et seq.	Two separate judicial filings required
Tenn. Code Ann. §§ 8-50-501 et seq.	Ethics Commission	Tenn. Code Ann. §§ 8-50-501 et seq.	Two separate judicial filings required
Tex. Gov't Code §§ 572.021 et seq.	Ethics Commission	Tex. Gov't Code §§ 572.021 et seq.	Judicial filing only under the statute

State	Executive Agency Name	Executive Statute	Legislative Agency Name
Utah	Lieutenant Governor; Attorney General	Utah Code Ann. §§ 20A-11-1604, 67-16-7	Secretary of the Senate/ Chief Clerk of the House
Vermont		No executive disclosure required	
Virginia	Conflict of Interest and Ethics Advisory Council	Va. Code Ann. §§ 2.2-3114 et seq.	Conflict of Interest and Ethics Advisory Council
Washington	Public Disclosure Commission	Rev. Code Wash. §§ 42.17A.700 et seq.	Public Disclosure Commission
West Virginia	Ethics Commission	W. Va. Code §§ 6B-2-6 et seq.	Ethics Commission
Wisconsin	Elections Commission	Wis. Stat. § 19.43	Elections Commission
Wyoming	Secretary of State, Ethics Division	Wyo. Stat. § 9-13-108	Secretary of State, Ethics Division

State Financial Disclosure Statutes

Legislative Statute	Judicial Agency Name	Judicial Statute	Judicial Filings under Code or Statute?
Utah Code Ann. § 20A-11-1604		No statutory requirement	No judicial disclosure required
No legislative disclosure required		No statutory requirement	Judicial filing only under the code of judicial conduct
Va. Code Ann. §§ 30-109 et seq.	Conflict of Interest and Ethics Advisory Council	Va. Code Ann. §§ 2.2-3114 et seq.	No, same as executive filings
Rev. Code Wash. §§ 42.17A.700 et seq.	Public Disclosure Commission	Rev. Code Wash. §§ 42.17A.700 et seq.	No, same as legislative/executive filings
W. Va. Code §§ 6B-2-6 et seq.	Ethics Commission	W. Va. Code §§ 6B-2-6 et seq.	Two judicial filings
Wis. Stat. § 19.43	Elections Commission	Wis. Stat. § 19.43	No, same as legislative/executive filings
Wyo. Stat. § 9-13-108		No statutory requirement	Judicial filing only under the code of judicial conduct

CHAPTER 5

Who Is the Client of the Government Lawyer?

Jane T. Feldman

This is a revision of a chapter originally prepared by Jeffrey Rosenthal.[1]

> Government lawyers at all levels often have several, sometimes competing, clients. Although some say that a government lawyer's primary duty is to "do justice" or represent "the people," it may not be clear how to represent those ideals, or who best embodies them. Privilege, confidentiality, and ethics issues may also be complicated depending on the relationships among the different client entities involved.

Whenever a lawyer is engaged in a legal matter, regardless of the nature of the work, there is a threshold question: Who is the client? In the usual private practice situation, a lawyer is retained for a particular purpose or matter by an identifiable client—an individual, a business, a corporation. Under the Model Rules of Professional Conduct,[2] a lawyer has very specific responsibilities and obligations to clients. Often there is a retention agreement that delineates both the scope of a representation and who the decision maker is within a client entity. For a lawyer engaged in government practice, however, the client of the government attorney may not be so easily identified. A government lawyer may have numerous "clients" as the lawyer may represent multiple agencies and individual officials as well as, potentially, "the public" or "public interest. Dilemmas concerning who a government lawyer represents and potential conflicts of interest will arise for the government lawyer. Parallels or comparisons with a private attorney are not always appropriate. Thus, while a lawyer engaged in private practice generally owes allegiance to a single client on a particular matter, the government lawyer may owe ethical responsibilities to a number of "clients" in the same or related matters. The purpose of this chapter is, first, to identify a number of a government lawyer's possible clients and, second, based on ethical considerations applicable to all attorneys, determine to whom the government lawyer owes duties of confidentiality and to whose communications privileges attach.

PRIVATE SECTOR PRACTICE: ALLEGIANCE TO A CLIENT

The typical lawyer in a private law firm is assigned a case concerning a certain client of the firm who has a particular legal issue or problem that needs to be addressed, which may be a litigation, regulatory, or corporate matter. In most instances, there is a retention agreement that identifies the client, and describes the nature of the case and the scope of the representation. The lawyer's responsibility to the client is to advocate, within legal and ethical boundaries, and to achieve the desired outcome on behalf of such client. Parallels to cases that support the client's position will be developed; cases that do not support the desired outcome will be distinguished. When interviewing employees of the client, a lawyer may need to remind the employee that she represents the corporation and not the employee. The responsibilities of the private attorney are directed toward developing a strategy that will best serve that client's interests within the legal framework. These issues will be discussed with the client, and with other lawyers in the firm if applicable.

GOVERNMENT PRACTICE: TO WHOM ARE LEGAL RESPONSIBILITY AND ALLEGIANCE OWED?

A lawyer employed by a government agency[3] may not have as clear or as delineated a focus. The government lawyer may be assigned to represent a particular client agency, to perform a variety of legal tasks, including providing general legal advice on statutory and regulatory interpretation, engaging in litigation on behalf of the client in enforcement matters, and drafting regulations or legislative initiatives. The lawyer also may be assigned to represent multiple agencies, and multiple attorneys may represent the same client agencies. The lawyer may be supervised by another agency lawyer but get directions and assignments from a policy or program staff member or the head of a client agency. These people may have different policy and legal agendas and perspectives.

Several commenters[4] have suggested that a government lawyer may have at least five potential clients; some are more obvious, some less so:

- The public interest
- The public
- The government as a whole
- The branch of government
- The particular agency or agencies represented by the lawyer
- A particular government official

I worked in the Colorado Attorney General's office for many years, mostly in the Natural Resources Section, representing both the Colorado Department of Public Health and Environment (CDPHE) and the Colorado Department of Natural

Resources (DNR) on matters relating to hazardous waste and superfund cleanups. I communicated on a regular basis, sometimes daily, about matters relating to the particular cases and issues I was working on with employees of those agencies. Those employees had supervisors who were the decision makers on larger issues, such as whether to bring an enforcement action, enter into settlements, and/or impose fines. Because of the nature of my work, I worked frequently with several divisions within both agencies, as well as with the Governor's Office, and occasionally with other state agencies, including the Colorado Department of Transportation (CDOT), and the Department of Local Affairs (DOLA), although typically CDOT and DOLA had other attorneys as their primary representatives.

To complicate matters further, the two primary state agencies I represented often had different priorities and concerns, and meeting all of them required a delicate balance. Frequently, colleagues in the Attorney General's Office represented these agencies as well.[5] Therefore, in a sense, both the agencies, including several divisions in them and the state of Colorado were my clients. The state can only speak through individuals, so in that sense the governor was a client, since ultimately, he directed the activities of all of my other clients, except for the attorney general. Realistically, however, my clients were the staff members I worked with on a regular basis, and their supervisors, with whom I interacted occasionally.[6]

Technically, I was employed by the Colorado Department of Law, and reported to the attorney general. For most of the dozen or so years I worked on these issues, the independently elected attorney general was from a different political party and had different views regarding environmental law and policy than the governor and his appointees.[7] There were frequent discussions within the Attorney General's Office regarding how to address these differing views and positions. I also had conversations with representatives at the client agencies regarding whether the attorney general would agree with a proposed litigation or settlement. Disagreements and controversies were not uncommon.

In some cases I worked on, the attorney general had independent jurisdiction under statutes and therefore he or she was both my supervisor and my client. In other cases, the AG's only interest in a case was in seeing that CDPHE and DNR received good legal representation. Who then was the client from whom I should take direction? It would be convenient to say that the attorney general should make the decisions on purely legal issues, and the client agencies on policy and technical issues, but often there was no controlling precedent or there were few cases on point and no consistent holdings. Few cases, moreover, involved strictly legal issues. Most involved mixed questions of law and policy, at least in the environmental law arena. Often some decision maker, whether an agency head or the attorney general wanted to expand or restrict a judicial decision or establish "new law" or guidelines. Legal costs, however, generally came out of an agency's budget, so even if the lawyers wanted to pursue a case to establish a legal precedent, the agency was sometimes loath to initiate or continue litigation. And, conversely, agency heads often wanted to pursue enforcement actions when the line attorneys, or even the attorney general, felt that the case was very weak or could result in a bad precedent that could adversely affect cases in the future. These cases were not necessarily frivolous, as that term is defined in Rule 11 of the Federal Rules of Civil Procedure, but could be problematic.[8]

Generally, disagreements between agencies or even between the governor and the attorney general, were resolved internally, with discussions among the interested parties until a consensus was reached, thereby avoiding a direct conflict for the attorneys involved. However, in 2015, long after I had left the Attorney General's Office, the then-Colorado attorney general joined a multi-state challenge to the Obama administration's clean power plant emission rules. The then-Colorado governor, John W. Hickenlooper, supported the stricter emissions standards, and had directed CDPHE to draft guidance on how to comply. The technical staff of CDPHE believed that the rules were not onerous and that most Colorado companies could comply with little difficulty. Governor Hickenlooper filed a petition for a declaratory judgment in the Colorado Supreme Court asking the court to hold that the attorney general does not have the authority to file a lawsuit against the federal government on behalf of the state, without the permission of the governor. He argued that only he, as the chief executive, has the authority to file litigation in this context.[9] The Colorado Supreme Court dismissed the action, holding that the governor had "adequate alternative remedy," although what that remedy might be was not specified.[10] The multi-state case continued in the District of Columbia Circuit for several years. The clean power plant rules were repealed by the Trump administration in 2017,[11] and the case was dismissed by the court in 2019.[12] However, during the pendency of this case, there were attorneys in the Colorado Attorney General's Office working on drafting guidance and regulations to comply with those rules, while others in the office, including their ultimate supervisor, the attorney general, were fighting their implementation in the D.C. Circuit. This is an extreme example of the dilemmas and conflicts potentially faced by a government attorney representing a client agency, but similar conflicts are not uncommon. The attorneys in this case were placed in a very difficult, if not untenable, position.

Attorneys working in similar situations (as well as attorneys general) should be careful not only to establish in writing a confidentiality wall between themselves and others working on similar issues from a different side, or perspective; they should also be careful not to violate attorney–client confidentiality when discussing issues with supervisors. The attorneys on both sides of this controversy (and there were other legal disputes between Governor Hickenlooper and Attorney General Cynthia Coffman) had identifiable clients, however, and they fulfilled their obligations to those clients. An information wall's validity as an ethical way to manage a conflict of interest is typically based on the informed consent of the conflicting parties.[13] Confidentiality walls may not always be an effective way to preserve confidentiality given physical and technological constraints in a typical government office. A more secure, although expensive, alternative would be hiring outside counsel to represent conflicting interests within government.

Another complicating factor of a government attorney's advocacy on behalf of an agency results from the fact that the head of an agency, the individual who sets the policy and speaks for the agency is likely to change during any administration, sometimes several times. The views held by a successor agency head may differ from his or her predecessor. Moreover, an agency head will undoubtedly be changed when a new executive is elected. Changes of agency heads, particularly in a new administration, may bring significant changes in the goals and policies to be carried out by the agency. The agency's position on a particular issue or program interests will necessarily change. Such changes may require the agency lawyer to alter strategies and recommendations even if the legal analysis and advice remains the same.

IDENTIFYING HYPOTHETICAL "PUBLIC INTEREST" OR THE "PUBLIC" AS CLIENTS

In the preamble to the Colorado Rules of Professional Conduct, as in the ABA Model Rules of Professional Conduct, the very first sentence, reads: "A lawyer, as a member of the legal profession, is a representative of clients, an officer of the legal system and a public citizen having special responsibility for the quality of justice."[14] Most lawyers, but especially government and public sector lawyers, believe that they have a special responsibility as "officers of the court" to work in the legal system honestly and fairly. This obligation may be analogous to the special duties owed by prosecutors in the criminal context.[15] Thus, many government attorneys often say that they represent the public or the "public interest" in addition to representing specific government agencies or officials. Of course, what constitutes the interest of the public depends on your own personal political or philosophical bent, and what one person believes to be in the public interest may be different from what another person believes. Moreover, the "public" does not even agree regarding what is in their best interest.[16]

"Public interest" is therefore too amorphous and hypothetical a concept to be the "true client" of a government lawyer. The public interest is necessarily expressed through the decisions of elected officials at all levels. Whether one believes that this interest is better expressed through the legislative, judicial, or executive branches, or at the local or state or federal level is not part of this discussion. If an individual attorney were free to declare that a decision is in the "public interest," a sort of legal chaos could ensue where individual attorneys or agencies are interpreting the law differently, giving the public and the regulated community no guidance on how to behave.[17] Interestingly, however, elected states attorneys general have increasingly refused to defend state statutes that they believe are unconstitutional.[18] Similarly, U.S. Attorney General Eric Holder refused to defend the Defense of Marriage Act (DOMA).[19] Attorney General Holder reasoned that challenges to the law in the Second Circuit caused the Department of Justice to reevaluate the applicable standard for review, and having done so, the president believed that defense of the law was inappropriate.[20] However, these decisions are not generally within the duties of the average government attorney.

This does not mean, however, that an attorney representing a government agency cannot have a legal opinion on the proper scope of enabling legislation, or on whether a proposed regulation is within an agency's statutory responsibilities, or whether a particular legal position is stronger than another. That is precisely what an agency attorney's duties should entail. However, it is the government lawyer's responsibility to preserve and advocate the interests of the agency, as so expressed by the head of the agency, assuming that those interests are legally and ethically defensible. The government lawyer has the obligation, both ethically and practically, to advance those interests as set out by the client.[21]

At the same time, the government lawyer must exercise professional judgment in pointing out the strengths and weaknesses in pursuing the agency head's desired course of action. A government attorney should always provide the best possible advice regarding how an agency's goals can be accomplished lawfully and within the statutory framework. A government lawyer, if possible, should present alternative interpretations so that the decision maker in any given situation can make the best-informed decision. The government lawyer must, however, recognize that, as in the private sector, the ultimate decision regarding how to proceed lies with the client and proceed accordingly.

Another obvious question that follows from the discussion of who the client is, is how the attorney–client privilege, rules of confidentiality, and conflict of interest rules apply when the client is the government. Most courts and commentators have noted that in a civil litigation context, the traditional rules of attorney–client privilege apply, but may fall in the criminal context, especially when the client is the target of the investigation.[22] My ethical obligations, I believe, were to all of my potential clients, their official capacities, as well as to the agencies as a whole. My conversations with my immediate clients, as well as with their supervisors, including the agency heads, were confidential, privileged, and protected under attorney–client privilege rules. These people, I believe, had the same right to rely on my discretion, confidentiality, as any other client in a private sector situation. When I reviewed documents, notes, and other materials pursuant to a discovery or open records request, I proceeded accordingly. No opposing attorney or court ever held that these privileges were limited to the governor, the attorney general, an agency head, or anyone else after reviewing lists of documents withheld as privileged.[23] Of course, these were, for the most part, people with whom I had an ongoing attorney–client relationship or met with to discuss a particular litigation issue or strategy. It may be a different situation, however, if I had merely attended a meeting involving other government officials and was not there to render legal advice.

As in private practice, there are situations where a government attorney needs to be a whistleblower. The situations where such disclosure is permitted are set forth in the ethical rules applicable to a particular jurisdiction. In private practice, disclosure of misconduct would first be made to the supervising attorney, but if the whistleblower found the response seriously inadequate it could be his or her duty to take the disclosure of known misconduct to the client's general counsel or ultimately the board of directors or regulatory authorities. In government, statutes or regulations may specify to whom disclosure of known conduct must be made. This topic is covered at greater length elsewhere in this volume.

SUMMARY OF KEY POINTS

- A government lawyer often has multiple, and nonaligned, even antagonistic, clients.
- A lawyer representing disparate agencies and people must be careful to keep these interests in mind and to operate as if all the relevant agencies and individuals were clients. This may require a difficult balancing act on a legal and policy basis and may present difficult issues of privilege and confidentiality.
- If conflicts prevent this posture, the attorney should err on the side of erecting confidentiality walls to ensure client confidentiality and an intact privilege and should consider retaining outside counsel if possible.
- Government agencies are entitled to the same commitments to confidentiality and zealous advocacy as private clients.

NOTES

1. The views expressed in this chapter are those of the writers and are not intended to represent those of the Colorado Department of Law, the NYS Governor's Office of Regulatory Reform or the State of New York, or any other entity.

2. https://www.americanbar.org/groups/professional_responsibility/publications/model_rules_of_professional_conduct/.

3. The term "agency" will be used throughout to mean any governmental agency, unit, authority, department, bureau, division, or other body of the executive branch of the state, federal, or local municipal government.

4. Kathleen Clark, *Conflicts, Confidentiality and the Client of the Government Lawyer*, Part I, *in* THE PUBLIC LAWYER, Vol. 21, No. 1 (2013).

5. An example of this multiple representation occurred when my primary client, the Hazardous Waste Division at CDPHE wanted a change in the applicable groundwater standard for a particular chemical found at the Rocky Mountain Arsenal. I represented the Hazardous Waste Division, a colleague represented the Water Quality Control Division, another represented the Water Quality Control Commission. We all had our unique roles and responsibilities.

6. In the context of federal governmental litigation, the Department of Justice espouses the "unitary executive theory" which maintains that the Department represents all federal agencies, sometimes even in opposition to each other. When I worked on the cleanup of the Rocky Mountain Arsenal, the same government lawyer represented both the Plaintiff Environmental Protection Agency, as well as the Defendant, the Department of the Army.

7. Most attorneys general are separately elected; only five state attorneys general are appointed by the governor, one is appointed by the state legislature, and one by the State

Supreme Court. https://ballotpedia.org/Attorney_General_office_comparison. The attorneys general I worked for were a Democrat, a Republican, and a Democrat; during that same time, Colorado's governors were a Democrat, and then a Republican. Only from 1989 to 1991 were the governor and the attorney general from the same political party.

8. Fed. R. Civ. P. 11. Government attorneys are of course subject to that Rule.

9. The governor was represented by a private law firm as outside counsel. To preserve confidentiality and avoid conflicts, it would have been preferable if both sides had been represented by outside counsel, thereby avoiding any potential conflicts, as well as an appearance of impropriety.

10. 2015SA296 (Co. S. Ct. 2015).

11. 84 Fed. Reg. 32,520 (July 8, 2019).

12. http://blogs2.law.columbia.edu/climate-change-litigation/wp-content/uploads/sites/16/case-documents/2019/20190917_docket-15-1363_order.pdf.

13. See ABA Model Rules of Pro. Conduct r. 1.7(b).

14. Colorado Rules of Pro. Conduct, as amended, April 2018. Model Rules of Pro. Conduct (2021).

15. Model Rules of Pro. Conduct r. 3.8.

16. One only has to look at the numerous articles, complaints regarding the wearing of face masks during COVID-19 to know that the perception of the "public interest" is not universal.

17. *See generally* Geoffrey P. Miller, *Government Lawyers' Ethics in a System of Checks and Balances*, 54 U. Chi. L. Rev. 1293 (1987).

18. *See* Neil Devins & Saikrishna Bangalore Prakash, 124(6) Yale L.J. (Apr. 2015).

19. Letter from Eric H. Holder, Jr., Att'y Gen. of the United States, to John A. Boehner, Speaker, U.S. House of Representatives (Feb. 23, 2011), http://www.justice.gov/opa/pr/letter-attorney-general-congress-litigation-involving-defense-marriage-act.

20. https://www.justice.gov/opa/pr/statement-attorney-general-litigation-involving-defense-marriage-act.

21. Model Rules of Pro. Conduct r. 1.2(a).

22. *See, e.g.*, Nancy Leong, *Attorney-Client Privilege in the Public Sector: A Survey of Government Attorneys* (2007). Wm & Mary, Faculty Publications 216, https://scholarship.law.wm.edu/facpubs/216; Joel D. Whitley, *Protecting State Interest: Recognition of the State Government Attorney-Client Privilege*, U. Chi. L. Re., 2005. *See also In re* Grand Jury Investigation, 399 F.3d 527 (2d Cir. 2005).

23. Where there is disagreement between staff and supervisors, the attorney must follow the lead of the higher ranking official, but that does not negate the confidentiality or privilege rules.

CHAPTER 6

The Government Attorney–Client Privilege

Ross Garber[1]

> The governmental attorney–client privilege is almost uniformly recognized in the civil context, but circuit courts are split as to the extent to which a government lawyer may be compelled to reveal client confidences in the face of a federal grand jury investigation. Adding to the confusion is the multitude of individual state statutes and case law governing privilege—some expressly recognizing the attorney–client privilege for government attorneys, and others rejecting it.

INTRODUCTION

Government lawyers serve a vital function, providing advice and counsel to public officials and offices on a variety of matters necessary for proper governmental function. They provide critical guidance to public officials on appropriate methods of executing existing laws and creating new laws, in addition to their guidance as to the extent to which government policies and the actions of public officials may run afoul of the law. To be effective, government lawyers must have candid and open communications with their clients. This will happen only if their conversations will remain private—exempt from compelled disclosure by way of the attorney–client privilege.

A series of underappreciated cases have, however, created uncertainty about the application of the government attorney–client privilege. As discussed here, some courts have held that the attorney–client privilege for government clients is more limited than for those in the private sector. These courts have reasoned that government lawyers serve two clients: their government client and the general public. This dual role, according to these courts, places upon government attorneys a higher duty to the public at large than is placed on their counterparts in private practice. The public interest in full disclosure by government officials and in truth seeking in the name of justice has thus been held to outweigh an official's assertion of the attorney–client privilege in the criminal context.

Nevertheless, state rules of professional conduct require that a government attorney keep his or her client's confidences, except in limited circumstances when the attorney reasonably believes disclosure to be necessary.[2] The Model Rules' requirement of confidentiality offers broader protection to the client than the attorney–client privilege. In the government realm, however, the application of the rule requiring confidentiality is not always clear.

Certainly, application of the attorney–client privilege to government attorneys and their clients presents problems that are less likely to occur in the private sector. For example, it may be difficult for a government attorney to identify her client with precision, as the client may be a government official or a government office generally or both. Furthermore, the line between what is said in execution of the office and what is said personally can become blurry, and it is correspondingly unclear whether a communication is made for the purpose of obtaining or providing legal advice. Additionally, policy advice, such as how to craft laws that are constitutional or execute the existing laws, may be found to be outside of the privilege because it is seen to be nonlegal in nature. Lastly, the issue of waiver further confounds the problem because courts are unsettled when it comes to waiver of privilege by subsequent officeholders.

THE RULES OF PROFESSIONAL CONDUCT AND CONFIDENTIAL COMMUNICATIONS

State rules of professional conduct apply to government lawyers as well as those in private practice. The ABA Model Rules of Professional Conduct, on which most state ethics rules are based, provides that "[a] lawyer shall not reveal information relating to the representation of a client."[3] The exceptions to this rule are narrow and clearly enumerated. A client may expressly or impliedly consent to disclosure or an attorney has the option to disclose under seven carefully described situations, one of which is "to comply with other law or a court order."[4]

The comments to Model Rule 1.6 discuss the broad reach of the duty of confidentiality. Those comments explain that "[a] fundamental principle in the client-lawyer relationship is that, in the absence of the client's informed consent, the lawyer must not reveal information relating to the representation."[5] The comments go on to state that the purpose of the duty of confidentiality is to encourage and foster candid conversation between the attorney and the client.[6] Absent such confidentiality, clients might not share pertinent, but sensitive, facts with their attorneys. The comments also recognize that, "[b]ased upon experience, lawyers know that almost all clients follow the advice given, and the law is upheld."[7]

The comments to Rule 1.6 also suggest procedures for an attorney to follow when presented with a court order or the like to compel disclosure of client confidences.[8] Of course, a client may give his or her informed consent and the attorney may then disclose client confidences; however, absent such consent, "the lawyer should assert on behalf of the client all nonfrivolous claims that the order is not authorized by other law or that the information sought is protected against disclosure by the attorney–client privilege or other applicable law."[9] Should the court rule adversely, the lawyer has the additional duty to counsel his or her client on the possibility of appeal; only if review is not sought may the attorney reveal the client's confidences to the applicable authority.[10]

STATE STATUTES GOVERNING ATTORNEY–CLIENT PRIVILEGE FOR GOVERNMENT ATTORNEYS

State law varies in its application of the attorney–client privilege to client confidences held by government attorneys. As a result, it is up to individual government attorneys to look at the laws of their own states to determine the scope of the privilege in their jurisdictions. Generally, however, the attorney–client privilege applies in civil cases in much the same way for government attorneys as it does for private attorneys.[11]

Connecticut

The Connecticut Supreme Court has recognized Connecticut's "long-standing, strong public policy of protecting attorney-client communications."[12] Additionally, the court has recognized that the threat of potential disclosure of confidential communications, by way of exceptions to the privilege, would work to weaken "attorneys' ability to advocate for their clients while preserving their ethical duty of confidentiality."[13]

Due to Connecticut's stance on a strong attorney–client privilege, the Connecticut legislature and courts recognize the attorney–client privilege as applied to government attorneys in civil, criminal, and administrative proceedings.[14] Indeed, section 52-146r of the Connecticut General Statutes states that "[i]n any civil or criminal case or proceeding or in any legislative or administrative proceeding, all confidential communications shall be privileged and a government attorney shall not disclose any such communications unless an authorized representative of the public agency consents to waive the privilege and allow such disclosure."[15] The governmental attorney–client privilege is applicable in Connecticut state courts when "(1) the attorney is acting in a professional capacity for the agency, (2) the communications are made between the attorney and a current member of the public agency, (3) the communications relate to legal advice sought by the agency from the attorney and (4) the communications are made in confidence."[16]

New York

New York law recognizes a governmental attorney–client privilege in the civil setting; however, New York law remains unsettled when it comes to the governmental attorney–client privilege in the face of a state grand jury investigation.[17]

The attorney–client privilege in New York is governed by statutory and common-law principles. Section 4503 of the New York Civil Practice Law and Rules (CPLR) codifies the privilege.[18] Additionally, the courts of New York have articulated a two-step inquiry to determine the applicability of the attorney–client privilege. First, the proponent of the privilege must show (1) the existence of an attorney–client relationship; (2) that the attorney is acting in his or her professional capacity; (3) that the communication in question was confidential; and (4) that the communication was made for the purpose of rendering legal advice or services.[19] Second, the opponent of the privilege has the opportunity to demonstrate that the privilege is inappropriate in application due to overwhelming public policy concerns.[20]

New York state courts have not squarely determined whether the attorney–client privilege applies to government attorneys and their public-sector clients in the face of a state grand jury investigation; nevertheless, the Second Circuit has ruled that the privilege does apply in these circumstances.[21] Consequently, at least one commentator predicts that New York state courts would extend the privilege to state grand jury proceedings if the issue were presented.[22]

Ohio

In Ohio state courts, the attorney–client privilege applies to government attorneys and their clients in the same manner as it applies to private attorneys, at least in civil matters.[23] Indeed, the Ohio Supreme Court determined the prevailing rule to be that public agencies and their government attorneys enjoyed protection from forced disclosure of confidential communication by way of the attorney–client privilege.[24] The Chief Justice, writing for the court, stated that, "[i]n Ohio, courts have consistently recognized that 'records of communications between attorneys and their state-government clients pertaining to the attorneys' legal advice are excepted from disclosure . . . since the release of these records is prohibited by state law'—i.e., they are protected by this state's attorney-client privilege."[25] Furthermore, the court determined that the attorney–client privilege would likely not be abused by government officials in order to skirt public record laws; indeed, the court believed that the privilege's application was limited by its definition and, thus, would not easily be abused.[26] Lastly, the Ohio Supreme Court held that the attorney–client privilege applies even if the attorney had not been appointed or approved by the Ohio attorney general, which had previously been required for application of the privilege.[27]

Massachusetts

The Supreme Judicial Court of Massachusetts has held that the attorney–client privilege applies with equal force to government attorneys and their public-sector clients.[28] Indeed, the court stated that "[c]onfidential communications between public officers and employees and governmental entities and their legal counsel undertaken for the purpose of obtaining legal advice or assistance are protected under the normal rules of the attorney-client privilege."[29] The court noted that public policy mandates a strong attorney–client privilege because public officials "must routinely seek advice from counsel on how to meet their obligations to the public."[30] Furthermore, the court explained that the public interest benefits from full disclosure by public-sector clients to their government attorneys because, if these attorneys are unable to gather all relevant facts, "they will less likely serve the public interest in good government by preventing needless litigation or ensuring government officials' compliance with the law." As such, government attorneys will not be able to fulfill their duties effectively without the privilege.[31] Therefore, "[b]ecause the attorney-client privilege serves the same salutary purposes in the public as in the private realm, 'it is now well established that communications between government agencies and agency counsel are protected by the privilege as long as they are made confidentially and for the purpose of obtaining legal advice for the agency.'"[32]

THE FEDERAL ATTORNEY–CLIENT PRIVILEGE

The federal attorney–client privilege is governed by the common law.[33] The privilege generally protects communications between attorneys and their clients when the communications are intended to be confidential and are made for the purpose of securing legal advice.[34] The privilege, which dates back to the 16th century, rests upon the principle that clients must be able to consult candidly with their attorneys regarding legal concerns without fear that their words will later be disclosed.[35] Its purpose is to promote "full and frank communication between attorneys and their clients and thereby promote broader public interests in the observance of law and administration of justice."[36] In other words, the attorney–client privilege promotes candid discussions between clients and their attorneys, which, in turn, leads to an attorney's ability to give sound legal advice and engage in effective lawyering.

Courts have long recognized the existence of an attorney–client privilege for government lawyers.[37] The privilege, however, has historically been construed narrowly because the privilege has the effect of withholding relevant information from the finder of fact.[38] The privilege applies when the invoking party shows (1) the existence of an attorney–client relationship; (2) that the communication was intended to be and remained confidential; and (3) that the communication was made for the purpose of obtaining or providing legal advice.[39]

The Attorney-Client Privilege for Government Lawyers and Their Public-Sector Clients

In some contexts, the attorney–client privilege has been construed and applied differently with respect to government attorneys and their public-sector clients. Although most courts agree that an attorney–client privilege applies to government lawyers under certain conditions,[40] some courts have found that there are competing interests that influence the extent to which the privilege applies to communications between government attorneys and government officials or offices.

By facilitating candid lawyer–client communications, a government attorney–client privilege advances societal interests in promoting compliance with law and administration of justice.[41] Indeed, if conversations between public officials and government attorneys are not protected by the privilege, public officials might refrain from seeking advice regarding sensitive legal matters, potentially leading to public officials' violation of the law and increased corruption within the government. Government officials frequently rely on the advice of their attorneys to craft public policies and implement government programs. If government officials are uninformed about the legal ramifications of their actions because of the potential that confidential information may be subsequently disclosed, they may be unable to carry out government programs effectively or to implement government policies. In the end, a weakened or nonexistent governmental attorney–client privilege may even discourage otherwise qualified persons from serving in public office in the first place. Such concerns favor the recognition of a strong government attorney–client privilege.

Nevertheless, government attorneys' obligations and responsibilities are different from those of private attorneys and the nature of the public-sector client is different from that of a private individual or even a private entity. Some courts have, therefore, modified the attorney–client privilege to address these nuances.[42] Courts have noted that government lawyers are not only responsible to their clients but also have a "higher, competing duty to act in the public interest."[43] Government attorneys take oaths to uphold the U.S. Constitution and governing laws, and they are compensated by public funds.[44] These considerations have led some courts to narrow the application of the government attorney–client privilege in some situations, particularly those that involve potential criminal activities.[45]

Additionally, although the Freedom of Information Act generally supports openness in government,[46] an exemption to the act provides expansive protection to attorney–client communications, as explained in the next section.[47]

Finally, it should be noted that the attorney–client privilege is an evidentiary privilege, the scope of which is defined by "the principles of the common law . . . as interpreted by the courts . . . in the light of reason and experience."[48] Starting from the principle that the public has the right to examine all relevant evidence, courts have construed privileges narrowly, only to the extent that excluding evidence would, in some other way, serve the public good.[49] Some courts have employed these concepts to narrow the scope of the privilege in the government context.

The Freedom of Information Act

The applicability of the attorney–client privilege to government attorneys and their public-sector clients is supported by Exemption Five of the federal Freedom of Information Act (FOIA).[50] In a general sense, the FOIA directs government agencies to make their records and communications available to the public.[51] The FOIA, however, contains exemptions to this disclosure requirement for particular categories of information.[52]

Much of the litigation surrounding the governmental attorney–client privilege concerns Exemption Five, which provides that "intra-agency memorandums or letters which would not be available by law to a party other than an agency in litigation with the agency" are exempt from disclosure under the FOIA.[53] Courts have construed Exemption Five to "exempt those documents, and only those documents, normally privileged in the civil discovery context."[54] Included are materials traditionally protected under the attorney–client privilege.[55]

Exemption Five does not create the attorney–client privilege; indeed, the FOIA does not expand or restrict any existing privileges.[56] Instead, "Congress intended that agencies should not lose the protection traditionally afforded through the evidentiary privileges simply because of the passage of the FOIA."[57] Still, courts have cited this exemption as further support that some form of attorney–client privilege should apply to government attorneys.[58]

The Attorney–Client Privilege in Criminal Cases

Generally, courts agree that the attorney–client privilege applies to government attorneys in civil and regulatory matters.[59] Despite the fact that the U.S. Supreme Court has directly stated that the attorney–client privilege should not be applied differently in civil and criminal contexts,[60] there is a circuit split on this very issue when communications with government lawyers are involved.[61]

SECOND CIRCUIT

The Court of Appeals for the Second Circuit broke with several other circuits, holding that the attorney–client privilege applies to communications between government lawyers and their clients, even in the face of a federal grand jury subpoena.[62] The case, *In re Grand Jury Investigation (Grand Jury)*, involved an appeal from an order of the U.S. District Court for the District of Connecticut compelling the former chief legal counsel to the Office of the Governor of Connecticut to testify before a federal grand jury about conversations she had with the governor and his staff for the purpose of providing legal advice.[63] The conversations at issue were made in confidence and for the purpose of providing legal advice to the chief counsel's client, the Office of the Governor.[64] Asserting the attorney–client privilege, the chief counsel refused to provide substantive testimony.[65] The district court ordered the attorney to testify, stating that "in the grand jury context, any governmental attorney-client privilege must yield because the interests served by the grand jury's fact-finding process clearly outweigh the interest served by the privilege."[66] The court added that "a government lawyer's duty does not lie solely with his or her client agency," but also with the public at large.[67]

On appeal, the Second Circuit reversed.[68] The court reasoned that "the attorney-client privilege is one of the oldest recognized privileges for confidential communications."[69] The court noted that "a consistent application of the privilege . . . is necessary to promote the rule of law by encouraging consultation with lawyers, and ensuring that lawyers . . . are able to render to their clients fully informed legal advice."[70] The court concluded that although it is in the public interest for a grand jury to be able to examine relevant information, the interest in disclosure is outweighed by the public interest in giving government officials access to effective legal advice.[71] The court noted that "[i]t is crucial that government officials, who are expected to uphold and execute the law and who may face criminal prosecution for failing to do so, be encouraged to seek out and receive fully informed legal advice," which is more likely to occur if government officials are ensured that conversations with counsel will remain confidential.[72] The Second Circuit noted its holding was directly contrary to the holdings of the Seventh, Eighth, and District of Columbia Circuits.[73]

EIGHTH CIRCUIT

The Eighth Circuit Court of Appeals held, in *In re Subpoena Duces Tecum*, that even though a governmental attorney–client privilege may apply in civil cases, it may not be used in the criminal context to withhold relevant information from a federal grand jury.[74] *In re Subpoena Duces Tecum* involved the Whitewater investigation of the President and Mrs. Clinton in the late 1990s.[75] The Office of Independent Counsel (OIC) appealed from a district court order that denied the OIC's motion to compel production of notes taken by an attorney during a meeting between the attorney and Hillary Rodham Clinton.[76] The district court never reached the question of whether a federal government entity may assert an attorney–client privilege to avoid a grand jury subpoena, but instead rested its decision on the fact that, because Mrs. Clinton had a "genuine and reasonable belief" that the conversations were privileged, the attorney–client privilege applied.[77]

The Eighth Circuit Court of Appeals reversed.[78] The court began its analysis by acknowledging that even though a government entity may be a client for the purposes of the attorney–client privilege, there were no clear rules concerning the privilege's application in the criminal context.[79] Additionally, it noted that because privileges exclude relevant evidence, they should be construed narrowly and may be set aside in the interests of the criminal justice system.[80] As such, the court concluded that "[t]he strong public interest in honest government and in exposing wrongdoing by public officials would be ill-served by recognition of a governmental attorney-client privilege applicable in criminal proceedings inquiring into the actions of public officials."[81] Instead, it would be "misuse of public assets" to allow the government officials to shield potential wrongdoings via the attorney–client privilege.[82] Additionally, government attorneys are held to a higher duty that obligates them to guard the public interest over and above that of their government client to ensure honest government and prevent official wrongdoing.[83] The Eighth Circuit concluded, therefore, that a government office is not able to assert the attorney–client privilege to shield relevant information from a federal grand jury investigation.[84]

DISTRICT OF COLUMBIA CIRCUIT

The District of Columbia Court of Appeals (D.C. Circuit) has recognized an attorney–client privilege for government entities in certain contexts, but it has also held that government entities may not invoke the attorney–client privilege to avoid responding to a federal grand jury subpoena.[85] The case, *In re Lindsey*, involved a federal grand jury subpoena directed toward Bruce Lindsey, deputy White House counsel and assistant to President Clinton.[86] The subpoena mandated Lindsey's testimony regarding conversations between him and the president concerning possible criminal conduct in which the president may have been involved.[87] Lindsey refused to testify, and, as a result, the Office of Independent Counsel moved to compel his testimony.[88] The district court granted the motion, ruling that although the president has an attorney–client privilege when consulting with White House counsel in his official capacity, that privilege may be overcome in a grand jury context by a sufficient showing of need.[89]

On appeal, the D.C. Circuit affirmed, holding that government entities may not assert the attorney–client privilege to withhold relevant information from a federal grand jury.[90] The D.C. Circuit did recognize that the attorney–client privilege applies to government attorneys and their public-sector clients under certain circumstances, particularly in the context of civil litigation.[91] It noted, however, that government attorneys have duties extending beyond those owed to their clients; indeed, government attorneys are obligated to "uphold the public trust" and may not conceal the wrongdoing of public officials by way of the attorney–client privilege.[92] Furthermore, the D.C. Circuit reasoned that

> it would be contrary to tradition, common understanding, and our governmental system for the attorney-client privilege to attach to White House Counsel in the same manner as private counsel. When government attorneys learn, through communications with their clients, of information related to criminal misconduct, they may not rely on the government attorney-client privilege to shield such information from disclosure to a grand jury.[93]

Therefore, although the governmental attorney–client privilege remains applicable in civil proceedings, it crumbles in the face of a federal grand jury.

SEVENTH CIRCUIT

Like the Eighth and D.C. Circuits, the Seventh Circuit Court of Appeals has held that although a governmental attorney–client privilege exists in civil proceedings, it does not extend its protection to criminal proceedings.[94] The case *In re Witness Before the Special Grand Jury 2000-2* involved a state government lawyer who was subpoenaed to testify before a special grand jury about advice that he provided to a former government official.[95] The attorney refused to testify, and the former official asserted the attorney–client privilege.[96] Then, the current officeholder waived the privilege as applied to the office by writing to the federal prosecutor.[97] The district court granted the prosecutor's motion to compel, finding that no attorney–client privilege had attached and, alternatively, that if a privilege attached, the current officeholder had waived it.[98]

On appeal, the Seventh Circuit affirmed and held that there was no governmental attorney–client privilege in the criminal context.[99] The court reasoned that even though the governmental attorney–client privilege in civil cases is identical with that of private attorneys, the privilege is limited in the criminal context because of several factors.[100] First, the court stated that government lawyers are held to a higher duty to act in the public interest and are obligated to uphold the laws of the nation and their individual state.[101] Second, government lawyers are compensated by the state itself, and, as such, it would be misuse of state resources to allow government officials to shield potentially criminal activities by asserting that their government attorneys are bound by the attorney–client privilege.[102] Therefore, under present Seventh Circuit law, government attorneys in that circuit may not use the attorney–client privilege to withhold relevant information regarding potential criminal wrongdoing of public officials, despite the information being confidential in nature and related to the giving of legal advice.[103]

IMPLEMENTATION CONCERNS FOR GOVERNMENT LAWYERS

The party asserting the attorney–client privilege has the burden to prove (1) that the communication was made within the confines of the attorney–client relationship; (2) that the communication was intended to be and remained confidential; and (3) that the communication was made for the purpose of giving or obtaining legal advice.[104] In the context of government attorneys and their public-sector clients, this burden is sometimes difficult to meet.

There is very little case law to guide attorneys in determining the precise identity of a government attorney's client. The Eighth Circuit Court of Appeals notes that according to the Federal Rules of Evidence "a governmental body may be a client for purposes of the attorney-client privilege."[105] The court, however, failed to elaborate on the status of employees of governmental bodies.[106] In a dissenting opinion, Judge Kopf expanded on the issue, noting that even though a governmental body can be a client for the purposes of the privilege, the client must act through its representative, the officeholder.[107] Therefore, the attorney–client privilege may extend to communications between the attorney and the officeholder, as the client's representative.[108]

Commentators cite five possible clients of a government lawyer:

1. The responsible official;
2. The government agency . . . [for example, the White House or a particular agency];
3. The branch of government (i.e., executive branch or legislative branch);
4. The government as a whole (including all of the above); or
5. The public.[109]

All of these have been deemed clients in various settings.[110]

Although the question is far from settled, based on statements by the Second, Eighth, and D.C. Circuits, a government attorney should be comfortable in treating the office itself, represented by the officeholders, as the client for purposes of the attorney–client privilege. Officeholders' conversations with government attorneys may be protected if those conversations were held in the course of fulfilling the duties of the office and otherwise satisfy the elements of the privilege.[111] Government attorneys, however, must be careful to warn government officials about the uncertainty of the privilege as it pertains to them personally and in the criminal context.[112]

The purpose prong of the attorney–client privilege is equally problematic in the context of the governmental attorney–client privilege. For a conversation between an attorney and a client to be privileged, its purpose must be to provide legal advice. Because government attorneys frequently offer advice about how to structure laws and policies in keeping with current laws or to avoid litigation,[113] rather than addressing strictly legal questions, the purpose of the communication may be difficult to discern. Several courts have held that such conversations are policy based and, therefore, are unprotected by an attorney–client privilege.[114]

The D.C. Circuit examined the purpose question strictly in determining what communications encompass legal advice. The court noted that "consultation with one admitted to the bar but not in that other person's role as lawyer is not protected. Where one consults an attorney not as a lawyer but as a friend or business adviser or banker, or negotiator, the consultation is not professional nor the statement privileged."[115] Furthermore, the court held that the privilege applies only when the purpose of the communication was to seek (1) an opinion on the law; (2) legal services; or (3) assistance with a legal proceeding.[116] Based upon the D.C. Circuit's analysis, only specific legal advice concerning strictly legal issues would fall within the realm of the privilege.

However, other courts apply a more liberal standard to determine whether a communication was made for the purpose of seeking legal advice. The Second Circuit Court of Appeals adopted the predominant purpose test in evaluating the purpose prong of the attorney–client privilege.[117] The Second Circuit explained that the line between strict legal advice and nonlegal advice is often blurry because "legal advice involves the interpretation and application of legal principles to guide future conduct or to assess past conduct."[118] Furthermore, the court found that, because a lawyer often provides legal advice by explaining costs and benefits, proposing alternative approaches, and providing suggestions on implementation, holding a communication to a strict determination of purpose may hamper a lawyer in the performance of his or her duties.[119] As such, the Second Circuit held that where the predominant purpose of a communication is legal advice, collateral benefits do not abrogate the privilege.[120] In determining the purpose of a communication, the Second Circuit explained that "it should be assessed dynamically and in light of the advice being sought or rendered, as well as the relationship between advice that can be rendered only by consulting the legal authorities and advice that can be given by a non-lawyer."[121]

PRACTICAL CONSIDERATIONS FOR GOVERNMENT ATTORNEYS

Government attorneys must take care to appreciate the complexities of the attorney–client privilege and to ensure those who seek their advice are informed about the extent and uncertainties of confidentiality. Generally, confidential communications between a government attorney and his or her public-sector client will be privileged, at least in the civil context. If, however, a criminal investigation is initiated, the attorney–client privilege may yield to the interests of fact-finding and justice. In light of these concerns, the following principles may assist government attorneys in protecting their clients' confidences.

Advise Client of the Uncertainty of the Privilege

Communication with one's client is indispensable. In order for a government attorney to represent a public office or official adequately, the attorney must effectively communicate to the client the uncertain nature of the attorney–client privilege as to government attorneys and their public-sector clients. Full disclosure to all members of a public office will alert those persons within the represented agency or office of the potential for forced disclosure of confidential communications.

Determine Who the Client Is

A government attorney must clearly define the identity of the client, be it an individual, an office, or an agency. Defining the client's identity is important to the issue of waiver. Indeed, the attorney–client privilege applies only to confidential communications. Therefore, if information is communicated in the presence of third parties, the communication is not confidential and, thus, not privileged.[122]

There is no question that the attorney–client privilege applies to private organizations.[123] In many jurisdictions the privilege has been explicitly applied, by virtue of statute or case law, to legally cognizable government entities, such as agencies.[124] Special care should be taken, however, when considering the representation of an entity that is not explicitly defined by law. Consider, for example, the "office" of a governor or member of Congress or the "chambers" of a judge. They are, for practical purposes, treated as organizations, but are not explicitly defined as legal entities. One potential approach is for the lawyer to define the individual personnel at issue as the clients in their official capacities, either instead of or in addition to representing the entity. It must be made clear to the individuals in question that the government lawyer does not represent them in their personal capacity. In addition, the government lawyer should ensure that he or she has authority to undertake the representation, as opposed to, in the federal system, the Department of Justice, or for state attorneys, an attorney general's office.

Take Note of the Purpose of One's Communication

As previously discussed, a communication between attorney and client is only privileged if its purpose is to render legal advice. First, it is imperative that a government attorney ascertain how courts in his or her jurisdiction determine the purpose of a communication.[125] To secure the protection of the attorney–client privilege, government attorneys should ensure that the communications address a legal question at the outset, such as whether a particular procedure violates the law. Government attorneys should be aware that communications regarding political questions generally are not privileged.[126] Communications between attorney and client that flow from legal questions, however, will likely be considered to be legal advice.[127] Therefore, government attorneys should structure communications so that they address legal issues at the outset; this tactic will likely ensure that the predominant purpose of the communication is the giving or obtaining of legal advice.[128]

Advise Individual Government Officials to Obtain Independent Legal Counsel for Criminal Matters

Currently, only the Second Circuit has held that the attorney–client privilege protects confidential communications in the face of a federal grand jury investigation. The Eighth, Seventh, and D.C. Circuits have explicitly held that the attorney–client privilege does not shield confidential communications between public officials and their government attorneys in the criminal context. Additionally, most states have yet to explicitly determine whether the governmental attorney–client privilege applies in the criminal context. Consequently, public officials would be well-advised to consult private counsel if their conduct has strayed close to the line of criminal liability.[129]

SUMMARY OF KEY POINTS

- A lawyer must maintain the confidentiality of information relating to the representation of a client.
- The scope and applicability of the privilege are sometimes unclear; as a result, government lawyers must be aware of the implications of their dual role in serving the public at large as well as their client government agency.

- Some courts have held that the privilege's protection is significantly weaker in the context of a criminal proceeding.
- Government lawyers should structure their consultations as much as possible to honor their professional obligations, including honoring the attorney–client privilege.

NOTES

1. The author wishes to express appreciation to Brooke Havard and Michele Querijero, former associates at the firm of Shipman & Goodwin LLP, for their assistance in preparing an earlier draft of this chapter.
2. MODEL RULES OF PRO. CONDUCT r 1.6(a)–(b).
3. *Id.* at 1.6(a).
4. *Id.* at 1.6(b)(1)–(7). A lawyer may reveal confidential client information if the lawyer believes it to be necessary: "(1) to prevent reasonably certain death or substantial bodily harm; (2) to prevent the client from committing a crime or fraud that is reasonably certain to result in substantial injury to the financial interests or property of another and in furtherance of which the client has used or is using the lawyer's services; (3) to prevent, mitigate or rectify substantial injury to the financial interests or property of another that is reasonably certain to result or has resulted from the client's commission of a crime or fraud in furtherance of which the client has used the lawyer's services; (4) to secure legal advice about the lawyer's compliance with [the Model Rules]; (5) to establish a claim or defense on behalf of the lawyer in a controversy between the lawyer and the client, to establish a defense to a criminal charge or civil claim against the lawyer based upon conduct in which the client was involved, or to respond to allegations in any proceeding concerning the lawyer's representation of the client; (6) to comply with other law or a court order; or (7) to detect and resolve conflicts of interest arising from the lawyer's change of employment or from changes in the composition or ownership of a firm, but only if the revealed information would not compromise the attorney-client privilege or otherwise prejudice the client." *Id.*
5. *Id.* at cmt. 2.
6. *Id.*
7. *Id.*
8. *See id.* at cmt. 15.
9. *Id.*
10. *See id.*
11. *See generally* RESTATEMENT (THIRD) OF THE LAW GOVERNING LAWYERS § 74 (stating the prevailing rule to be that government attorneys and their clients enjoy the same protections from the attorney–client privilege as do their private practice counterparts).
12. Metropolitan Life Ins. Co. v. Aetna Cas. & Surety Co., 730 A.2d 51, 58 (Conn. 1999).
13. *Id.* (citing Hickman v. Taylor, 329 U.S. 495, 511 (1947)).
14. *See* CONN. GEN. STAT. § 52-146r (2005).
15. *Id. at* § 52-146r(b).
16. McLaughlin v. Freedom of Info. Comm'n, 850 A.2d 254, 259 (2004) (citing Shew v. Freedom of Info. Comm'n, 714 A.2d 664 (1998)).
17. *See* Stacy Lynn Newman, Comment, *The Governmental Attorney-Client Privilege: Whether the Right to Evidence in a State Grand Jury Investigation Pierces the Privilege in New York*, 70 ALB. L. REV. 741 (2007).
18. *See* N.Y. C.P.L.R. § 4503(a) (1992).
19. *See* People v. Mitchell, 448 N.E.2d 121, 123 (N.Y. 1983).
20. *See* Priest v. Hennessy, 409 N.E.2d 983, 986 (N.Y. 1980).
21. *See infra* notes 62–73 and accompanying text.
22. *See* Newman, *supra* note 17, at 768.

23. State ex rel. Leslie v. Ohio Housing Finance Agency, 824 N.E.2d 990, 997 [hereinafter Ohio 2005]. The case presented to the Ohio Supreme Court addressed only a civil matter, and, as such, the court did not make any ruling as to the governmental attorney–client privilege with respect to criminal matters or grand jury investigations. See id.
24. Id. at 995 (stating that "the weight of existing authority applies the attorney-client privilege to confidential communications between government agencies and their attorney-employees").
25. Id. at 995–96 (quoting State ex rel. Thomas v. Ohio State Univ., 643 N.E.2d 126 (1994)).
26. See id. at 997. More specifically, in order to be protected by the attorney–client privilege, the communication must be made to the attorney in his or her role as a legal adviser. This means that a public official is not able to shield nonlegal information from the public by simply disclosing it to the government attorney. Additionally, the communication must be confidential and must relate to the purpose of giving legal advice. Id.
27. See id. at 998–99.
28. See Suffolk Constr. Co. v. Div. of Capital Asset Mgmt., 870 N.E.2d 33, 38 (Mass. 2007).
29. Id.
30. Id. at 39.
31. Id.
32. Id. (quoting E.S. EPSTEIN, THE ATTORNEY-CLIENT PRIVILEGE AND THE WORK-PRODUCT DOCTRINE 127 (4th ed. 2001)).
33. See FED. R. EVID. 501 ("The common law—as interpreted by United States Courts in the light of reason and experience—governs a claim of privilege unless any of the following provide otherwise: the United States Constitution; a federal statute; or rules prescribed by the Supreme Court.").
34. In re Lindsey, 158 F.3d 1263, 1269 (D.C. Cir. 1998).
35. Patricia E. Salkin & Allyson Phillips, Eliminating Political Maneuvering: A Light in the Tunnel for the Government Attorney-Client Privilege, 39 IND. L. REV. 561, 562–63 (2006). See also Hunt v. Blackburn, 128 U.S. 464, 470 (1888) (noting that the attorney–client privilege "is founded upon the necessity, in the interest and administration of justice, of the aid of persons having knowledge of the law and skilled in its practice, which assistance can only be safely and readily availed of when free from the consequences or the apprehension of disclosure").
36. Upjohn Co. v. United States, 449 U.S. 383, 389 (1981).
37. Lindsey, 158 F.3d at 1268.
38. Fisher v. United States, 425 U.S. 391, 403 (1976).
39. In re Cnty. of Erie, 473 F.3d 413, 419 (2d Cir. 2007), citing United States v. Constr. Prods. Rsch., 73 F.3d 464, 473 (2d Cir. 1996).
40. See In re Grand Jury Investigation, 399 F.3d 527, 532–33 (2d Cir. 2005).
41. See Upjohn Co. v. United States, 449 U.S. 383, 389 (1981).
42. Id.
43. Id. (citing Lindsey, 158 F.3d at 1273).
44. Id.
45. See id. at 293–94.
46. Salkin & Phillips, supra note 35, at 566.
47. Lindsey, 158 F.3d at 1268.
48. FED. RULE EVID. 501; Swidler & Berlin v. United States, 524 U.S. 399, 403 (1998).
49. See Swidler & Berlin at 411–12 (O'Connor, J., dissenting).
50. Lindsey, 158 F.3d at 1268.
51. See generally 5 U.S.C.S. § 552(a) (2016).
52. See 5 U.S.C.S. § 552(b) (2007).
53. Lindsey, 158 F.3d at 1268, quoting 5 U.S.C.S. § 552(b)(5) (2007).
54. Nat'l Labor Relations Bd. v. Sears, Roebuck & Co., 421 U.S. 132, 149 (1975).
55. See id. at 149. See also Lindsey, 158 F.3d at 1268; Baker & Hostetler LLP v. U.S. Dep't of Commerce, 473 F.3d 312, 321 (D.C. Cir. 2006).

56. *See* Ass'n for Women in Sci. v. Califano, 566 F.2d 339, 342 (D.C. Cir. 1977).
57. Coastal States Gas Corp. v. Dep't of Energy, 617 F.2d 854, 862 (D.C. Cir. 1980).
58. *Lindsey*, 158 F.3d at 1268.
59. *Id.*
60. Swidler & Berlin et al. v. United States, 524 U.S. 399, 408–09 (1998) (stating that "there is no case authority for the proposition that the privilege applies differently in criminal and civil cases," and noting that "a client may not know at the time he discloses information to his attorney whether it will later be relevant to a civil or a criminal matter").
61. *In re* Cnty. of Erie, 473 F.3d 413, 418 (2d Cir. 2007) (collecting cases and noting that "[i]n civil suits between private litigants and government agencies, the attorney-client privilege protects most confidential communications between government counsel and their clients that are made for the purpose of obtaining or providing legal assistance"). *Cf.* Ross v. City of Memphis, 423 F.3d 596, 602–03 (6th Cir. 2005) (stating "a split has emerged among several of our sister circuits regarding whether a state or federal government entity can assert attorney-client privilege in grand jury proceedings" and reviewing cases).
62. *In re* Grand Jury Investigation v. Doe, 399 F.3d 527 (2d Cir. 2005).
63. *Id.* at 528.
64. *Id.*
65. *Id.* at 529–30.
66. *Id.* at 530.
67. *Id.*
68. *Id.* at 528.
69. *Id.* at 530.
70. *Id.* at 531.
71. *Id.* at 534.
72. *Id.*
73. *Id.* at 536, n.4.
74. *In re* Subpoena Duces Tecum, 112 F.3d 910, 921, 924 (8th Cir. 1997) (stating that "a government attorney is free to discuss anything with a government official—except for potential criminal wrongdoing by that official—without fearing later revelation of the conversation" and holding that a government entity may not assert the attorney-client privilege to withhold relevant information from a federal grand jury investigation).
75. *Id.* at 913.
76. *Id.*
77. *Id.* at 914.
78. *Id.* at 913.
79. *Id.* at 916.
80. *Id.* at 918–19.
81. *Id.* at 921.
82. *Id.*
83. *See id.*
84. *Id.* at 924.
85. *See Lindsey*, 158 F.3d at 1266.
86. *Id.* at 1267.
87. *Id.*
88. *Id.*
89. *Id.*
90. *Id.* at 1266.
91. *Id.* at 1269, 1271.
92. *Id.* at 1272, 1273.
93. *Id.* at 1278.
94. *In re* A Witness Before the Special Grand Jury 2000-2, 288 F.3d 289, 290, 291 (7th Cir. 2002).
95. *Id.* at 290.

96. *Id.*
97. *Id.* at 291.
98. *Id.*
99. *Id.* at 293.
100. *Id.* at 293–95.
101. *Id.* at 293.
102. *Id.*
103. *Id.* at 294.
104. Salkin & Phillips, *supra* note 35, at 568; *In re Cnty. of Erie*, 473 F.3d at 419.
105. *In re Grand Jury Subpoena Duces Tecum*, 112 F.3d at 916.
106. *See id.*
107. *Id.* at 933 (Kopf, J., dissenting).
108. *Id.*
109. Patricia E. Salkin, *Beware: What You Say to Your [Government] Laywer May Be Held Against You—The Erosion of Government Attorney-Client Confidentiality*, 35 URB. LAW. 283, 291–92 (2003).
110. *See id.*
111. *See Lindsey*, 158 F.3d at 1268–69; *In re Grand Jury Subpoena Duces Tecum*, 112 F.3d at 915–16; *In re Grand Jury Investigation*, 399 F.3d at 533.
112. Salkin & Phillips, *supra* note 35, at 608.
113. *See, e.g., Lindsey*, 158 F.3d at 1270.
114. *See id.* at 1270–71.
115. *Id.* at 1270 (internal citations and quotations omitted).
116. *Id.* (quoting United States v. United Shoe Mach. Corp., 89 F. Supp. 357, 358–59 (D. Mass. 1950)).
117. *See In re Cnty. of Erie*, 473 F.3d at 420.
118. *Id.* at 419.
119. *Id.* at 420–21.
120. *Id.* at 421.
121. *Id.*
122. *See* Reed v. Baxter, 134 F.3d 351, 357 (6th Cir. 1998).
123. *See, e.g.*, Upjohn Co. v. United States, 449 U.S. at 397.
124. *See supra* section titled State Statutes Governing Attorney–Client Privilege for Government Attorneys.
125. *See supra* sections explaining D.C. and Second Circuit approaches to determining purpose of communication between attorneys and clients.
126. *See Lindsey*, 158 F.3d at 1270.
127. *See In re Cnty. of Erie*, 473 F.3d at 420.
128. *See id.*
129. *In re Grand Jury Subpoena Duces Tecum*, 112 F.3d at 921.

CHAPTER 7

Safeguarding against Government for Purchase: Restrictions on Gifts and Honoraria

Martha Harrell Chumbler

"We have the best government that money can buy."

—Mark Twain[1]

"Public confidence in the integrity of Government is indispensable to faith in democracy; and when we lose faith in the system, we have lost faith in everything we fight and spend for."

—Adlai Stevenson[2]

> This chapter provides guidance about what kinds of remuneration are restricted for public sector employees, the nature of those restrictions, and the extent to which the restrictions vary depending on whether the giver is in the public or private sector.

While political satirists like Mark Twain have long joked about the susceptibility of government officials to monetary and other economic persuasions, it is a fundamental tenet of government ethics that democracy is better served when government decision making is not influenced by gifts or other private remuneration. One source succinctly identifies as an important goal of government ethics codes "prevent[ing] the perception or the reality that gift giving influences public official's actions. This is because public agency actions should always promote the public's interests, as opposed to narrow personal or political interests."[3]

In service of this goal, all levels of government impose restrictions on the extent to which government officials and certain government employees may accept—and certain private parties may offer or convey—gifts and other types of remuneration over and above the officials' or employees' designated government salaries. Those restrictions vary significantly, however, depending on the type of remuneration and its source.

DEFINITION OF "GIFT"

There is no uniform definition of "gift"[4] for purposes of government ethics laws and regulations. However, the definition found in the Connecticut ethics code is illustrative of the broad meaning often assigned the term: "anything of value, which is directly and personally received, unless consideration of equal or greater value is given in return."[5] In some instances, the definition is fleshed out further by including specific types of items or services regarded as gifts, but a catchall synonymous with anything else of value is generally included.[6] The Florida ethics code further broadens the term by requiring repayment or the exchange for something of equal value to occur within 90 days after conveyance of something of value to a public official in order to avoid being regarded as a gift.[7] Forgiveness of a preexisting debt is also frequently included in the list of items considered a gift for purposes of ethical restrictions.[8]

Whether expressly stated or not, limitations on gift giving and receipt are designed to prevent the improper influence that gifts may have on government decision makers and, often, to prevent the appearance of such influence. Some ethics codes state the prohibition in just that manner. For example, Connecticut's ethics code bars gifts "based on any understanding that the vote, official action or judgment of the public official, state employee or candidate for public office would be or had been influenced thereby.[9] Hawaii, even more expansively, bars gifts where "it can reasonably be inferred that the gift is intended to influence" the official actions of a public official or employee.[10] Gifts of nominal value are often excluded from ethical constraints, either expressly by statute[11] or through judicial interpretation, since they would not be expected to exert influence on decision making. Thus, for example, payments made by a regulated utility to a local athletics club to make basketball courts available for use to utilities commissioners while at conferences were found to be of such minimal benefit to the commissioners as to be unlikely to influence their actions and, therefore, not a gift for purposes of the New Jersey ethics code.[12] Similarly, the gift law was not violated where there was insufficient evidence that a university official knew or reasonably should have known that he had received a significant discount for the re-roofing of his residence from the contractor being considered for award of a university construction contract.[13]

In contrast, contributions by a utility of $1,000 for sponsorship of an event organized by a utility commissioner were found to be prohibited gifts—not because of any evidence that the commissioner was actually swayed to take certain action—but, instead, because the contributions "would tend to improperly influence 'a reasonable person' in [the commissioners] position."[14] Similarly, a parole officer's acceptance of a share of a parolee's estate, even when the officer did not open the envelope revealing the parolee's devise until after the parolee's death, was found to violate the prohibition on accepting gifts "meant to influence or reward for official action taken."[15]

The statutes specifying an amount considered sufficient to suggest improper influence vary significantly, ranging from a high of $300[16] to a low of $25,[17] with some statutes barring gifts given with an intent to try to gain influence regardless of how nominal the gift's value.[18] Some of these monetary thresholds are established as aggregate thresholds of the value of what is conveyed over a prescribed time period, for example an amount given by a single benefactor during a single day,[19] month,[20] or year.[21]

Thus, while the specific scope of gift laws varies among jurisdictions, the advisory provided by the Massachusetts Ethics Commission identifies two threshold questions that public officials and employees should ask themselves when offered a gift from a private party:

> (1) whether the thing being offered is of "substantial value" and, if so, (2) whether it is being offered for or because of any official act or act within [their] official responsibility that [they] performed or will perform.[22]

As indicated earlier, in some jurisdictions, an additional query should be whether the thing being offered would suggest to a reasonable person that it was being offered to influence an official decision or action.

EXCEPTIONS BASED ON THE NATURE OF THE GIFT OR CIRCUMSTANCES IN WHICH GIVEN

The broad definitions of "gift" found in most ethics codes are narrowed—sometimes significantly—by exception from the definition itself or as exemptions from restrictions that would otherwise apply. In each instance, as with gifts of nominal value, the exception or exemption results from the presumption that the acceptance of the item or service will have little likelihood of influencing official action and, therefore, does not require restriction. The exceptions generally fall within four categories: (1) exceptions related to the nature of the gift, (2) exceptions related to the nature of the circumstances in which given, (3) exceptions based on the ultimate recipient of the gift, and (4) exceptions based on the source of the gift. The first two of these are discussed here, with the latter two addressed later in this chapter.

In virtually every jurisdiction, campaign contributions are controlled by statutes or regulations that specifically focus on elections and campaign finance issues. Thus, contributions made to a campaign—rather than directly to a candidate—are typically excluded from the definition of "gift."[23]

Aside from exceptions based on the value of the gift, another common exception based on the nature of the gift itself relates to food and beverages, with some jurisdictions excluding such consumables from the definition altogether[24] or establishing a rebuttable presumption that food and beverages are unlikely to influence a government official's actions.[25] In some instances, the food and beverage exception applies only to that which can be consumed immediately[26] or that is served at specific events.[27] In others, gifts of food and beverages are restricted only if they exceed a certain value, despite the absence of a threshold value for other categories of restricted gifts.[28]

Other items often deemed by their very nature to have little potential for influencing official actions and, therefore, exempted from gift restrictions include the following:

- Greeting cards[29]
- Promotional, educational, or instructional materials[30]
- Plaques, certificates, and trophies[31]
- Flowers and plants[32]

In some instances, it is the nature of the event or circumstances, either alone or in combination with the type of gift item given, that serves as the basis for an exemption. For example, condolence gifts are frequently excluded from restriction, although sometimes with a maximum value attached or other conditions relating to the type or timing of the gift.[33] Gifts received through inheritance, regardless of value or type, are also often exempted.[34]

GIFT RESTRICTIONS AND EXCEPTIONS BASED ON THE IDENTITY OF THE RECIPIENT

While there is no uniform delineation of those persons subject to restrictions on acceptance of gifts, the restrictions are fairly consistent in their application to elected and appointed government officials and at least certain categories of government employees, although the meanings ascribed to those terms vary. In some instances, the restrictions are all-encompassing, including within their scope government employees at all levels, without regard to their decision-making authority. For example, the prohibition found in the Arkansas ethics code against acceptance of gifts applies to all "public servants," a term that includes not only all elected and appointed officials but also all employees of any government body.[35] More often, the restrictions apply only to those officials and employees charged with specific regulatory, decision-making, or policy-making authority. Idaho, for example, proscribes the acceptance of gifts by "regulatory and law enforcement officials," "officials concerned with government contracts and pecuniary transactions," "judicial and administrative officials," and "legislative and executive officials."[36] In some states, candidates for elected office are also subject to prohibitions on receipt of gifts.[37]

The intent of all these more limited provisions is to prevent those government officials and employees in decision-making positions from accepting gifts that influence, who would tend to influence, such decision making. Recognizing that gifts benefiting a family member also have the potential to unduly influence government decision makers, some states have specifically prohibited acceptance of gifts by an official's or public employee's family members. The reach of the prohibition in some states is limited to the official's or employee's spouse,[38] spouse and dependent children,[39] or persons living in the same household,[40] while other states cast a much broader net. For example, Alabama prohibits a public official from accepting gifts for the benefit of their spouse, dependents, adult children, parents, and siblings, as well as their spouse's parents, children's spouses, and siblings' spouses,[41] while the Oregon gift bar includes stepparents, stepsiblings, anyone who receives benefits resulting from the public official's employment, and anyone whose employment benefits cover the public official.[42] Other states place no restrictions on the acceptance of gifts by family members.[43]

In a few jurisdictions, entities subject to restrictions on acceptance of gifts include business affiliates of a public official or employee. Connecticut and Pennsylvania, for example, prohibit offering or giving gifts to a business with which a public official or employee is associated,[44] while Rhode Island bars business associates of a public official or employee from soliciting or accepting a gift if given with the understanding that the official or employee's actions would be influenced.[45] Missouri and Utah restrict gift giving to any third party if given to[46] or solicited by[47] a public official to influence an official action.

Given that the object of gift restrictions is to guard against the purchase of favorable treatment by government officials or employees, some ethics codes expressly exclude gifts either intended for, or ultimately given to, a recipient other than the government official, government employee, or a member of their family. For example, while a gift may be delivered by a third party to a government official, if it is intended as a gift to the public body, rather than to the official personally, it is generally not regarded as a prohibited or restricted gift.[48] Some ethics codes also exclude gifts that the public official or employee donates to a charitable organization.[49]

RESTRICTIONS AND EXCEPTIONS BASED ON THE SOURCE OF THE GIFT

While ethics codes uniformly bar government officials and employees from accepting gifts that actually influence their decision making, greater restrictions, or outright prohibitions, are often imposed on gifts offered by certain categories of givers, while expressly allowing gifts received from others. The list of "restricted donor[s]" included in New Mexico's ethics code is typical of the gift sources subject to greater restrictions.

> "[R]estricted donor" means a person who:
> (1) is or is seeking to be a party to any one or any combination of sales, purchases, leases or contracts to, from or with the agency in which the donee holds office or is employed;

(2) will personally be, or is the agent of a person who will be, directly and substantially affected financially by the performance or nonperformance of the donee's official duty in a way that is greater than the effect on the public generally or on a substantial class of persons to which the person belongs as a member of a profession, occupation, industry or region;

(3) is personally, or is the agent of a person who is, the subject of or a party to a matter that is pending before a regulatory agency and over which the donee has discretionary authority as part of the donee's official duties or employment within the regulatory agency; or

(4) is a lobbyist or client of a lobbyist with respect to matters within the donee's jurisdiction; . . . .[50]

Thus, for example, while Florida's ethics code prohibits the solicitation or acceptance of any gift given with the understanding that the gift would influence official action,[51] it also prohibits public officials and certain public employees from soliciting any gifts from political committees, lobbyists, the principals of lobbyists, or vendors doing business with the official or employee's agency. Gifts from those sources valued at more than $100 cannot be accepted; gifts valued at more than $25 but not in excess of $100 must be reported.[52]

Lobbyists and the parties represented by lobbyist are the gift source most commonly subjected to stricter gift restrictions than either the general public or other categories of givers. Approximately half of the states single out lobbyists and the entities they represent for special treatment, either prohibiting or requiring the reporting of gifts of lower value than those received from other sources,[53] or banning all but very limited types of gifts from lobbyists and their principles.[54]

Restrictions placed on lobbyists have faced legal challenges. In *Vannatta v. Oregon Government Ethics Commission*,[55] Oregon's restrictions on both the acceptance of gifts by public officials and the offering of gifts from a lobbyist was challenged on the ground that such restriction impaired lobbyists' state and federal constitutional rights of free speech. The court rejected that argument with respect to the bar on acceptance of lobbyists' gifts by public officials and employees, concluding that acceptance did not necessarily involve any type of expression and, therefore, did not implicate lobbyists' free speech rights.[56] The prohibition on lobbyists' offering of gifts, however, was found to be unconstitutional, given that such prohibition was imposed without respect to the time, place, or manner in which the offer occurs.[57]

Similarly, in *Schickel v. Dilger*,[58] a federal district judge entered summary judgment in favor of groups of lobbyists who challenged an amendment to Kentucky's gift statute that removed an exception for gifts of de minimus value. Finding that the amended gift bar had an unconstitutional chilling effect on protected speech, the court explained that

> a speaker-based ban which suppresses political speech requires the government to show that the ban is narrowly tailored to achieve the purpose of combatting *quid pro quo* corruption.[59]

The appellate court rejected this conclusion, however, holding that the gift ban was "closely drawn to further Kentucky's anticorruption interest"[60] and therefore passed constitutional muster.

Pennsylvania's and Florida's restrictions on lobbyist gifts have both been challenged as unconstitutional infringements on the practice of law, albeit with different outcomes. Both states' constitutions provide that regulation of the practice of law falls under the jurisdiction of those states' supreme courts, rather than their legislatures. In *Gmerek v. State Ethics Commission*,[61] the Pennsylvania supreme court considered a statute that defined "lobbyist" as any individual or entity that sought to influence legislative or administrative action and expressly stated that "the term includes an attorney who engages in lobbying."[62] Related provisions imposed requirements on all lobbyists, including the requirement to report all gifts given to state officials, state employees, or members of their families.[63] The court rejected the state ethics commission's arguments that the statute regulated lobbying rather than the practice of law, concluding, instead, that direct and indirect communications by a lawyer/lobbyist on behalf of their client clearly encompasses the practice of law. Thus, the Pennsylvania statutes were held to be a violation of the separation of powers.

Florida's supreme court reach the opposite conclusion.[64] That state's statute prohibited lobbyists from providing anything of value to state officials and employees, but expressly excluded any person—including lawyers—representing someone in a judicial or formal administrative proceeding.[65] The Florida court adopted a much more limited view than that of the Pennsylvania court, adopting the view that the practice of law includes only representation in formal proceedings, providing legal advice, and preparation of legal instruments. Lobbying, in the Florida court's opinion, falls outside those categories. Thus, the bar on gifts from lobbyists was found not to infringe on the state supreme court's exclusive authority over the regulation of lawyers.[66]

Just as gift restrictions often apply more rigorously to certain categories of gift givers, virtually every jurisdiction imposes little to no restrictions on gifts offered or given by certain other sources. Most commonly, gifts from family members fall outside the scope of restrictions on both gift giving and gift acceptance, although the definition of "family" for purposes of this exception varies significantly. Gifts from a public official's or employee's spouse, parents, siblings, children, and children's spouses are typically excluded.[67] However, the list of family members from whom unlimited gifts may be received is sometimes much longer, including grandparents, aunts, uncles, cousins, step-relatives, and the spouses of each of those individuals.[68] Some states allow the acceptance of gifts from relatives of certain defined degrees of consanguinity.[69] Idaho exempts gifts given from someone of any degree of kinship, as long as the recipient's status as a public official or employee is not the reason for the gift.[70]

In some jurisdictions, gifts from nonfamily members who have a personal or business relationship with the public official are also exempted, although generally with some caveat attached to guard against such gifts being given to influence an official action or decision.[71]

HONORARIA

As with gift laws, those ethics codes that include restrictions on acceptance of honoraria are intended to diminish the opportunity for government officials and employees to be unduly influenced, as well as to prevent officials and public employees from using their position for their private enrichment. Some jurisdictions, therefore, do not have specific provisions relating to honoraria but, instead, treat honoraria just as they do other items or services of value given to a public officer or employee.[72] However, a majority of the states' ethics codes include provisions specifically relating to honoraria.

Just as there is no uniform definition of "gift," the definitions ascribed to "honorarium" vary from jurisdiction to jurisdiction. Merriam-Webster defines the term as "a payment for a service (such as making a speech) on which custom or propriety forbids a price to be set."[73] A fundamental concern regarding the payment of honoraria to public officials and employees is that—without a standardized payment scale—there exists a heightened opportunity for private parties to gain influence by payment of generous honoraria. Thus, many, but not all, states have elected to impose specific restrictions, and sometimes bans, on the payment or acceptance of such honoraria.

Maryland's honorarium law exemplifies the most restrictive approach. That state defines "honorarium" as

> the payment of money or anything of value for:
> (i) speaking to, participating in, or attending a meeting or other function, or
> (ii) writing an article that has been or is intended to be published.[74]

This restriction applies regardless of the subject matter of the speech or article. The only permitted exceptions—aside from the exceptions that apply generally to all types of gifts—are reimbursement for reasonable travel and dependent care expenses incurred as a result of the speaking engagement and payment to government officials who are also faculty members at a state college or university.[75] Even the general gift exclusions do not apply if the source of the honorarium has an interest different from the general public that is affected by the official's decision making or the honorarium offer is related to the official's public position.[76]

Such content-neutral restrictions have been successfully challenged, most notably in *U.S. v. National Treasury Employees Union (NTEU)*.[77] In that case, executive branch employees below the grade GS-16 challenged a provision in the Ethics in Government Act, which barred congressmen, federal officers, and federal employees from receiving an honorarium for making a speech or writing an article, alleging that the bar violated the employees' First Amendment rights. Focusing on the impacts felt by the "rank and file" of federal employees, the Court found that the "prohibition on compensation imposes a significant burden on expressive activity,"[78] particularly when applied as a "blanket burden on the speech of nearly 1.7 million federal employees."[79] The Court described the burden placed on government to justify restrictions on officials' and employees' expression, including restrictions on honorarium, as follows:

The government must show that the interests of both potential audiences and a vast group of present and future employees in a broad range of present and future expression are outweighed by that expression's "necessary impact on the actual operation" of the government.[80]

Notably, the Supreme Court declined to find the honorarium ban unconstitutional on its face, instead limiting its ruling to the statute's applicability to the class of federal employees who brought the challenge.[81] The Court's holding suggests two possible safe harbors that could protect honorarium restrictions from successful constitutional challenge: (1) limitation of the bar to high level public officers; and (2) limitation of the bar to speeches and writings that have some nexus to a public official's or employee's official duties. Most ethics codes incorporate at least one of these safe harbor provisions.

First, the Supreme Court noted that the balancing factors applicable to any restriction on rights of free expression might weigh in favor of an honorarium ban applied only to high-level officials, since legislators and other high-level officers more often receive invitations to speak or write as a result of their official positions.[82] Thus, Illinois bars acceptance of honoraria only by members of its general assembly.[83] Georgia restricts acceptance of honoraria to a broad range of public official and employees, but with differing degrees of rigor. Statewide elected officials are prohibited from accepting "any monetary fee or honorarium for a speaking engagement, participation in a seminar, discussion panel, or other such activity," while other public officers may accept honoraria of up to $100, as long as the speaking or writing engagement does not relate to the officer's official duties.[84]

Second, the *NTEU* opinion expressly cites the absence of a sufficient justification for the honorarium restriction where "the vast majority of the speech at issue in this case does not involve the subject matter of Government employment and takes place outside the workplace."[85] The official nexus test suggested by this language was itself challenged in *Wolfe v. Barnhart*.[86] Wolfe, a federal administrative law judge for the Social Security Administration, co-authored a text book relating to Social Security law for which he expected to receive royalties. After receiving an advisory opinion that federal regulation prohibited him from receiving compensation for speeches and written products related to his public duties,[87] Wolfe brought a First Amendment challenge to the regulation. The federal district court denied relief, noting that "[w]hile the Court in *NTEU* declined to impose a nexus requirement on the challenged regulation, the opinion indicates tacit approval for such a limitation."[88]

Many jurisdictions have incorporated this nexus requirement into their honorarium laws. Alaska, for example, expressly allows legislators and legislative employees to accept honoraria "if the appearance or speech is not connected with the person's legislative status."[89] Connecticut includes within its honorarium restriction only those articles and speeches made in the official or employee's "official capacity."[90]

Other jurisdictions have adopted a slightly different nexus test, by allowing acceptance of honoraria for speeches and sometimes writings given during the course of a government official's private business or occupation. For example, California's statute has a carve-out for speeches related to an official's "bona fide business, trade, or profession"—but disqualifies businesses or occupations that consist primarily of making speeches.[91] Tennessee allows acceptance of honoraria for speeches made and articles written in the official's "capacity as a private business person, professional or tradesperson," without limitation on the types of businesses, professions, or trades that qualify.[92]

A few jurisdictions require public officers and employees to obtain specific approval before accepting an honorarium. Washington, for example, only allows state officers and employees to accept honoraria if specifically approved by their agency.[93] This case-by-case approval may be constitutionally suspect, since they present the risk that approval will be conditioned upon the acceptability of the speech or article's content. The validity of this approach was tested in *Sanjour v. U.S. Environmental Protection Agency*.[94] The regulation at issue in *Sanjour* dealt not with the acceptance of fees for speaking or writing engagement but, instead, with a public employee's acceptance of reimbursement for travel expenses incurred in connection with making a speech. Nonetheless, the rationale applied by the *Sanjour* court may be equally applicable to ethics statutes or regulations that require case-by-case approval of honoraria that exceed mere reimbursement. The *Sanjour* court struck the regulation, stating that:

> the broad discretion that the regulations vest in the agency reinforces our belief that they are impermissible. . . .
>
> [A] law or policy permitting communication in a certain way for some but not for others raises the specter of content and viewpoint censorship. This danger is at its zenith when the determination of who may speak and who may not is left to the unbridled discretion of a government official. [W]e have often and uniformly held that such statutes or policies impose censorship on the public or press, and hence are unconstitutional.[95]

Most, but not all, jurisdictions do allow public officials and employees to accept reimbursement for their travel and other actual expenses incurred as a result of making a speech or authoring written materials. For example, while Alaska prohibits the acceptance of honoraria for speeches connected to a legislator's or legislative employee's government responsibilities, it allows reimbursement of "actual and necessarily incurred travel expenses."[96] Florida allows reimbursement for actual and reasonable transportation, lodging, and food and beverage expenses related to the honorarium event, including any event or meeting registration fee" for both covered officials and employees and their spouses, but requires that reimbursements received from a lobbyist be reported to the state ethics commission.[97]

Finally, of those jurisdictions that specifically regulate honoraria, some merely require that fees received for speeches, written materials, or similar activities be disclosed, generally to the state ethics commission.[98] In some instances, reporting is required only for honoraria received from certain designated categories of sources. For example, Massachusetts requires reporting of honoraria in excess of $100 if received by a legislator from a lobbyist or someone with a direct interest in legislation or received by another public official or employee from a source with a matter pending before the official or employee's agency.[99]

Whether provided in the guise of an honorarium, or as an outright gift, all jurisdictions prohibit public officials, and at least those public employees in decision-making positions, from accepting money or other items of value in return for favorable treatment for the source or others associated with the source. The objective is to assure the public that their government is not "the best that money can buy,"[100] but, instead, reflects the "integrity . . . [that] is indispensable to faith in democracy."[101]

SUMMARY OF KEY POINTS

- Gifts to public sector employees are restricted to prevent improper influence or the appearance of improper influence on governmental decision makers.
- In setting the gift laws, officials should consider whether the thing being offered is of substantial value, and, if so, whether it is being offered for or because of an official act or the expectation thereof.
- Gifts laws usually include exemptions related to (1) the nature of the gift, (2) the circumstances under which the gift is provided, (3) the gift's ultimate recipient, and (4) the source of the gift.
- Many jurisdictions also specifically restrict the giving of honoraria to diminish the opportunity for government officials and employees to be unduly influenced or to use their positions for private enrichment.

NOTES

1. *Popular Quotes by Mark Twain*, ALLAUTHOR.COM, https://allauthor.com/quotes/author/mark-twain/?p=18 (last visited Apr. 2, 2019).
2. Adlai Stevenson, SPEECHES OF ADLAI STEVENSON 31 (Debs Meyers & Ralph Martin eds., 1952).

3. *Understanding California's Gift Rules for Public Officials*, Institute for Local Gov't: Gift Resource Ctr. Updated to 2017–2018 Limits 1, https://www.ca-ilg.org/GiftCenter (last visited Apr. 12, 2022).

4. While the term "gift" is widely used across jurisdictions, some ethics codes use such terms as "anything of value," "compensation," or "gratuitous transfer," either in place or, or in addition to, the term "gift." *See* Ky. Rev. Stat. Ann. § 6.611(2) (2021) (anything of value); Miss. Code Ann. § 25-4-3(e) (2020) (compensation); Ga. Code Ann. § 21-5-3(14) (2020) (gratuitous transfer).

5. *E.g.*, Conn. Gen. Stat. Ann. § 1-79(e) (2020).

6. *E.g.*, Ark. Code Ann. § 21-8-402(5)(A) (2020) ("[a]ny payment, entertainment, service, or anything of value . . ."); Del. Code Ann. tit. 29, § 5812(h) (2021) ("a payment, subscription, advance, forbearance, rendering or deposit of money, services or anything of value . . . "); Ky. Rev. Stat. Ann. § 6.611(2) (2021) (identifying a list of 13 categories of items and adding "[a]ny other thing of value . . .").

7. Fla. Stat. Ann. § 112.312(12)(a) (2021) ("[t]hat which is accepted by a donee or by another for or on behalf of a donee, directly, indirectly, or in trust for the donee's benefit or by any other means, for which equal or greater consideration is not given within 90 days").

8. *See, e.g.*, La. Bd. of Ethics, 236 So. 3d 593 (La. 2017) (forgiveness of debt owed on sublease of university stadium suite found to be a prohibited gift); Me. Rev. Stat. tit. 1, § 1012.4 (2021).

9. Conn. Gen. Stat. Ann. § 1-84(f) (2020).

10. Haw. Rev. Stat. Ann. § 84-11 (2021).

11. *E.g.*, N.Y. Legis. Law § 1-c (j) (2021).

12. Exec. Comm'n on Ethical Standards v. Salmon, 684 A.2d 930, 939 (N.J. 1996).

13. Goin v. Comm'n on Ethics, 658 So. 2d 1131 (Fla. 1st DCA 1995).

14. Molnar v. Fox, 301 P.3d 824, 832 (Mont. 2013); *see also* Rubenfield v. N.Y. State Ethics Comm'n., 841 N.Y.S.2d 397 (N.Y. 2007) (transportation official's acceptance of gala tickets from contractor found to be a prohibited gift because received under circumstances that inferred a promise of influence).

15. Mont. Dep't of Corr. v. State Dep't of Labor & Indus., 148 P.3d 619, 625 (Mont. 2006).

16. Me. Rev. Stat. Ann. tit. 1, § 1012(4)(A) (2021) (relating to gifts from a single source).

17. N.H. Rev. Stat. Ann. § 15-B:2(V)(a)(2) (2020).

18. Fla. Stat. Ann. §112.313(2) (2021) (prohibiting those executive branch officials and employees required to file financial disclosures from accepting anything of value from a lobbyist or an entity that employs a lobbyist when the gift is given for the purpose influencing a decision or gaining goodwill).

19. *See, e.g.*, Utah Code Ann. § 36-11-304 (2021) (prohibiting gifts with an aggregate daily value of more than $10 for all but food and beverages).

20. *See, e.g.*, Neb. Rev. Stat. Ann. § 49-1490 (2021) (prohibiting public officials from accepting gifts with an aggregate value over the course of a month of more than $50).

21. *See, e.g.*, Kan. Stat. Ann. § 46-237(a) (2020) (prohibiting gifts of hospitality valued at $100 or more in a calendar year and any other type of gifts valued at more than $40 in a calendar year).

22. Advisory 04-02: Gifts and Gratuities, Mass. Ethics Comm'n 3 (2004).

23. *E.g.*, Ark. Const. art. 19, § 30(b)(2)(B)(vii) (2020); Alaska Stat. Ann. § 24.60.080(e) (2020); Cal. Gov't Code § 82028(b)(4) (2020); Del. Code Ann. tit. 29, § 5812(h) (2021); Mich. Comp. Laws Ann. § 4.414(1)(a) (2021); S.D. Codified Laws § 2-12-18(2) (2021); Va. Code Ann. § 30-101 (2021). For a discussion of federal campaign finance regulation, *see* Ann M. Ravel, *The Work and Responsibilities of the Federal Election Commission*, *in* America Votes!: Challenges to Modern Election Law and Voting Rights 3 (Benjamin E. Griffith, ed., 2016).

24. *E.g.*, Ohio Rev. Code Ann. § 102.031(C)(3) (2020); 65 Pa. Const. Stat. § 13A03 (2021); Tex. Gov't Code Ann. § 305.024(a)(7)(B) (2021); Utah Code Ann. § 36-11-304 (2022); Wyo. Stat. Ann. § 9-13-102(a)(vi)(E) (2021).

25. W. Va. Code Ann. § 6B-2-5(2)(A) (2020).

26. *E.g.*, Alaska Stat. Ann. § 24.60.080(a)(2)(A) (2020) (exempting food and beverages when the food or beverage is for immediate consumption); Mich. Comp. Laws Ann. § 4.414(1)(d) (2021) (exempting food and beverages from any source when for immediate consumption).

27. *E.g.*, Alaska Stat. Ann. § 24.60.080(c)(1)(B) (2020) (exempting acceptance of food and beverages when served at a social event); Me. Rev. Stat. Ann. tit. 1, § 1012.4.F. & G (2021) (exempting meals served at prayer breakfasts and meals served as part of an information program for public servants); Mont. Code Ann. § 2-2-102(3)(b)(ii) (2021) exempting food and beverages served at civic, charitable, and community events that relate to the official's position or where the official is attending in an official capacity).

28. *E.g.*, Ala. Code § 36-25-1(34)(b)16 (2021) ($25 per meal and $50 per year); Kan. Stat. Ann. § 46-237(d) (20202) ($40).

29. *E.g.*, Ala. Code Ann. § 36-25-1(34)b.4 (2021) (greeting cards).

30. *E.g.*, Ark. Const. art. 19, § 30(b)(2)(B)(i)(*a*) (2020) (informational material regarding an official's duties); Cal. Gov't Code § 82028(b)(1) (2020) (informational material); 5 Ill. Comp. Stat. Ann. 430/10-15(4) (2021) (educational programs & materials); Ky. Rev. Stat. Ann. § 6.611(2)(b)5-7 (2021) (promotional items worth less than $50, educational items, & informational items); Tenn. Code Ann. § 3-6-305(b)(4) (2020) (promotional items of the type routinely given to customers).

31. *E.g.*, Ala. Code Ann. § 36-25-1(34)b.4 (2021); Colo. Const. art. 29 § 3(3)(a) (if valued at less than $100); Iowa Code Ann. § 68B.22.4.h (2021) (plaques of negligible value).

32. *E.g.*, Wash. Rev. Code Ann. § 42.52.150(2)(a) (2021) (unsolicited flowers, plants, and floral arrangements).

33. *E.g.*, N.C. Gen. Stat. § 138A-2(32)f (2021) (expressions of condolence limited to cards, flowers, meals, and charitable donations given within a reasonable time of the death).

34. *E.g.*, Cal. Gov't Code § 82028(b)(5) (2022); Haw. Rev. Stat. Ann. § 84-11.5(d)(1) (2021); Iowa Code Ann. § 68B.22.4.d (2022); *but see* Mont. Dep't of Corrections, 148 P. 3d at 625 (holding that parole officer's acceptance of a devise from a probationer violated state gift prohibitions).

35. Ark. Const. art. 19, § 30(b)(10)–(13) (2021) (defining "public appointee," "public employee," "public official," and "public servant," with the last of these terms defined to include the other three, and including public officials after the date of their election but before being seated).

36. Idaho Code Ann. §§ 18-1356(1)–(4) (2022).

37. *E.g.*, Conn. Gen. Stat. Ann. § 1-84(f) & (g) (2020); Iowa Code Ann. § 68B.22.1 (2021); Kan. Stat. Ann. § 46-236 (2020).

38. *E.g.*, Ky. Rev. Stat. Ann. § 6.751(2) (2021) (extending the prohibition on acceptance of gifts only to a spouse).

39. *E.g.*, Iowa Code Ann. §§ 68B.2.11 (2021) (defining "immediate family members") & 68B.22.1 (prohibiting acceptance of gifts by immediate family members); N.Y. Legis. Law § 1-m (2021) (prohibiting gifts to the spouse and unemancipated children of a public official).

40. *E.g.*, N.H. Rev. Stat. Ann. §§ 15-B:2.VII & 15-B:3.II (2020) (defining "family member" as persons living in the same domicile who share a common interest in the household's daily expenses & prohibiting giving a gift to a public official or employee's family member).

41. Ala. Code §§ 36-25-1(15) & 36-25-7 (2021) (defining "family member of a public official" & prohibiting gifts given for the benefit of a public official's family member).

42. Or. Rev. Stat. Ann. §§ 244.020 (16) & 244.025(1) (2021) (defining "relative" & prohibiting gifts to the relatives of public officials and candidates).

43. *E.g.*, Fla. Stat. 112.313(2) (2021) (omitting any mention of family members).

44. Conn. Gen. Stat. Ann. § 1-84(f) (2020); tit. 65 Pa. Const. Stat. Ann. § 1103(b) (2021).

45. R.I. Gen. Laws § 36-14-5(g) (2021).

46. Mo. Ann. Stat. § 105.452.1(1) (2021).

47. Utah Code Ann. § 67-16-5(2)(2021).

48. *E.g.*, Ark. Code Ann. § 21-8-804(a) (2020) (allowing designated state officials to accept gifts on behalf of the state).

49. *E.g.*, Alaska Stat. Ann. § 24.60.080(g) (2020) (excluding gifts received on behalf of a nonpolitical charitable organization); Cal. Gov't Code § 82028(b)(2) (2020) (excluding unused gifts that are donated to a § 501(c)(3) organization within 30 days of receipt).

50. N.M. Stat. Ann. § 10-16B-2.D (2020); *see also* Idaho Code Ann. § 18-1356(1)-(4) (2021) (describing the prohibiting gift sources for each of four categories of public officials and employees).

51. Fla. Stat. Ann. § 112.313(2) (2021).

52. *Id.* § 112.3148(4) & (5) (2021); *see also* Fla. Comm'n on Ethics Op. 16-1 (Jan. 27, 2016) (stating that a school board member may not accept gifts of travel, lodging, and meals from her boyfriend, an attorney with a law firm that provides bond services to the school district and that employs a lobbyist).

53. *E.g.*, Cal. Gov't Code § 86203 (2020) (prohibiting gifts from lobbyists having an aggregate value of $10 during a calendar month); Neb. Rev. Stat. Ann. § 49-1490(1) & (2) (2021) (prohibiting gifts from lobbyists and their principles having an aggregate value of $50 in one calendar month).

54. *E.g.*, Colo. Const. art. 29, § 3(4) (2021) (barring all gifts from lobbyists with the exception of lobbyists who are family members of the public official or employee).

55. 222 P.3d 1077 (Ore. 2009). The statute's prohibition on the solicitation of such gifts was also challenged, but the court determined that the appellant lobbyists did not have standing to raise that issue.

56. *Id.* at 1081–84. The applicability of the gift restriction only to gifts with an annual aggregate value of $50—essentially about the value of a coffee and doughnut once a month—did not seem to have any bearing on the court's decision. *See* Or. Rev. Stat. Ann. § 244.025(2) (2007) (which prohibited a lobbyist from offering and a public official, candidate, or family member of either from accepting "any gift or gifts with an aggregate value in excess of $50" during a calendar year).

57. *Vannatta*, 222 P.3d. at 1084–86.

58. No. 2:15-CV-155, 2017 WL 2464998 (E.D. Ky. June 6, 2017).

59. *Id.* (citing Citizens United v. Fed. Election Comm'n, 558 U.S. 310, 340 (2010)).

60. Schickel v. Dilger, 925 F.3d 858, 881 (6th Cir. 2018).

61. 807 A.2d 812 (Pa. 2002).

62. 65 Pa. Const. Stat. Ann. § 1302, subsequently repealed by 2006 Pa. Laws 134, § 2.

63. 65 Pa. Const. Stat. Ann. § 1305, subsequently repealed by 2006 Pa. Laws 134, § 2.

64. Fla. Ass'n of Prof'l Lobbyists v. Div. of Legislative Info. Servs., 7 So. 3d 511 (Fla. 2009).

65. Fla. Stat. Ann. § 112.3215 (2008), quoted in Fla. Ass'n of Prof'l Lobbyists v. Div. of Legislative Info. Servs., 7 So. 3d at 516–17.

66. Florida's prohibition on gifts from lobbyists to legislators and other officials and employees is now divided between two statutes: Fla. Stat. § 11.045(4)(a) (2021) (legislators) and § 112.3215(6)(a) (2021) (those state official and employees required to file financial disclosures).

67. *E.g.*, Conn. Rev. Stat. Ann. § 1-79(5)(D) (2020) (limiting the exception to spouses, fiancés, parents, siblings, children, and children's spouses).

68. *E.g.* Cal. Gov't Code § 82028(b)(3) (2020) (including within the exception spouses, children, parents, grandparents, grandchildren, siblings, parents-in-law, siblings-in-law, nephews, nieces, aunts, uncles, first cousins, and the spouses of each of these).

69. Del. Code Ann. tit. 29, § 5812(h) (2021) (three degrees of consanguinity); Haw. Rev. Stat. Ann. § 84-11.5(d)(3) (2021) (four degrees); Mich. Comp. Laws. Ann. § 4.414(1)(c) (2021) (seven degrees).

70. Idaho Code Ann. § 18-1356(5)(b) (2021).

71. *E.g., id.* (exempting gifts unrelated to the public official or employee's position); *cf.* Conn. Gen. Stat. Ann. § 1-79(12) (2020) (allowing gifts from nonrelatives given for "major life events," but limiting their value to $1000); Va. Code Ann. § 30-101 (2021) (exempting gifts from personal friends unless the friend is either a lobbyist or someone represented by a lobbyist).

Safeguarding against Government for Purchase: Restrictions on Gifts and Honoraria • 129

72. *E.g.*, Haw. Rev. Stat. Ann. ch. 84 (2021); Mont. Code Ann. §§ 2-2-101 through 2-2-145 (2021).
73. Merriam-Webster, https://www.merriam-webster.com/dictionary/honoraria (last visited Apr. 3, 2022).
74. Md. Code Ann. GP § 5-101(r)(1) (2022). Payment for writing a book that will be published is excluded. *Id.* § 5-501(r)(2) (2022).
75. *Id.* § 5-505(d)(2) (2022); *see also* Ga. Code Ann. § 21-5-11 (2020) (barring statewide elected officials from accepting any honoraria, but allowing reimbursement of travel expenses).
76. Md. Code Ann. GP § 5-505(d)(3) (2021).
77. 513 U.S. 454 (1995).
78. *Id.* at 468.
79. *Id.* at 474.
80. *Id.* at 468.
81. *Id.* at 477–78.
82. *Id.* at 469, 478.
83. *E.g.* 5 Ill. Comp. Stat. 420/2-110 (2021) (barring members of the state general assembly from accepting honoraria).
84. Ga. Code Ann. § 21-5-11 (2020).
85. *NTEU*, 513 U.S. at 470 & 479 (declining to define what a constitutionally defensible nexus would be).
86. 354 F. Supp. 2d 1226 (N.D. Okla. 2004).
87. 5 C.F.R. § 2635.807(a) (2021).
88. *NTEU*, 354 F. Supp. 2d at 1241.
89. Alaska Stat. Ann. § 24.60.085(b) (2020).
90. Conn. Gen. Stat. Ann. § 1-84(k) (2020); *cf.* N.H. Rev. Stat. Ann. § 15-B:2.VI (2020) (defining "honorarium" to exclude speeches and written products "not related to or associated with any public office or government employment"); Fla. Stat. Ann. § 112.3149(2) (2021) (prohibiting those officials required to file financial disclosures and certain procurement employees from soliciting an honorarium "relating to the reporting individual's or procurement employee's public office or duties"); N.M. Stat. Ann. § 10-16-4.1 (2020) (prohibiting acceptance of honoraria in excess of $100 if related to official duties).
91. Cal. Gov't Code § 89501(b)(1) (2020) (describing as examples of a bona fide business, trade, or profession, "teaching, practicing law, medicine, insurance, real estate, banking, or building contracting, unless the sole or predominant activity of the business, trade, or profession is making speeches").
92. Tenn. Code Ann. § 2-10-116.B (2020).
93. Wash. Rev. Code Ann. § 42.52.130 (2021).
94. 56 F.3d 85 (D.C. Cir. 1995).
95. *Sanjour*, F.3d at 97, quoting City of Lakewood v. Plain Dealer Publishing Co., 486 U.S. 750, 763 (1988).
96. Alaska Stat. Ann. § 24.60.085(a)(2) (2020).
97. Fla. Stat. Ann. § 112.3149(1) & (6) (2021).
98. *E.g.*, Del. Code Ann. tit. 29, § 5813(a)(4)d (2021) (requiring the filing of annual financial disclosures of any honorarium received state officials); Me. Rev. Stat. Ann. tit. 1, § 1016-G.1.H (2021) (requiring legislators to report all sources of honoraria of $2000 or more); *see also* D.C. Code § 1-1162.24(a)(1)(A)(i) (2021) (requiring financial disclosure of every business entity from which an official received any income in excess of $200).
99. Mass. Gen. Laws Ann. ch. 268B, § 5(g)(4) & (7) (2020) (requiring reporting of honoraria aggregating more than $100 if received from certain sources, as well as any reimbursement in excess of $100 from any of the same sources).
100. *Popular Quotes by Mark Twain*, *supra* note 1.
101. Stevenson, *supra* note 2.

CHAPTER 8

Postemployment Restrictions on Government Employees: Closing the "Revolving Door"

Michael Donaldson*
Benjamin Stearns**

This is a revision of a chapter originally prepared by George F. Carpinello.***

> This chapter explores special considerations that arise for public sector lawyers when they leave public service, specifically with respect to postemployment restrictions. There are easily identifiable federal and state statutes on point, but at the local government-level practitioners must also consult local ethics laws and applicable case law. Furthermore, lawyers would be wise to weigh relevant postemployment restrictions prior to accepting employment and/or contracts for service with governmental entities.

A number of ethical issues arise when a public employee leaves public service. One concern is that employees not use confidential information they have gained while working for the government to their private advantage or the private advantage of others. Second, public employees might use their acquaintance with former colleagues as an opportunity to curry special favor, on behalf of a private interest, from their former agency. Additionally, public employees might be influenced in the performance of their job by the prospect of future employment. In carrying out their duties, public employees may seek to favor a potential future employer. Finally, a high degree of mobility between the regulators and the regulated may create the appearance of impropriety in the eyes of the public and give the impression that the government entities are captives of the industries they regulate.[1]

This chapter discusses the various rules that have been adopted by government at the state, local, and national levels to regulate postemployment activity. Those rules fall into four categories. The first type is a ban on any appearance before one's former agency for a specific period of time (the "agency ban"). The second is a prohibition, often indefinite, on a former government employee's involvement in any matter the employee worked on as a government official (the "matter ban"). The third is a prohibition on the use, for personal advantage, of any confidential information obtained by an individual while in government employment. Finally, many states and municipalities prohibit government employees from seeking future employment from private entities appearing before their agency.

In addition to state and federal statutory controls on postemployment activities of former government employees, government lawyers are bound by the ethics rules adopted by their jurisdictions relating to representing clients in matters in which those lawyers were involved as government officials.

All of these restrictions are discussed in more detail in the sections that follow.

THE BAN ON APPEARANCES BEFORE A FORMER EMPLOYEE'S AGENCY (THE "AGENCY BAN")

Many states prohibit former employees from appearing, on behalf of a private party, before their former agency for a period of one to two years after the termination of their employment. New York and Florida, two of the strictest states, have enforced a two-year ban.[2] The federal government has imposed a one-year ban on senior government officials from appearing before their former agencies and a ban for very senior officials, such as the vice president, cabinet level officers, and other officers appointed by the government, from appearing before *any* agency of the government for a period of one year.[3] A one-year ban on most government employees from appearing before their own agency is quite common.[4]

Restrictions are both criminal and civil in nature and can lead to serious sanctions. For example, the federal statute is a criminal statute, and violators are subject to up to five years' imprisonment, a $50,000 civil penalty, and any other remedies available to any other person.[5] Like the federal regulation, Ohio's statute is also criminal, and violation of it constitutes a misdemeanor in the first degree.[6] New York's statute subjects its violators to a civil penalty of up to $40,000 and the value of any benefit received, or, upon referral by the ethics committee to the appropriate prosecutor, punishment as a Class A misdemeanor.[7]

The purpose of these regulations is obviously to create a cooling-off period between the time an employee leaves government service and the time the employee reappears before the agency as an advocate for private interests. It is questionable that a truly influential government official would lose that influence within a one- or two-year period; however, the inability to lobby former colleagues for that period of time often induces former government officials to opt for private positions that entirely avoid any potential conflict.

For certain public officials, especially lawyers, a one- or two-year ban can cause considerable hardship. For example, a lawyer involved for a number of years in any area subject to pervasive state regulation, such as environmental or public utility law, would have difficulty leaving government service and entering into private practice, where the bulk of such practice would require an appearance before the lawyer's former agency. This hardship can be especially acute when the lawyer leaves involuntarily because of a workforce reduction. In such a case, the lawyer obviously is not entering into private practice to take advantage of state connections; the lawyer has no choice but to enter private practice. New York, in recognition of this fact, enacted temporary legislation exempting some employees terminated in downsizing from the application of the agency ban.[8] In Florida, the ban does not apply to employees employed with the agency prior to the enactment of the statute in 1989.[9]

The agency ban most routinely applies to executive branch officials. However, some states and the federal government have enacted restrictions on former legislators. For example, the federal government prohibits a member of Congress or certain legislative congressional staffers from lobbying Congress for a one-year period.[10] Similarly, New York and California prohibit former legislators from lobbying the state legislature for two years[11] and one year, respectively.[12] Florida also bans members of the legislature, appointed state officers, and statewide elected officers from personally representing another person or entity for compensation before that person's agency or governmental body for two years.[13] Texas prohibits legislators from representing, for compensation, another person before a state agency in the executive branch of state government unless the representation relates to a criminal matter or involves the filing of documents that only involve ministerial acts on the part of the government agency.[14] New York's two-year ban also applies to staffers.[15]

Some states have also enacted restrictions on former judges. For example, the New York Court of Appeals has prohibited former judges from appearing before their courts for a period of two years after leaving employment.[16] Additionally, in some places restrictions have been placed on the employees of judges, such as their law clerks or law secretaries. These restrictions, whether found in statute or in rules adopted by individual judges, restrict former law assistants' appearances before their former court for a certain period of time after they leave their position as clerk.[17] Some rules also prohibit former law clerks from practicing in connection with any case that was pending during the time of their clerkship.[18] See discussion of the matter ban on pages 138–141.

What Services Are Prohibited?

The agency ban applies to appearances on *any* matter before one's former agency. (Compare with the matter ban discussed on pages 138–141.) Moreover, it does not depend upon the employee's motivation or whether or not he or she will contact acquaintances in the agency. However, rules vary considerably among the states as to what form of contact or activity is prohibited. For example, the federal government prohibits the making of any communication to, or appearance before, the employee's former agency with the intent to influence that agency.[19] However, a former employee is not specifically prohibited from offering "behind-the-scenes advice and assistance" to those dealing directly with the agency.[20] Similarly, Rhode Island prohibits a former employee from representing any person before the employee's former agency.[21] New York City prohibits "any communication, for compensation, other than those involving ministerial matters."[22] Wisconsin bans for a period of one year former state public officials from making for compensation "any formal or informal appearance before, or negotiat[ing] with, any officer or employee of the department with which he or she was associated as a state public official."[23]

New York state, in contrast, prohibits former employees from appearing or practicing before their former agency *or* receiving compensation for any services rendered on behalf of any person "in relation to any case, proceeding or application or other matter before such agency."[24] Because the statute is in the disjunctive, a former employee who does not appear or practice before the agency, but who aids in the preparation of a matter that is presented to the agency and receives compensation for such preparation, violates the statute.[25] The former employee therefore cannot submit to his or her former agency permit and grant applications, contract proposals, and/or any work that contains the individual's professional stamp or seal.[26] Former employees may give general advice to their new employer as to the requirements of their former agency or prepare a general report that could be used by potential funding applicants to their former agency, but they may not be involved in preparing a specific application that would be submitted to the agency.[27] "[I]f the former employee can reasonably assume that his/her work product will reach the individual's former agency," the former employee would be appearing before that agency and would violate the statute.[28] Indeed, even the making of a Freedom of Information Act request to one's former agency, whether compensated or not, is barred by New York's revolving door provisions.[29]

Florida, in contrast, limits its two-year ban to actual "representation" before an agency, which means "actual physical attendance on behalf of a client in an agency proceeding, the writing of letters or filing of documents on behalf of a client, and personal communications made with the officers or employees of any agency on behalf of a client."[30] Thus, it appears that behind-the-scenes work by a former employee would not come within the scope of the ban. However, the Florida Commission on Ethics has cautioned that representation includes any contact with the agency that might influence agency action in a matter that is not purely ministerial.[31] Acting as a mediator in cases that may go before one's former agency is not representation because the former official is not representing either of the parties to the mediation before the agency.[32]

What Is Considered a Former Employee's Agency?

Ambiguities often arise as to the scope of the "agency" before which the former employee cannot appear. Ambiguities in the federal revolving door laws created considerable controversy and provided an opportunity for loopholes through compartmentalization of individual agencies or departments. For example, because the Office of the President was divided into a number of agencies, former top aides of President Reagan were allowed to lobby former colleagues because they were designated as being employees of different agencies. This dubious practice was eventually resolved by legislation that prohibited the breaking up of the Executive Office of the President to separate agencies.[33]

However, current federal law still provides that a former employee may make appearances before unrelated bureaus or agencies within the same department.[34] Further, federal law gives the Office of Government Ethics authority to designate various agencies or bureaus as separate and distinct for purposes of the agency ban.[35]

New York law does not provide for any compartmentalization of agencies. However, ambiguities may nonetheless arise as to whether an employee is lobbying his former agency or department. For example, the New York Ethics Commission has held that a former executive branch employee and assistant counsel to the governor could appear before the much larger Executive Department since the Executive Chamber is not statutorily a part of the Executive Department.[36] New York also has held that an official could be considered to be an employee of more than one agency if the official performed substantial and continuous work for an agency other than the one to which he or she was officially assigned. Moreover, technical or statutory designations between agencies or bureaus are to be ignored when the official exerts substantial control beyond official lines of authority.[37] At the same time, the commission has applied the ban only to a former employee's particular office or bureau, and not to the whole department, where that office or bureau operated independently, with its own power of appointment and funding separate from that of the department.[38]

Ambiguities also arise from changes in agency structure. For instance, an employee's former agency may merge with another agency, resulting in an entirely different entity. Florida has defined "agency" as the "lowest departmental unit within which [the former official's] influence might reasonably be considered to extend."[39] The commission further sought to limit the definition of "agency" to those segments where the former official's influence would naturally extend and which the former official should be prohibited from exploiting after leaving state employment.[40] The Florida Commission on Ethics held that the restricted agency was not the entire entity, as it stood post-merger. Rather, the former employee was restricted only from the department of the new agency with which he or she worked before the merger.[41] The federal Office of Government Ethics has held that the one-year ban does not apply at all to postemployment appearances of former employees of the Civil Aeronautics Board (CAB) before the Department of Transportation (DOT), even though CAB had been merged into DOT.[42] New York has taken a case-by-case approach. In one case, where two agencies were entirely merged and their staffs intermingled, employees from both predecessor agencies were barred from appearing before the entire merged entity.[43] However, where the functions of two merged agencies were distinct, the commission limited the ban on a former official to only the types of matters that would have been submitted to the official's former agency.[44]

Because the goal of the one- and two-year bans is to reduce the former employee's influence with the employee's own agency, these bans generally do not apply to appearances before a court.[45] Thus, former employees are generally free to litigate against their former agency in a court of law and to enter into settlement discussions with their former agency.[46] It should be noted, however, that with regard to matters with which a former employee was personally involved, employees are generally prohibited from any involvement in that matter on behalf of a private entity, even in a court of law. See discussion of the matter ban on pages 138–141.

Applicability to Partners and Associates of Former Employees

An important consideration for any lawyer leaving government service is whether any ban on future government work would apply to other members of the former employee's new firm.

Generally, most states and the federal government have construed postemployment statutes to be limited solely to the individual lawyer and not to apply to the entire firm.[47] It should be noted, however, that the rule may very well be different with regard to appearances on particular matters with which the lawyer was involved during government service.[48] See discussion of the matter ban on pages 138–141.

In this area as well, New York has taken a relatively strict stand. Although the New York statute does not prohibit a former employee's firm from appearing before that employee's former agency, the ethics commission has emphasized that if the firm is "so identified with the individual, for example, [that it] utilizes his name as its organizational name or he is the only principal [of the entity]," then all appearances would be prohibited under New York's statute.[49] Moreover, if a former government employee's partner or associate appears before that former employee's agency, that employee may not receive any of the "net revenue" derived from that representation.[50]

If a former employee's new role includes responsibility over all aspects of the entity with which he or she is employed, he or she may not avoid the ban by delegating responsibilities to others. Thus, the Ohio Ethics Commission prohibited a member of that state's public utilities commission from becoming the consumer counsel, who must appear before that board. The employee could not avoid the ban by delegating such matters to a subordinate because the counsel would be required by law to be involved in all matters before the agency.[51]

Applicability of the Ban to Representation of, or Further Employment with, the Government

A recurring issue in the interpretation of the various states' statutes is the question of whether the agency ban applies to service on behalf of another government entity. The federal government allows bureau officers to contact their former agency on behalf of the U.S. government.[52] New York also excludes from the reach of the statute former officials who appear before their former agencies carrying out official duties as elected officers or employees of any other level of government.[53] However, a former state employee who is a paid consultant to a municipality or is retained as a paid private lawyer by the municipality is not exempt from the ban.[54] Other states have broader provisions allowing any representative activities on behalf of other governments.[55]

In what appears to be a particularly strict interpretation of the statute, the New York State Ethics Commission has held that an agency may not even hire its own former employee as a consultant for a period of two years after public service.[56] Obviously, in such cases, former employees are not attempting to use their influence with the agency on behalf of a private entity. The only private gain would be their own compensation, which would not appear to be significantly different from their receipt of a salary as public officials. Nonetheless, the commission apparently was concerned about sweetheart deals between an agency and its former officials wherein the employee would leave the agency and then perform the same work at a much higher rate of pay. Ohio, in contrast, expressly allows a former public official to be retained by, or to represent, the agency with which he or she was previously employed.[57]

The New York City Conflicts of Interest Board has allowed a former employee to be retained by the employee's agency as a consultant, but refused to allow a private firm that hired the former government official from an agency to be retained by the agency for the purpose of utilizing the services of the former public official. In such a case, the board concluded, the firm would be obtaining a contract solely by virtue of its hiring of a former government employee.[58] The federal Office of Government Ethics, in contrast, has held that a former employee's new employer could be retained for the purpose of employing the former official to complete work on a manual for the employee's former agency. The office found that none of the concerns that motivated Congress to pass the revolving door rules were implicated.[59]

A closely related question is whether or not the prohibition on postemployment appearances before one's former agency applies to representation of employees as a union or collective bargaining representative. In an advisory opinion, the New York City Conflicts of Interest Board held that the city's postemployment restrictions technically applied to a former employee who, while employed with the agency, acted as the union representative and who, upon leaving government service, continued to act as a union representative in collective bargaining with the former agency. Nonetheless, the board, finding that the former employee's continued representation as a union official did not create a conflict of interest, granted a waiver from the provisions of the statute.[60]

THE BAN ON INVOLVEMENT IN MATTERS HANDLED WHILE IN GOVERNMENT (THE "MATTER BAN")

Many states, localities, and the federal government have a ban that prohibits former employees from becoming involved in any matter with which they had a personal involvement during their employment.[61] It differs from the agency ban in two important respects. First, the ban usually prohibits *any* post-government involvement in any matter handled while in government. It is not limited to appearances before the employee's former agency.[62] It usually prohibits appearances before all agencies, courts, and the legislature.[63] Second, the ban is often, but not always, of indefinite, or "lifetime," duration.[64] The reason for the ban is obvious: a government official, having represented the government on a particular matter, should not be able to "switch sides" and represent a private party in the same matter. The danger that confidential information gained as a public employee could be used in such situations for private advantage is manifest. Indeed, former government lawyers who work in states having relatively shorter matter bans or no bans at all should be aware that professional codes of responsibility severely restrict their ability to represent a private client on matters handled while in government. See the discussion of professional codes of responsibility that follows. Moreover, the Ohio Ethics Commission, in applying that state's matter ban, advised a former public servant that, although the disqualification applied only for a period of 12 months, "disqualifying yourself from participation in such matters beyond the twelve-month period imposed by [the statute] would help to avoid an appearance of impropriety."[65]

South Carolina imposes a one-year prohibition on representation of clients by former public employees before their former agency or department with regard to matters on which the official or employee directly and substantially participated during his or her public employment.[66]

Some governments, such as the federal government and the California state government, apply the ban only to matters in which the respective government has a direct or substantial interest.[67] Thus, former federal employees can be involved in litigation relating to matters that they worked on in the government if their former agency had no interest in the litigation.[68] The New York state government, on the other hand, has no such limitation, and the subject matter ban applies to all matters with which the former attorney had direct personal involvement.[69]

How Involved Must the Employee Have Been in the Matter?

The federal government imposes a permanent restriction on representation of a particular matter in which the former employee participated substantially while in government service. Substantial participation "requires more than official responsibility, knowledge, perfunctory involvement, or involvement on an administrative or peripheral issue."[70] The statute requires a direct relationship and "contemplates a responsibility requiring the official to become personally involved to an important, material degree, in the investigative or deliberative processes."[71] However, federal law also imposes a two-year ban on post-government involvement in any matter that a former government employee had "under his or her official responsibility" within a year of his or her termination.[72]

In New York, the statute applies to any matter that the employee was directly concerned with and in which he personally participated.[73] Personal participation includes participation through "decision, approval, recommendation, investigation or other similar activities."[74] "[M]ere acquaintance with or knowledge of a fact or circumstance is insufficient to trigger the lifetime bar."[75] Advisory opinions have held that one's mere presence in a room when a particular matter is discussed does not constitute personal participation[76] and suggested that the former official must have had some official role in effecting the outcome of the matter.[77] However, the New York State Ethics Commission has also taken the position that a very senior official, such as an agency head, will be deemed to have participated personally in major policy decisions made by his or her close, senior staff, even though he or she actually had no personal involvement.[78] Ohio includes within the term *personal participation* the supervision or general oversight of other personnel and their work on the particular matter.[79]

What Postemployment Activities Are Covered?

The previous section dealt with the question of how involved with a matter the former employee had to be while in government for the ban to apply. This subsection deals with the degree of *postemployment* involvement necessary for the ban to apply. As with the agency ban, New York state prohibits the former employee from appearing or communicating before any state agency on the matter or receiving compensation for any services related to the matter.[80]

New York City has taken a similar view. That city's one-year ban on appearances before an official's former agency prohibits only communications "for compensation" with the agency. In contrast, the city's matter ban applies to a former official's appearance "whether paid or unpaid" before the agency, or the receipt of compensation "for *any* services rendered" in relation to the matter in which the party was formerly involved as a public official.[81] The federal government, in contrast, bans only representation before agencies or courts of the United States and does not prohibit behind-the-scenes activities.[82]

Ohio has interpreted its regulations in a similar way. To "[r]epresent a client or act in a representative capacity" has been interpreted to mean any written or oral communication, formal or informal, including preparation of communications even if the former officer does not sign the communication.[83] It includes both formal advocacy and informal lobbying. However, if the former officer "merely consulted with the attorneys or other personnel who prepared the documents, letters, or notes [which were submitted to the agency] the prohibition would not apply."[84]

How Is "Matter" Defined?

A significant question of interpretation that arises in these regulations is the definition of the term "matter." Matter can include almost any action, including administrative proceedings, legislation, rule promulgation, negotiation, or contracts. Many states, such as Ohio, however, draw a distinction between cases, proceedings, and applications, which are included in the ban, and the promulgation of rules, regulations, and statutes, which are not.[85] A discrete administrative proceeding or contract is generally of limited duration, and the issues raised are usually applicable only to the parties before the agency. It is appropriate in such circumstances to prohibit a former public official from becoming involved in *that* proceeding or application at any time after leaving public service. A statute, rule, or regulation, in contrast, is generally applicable to a wide class of parties and individuals, and it seems unreasonable and unduly burdensome to prohibit a former employee from having any involvement with a particular law, rule, or regulation for the rest of his or her professional career.

The New York City Charter does not, by its terms, include legislation within the scope of the matter ban.[86] However, the Conflicts of Interest Board has interpreted the provision to include legislation with which a former employee has been involved, but only during the particular legislative session. Once the session has ended and a similar or exact bill is introduced in a subsequent session, the new bill would be considered a different matter, and the former employee would be free to become involved in that legislation in a private capacity.[87]

In contrast, the New York State Ethics Commission has taken the position that legislation can constitute a matter and that bills introduced in the same or even different legislative sessions may constitute the same matter if they affect the same or substantially the same population or issues.[88] "This can be true even when the form in which the issue is presented is not identical."[89] Additionally, the commission has held that a former government employee involved in development of legislation was barred upon leaving state service from any involvement in the promulgation of regulations based upon that legislation.[90] Indeed, the commission has gone so far as to caution a former government employee who was involved in drafting legislation relating to the personal income tax to refrain from any postemployment involvement in any legislation involving the income tax without first seeking approval from the commission on a case-by-case basis.[91]

The federal Office of Government Ethics has held that legislation can be a matter for purposes of section 207(a), the federal matter ban, but that former employees would rarely be barred from appearing before the government on that same legislation because section 207(a) also requires that the former official's involvement with legislation, while in the government, has to "involve a particular party or parties."[92] The office found that such a situation would usually arise only in the context of private relief bills or bills establishing grant programs "for which only one known organization was eligible."[93]

In the area of contracts, the matter ban usually will apply to any subsequent involvement with the contract, including providing services under that contract or negotiating any change in the contract.[94] Moreover, for purposes of the ban, a contract remains the same matter (and is therefore subject to the ban), even though it may have been amended in a number of respects or assigned to a new party.[95]

To determine whether two matters are in fact the same matter, the federal Office of Government Ethics looks at whether the matters "involve the same basic facts, the same or related parties, related issues . . . [and the] same confidential information."[96] They also look at the amount of time elapsed and the continuing existence of an important federal interest.[97]

RESTRICTING THE USE OF CONFIDENTIAL INFORMATION

The third type of revolving door statute prohibits the use of confidential information that is gained during the course of public employment for an employee's personal benefit or gain. For example, Florida's statute provides that a public employee cannot disclose or use "information not available to members of the general public . . . for his or her personal gain or benefit."[98] These statutes not only prohibit the use of information for the former employee's own benefit but also prohibit its use for the gain of any other person, including a relative, business associate, friend, or acquaintance. For example, South Carolina prohibits public officials from using or disclosing "confidential information gained in the course of or by reason of his official responsibilities in a way that would affect an economic interest held by him, a member of his immediate family, an individual with whom he is associated, or a business with which he is associated."[99] Texas bans state employees from accepting employment or business or professional activities that an employee "might reasonably expect would require or induce . . . the employee to disclose confidential information acquired by reason of the official position."[100]

A "gain" or "benefit" can include different things, such as selling information to an interested party, or using this information to acquire future clients or to acquire a contract. Additionally, an employee could benefit by using his position as a public employee to seek potential employment offers, as discussed in the next section.

USING ONE'S PUBLIC POSITION TO OBTAIN PRIVATE EMPLOYMENT

Many states and municipalities expressly prohibit a public officer or employee from accepting or soliciting, or using one's position to secure, a promise of future employment with any party that is regulated by, doing business with, seeking to do business with, or having any matters before the agency that the public official serves, unless the public officer withdraws from the matters affecting the interest of that party.[101] South Carolina prohibits public officials or employees who are participating directly in a procurement from "resign[ing] and accept[ing] employment with a person contracting with the governmental body if the contract falls or would fall under the public official's . . . or public employee's official responsibilities."[102] Texas prohibits state officers and employees from accepting employment or compensation "that could reasonably be expected to impair the officer's or employee's independence of judgment in the performance of the officer's or employee's official duties."[103]

If a federal employee hires a search firm to secure future employment, the employee must remove himself or herself from all matters involving the financial interest of any prospective employer whom the employee knows has been contacted by the search firm. The Office of Government Ethics has declined to endorse a procedure whereby the search firm "screens" the employee from any knowledge of the initial contacts made by the firm. The office noted that the employee may have constructive knowledge of which firms are contacted, and that, in any event, the procedure creates an appearance of impropriety.[104]

A corollary provision is a ban on a former public official profiting from any public contract that is authorized by the official or by a body of which he or she was a member while in public employment.[105] To that end, Idaho provides that "members of the legislature, state, county, city, district and precinct officers, must not be interested in any contract made by them in their official capacity, or by any body or board of which they are members."[106] However, an Idaho public officer is not deemed to be "interested in a contract," if he or she only has a "remote interest" in the contract and if that interest is disclosed to and authorized or approved by the body of which the person is a member.[107] A "remote interest" is defined as (1) that of a non-salaried officer of a nonprofit corporation; (2) that of an employee or agent of a contracting party where the compensation of such employee or agent consists entirely of fixed wages or salary; (3) that of a landlord or tenant of a contracting party; or (4) that of a holder of less than one percent of the shares of a corporation or cooperative which is a contracting party.[108] The Ohio Ethics Commission interpreted this provision to prohibit a former agency lawyer from recommending that the agency hire private counsel, and then obtaining a position as that private counsel.[109] Similarly, a former official could not, for a period of one year, assume the directorship of an entity that received a substantial grant approved by the former official.[110] Ohio, however, allows a former public official to obtain a contract authorized while he or she was in office, if the contract is let by competitive bidding and the public official made the lowest and best bid.[111]

THE LIMITATIONS IMPOSED BY ABA MODEL RULES OF PROFESSIONAL CONDUCT

Rule 1.11 of the ABA Model Rules of Professional Conduct expressly prohibits a lawyer from representing a private client in connection with a matter in which the lawyer participated "personally and substantially" as a public officer or employee, unless the government agency expressly consents to such representation. Moreover, no lawyer in a firm with which that lawyer is associated may undertake or continue representation of such a matter unless the disqualified attorney is screened from any participation in the matter and written notice is given to the government agency so that the agency can ascertain whether there has been full compliance with this rule.[112] The lawyer is also barred from receiving any compensation from the firm for such work, even if performed by others. This requirement is necessary to avoid disqualification of the other lawyers in the firm.[113] Similar prohibitions are contained in the New York Rules of Professional Conduct.[114]

The Model Rules also prohibit any lawyer who has obtained confidential information about a person, acquired while the lawyer was in public service, from representing a private client whose interests are adverse to that person in any matter in which the information could be used to a material disadvantage to that person.[115] Furthermore, the law firm with which that lawyer is associated is prohibited from such representation unless the disqualified lawyer is screened from participation and receives no fee from such representation.[116]

Similarly, the rules prohibit a lawyer who is in public service from participating in a matter in which the lawyer participated personally and substantially while in private practice or nongovernment employment unless "the appropriate government agency gives its informed consent confirmed in writing."[117]

Finally, the rules also prohibit any government lawyer from negotiating for private employment with any person who is involved as a party or as a lawyer for a party in a matter in which the lawyer is participating personally and substantially.[118]

CONCLUSION

As detailed earlier, a substantial body of law governing postemployment restrictions on government employees has built up over time. These statutes and rules are important to both maintain the integrity of government employees and the public's faith in the fair and impartial operation of government. It is imperative that government employees understand their continuing obligations under these laws so as to avoid any violations or appearances of impropriety.

NOTES

* Michael Donaldson updated and revised the chapter both in 2007 and for the current version.

** Benjamin Stearns updated and revised the current version of this chapter.

*** George F. Carpinello originally authored this chapter as it was published in the first edition in 1999. Mr. Carpinello took no part in the update and revision of the current version of the chapter.

1. *See, e.g.*, New York City Conflicts of Interest Board Advisory Op. No. 95-1 (the purpose of postemployment restrictions is, "among other things, to prevent former public servants from exploiting public office for personal gain, subordinating the interests of the City to those of a prospective employer, or exerting undue influence on government decision-making"). *See also* Fla. Advisory Op. CEO 91-49 (postemployment restriction designed to "prevent influence peddling and the use of public office to create opportunities for personal profit once officials leave office"); N.Y.S. Formal Ethics Op. 95-15 (the purpose of the revolving door provision is to "preclude the possibility that a former State employee may leverage his or her knowledge, experience and contacts gained in State service to his or her advantage or to that of a client, thereby securing unwarranted privileges, consideration or action").

2. N.Y. Pub. Off. Law § 73(8)(a)(i); Fla. Stat. § 112.313(9)(a)3. *See also* La. Rev. Stat. § 42:1121(B).

3. 18 U.S.C. § 207(c)–(d). This provision applies to federal employees as specified in 5 U.S.C. § 5312-16, which include, generally, the numerous federal secretaries and deputy secretaries (of state, etc.), the chairpersons of the federal commissions, directors and members of federal boards, and other more specific executive positions.

4. For similar statutes in Arkansas, Indiana, California, and Hawaii, *see* Ark. Code Ann. § 19-11-709(b)(2); Ind. Code Ann. § 4-2-6-11(b)(3); Cal. Gov't Code § 87406(c); Haw. Rev. Stat. § 84-18(c).

5. 18 U.S.C. § 216.

6. Ohio Rev. Code § 102.99.

7. N.Y. Pub. Off. Law § 73(18).

8. *Id.* § 73(8)(b)(i).

9. Fla. Stat. § 112.313(9)(a)6.

10. 18 U.S.C. § 207(e).

11. N.Y. Pub. Off. Law § 73(8)(a)(iii).

12. Cal. Gov't Code § 87406(b). *See also* Haw. Rev. Stat. § 84-18(b) (Hawaii prohibits lobbying for one year).

13. Fla. Stat. § 112.313(9)(a)3.

14. Tex. Gov't Code § 572.052(a).

15. N.Y. Pub. Off. Law § 73(8)(a)(iii).

16. N.Y. Comp. Codes R. & Regs. tit. 22 § 16.1.

17. *See, e.g.*, U.S. Court of Appeals, First Circuit, Local Rules, Rule 46(e) (a law clerk may not "appear at the counsel table or on brief in connection with any case heard during a period of one year following separation from service with the court"), https://www.ca1.uscourts.gov/sites/ca1/files/rulebook.pdf; Missouri Supreme Court Rules, Rule 82.05(a) (a former law clerk "shall not appear at counsel table or sign any filing in any case before this Court for a period of six months after leaving this Court's employment"), http://www.courts.mo.gov/courts/ClerkHandbooksP2RulesOnly.nsf/c0c6ffa99df4993f86256ba50057dcb8/930d9ef4f01552f786256ca6005215be?OpenDocument.

18. *See, e.g.*, U.S. Court of Appeals, First Circuit, Local Rule 46(e); U.S. District Court for the District of Columbia, Local Rule 83.5, https://www.dcd.uscourts.gov/sites/dcd/files/LocalRulesJuly_2019.pdf; U.S. District Court for the Western District of Missouri, Local Rule 83.1(a), https://www.mow.uscourts.gov/sites/mow/files/Local_Rules.pdf.

19. 18 U.S.C. § 207(c)(1).

20. *Id. See also* OGE Inf. Adv. Letter 81-35.
21. R.I. Gen. Laws § 36-14-5(e).
22. N.Y.C. Charter ch. 68 §§ 2601(4), 2604(d)(4), http://public.leginfo.state.ny.us/menuf.cgi (follow the "Laws of New York" link, then follow the "New York City Charter" link).
23. Wis. Stat. § 19.45(8)(a).
24. N.Y. Pub. Off. Law § 73(8)(a)(i).
25. *See* N.Y.S. Formal Ethics Op. 89-7. New York goes so far as to prohibit a former employee from appearing or working on a matter before an agency that involves or seeks input from the former employee's agency. *See id.* However, where the former employee has no reason to know or anticipate that his or her former agency will be involved, and there is no statute, law, or policy requiring involvement, there is no violation of the statute. *Id.*
26. *See* N.Y.S. Formal Ethics Op. 94-6.
27. *See* N.Y.S. Formal Ethics Ops. 94-18, 90-3.
28. *See* N.Y.S. Formal Ethics Op. 94-6.
29. *See* N.Y.S. Formal Ethics Op. 89-7.
30. *See* Fla. Stat. §§ 112.312(22), 112.313(9).
31. Fla. Advisory Op. CEO 91-49.
32. *Id.*
33. *See* 18 U.S.C. § 207(h)(2) (specifically providing that "no agency or bureau within the Executive Office of the President may be designated . . . as a separate department or agency"). This provision was added by Public Law 101-194, the Ethics Reform Act of 1989.
34. *See* 18 U.S.C. § 207(h).
35. *Id.*
36. N.Y.S. Formal Ethics Op. 89-3.
37. N.Y.S. Formal Ethics Op. 95-33.
38. N.Y.S. Formal Ethics Op. 95-1.
39. Fla. Advisory Op. CEO 91-49.
40. Fla. Advisory Op. CEO 94-029.
41. Fla. Advisory Op. CEO 02-12.
42. OGE Inf. Adv. Letter 85-5.
43. N.Y.S. Formal Ethics Op. 93-11.
44. N.Y.S. Formal Ethics Op. 96-7.
45. *See, e.g.,* Ohio Ethics Op. 93-014, 87-001; R.I. Gen. Laws Ann. § 36-14-5(e)(4).
46. *See* N.Y.S. Formal Ethics Op. 95-28.
47. *See, e.g.,* N.Y.S. Formal Ethics Op. 90-14.
48. *See* Cal. Ethics Op. 1993-128.
49. N.Y.S. Formal Ethics Op. 89-12. *See also* N.Y.S. Formal Ethics Ops. 94-6, 90-14.
50. N.Y.S. Formal Ethics Ops. 94-6, 90-14.
51. Ohio Ethics Op. 93-011.
52. 18 U.S.C. § 207(j)(1)(a); *see* OGE Inf. Adv. Letter 91-29.
53. N.Y. Pub. Off. Law §§ 73(7)(h), (8)(e).
54. N.Y.S. Formal Ethics Op. 89-7; *see also* N.Y.S. Formal Ethics Op. 93-15 (matter ban does not apply to a lawyer who works for a municipality pro bono).
55. *See, e.g.,* Cal. Gov't Code § 87406(e) (the restrictions shall not apply to an employee "of another state agency, board, or commission if the appearance or communication is for the purpose of influencing legislative or administrative action on behalf of the state agency"); N.Y.C. Charter ch. 68 § 2604(d)(6) (the ban does not apply to "positions with or representation on behalf of any local, state or federal agency").
56. N.Y.S. Formal Ethics Ops. 89-9, 91-9. The commission has held, however, that the former employee may serve in an unpaid capacity. N.Y.S. Formal Ethics Op. 93-3.
57. Ohio Rev. Code § 102.03(A)(6); *see* Ohio Ethics Ops. 92-005, 91-009, 91-005.
58. N.Y.C. Conflicts of Interest Board Advisory Op. No. 95-1. Similarly, the New York State Ethics Commission has held that an agency cannot "outsource" work by hiring private companies that, in turn, hire recently departed former employees from the agency. N.Y.S.

Formal Ethics Op. 95-31. The New York legislature provided some relief from this ban by allowing temporary workers who perform some clerical duties to work for an outsource firm within two years of their departure. N.Y. Pub. Off. Law § 73(8)(f).

59. OGE Inf. Adv. Letter 81-29 (interpreting the federal "matter" ban).

60. N.Y.C. Conflicts of Interest Board Advisory Op. 96-1. *See also* N.Y. Pub. Off. Law § 78(7)(e).

61. *See, e.g.*, 18 U.S.C. § 207(a)(1); Ark. Code Ann. § 19-11-709(b)(1); Cal. Gov't Code § 87401; N.Y. Pub. Off. Law § 73(8)(a)(ii); Ohio Rev. Code § 102.03(A)(1); L.A. Mun. Code § 49.5.13(B).

62. *See, e.g.*, 18 U.S.C. § 207(a)(1), (2); Ohio Rev. Code § 102.01(C) (including courts within the definition of "agency"); Ohio Ethics Op. 87-001 (defining representation as any formal or informal appearance before any public agency); N.Y. Pub. Off. Law § 73(8)(a)(ii); N.Y.S. Formal Ethics Op. 93-13 (ban applies to involvement "anywhere," including appearances before Congress).

63. *See, e.g.*, N.Y.S. Formal Ethics Op. 93-13, where the New York Ethics Commission held that the state's law would prohibit a former state official who, as an official, lobbied Congress for legislation aiding businesses converting from defense work, from lobbying Congress on behalf of those businesses to amend that legislation. In the case before it, however, the commission found that the employee was not barred because he was not sufficiently involved in the matter while working for the state.

64. For examples of lifetime bans, *see, e.g.*, 18 U.S.C. § 207(a)(1); Mass. Gen. Laws Ann. ch. 268A § 5(a); Conn. Gen. Stat. § 1-84b(a); N.Y. Pub. Off. Law § 73(8)(a)(ii); N.Y.C. Charter ch. 68 § 2604(d)(4). For examples of shorter bans, *see, e.g.*, Ala. Code 36-25-13(g) (two years); Del. Code Ann. tit. 29 § 5805(d) (two years); La. Rev. Stat. § 42:1121(B)(1) (two years); Ohio Rev. Code 102.03(A)(1) (one year).

65. Ohio Ethics Op. 92-005.

66. S.C. Code § 8-13-755.

67. 18 U.S.C. § 207(a)(1); Cal. Gov't Code § 87401. *See also* Ala. Code § 36-25-13 (state must be a party or have a direct and substantial interest).

68. *See* OGE Inf. Adv. Letter 82-2.

69. *See* N.Y. Pub. Off. Law § 73(8)(a)(ii).

70. United States v. Josten, 1989 WL 112310, at *3 (N.D. Ill.1989).

71. *Id.*

72. 18 U.S.C. § 207(a)(2)(B).

73. N.Y. Pub. Off. Law § 73(8)(a)(ii).

74. N.Y.C. Conflicts of Interest Board Advisory Op. 96-7.

75. N.Y.S. Formal Ethics Op. 90-16. *See also* N.Y.S. Formal Ethics Op. 89-3.

76. N.Y.S. Formal Ethics Op. 95-7.

77. N.Y.S. Formal Ethics Op. 95-16.

78. N.Y.S. Formal Ethics Op. 92-20.

79. Ohio Ethics Ops. 93-001, 91-009, 91-005.

80. N.Y. Pub. Off. Law § 73(8)(a)(ii).

81. *Compare* N.Y.C. Charter ch. 68 §§ 2604(d)(2), 2601(4) *with* 2604(d)(4) (emphasis added).

82. 18 U.S.C. § 207(c); *see* OGE Inf. Adv. Letter 91-29.

83. Ohio Ethics Op. 86-001.

84. *Id.*

85. *See, e.g.*, Ohio Rev. Code § 102.03(A)(5); *see also* Ohio Ethics Op. 91-009.

86. N.Y.C. Charter ch. 68 § 2604(d)(4).

87. N.Y.C. Conflicts of Interest Board Advisory Op. No. 95-23.

88. N.Y.S. Formal Ethics Op. 92-20.

89. *Id.* However, each year's budget is a separate matter as is each separate application for a rate increase by the same utility. N.Y.S. Formal Ethics Op. 95-32.

90. N.Y.S. Formal Ethics Op. 93-2.

91. N.Y.S. Formal Ethics Op. 94-6.

92. OGE Inf. Adv. Letter 87-3.
93. *Id.*
94. *See generally* Ohio Ethics Op. 89-009.
95. *See* OGE Inf. Adv. Letter 91-24.
96. *Id.*
97. *Id.*
98. Fla. Stat. § 112.313(8). *See also* R.I. Gen. Laws § 36-14-5; Ohio Rev. Code § 102.03(B); N.Y.C. Charter ch. 68 § 2604(d)(5).
99. S.C. Code § 8-13-725(A).
100. Tex. Gov't Code § 572.051(a)(2).
101. *See, e.g.*, 18 U.S.C. § 208 (officer or employee cannot participate in matter involving the financial interest of an entity with which the employee "is negotiating or has any arrangement concerning prospective employment"); Fla. Stat. § 112.313(2); Ohio Rev. Code § 102.03(D) ("no public official or employee shall solicit or accept anything of value"); Ohio Advisory Ops. 82-002, 87-004, 89-010; N.Y.C. Charter ch. 68 § 2604(d)(1) ("no public servant shall solicit, negotiate for or accept any position . . . with any person or firm who or which is involved in a particular matter with the city"); R.I. Gen. Laws § 36-14-5(g). *But see* Ark. Code Ann. § 19-11-709(e)(1) ("this section is not intended to preclude a former employee from accepting employment with private industry solely because his or her employer is a contractor with this state").
102. S.C. Code § 8-13-760.
103. Tex. Gov't Code § 572.051(a)(3)
104. OGE Inf. Adv. Letter 92-17.
105. *See, e.g.*, Ohio Rev. Code § 2921.42(A)(3).
106. Idaho Code § 74-501.
107. *Id.* § 74-502(1).
108. *Id.*
109. Ohio Ethics Op. 92-005.
110. Ohio Ethics Op. 87-004.
111. Ohio Rev. Code § 2921.42(A)(3).
112. Valid screening requires that the former employee (1) receives no part of the compensation from the matter and (2) provides prompt, written notice to the appropriate agency. Model Rules of Pro. Conduct r. 1.11; *see also* Fla. Advisory Op. CEO 72-41.
113. Although a lawyer is prohibited from receiving a fee from such representation, the comment to the rule explains that a lawyer is not prohibited from receiving a salary or a partnership share "established by prior independent agreement." The rule only prohibits a lawyer from receiving a fee that is directly related to the matter from which the lawyer is disqualified. Model Rules of Pro. Conduct r. 1.11, cmt. 6.
114. *See* N.Y. Rules of Pro. Conduct r. 1.11; *see also* Cal. Bus. & Prof. Code § 6131(b), which makes it a misdemeanor for a current or former prosecutor, after having aided in the prosecution of any matter, to directly or indirectly advise in relation to or take any part in the defense of that matter. In interpreting this provision, the California State Bar concluded that a former district attorney could join a law firm that was retained to represent a defendant who was prosecuted by the former district attorney as long as the firm established an elaborate screening procedure to assure that the district attorney was screened from any involvement in the defense. Cal. Ethics Op. No. 93-128.
115. Model Rule of Pro. Conduct 1.11(c).
116. *Id. See generally* Armstrong v. McAlpin, 625 F.2d 433 (2d Cir. 1980) *en banc vacated on other grounds*, 449 U.S. 1106 (1981).
117. Model Rules of Pro. Resp. 1.11(d)(2)(i).
118. Model Rules of Pro. Resp. 1.11(d)(2)(ii).

CHAPTER 9

Considering Ethics at the Local Government Level

Mark Davies[1]

> This chapter offers practical insights for municipal lawyers faced with drafting local ethics laws. A comprehensive discussion of over a dozen issues that may be appropriately addressed in an ethics law is provided, as well as references to how different jurisdictions have chosen to legislate ethics guidance for their officers and employees.

INTRODUCTION

A local government ethics law is a municipal official's best friend and a private citizen's greatest ally.[2] It tells the official what the rules are and how to avoid breaking them. It protects the official against unjustified accusations of ethical impropriety. It promotes a more ethical government.[3]

The purpose of a municipal ethics law lies in promoting both the reality and the perception of integrity in local government by preventing unethical conduct *before* it occurs. These laws thus seek:

1. To provide ethics guidance to the municipality's officials;
2. To provide reassurance to the public that their public servants are acting in the best interests of the community; and
3. To encourage private citizens to participate in public service.

A municipal ethics law that does not meet these standards is worthless. Indeed, it is worse than worthless because it gives officials a false sense of comfort and the public a false sense of confidence. Such a law will utterly fail to meet the expectations it raises and will consequently create only bitterness and disillusionment.

Underlying the threefold purpose of a municipal ethics law are several assumptions. First and foremost, municipal ethics laws assume that the vast majority of municipal officials are honest and want to do the right thing. In the experience of the principal author of this chapter, actual corruption at the local level is relatively rare. It happens, but far less often than people think.

Second, it is far better to prevent unethical conduct from occurring in the first place than to punish it after it occurs. Once tolled, the ethics bell can never be unrung. Once the ethics violation occurs, the damage is done and the public loses just that much more confidence in the integrity of government. In the current political climate, where politicians and public servants rank somewhat below used car salesmen and carriers of loathsome diseases, even the slightest such loss hurts.

Third, local government differs in many respects from state government, and the locality's ethics law must reflect those differences. The geographic and subject matter jurisdiction of local government is far more restricted than that of state government. Thus, restrictions or disclosure requirements that appear wise at the state level may make no sense at the local level. So, too, municipal officials often have less access than their state counterparts to sophisticated legal counsel. Thus, a code of ethics written in lay terms becomes critical. Most importantly, local government, unlike state government, depends heavily on volunteers. Zoning board members, planning board members, ethics board members, and even many municipal legislators are often unpaid or only minimally paid. To subject these volunteers to onerous financial disclosure and ethics requirements will drive good people out of municipal government.

Fourth, "ethics laws" do not really regulate ethics. They regulate, primarily, financial conflicts of interest. A school superintendent who spends $10,000 to install a bathroom in his office while his students lack textbooks may have acted "unethically," but he has probably not, on those facts alone, violated any "ethics law." If, on the other hand, he spends the $10,000 to buy textbooks from his brother, he will have violated most municipal codes of ethics.

Fifth, ethics laws must be largely self-enforcing—by the official, by peer pressure, by whistleblowers, by the media, and by the public. Ethics boards must view their enforcement actions largely as educational tools.

These purposes and assumptions dictate the content and structure of a good municipal ethics law. Specifically, such a law should be:

1. *Clear and concise.* A municipal officer or employee cannot obey an ethics law unless he or she can understand it. Therefore, it must be intelligible to the lay person without the need to consult lawyers or plain language guides.
2. *Comprehensive.* An ethics law riddled with gaps provides a trap for the unwary official and a source of endless frustration for private citizens.
3. *Bright-line*, whenever possible. Officials need a beacon in the night, not a penlight in the fog. The work of a three-handed lawyer (on the one hand this, on the other hand that, on the third hand something else) may make a great law school exam, but it makes a lousy ethics law.
4. *Flexible.* Ethics laws regulate a rather vague area of human endeavor and will inevitably, albeit only occasionally, produce inequitable results. Some mechanism, such as waivers by a local ethics board, must exist to address those problems.

5. *Sensible*. Above all, a municipal ethics law must make sense—to the public official, to the media, and to the public. Officials may well refuse to obey, or obey only grudgingly, an ethics law that does not make sense to them.

A local ethics law should thus focus less on punishment than on prevention, and less on prohibition than on disclosure and recusal. It must also be easy and inexpensive to administer and enforce. It must establish an independent ethics board that, while possessing the power to investigate and punish, views its primary mandate as giving quick advice and providing comprehensive ethics training and education.

Accordingly, a good ethics laws rests upon three pillars:

1. A code of ethics
2. Disclosure
3. Administration—ethics training, legal advice, disclosure, and enforcement—by an independent ethics board

Unfortunately, few municipal ethics laws in this country meet these standards. Most are deficient (often seriously deficient) in one respect or another. Too often, in developing municipal ethics laws, state or local governments appear simply to have thrown a bunch of provisions against the wall and kept what sticks. Knee-jerk reactions to public pressure generated by scandal have often prevailed over calm analyses of the necessity, purpose, and contents of an ethics program. Applying a corollary to Occam's razor, government should include in an ethics law the fewest and simplest provisions that achieve the law's goals. The enactors should thus first determine those goals and then measure every provision of the proposed ethics law against that yardstick. Provisions that further the law's goals should be included. Provisions that do not should be eliminated. If in doubt, leave it out.

This chapter seeks to facilitate that process and also to lay out in a rather general way, from the municipal perspective, the contents and workings of a good ethics law—to alert the private practitioner to the types of municipal ethics provisions he or she may encounter and to guide the municipal attorney in drafting a new ethics law for his or her client. In other chapters in this book, the reader will find these topics discussed in greater detail.

SOURCES OF LOCAL GOVERNMENT ETHICS LAWS

Unfortunately for municipal officials and lawyers, ethics restrictions applicable to a municipality's officers and employees often lie scattered among a number of state and local laws. Such restrictions may be found not only in the municipality's own ethics law, and interpretative opinions of the ethics board, but also in:

1. The state constitution;
2. State statutes;

3. Local laws other than the municipality's ethics law;
4. Agency regulations; and
5. Common law.

Each of these possible sources is discussed in the sections that follow.

For example, to determine the permissibility of a gift to a Philadelphia official, one would need to consult the Pennsylvania State Ethics Act, the Standards of Conduct and Ethics in the Philadelphia Code, the Philadelphia Home Rule Charter, and Executive Order 16-92 on gifts.[4] In addition, one should examine the rules and advisory opinions of the Pennsylvania State Ethics Commission and the Philadelphia Board of Ethics, as well as any applicable case law.

State Constitutions

A few states provide municipal conflicts of interest restrictions in their state constitutions. For example, the Rhode Island Constitution pronounces that "[t]he people of the State of Rhode Island believe that public officials and employees must adhere to the highest standards of ethical conduct, . . . avoid the appearance of impropriety and not use their position for private gain or advantage."[5] In addition, the Rhode Island Constitution requires the general assembly to "establish an independent non-partisan ethics commission which shall adopt a code of ethics[,]" provides that "[a]ll elected and appointed officials and employees of state and local government, of boards, commissions and agencies shall be subject to the code of ethics[,]" and empowers the commission to remove officials from office for unethical conduct, unless they are subject to impeachment.[6]

State constitutions may also contain restrictions aimed at specific types of unethical conduct. For example, the New York State Constitution prohibits municipalities from "giv[ing] or loan[ing] any money or property to or in aid of any individual, or private corporation or association, or private undertaking."[7]

State Statutes

A number of states regulate municipal ethics by state statute. In many instances these statutes include a conflicts of interest code, a financial disclosure law, and an enforcement mechanism.[8] These state regulations may or may not contemplate supplementation by local ethics codes.[9] For example, the California Government Code requires that every agency, which includes local government agencies, adopt and promulgate a conflicts of interest code.[10] At the same time, that state law imposes certain ethics requirements on municipal officers and employees.[11]

In addition, most, if not all, states have enacted statutes regulating certain specific types of ethics problems or providing specific remedies to address certain types of unethical conduct. For example, New York State prohibits certain hiring and retention decisions from being made on the basis of political affiliations and also permits a private citizen to sue to prevent an illegal official act by a municipal officer or employee.[12]

Local Laws Other Than Ethics Laws

To regulate unethical conduct, a municipality may enact local laws distinct from a code of ethics. For example, the New York City Charter, separate and apart from its ethics code, prohibits designated officers and employees of the Department of Citywide Administrative Services involved in citywide personnel matters and members, officers, and employees of the Civil Service Commission from holding certain political party positions.[13]

Agency Regulations

Individual agencies within a municipality may impose restrictions relating to the ethical conduct of the agency's employees. For example, the police chief of the city of Syracuse (New York) promulgated rules and regulations relating to off-duty employment of police officers, and the New York City Police Department has adopted guidelines regulating the acceptance of cash rewards and personal gifts.[14] Chicago's ethics law expressly authorizes city agencies to adopt rules that are more restrictive than that law.[15]

Common Law

Wholly apart from any statutory or administrative regulations, the common law has developed certain ethics restrictions on the conduct of local government officials.[16] For example, in some states, including New York, the common law prohibits municipal officials from contracting with their own municipality. Thus, in New York, an employment contract between a town board member and the town has been held void because the common law does not recognize a contract between a municipality and its officers.[17] Similarly, "[p]ublic policy forbids the sustaining of municipal action founded upon the vote of a member of the municipal governing body in any matter before it which directly or immediately affects him individually."[18]

Courts may also sometimes use an ethics statute as a springboard for a common law ethics restriction. For example, a court may find that "[i]t is not necessary . . . that a specific provision of [an ethics statute] be violated before there can be an improper conflict of interest."[19] Attorneys should, therefore, carefully check the annotations to the applicable statutes for cases that expand upon the scope of the statutory law.

A NOTE ON PROCESS

Adopting an effective municipal ethics law, more often than not, proves a daunting process, in part because public officials often view any proposal of such a law as an attack upon their integrity, and in part because, unlike virtually every other law, an ethics law regulates the officials themselves. Discussion of the adoption process lies beyond the scope of this chapter, but the reader may wish to consult other articles by the principal author on that process.[20]

FIRST PILLAR: CODE OF ETHICS

Generally

As noted previously, the first pillar of a good municipal ethics law is a comprehensive and comprehensible code of ethics. The contents of such codes may be grouped into more than a dozen types of provisions. Each of these types is discussed here, with illustrations from various state laws regulating municipal ethics, local ethics laws, a proposed state ethics law for local governments, and a model local ethics law.[21] However, one should note four preliminary matters.

Interests versus Conduct

Some ethics codes restrict interests. Most restrict conduct. Some restrict both. Restrictions on interests usually prohibit or limit a municipal official's interests in private firms that do business with the municipality or in contracts with the municipality. Restrictions on conduct prohibit the municipal officer or employee from engaging in certain specified conduct, such as using one's municipal position for private gain or accepting a gift from someone doing business with the municipality.

Definitions

In a good ethics law, the definitions narrow the scope of the code of ethics; they never expand it. So if a municipal employee reads and obeys the code of ethics but not the definitions, the official will not violate the law. In particular, substantive ethics provisions should not be buried in definitions. Indeed, definitions should be kept to a minimum.

Unfortunately, many ethics laws contain extensive and complex definitions that set a trap for unsuspecting officials. The attorney must parse the definitions of an ethics law carefully. Words like "appear" (any communication), "interest" (employment as well as ownership), and "position" (attorneys and consultants as well as officers, directors, and employees) present particular problems.[22]

In addition, definitions may, for example, deem a municipal official to have an interest in a contract if someone with whom the municipal employee is associated has an interest in the contract. Associated persons may include relatives, employers, business associates, or corporations in which the municipal official owns stock.[23] Such definitions can significantly expand the scope of the prohibition—to an extent that may, in fact, prove unacceptable in small municipalities. For example, the Anne Arundel County (Maryland) Public Ethics law includes not only biological, adopted, and stepchildren within the definition of "child," but also includes grandchildren and foster children.[24] Attorneys must, therefore, carefully review definitions for hidden ethics restrictions.

Exclusions

Virtually every ethics code contains exclusions from its provisions. The better codes contain narrowly drafted restrictions that require only a few exclusions that are set forth in a separate section.[25] Some ethics laws, however, provide broad restrictions, often with exceptions and even exceptions to the exceptions within the ethics provision itself, supplemented by a separate section with still more exclusions. For example, New York state's conflicts of interest law for municipalities—a model of how *not* to draft an ethics law—contains a broad prohibition on municipal officials having an interest in a contract with the municipality but then sets out an exception in that provision, another exception in the definition of "interest," and then 16 further exceptions in a separate section.[26] One must question what kind of ethics law requires 18 exceptions.

Waivers

As noted previously, because ethics laws regulate a rather vague area of human endeavor, they inevitably, albeit only occasionally, produce inequitable or even irrational results. For example, a revolving door prohibition may prevent a city from placing one of its employees as the head of a nonprofit organization that provides services critical to the city. To address these types of problems, some ethics laws permit the local ethics board to grant waivers.

For example, the Rhode Island Ethics Commission may, in the case of hardship, waive the prohibition against a municipal official representing himself or herself before his or her own agency.[27] So, too, Anne Arundel County permits the county ethics commission to waive that municipality's postemployment restrictions.[28] The District of Columbia authorizes the waiver of the misuse of office provision.[29] New York City's ethics law grants broad waiver power to the city's Conflicts of Interest Board.[30]

Waiver provisions present some danger to the integrity of the ethics law because they enable an ethics board to gut the law and may engender accusations of partiality. On the other hand, the lack of a waiver power can occasionally turn an ethics law into an unintended instrument of oppression that hurts not only the individual employee but the municipality itself. For example, the principal author of this chapter was once constrained to advise a town supervisor that his town would have to truck its bulk trash to another state, at considerable expense, because, under the state ethics law, the town could not contract to dump it in the local landfill owned by a town board member. Such results make the ethics law a joke. A waiver would have prevented this absurd outcome. However, waiver power should be vested only in an independent ethics board. Ethics laws that grant waiver authority to a legislative body are misguided, for they inevitably transform the waiver process into a political football.[31] Furthermore, waivers should be granted only when a defined standard is met, such as when the waived interest or conduct "would not be in conflict with the purposes and interests" of the municipality.[32] Finally, waivers must always be public because they allow otherwise prohibited interests or conduct.

Prohibited Interests

A restriction on interests typically prohibits a municipal officer or employee from having an interest (1) in a firm or organization that does business with the officer's or employee's own municipality or municipal agency and/or (2) in a contract with the municipality. A prohibited interest in a firm or organization might arise from a position with the firm or organization or from an ownership interest in the firm or organization. A position interest would include officers, directors, employees, and perhaps even attorneys, brokers, and consultants. An ownership interest would include shareholders and partners. A municipal official might be deemed to have an interest in an entity or a municipal contract if someone with whom the official is associated has such an interest, and "associated" might include relatives, businesses, employers, and customers or clients of the municipal official.

For example, the Honolulu ethics code prohibits officers or employees of the city from acquiring a financial interest in business enterprises that the officer or employee has reason to believe may be directly involved in official action to be taken by the person.[33] Chicago's Governmental Ethics Ordinance prohibits elected officials and employees from having a financial interest, inter alia, in any contract, work, or business of the city.[34] Some ethics laws contain prohibitions on specific types of interests, such as a prohibition against municipal officials having an interest in legislation or in property before the appeals and equalization board, or having a close relative serving on the same board or commission.[35] Prohibited interest provisions are sometimes read to prohibit a municipal official from holding a second, incompatible public office, although some ethics laws specifically regulate compatibility of public offices.[36]

Interest restrictions essentially presume that merely having an interest in an entity that is doing business with the municipality, or is in a contract with the municipality, constitutes a conflict of interest. Such restrictions may place severe restraints upon the ability of municipal officers and employees to moonlight for a private company or to own private businesses. These restrictions may be unpalatable in smaller communities where such interests are virtually unavoidable. In such communities, disclosure and recusal (discussed later in this chapter) often offer the preferable alternative.

Use of Public Office for Private Gain

The rest of the ethics restrictions discussed in this section address not interests but conduct. Many ethics codes contain a general prohibition against municipal officers and employees using their official position for private gain—for themselves or for someone with whom they are associated. For example, the California Conflicts of Interest law provides:

> No public official at any level of state or local government shall make, participate in making or in any way attempt to use his official position to influence a governmental decision in which he knows or has reason to know he has a financial interest.[37]

An official would, for example, have a financial interest in a decision if it is reasonably foreseeable that the decision will have a material financial effect on a business entity in which the official is a director, officer, partner, trustee, or employee.[38] Similarly, the Anne Arundel County (Maryland) Public Ethics law provides that "[a]n employee may not intentionally use the prestige of office or public position for that employee's private gain or the gain of another."[39]

Other ethics provisions prohibit the use of public resources for private purposes. For example, the ethics law of King County (Washington) states:

> No county employee shall request, use or permit the use of county-owned vehicles, equipment, materials or other property or the expenditure of county funds for personal convenience or profit. Use or expenditure is to be restricted to such services as are available to the public generally or for such employee in the conduct of official business.[40]

Similarly, Maui prohibits county officers or employees from using county property or personnel "for other than public activity or purpose."[41] Some ethics codes, such as Cook County's, set forth blackout provisions—that is, restrictions on the use of municipal funds for newsletters, brochures, public service announcements, or promotional materials for some prescribed period before an election.[42]

A number of codes contain a general prohibition against engaging in a business or transaction, or having a financial interest, in conflict with the proper discharge of one's official duties.[43] Numerous codes also contain a prohibition against using one's office to benefit a relative.[44] San Francisco requires that each city/county agency adopt, subject to Ethics Commission approval, a statement of incompatible activities, "list[ing] those outside activities that are inconsistent, incompatible, or in conflict with the duties of the officers and employees" of the agency.[45] Some ethics codes specifically restrict voting on a matter in which one has an interest.[46] Such provisions are not without problems. A general prohibition against acting in conflict with one's official duties provides, in the absence of interpretative rules, little guidance to the official and may be insufficiently specific to support criminal or even civil penalties. Restricting the voting rights of a legislative body raises thorny separation of powers and disenfranchisement issues; unlike the executive branch, where another official almost always stands ready to step into the shoes of a recusing officer or employee, in the legislative branch, no such alternates are permissible, with the result that the voters of that legislator's district receive no representation on that issue.

Such wrinkles aside, however, ethics codes that prohibit use of public office for private gain strike at the heart of ethical impropriety. Unfortunately, many codes contain no such prohibition.

Moonlighting

In addition to restrictions on having an interest in certain businesses or in using one's position for private gain, some ethics codes specifically regulate private employment by municipal officers and employees.[47] Some of these provisions, such as those of Anne Arundel County (Maryland), are quite detailed, while others are far more general.[48] For example, Westchester County (New York) merely provides that a county officer or employee "shall not engage in, solicit, negotiate for or promise to accept private employment or render services for private interests when such employment or service creates a conflict with or impairs the proper discharge of official county duties."[49] Such general prohibitions provide little guidance to officials and should either be eliminated or supplemented, if only by specific, narrowly tailored prohibited interest provisions, as discussed previously. In addition, some ethics codes, such as that of King County (Washington), require the approval of a supervisor before an employee may undertake non-municipal employment.[50]

Appearances, Representation, and Contingent Compensation

Municipal ethics codes often prohibit the municipality's officers and employees from appearing, or representing someone, before an agency of the municipality or at least before the municipal official's own agency. For example, the Honolulu Charter provides that no elected or appointed officer or employee shall "[r]epresent private interests in any action or proceeding against the interests of the city or appear in behalf of private interests before any agency, except as otherwise provided by law."[51] That prohibition would apply even if the official does not attempt to use his or her municipal office for private gain.

Ethics codes also sometimes prohibit receipt of compensation from a private person where the compensation is contingent upon any action by the official's municipality, even if the official does not appear before the municipality.[52] Such contingent compensation agreements are thought to be fraught with potential for abuse of office.

These provisions ordinarily present little difficulty for municipal officials, at least if the provisions are narrowly drafted. But, for example, in a large municipality, a ban on appearing before any agency of the municipality may make little sense for lower-level employees who have little influence over the actions of another agency. In addition, waivers should be available in appropriate cases. For example, if a city's land use law requires the city to appoint an architect to its planning board, waivers will be necessary to permit the firm of an architect board member to appear occasionally before the board, with appropriate disclosures and recusal. Otherwise, the only architects likely to accept service on the board are those having no knowledge or involvement with architecture in the city. Finally, restrictions on a municipal official appearing before a municipal agency must permit the official to appear on his or her own behalf. For example, a zoning board member must be permitted to appear, with appropriate disclosures and recusal, before the zoning board to obtain a variance to build a deck on his or her own home. However, in such situations, the board member should, if possible, appear through someone else, such as a builder, architect, or attorney, in order to avoid appearances of impropriety and allegations that "the fix is in."

Gifts

Even the most anemic ethics laws contain limitations on the solicitation and receipt of gifts by municipal officials.[53] Often the laws also regulate receipt of honoraria[54] and travel expenses.[55] The better ethics laws provide reasonably bright-line rules. For example, Anne Arundel County's ethics law prohibits the solicitation of gifts and further provides that:

> Except as provided in subdivision (c) ["Exceptions"], an employee may not knowingly accept a gift, directly or indirectly, from any person whom the employee knows or has reason to know:
>
> (1) does or seeks to do business of any kind, regardless of amount, with the County;
>
> (2) engages in an activity that is regulated or controlled by the employee's governmental unit;
>
> (3) has a financial interest that may be substantially and materially affected, in a manner distinguishable from the public generally, by the performance or nonperformance of the employee's official duties; or
>
> (4) is a lobbyist with respect to matters within the jurisdiction of the employee.[56]

Other ethics laws contain virtually unenforceable gifts provisions prohibiting, for example, the receipt of gifts "under circumstances in which it could reasonably be inferred that the gift was intended to influence [the official or employee], or could reasonably be expected to influence him, in the performance of his official duties or was intended as a reward for any official action on his part."[57] In general, whatever the ethics law requires, municipal officials are well advised to refuse any gift from someone with whom they deal or have recently dealt as a public official.

As a general rule, ethics laws do not treat political contributions as gifts.[58] Some ethics laws separately regulate political contributions.[59] Indeed, to avoid preemption and First Amendment problems, municipalities may be well advised to exclude campaign contributions from the definition of gift and to prohibit inappropriate political activities by municipal officials, as discussed later in this chapter.

Compensation by Private Entities for Municipal Work

In addition to prohibiting use of public office for private advantage and restricting receipt of gifts, some ethics codes bar a municipal officer or employee from receiving compensation from any source other than the municipality for performing municipal services. For example, the Honolulu Charter provides:

> No elected or appointed officer or employee shall . . . [r]eceive any compensation for such person's services as an officer or employee of the city from any source other than the city, except as otherwise provided by this charter or by ordinance.[60]

Although ordinarily a wise provision, such a restriction may significantly undercut the ability of the municipality to enter into public–private partnerships. For example, the provision may prevent parks department employees from being paid in part by a private foundation. Such problems can be remedied either by the passage of a law permitting the private payments or by the private entity donating the money as a gift to the municipality, earmarked for parks department salaries. Most municipal ethics codes permit gifts to the municipality, and such block donations obviate, to some extent, the danger that individual employees will favor the donor, provided that the municipality, not the donor, determines which municipal officials benefit from the gift. Nonetheless, municipalities and, if possible, their ethics boards should carefully consider the merits of each proposed public–private partnership because such arrangements pose the danger that the donor's private interests may be placed above the public interest or that the donor-vendor may be favored over a non-donor competitor.

Confidential Information

Most ethics codes prohibit the release of confidential information or the use of confidential information for private gain.[61] Confidential information, most broadly defined, as in San Francisco's ethics law, includes any information not subject to disclosure under the state freedom of information laws.[62] For example, Philadelphia's ethics law provides that no city officer or employee, including part-time and unpaid officials, "shall directly or indirectly disclose or make available confidential information concerning the property, government or affairs of the City without proper legal authorization, for the purpose of advancing the financial interest of himself or others."[63] Some statutes governing confidential information, like those of Philadelphia, prohibit release of information only if the release may result in a financial gain.[64] Other confidential information provisions, like those of Cook County (Illinois) and Seattle (Washington), prohibit release or use of the information even if it will result in no such gain.[65] Many confidentiality provisions, such as Cook County's and New York City's, contain exceptions for certain types of disclosure, such as disclosure made in the course of official duties, disclosure required by law, or disclosure made within the scope of a whistleblower law or relating to waste, inefficiency, corruption, criminal activity, or conflicts of interest.[66]

Restrictions on the release or use of confidential information protect the integrity of municipal records and the privacy of those who deal with the municipality and help prevent employee misuse of such information for personal advantage. However, attorneys should take care to determine the scope of the "confidentiality." In particular, some statutes, such as Chicago's, treat information as confidential unless its disclosure is *required* by the applicable freedom of information law. Other statutes, such as Los Angeles's, treat information as confidential only if its disclosure is *prohibited* by law.

Political Activities

Although partisan politics may play a smaller role at the local level, especially in small communities, than at the state or federal level, nonetheless many municipal governments rest upon a partisan political system. Restrictions on the political activities of municipal officials must, therefore, be approached with caution. In particular, one must avoid ethics restrictions that may cripple political parties, raise First Amendment problems, or so restrict the pool of volunteers that either the municipality or the local political parties will be unable to fill their vacant volunteer positions, such as zoning board members or ward leaders.

The purpose of political activity restrictions in ethics laws lies in the concern that mixing politics and municipal operations corrupts the public process, creates the appearance that political support will garner municipal favor, risks the displacement of the public good by partisan will, and generates pressure on nonpolitical municipal employees to provide political support to their elected superiors. Thus, for example, New York City prohibits its officers and employees from coercing other officers and employees to engage in political activities, requesting a subordinate to engage in a political campaign or make a political contribution, compelling or requesting anyone to make a political contribution under threat of prejudice or promise, or making a political contribution in consideration of becoming a city official or receiving a raise or promotion.[67] In addition, New York City prohibits certain high-level officials from requesting anyone to make a political contribution to certain candidates for elective office or from serving as a political party leader (a so-called two hats provision).[68] Similarly, San Francisco's ethics law prohibits city officers and employees from soliciting political contributions from other city officers or employees or from persons on employment lists of the city, from participating in political activities while in uniform, or from engaging in political activity during working hours or on city premises.[69] A so-called Little Hatch Act that seeks to prohibit all political activity may, however, raise First Amendment issues, although employees of federally funded municipal agencies may be subject to the federal Hatch Act.[70]

Superior–Subordinate Relationships

Restrictions on financial relationships between superiors and subordinates not only protect the subordinate but also prevent a municipal official from compelling a subordinate to take an action that benefits the superior, or his or her associate or business, to the detriment of the municipality or the public good. For example, the King County (Washington) Employee Code of Ethics prohibits a county employee from "[e]nter[ing] into a business relationship outside county government . . . with any other employee for whom he or she has any supervisory responsibility."[71] Similarly, the Alabama Code of Ethics prohibits a municipal officer or employee from soliciting anything of value from a subordinate.[72]

While fulfilling a salutary purpose, such restrictions may occasionally work as a hardship in individual cases. For example, the provisions could be read as prohibiting a superior and subordinate from maintaining a business, which they had entered into long before they were superior and subordinate, even though they are not in a direct chain of command. In appropriate cases, waivers should be available.

Pre-Employment Restrictions

Although many ethics laws contain postemployment (revolving door) restrictions, few address the pre-employment situation. Yet when a municipal official takes an action that benefits his or her immediate past employer, a public outcry is almost certain. For that reason, even in the absence of pre-employment restrictions, municipal officials would be well advised to disclose and recuse themselves in such instances. However, actual statutory provisions may provide greater guidance. For example, the King County (Washington) Employee Code of Ethics prohibits a county employee, within one year of entering county employment, from awarding a county contract "benefiting a person that formerly employed the employee," or participating in a county action benefiting a former employer absent disclosure and approval by the appointing authority.[73] So, too, the Seattle (Washington) Code of Ethics prohibits a city officer or employee from "[p]articipat[ing] in a matter in which a person that employed the [employee] in the preceding 12 months, or retained the [employee] or his or her firm or partnership in the preceding 12 months, has a financial interest."[74]

Payment for a Municipal Position

Some ethics codes prohibit a person from paying to obtain a municipal position or from being paid to accept a municipal position. For example, the Pennsylvania ethics law provides that "[n]o person shall solicit or accept a severance payment or anything of monetary value contingent upon the assumption or acceptance of public office or employment."[75] So, too, New York City's ethics law prohibits a public servant from giving or promising to give "any portion of the public servant's compensation, or any money, or valuable thing to any person in consideration of having been or being nominated, appointed, elected or employed as a public servant."[76]

Postemployment (Revolving Door)

Most ethics codes contain some kinds of restrictions on the activities of municipal officials after they leave municipal service.[77] Common restrictions include:

- A prohibition on an officer or employee negotiating for a job with an individual or company with whom or with which the officer or employee is dealing in an official capacity on behalf of the municipality;
- A ban on non-ministerial communications by a former official with the municipality or his or her former agency for some period, typically one or two years, after leaving municipal service (sometimes called an appearance ban);
- A lengthy or even permanent bar on the former official working on a particular matter on which the official personally did substantial work while in municipal service (sometimes called a particular matter bar); and
- A continuation after municipal service of the prohibition against the official disclosing confidential municipal information or using it for a private purpose.

Postemployment restrictions seek to prevent former municipal officials from trading on their contacts with their former agency or municipal employer to the detriment of the municipality or the public (e.g., sweetheart deals) and also seek to level the playing field between former municipal officials and their competitors in the private sector. However, overbroad postemployment restrictions may discourage qualified individuals from entering municipal service and may unfairly injure municipal officials who wish to return to the private sector. Accordingly, care must be taken to tailor such restrictions to the particular size and needs of the municipality and the particular position of the municipal official. For example, a small community may wish to impose only a one-year appearance ban but make it applicable to appearances before the entire municipality or, for example, where the official was involved in land use, to appearances before all departments and boards involved in land use matters. Alternatively, the municipality may wish to impose a municipal-wide appearance ban only on certain high-level officials whose influence on municipal government may extend beyond their former agency.

Few, if any, municipalities will find it necessary or advisable to prohibit a former official not only from appearing before the municipality for some period but also from working on matters involving the municipality for that period. That is, most municipalities will permit former officials during the appearance ban period to work for a company on a matter involving the municipality so long as they do not communicate with the municipality with respect to that matter or work on a particular matter they worked on in municipal service.

Postemployment restrictions can also work to the detriment of the municipality if they prevent the municipality from placing their employees in critical positions in the private sector (e.g., as the executive director of a foster care agency upon which the municipality heavily depends), from hiring highly qualified former employees as consultants, from contracting with a former employee who happens to offer the best deal on goods or services, or from transferring municipal employees to a privatized agency. For that reason, a good ethics code will contain a provision authorizing the municipal ethics board to grant a waiver of the postemployment restrictions in appropriate circumstances. In addition, the code may exempt from those restrictions former employees who leave municipal service to work for another municipality or for the state or federal government (a so-called government-to-government exception).[78]

Inducement of Violations

Few ethics codes prohibit a municipal official from ordering, aiding, or inducing another municipal official to violate the code. As a result, not infrequently a municipal officer or employee may, with virtual impunity, convince a colleague to commit an ethics violation. For example, if a secretary in the village hall buys all village stationery supplies from the secretary's husband at the suggestion of the village administrator, the secretary will almost certainly have violated the village's ethics law, but the village administrator will not have unless that law includes a catchall provision prohibiting a municipal official from taking any action incompatible with his or her official duties. To prevent such injustice, an inducement provision should be included in the ethics code. For example, the San Francisco Charter prohibits any person from causing any other person to violate any provision of the city charter, or of any city ordinance, relating to campaign finance, lobbying, conflicts of interest, or governmental ethics and from aiding and abetting any other person in such a violation.[79]

Avoidance of Conflicts of Interest

Some ethics codes require that the municipal officials avoid conflicts of interest. For example, Westchester County's (New York) code of ethics provides that a county officer or employee "shall not invest . . . directly or indirectly[ ] in any financial, business, commercial or other private endeavor or entity, which creates a conflict with official county duties."[80] Although not a critical component of a code of ethics, such provisions encourage municipal officials to be on the alert for potential conflicts of interest.

Whistleblower Protection

The officers and employees of many municipalities enjoy protection against retaliation by other municipal officials for blowing the whistle on waste, fraud, corruption, or ethics violations. Occasionally, this protection is set forth in the ethics law itself.[81] Without such protection, whether in the ethics code or elsewhere, municipal employees may well hesitate to report ethics violations or may resist cooperating in an investigation of an ethics violation.

RESTRICTIONS ON PRIVATE CITIZENS AND COMPANIES

Generally

Municipal ethics laws, by their very nature, focus primarily upon the actions and interests of municipal officers and employees. Yet, private citizens and companies should have a stake in the integrity of municipal government. In particular, they should not be permitted to induce a municipal official to violate the ethics code. However, only a few ethics laws contain such inducement prohibitions, and even those ordinarily address only specified provisions of the code of ethics. Other ethics laws restrict certain actions by private citizens that might bring a municipal official into violation of the ethics law. Examples of these various provisions are discussed in the sections that follow.

Inducement of Ethics Violations and Influencing Officials

If a bank, hoping to keep a town's financial business, gives a loan to the new town treasurer at a couple percentage points below the bank's usual rate, the treasurer may well be out of a job. Absent a quid pro quo, under most ethics laws, nothing will happen to the bank.

Thus, to permit a private company, with virtual impunity, to corrupt a municipal official undercuts significantly the efficacy of the ethics law and constitutes gross unfairness to the official. Accordingly, such laws should prohibit private citizens and companies from inducing a municipal official to violate the code of ethics. For example, the Temporary State Commission's proposed bill provides:

> No person, whether or not a municipal officer or employee, shall induce or attempt to induce a municipal officer or employee to violate any of the provisions of section 800 [the code of ethics] of this article.[82]

Unfortunately, few ethics laws contain such a prohibition.

> Alabama's code of ethics does prohibit any person from soliciting a municipal official or employee: to use or cause to be used equipment, facilities, time, materials, human labor, or other public property for such person's private benefit or business benefit, which would materially affect his or her financial interest, except as otherwise provided by law.[83]

Since such actions by a municipal official or employee violate the code of ethics, this provision has the effect of punishing a private individual or company for inducing a public servant to violate the ethics law.

A number of ethics laws prohibit private persons from giving gifts—or additional compensation—to municipal officers and employees. For example, Ohio prohibits anyone from promising to give, or giving, to a public official or employee anything of value "that is of such a character as to manifest a substantial and improper influence upon the public official or employee with respect to that person's duties."[84] Massachusetts prohibits any person from "knowingly, otherwise than as provided by law for the proper discharge of official duties, directly or indirectly giv[ing], promis[ing] or offer[ing] . . . compensation [from anyone other than the city or town or municipal agency in relation to any particular matter in which the same city or town is a party or has a direct and substantial interest]."[85] Cook County's Ethics Ordinance restricts contributions to candidates for county office or elected county officials by persons who are seeking to do business with the county or who have done business with the county during the previous four years.[86] Restrictions on lobbyists and on gifts by lobbyists to municipal officials, as well as pay-to-play regulations, lie beyond the scope of this chapter but are discussed elsewhere in this book.

Appearances by Officials' Outside Employers

Appearances by a municipal official's outside employer or business before the official's municipal agency can create the impression that "the fix is in," even if the official recuses himself or herself from acting on the matter either as a public servant or as an officer or employee of the firm. However, a flat prohibition on appearances by an official's private firm may effectively prevent many good people from serving in municipal government. For that reason, these situations are probably best handled by restrictions on appearances coupled with the availability of ethics board waivers. The mere fact that the ethics board has reviewed the matter—and attached appropriate conditions to any waiver—goes far toward reassuring those who deal with the affected agency of its integrity.

Thus, for example, New York City's conflicts of interest law provides that no public servant shall have a position or an ownership interest in a firm that does business with that public servant's city agency.[87] But the law further provides that the public servant may apply to the city's Conflicts of Interest Board for a waiver of the prohibition.[88] It should be noted that New York City's restriction falls on the public servant, not directly on his or her private employer or business. Other ethics laws, such as the Massachusetts law, directly restrict appearances by the private entity itself as well.[89]

SECOND PILLAR: DISCLOSURE

The second pillar of a good municipal ethics law is disclosure. Three types of disclosure exist: transactional disclosure, applicant disclosure, and annual disclosure. Each of these types is considered here.

Transactional Disclosure

Of the three types of disclosure, transactional disclosure—that is, disclosure of a potential conflict of interest when it actually arises—is the most important and the least controversial. Recusal often, though not always, accompanies this type of pinpoint disclosure: "I would like to state for the record that the applicant for this zoning variance is my employer, and I therefore recuse myself from acting on this matter."

One should emphasize, however, that transactional disclosure and recusal do not provide a panacea for ethics problems. Sometimes this approach is inadequate or ill advised. For example, real estate brokers who do substantial business in a town should probably not be appointed to the town planning board since their frequent recusal will significantly undermine their ability to function effectively in their municipal positions.[90] As discussed earlier, mandating recusal by legislators also raises thorny issues of separation of powers and disenfranchisement of voters. In any event, in those states that require a public body to adopt a resolution by a majority of the body's total members, not just by a majority of those members present and voting, a recusal is indistinguishable from a negative vote.[91]

Transactional disclosure ordinarily occurs on the record of a public body, if the disclosing official is a member of a public body, or in a written statement to the official's superior and/or to the municipal clerk or ethics board, if the official is not a member of a public body. Recusal, if required, may merely prevent the official from acting on the matter or may in effect serve as a gag order, prohibiting the official from even discussing the matter with anyone. The recusal language commonly employed by the New York City Conflicts of Interest Board, for example, reads:

> Recusal means that you may not be involved, directly or indirectly, in any dealings between XYZ and the City. This includes, but is not limited to, not participating at your City agency in any communications (including, but not limited to, emails, telephone conversations, and conference calls) concerning XYZ, not attending meetings with City officials and others to discuss XYZ, and not receiving copies of relevant documents or email messages.[92]

Whatever the scope of recusal contemplated by statute, attorneys should ordinarily advise their municipal clients to take the broadest possible view of recusal. Public perception of integrity in government suffers when municipal officials "recuse" themselves from voting on a matter in which they have a personal interest but then go on to discuss the matter at length "as a private citizen." In addition, recusal should ordinarily be accompanied with disclosure of the reason for the recusal, that is, of the nature and extent of the conflict of interest. Codes of ethics reflect these various permutations.[93]

Applicant Disclosure

Applicant disclosure represents the flip side of the transactional disclosure coin and thus provides a check on transactional disclosure. Applicant disclosure occurs when a person applying for a municipal permit or license, or a bidder for a municipal contract, discloses in the application or bid documents the name and office of any officers or employees of the municipality who have a financial interest in the applicant/bidder or in the application or bid. In fairness to the applicant or bidder, which may not know the identity of all such persons, the disclosure should be required only of those affected municipal officials actually known to the applicant or bidder or of whom the applicant or bidder should have knowledge. (An applicant should not be heard to claim that it was unaware that one of its five shareholders worked for the municipality.) Some applicant disclosure laws may limit the scope of the disclosure to affected officials who might be expected to act on the matter; other laws may expand the scope of the disclosure to include officials whose relatives or private businesses have a financial interest in the applicant/bidder or in the application or bid. In the event that the application is oral, the disclosure could be made either on the records of the body to which the application is made or in a separate writing.

Although courts often require that litigants disclose the names of parent and subsidiary companies (e.g., U.S. Supreme Court Rule 29.6), applicant disclosure is relatively uncommon. Nonetheless, some jurisdictions do require it, at least in certain contexts, such as land use.[94]

Annual Disclosure

Lengthy annual financial disclosure forms raise a fire storm among municipal officials. Yet, properly structured and understood, annual disclosure plays a critical role in a municipal ethics scheme.

Unlike state government, most municipalities rely heavily on volunteers or near-volunteers to staff many of their high-level positions, such as legislative bodies and planning and zoning boards. Overly intrusive financial disclosure poses a serious threat to the ability of municipalities to attract and retain qualified volunteer board members and even elected officials.

It is often said in defense of lengthy financial disclosure forms that "sunlight is the best disinfectant." Maybe, but sunlight also causes cancer. Indeed, the imposition of blunderbuss financial disclosure reflects a serious misunderstanding of the purpose of municipal ethics laws. The purpose of such laws, including their annual disclosure component, lies not in catching crooks but in improving the reality and the perception of integrity in municipal government by preventing conflicts of interest violations *before* they occur.

Viewed in this light, the specific objective of annual disclosure lies in revealing potential conflicts of interest violations before they arise and thus helping to prevent them. Annual disclosure compels municipal officials, at least once each year, to focus on the requirements of the municipality's ethics provisions. It also serves as a check on transactional disclosure by alerting officials, their colleagues, the public, and the media to those areas where the official will probably have to transactionally disclose (and, if required, recuse); those colleagues, citizens, and media will almost certainly remind the official of that obligation should the official forget.

Accordingly, an effective annual disclosure law:

1. Ties the disclosure to the code of ethics—for example, if under the ethics code stock ownership can become a conflict only where it exceeds a threshold value or percentage, the disclosure form should not require disclosure of stock interests falling below that threshold;
2. Tailors the disclosure to the official's particular agency and position—for example, if no conceivable action of the official could affect the value of his or her private investments, disclosure of those investments makes little sense in the ethics context (agencies such as a municipal department of investigation or office of internal affairs might wish such information to aid in the search for theft and corruption, but, fundamentally, ethics laws do not share those objectives);
3. Requires that the disclosure forms be available to the public and the media since it is largely they who enforce the ethics laws (although some financial disclosure laws, like those of Pennsylvania and Rhode Island, expressly prohibit use of the forms for commercial purposes);[95] and
4. Provides for computerization of information contained on the forms in order to permit their comparison with other databases, such as lists of vendors to the municipality.

Annual disclosure laws differ widely throughout the country with respect to the type and extent of the information sought, its public availability, and the type of officials, or candidates for office, required to file.[96] (New York State even sets forth in the law the text of the actual form,[97] a singularly poor idea that prevents the ethics board from clarifying the shockingly imprecise language of the statutory questions.) Some municipal codes explicitly prohibit the commercial exploitation of such disclosures.[98]

Disclosure of dollar amounts and of the finances of the filer's spouse has traditionally elicited the greatest objections from municipal officials. But one proposed law would require disclosure only of (1) the location of any real property within the municipality, or within one mile of the boundary of the municipality, in which the official or a relative has an interest and (2) the identity and nature of the source (not the amount) of the outside earned income of the official and the official's spouse.[99] Such disclosure would probably suffice in all but the largest municipalities.

THIRD PILLAR: ADMINISTRATION

Generally

Administration is the third pillar upon which an effective ethics law rests. Ethics laws must be easy and inexpensive to administer and enforce. The last thing that any municipality needs in an ethics law is yet another complicated and expensive mandate. Moreover, the success of an ethics law depends above all else on the efficacy of its administration and on the independence of the body enforcing it. For that reason, a good ethics law invests broad administrative responsibilities in an ethics board that is independent of the political process. So long as the reality and perception of that independence is maintained, the details of administration probably matter little. However, ethics boards should be lean and mean—a model of government efficiency.

The appointment and composition of ethics boards vary widely.[100] Some laws specify professions, such as lawyers, to be represented on the board and restrict the number of members who can be registered in the same political party.[101] Many ethics laws restrict the political activity of board members and may prohibit them from holding any other public office or employment.[102] For example, members of the Miami-Dade County Ethics Commission are prohibited from holding or campaigning for any elective political office, holding office in any political party or political committee, actively participating in or contributing to any political campaign or political action committee, being employed by the county or any municipality within the county, or allowing their names to be used by a campaign in support of or against any candidate for political office or any referendum or other ballot question.[103]

To help preserve the board's independence, ethics laws often involve both the executive and legislative branch in the appointment process (either by giving each branch appointments or by creating an advice and consent procedure), establish set terms of office for board members, stagger those terms, and make them overlap the term of the appointing authority; board members should be removable only for cause and after a hearing.[104] Municipalities are cautioned against appointments by multiple officials because such a system tends to politicize the ethics board, create factions, and risk breaches of confidentiality. To ensure the continuous flow of new blood, some ethics laws establish a term limit for board members.[105] Members usually either serve pro bono or receive only per diem compensation, perhaps with a cap.[106]

The powers and duties of an ethics board may be grouped into six areas:

1. Training and educating municipal officers and employees about the ethics law, including writing and distributing educational materials and DVDs, conducting training sessions, creating and maintaining a web site, and developing ethics compliance programs (in Chicago, any employee who fails to comply with the mandated training requirement is subject to employment sanctions, including suspension, and any employee who is found to have knowingly falsified compliance with the training requirement is subject to discharge,[107] putting real teeth in their ethics education program);
2. Providing oral and written advice, including staff opinions and formal advisory opinions of the board, to municipal officials and their supervisors as to whether the ethics law permits a proposed action or interest;

3. Enforcing the ethics law, including referring, investigating, prosecuting, and conducting hearings on alleged violations and imposing penalties;
4. Waiving conflicts of interest requirements, where appropriate;
5. Collecting, reviewing, and maintaining disclosure forms and making them publicly available; and
6. Engaging in miscellaneous related activities, such as enacting rules and regulations, proposing legislative changes, and issuing annual reports.[108]

If it is to be successful, an ethics board must undertake all of these duties. Only enforcement will be discussed here. For a discussion of the other duties, the reader is referred to the principal author's articles cited in endnotes 3, 20, 21, and 108.

Enforcement

As discussed previously, the primary purpose of ethics laws lies in prevention, not punishment. Enforcement, too, reflects that same purpose, for the primary goal of ethics enforcement is not punishment of the individual official but prevention of future ethics violations by all officials. Indeed, the seriousness and newsworthiness of an enforcement action makes it one of the most powerful teaching tools in an ethics board's work shed. For example, when the New York City Conflicts of Interest Board fined a former city employee $1,000 for sending his resume to a private company at the same time he was involved with that company in his city job, that enforcement action sent a powerful educational message to all city employees, alerting them to the existence and potency of the city's postemployment restrictions.

In addition, it has been shown time and again across the country that an ethics board without enforcement authority will not be taken seriously. Such a board instead becomes a toothless tiger, raising expectations it cannot meet and thus, paradoxically, increasing public cynicism. Historically, ethics laws that grant to an ethics board only advisory power simply do not work. No one listens. Enforcement therefore constitutes an indispensable part of an effective ethics scheme. Annexed as Appendix 9A to this chapter is a chart setting forth the enforcement and investigative authority of the ethics boards in the nation's largest cities.

Ethics enforcement may be divided into four stages: investigation; pleadings and negotiation; adjudication, including imposition of penalties; and judicial review. This process is briefly summarized in the following sections. For a detailed discussion of enforcement and penalties, the reader is referred to Chapter 12 of this book.

Stages of the Enforcement Process

Every respectable ethics board has the power to enforce the law it interprets.[109] Most boards may initiate investigations upon receipt of a complaint or upon their own initiative. (Virtually all boards have the prosecutorial discretion to dismiss a complaint at the outset if it appears that no possible violation of the ethics law has occurred. Some ethics laws, such as those of Pennsylvania, Rhode Island, Miami-Dade County, Philadelphia, and San Francisco provide penalties for frivolous or false complaints.[110]) Some boards act as their own investigators; other ethics boards use some other municipal agency, such as a department of investigation or inspectors general, as their investigators. Requiring the board to rely on a separate investigative agency has the advantage of reducing the board's costs and separating, to some extent, investigative and adjudicatory functions, but has the disadvantage of giving the board far less control over its investigations. As Appendix 9A shows, New York City would appear to be the only large municipality in the country whose ethics board has enforcement power but not investigative authority, a serious defect in that city's ethics program.

Following an investigation, the board's staff—or in some jurisdictions the board itself—will determine whether a possible violation of the ethics law may have occurred. At this point, in some jurisdictions, the board will serve a complaint or petition on the respondent official. In other jurisdictions, the board will first issue to the respondent a notice that the board has probable cause to believe that a violation may have occurred. The respondent will then have the opportunity to explain his or her actions. If the board accepts the explanation, it will dismiss the case. If the board sustains its previous finding of probable cause, a complaint or petition will be issued.

Once the ethics board has formally notified the respondent of the proceeding, whether by a notice of probable cause or by a pleading, settlement negotiations may ensue. Avoiding the publicity attendant upon a hearing and final imposition of a penalty provides the greatest incentive for a municipal officer or employee, particularly an elected official, to settle a case early. Although many ethics boards have a strong policy against private settlements, even a public settlement gives the official some control over the content of the settlement document and thus some control over adverse publicity, particularly if the board agrees not to comment on the case beyond what the settlement papers state.

Indeed, ethics boards probably have their greatest leverage at the non-public stages of the proceeding. For example, if under the applicable ethics law a petition is public but a notice of probable cause is not, then the board will probably be best able to force a settlement in the period between the probable cause notice and the petition. For that reason, in view of their limited resources, ethics boards should carefully consider the issuance of a publicly available accusatory instrument.

If the case is not settled, after the issuance of the complaint or petition and the receipt of the respondent's answer, the parties may engage in limited discovery and motion practice, preparatory to trying the case at a hearing before either the board itself or a hearing officer.

Most ethics boards suffer from a sort of multiple personality disorder engendered by the need both to prosecute and adjudicate the same claim. However, the inherent tension in that situation may be relieved by building a wall between those employees involved in the prosecution and those involved in the adjudication. For example, the ethics board members who will vote on whether a violation occurred and, if so, on the amount of the penalty, should be insulated from the investigation and prosecution of the allegations.

After the hearing, the board will need to determine, based on the evidence, whether a violation of the ethics law has occurred. If it finds a violation, the board will need to determine the type and amount of the penalty. Penalties are discussed in the next section. If the respondent contests the board's determination, he or she may seek judicial review.

Finally, an effective municipal ethics law must provide for the continuing jurisdiction of the ethics board over former public servants, lest a public servant thwart an ethics investigation merely by resigning.[111]

Penalties

Critical to the effective enforcement of an ethics law is the availability of a wide range of penalties, thereby permitting the ethics board to fit the punishment to the crime. In particular, the ethics board, either directly or through a court proceeding, must have the ability to impose penalties not only upon the municipal official who violated the ethics law but also upon any private individual or company that aided or abetted in that violation. Thus, the board should have the power, either directly or by the commencement of a civil court proceeding, to void any contract entered into in violation of the ethics law, such as a contract with a private vendor in which the official has a financial interest. So, too, the board should have the authority to commence a proceeding to debar from future municipal business any private individual or company that intentionally induced a violation of the ethics law. Other penalties against the non-municipal offender might include civil fines, criminal sanctions, restitution, damages, double or treble penalties, disgorgement of ill-gotten gains (even where the municipality suffered no loss as a result of the violation), civil forfeiture, and injunctive relief. Some jurisdictions, such as California, permit qui tam actions against violators of the ethics law.[112] The cap on civil fines should be sufficiently high to discourage intentional violations and offset any possible gain received by the violator as a result of the violation.

Permissible penalties against municipal officers and employees should include, in addition to the foregoing, letters of warning, censure, or reprimand by the ethics board; recommendations by the ethics board to the appointing authority for disciplinary action, including suspension or removal from office (most ethics laws do not permit the ethics board itself to impose disciplinary action); and disqualification from holding office in the future. However, the ethics laws of state and local governments applicable to municipalities rarely provide for all of these penalties.[113]

Confidentiality

The confidentiality of the records and proceedings of an ethics board presents one of the most controversial and contentious aspects of an ethics law. An unavoidable tension exists between the need to protect the privacy of the municipal officials, particularly those who have been unjustly accused of unethical conduct, and the need to educate officials, the media, and the public about the ethics law and alert them to potential conflicts of interest in order to avoid violations of the ethics law. States and municipalities have implemented varying rules, reflecting those often competing needs of confidentiality and openness to the public.[114] Too much openness deters officials and complainants from contacting the ethics board and discourages good people from serving in local government. Too much confidentiality creates the perception that the board is at best an irrelevancy and at worst a Star Chamber.

In particular, a prohibition against disclosure of pleadings and hearings fosters the impression that the ethics board is a do-nothing agency, as months may go by between the first press reports of a potential ethics issue and its resolution by the board. Permitting the board to release its disposition of a complaint only if the board finds a violation substantially aggravates that problem. Moreover, excessive privacy in enforcement proceedings—based largely on the fear of politicians that, for them, an accusation is as good as a conviction—runs counter to the current trend toward greater openness in professional disciplinary proceedings.

Accordingly, as a general rule, the records and proceedings of ethics boards should be no less open than those of other agencies under the applicable open meetings and freedom of information laws. Such laws ordinarily protect investigative, litigation, intra-agency, and disciplinary matters. Enforcement proceedings should be public once the complaint or petition has been served. Criminal procedure laws provide a guide in that regard. Thus, discussions and documents relating to investigations would remain confidential, as would the initial proceeding to determine whether probable cause exists to believe that an ethics violation occurred. Pleadings and all other post-pleading litigation documents served on either side would be public, as would hearings and oral arguments. The deliberations of the board, like those of a court, would be confidential since, as the adjudicative body, the board is acting in a quasi-judicial capacity. Adopting this approach to confidentiality not only provides a fair balance between privacy and openness but also promotes integrity in government by focusing attention upon the ethics law and revealing how it plays out in practice.

In the words of Robert Service, "Now a promise made is a debt unpaid."[115] And municipal ethics laws typically scatter promises like grass seed across the political landscape. But unless those laws are prudently structured and effectively administered—and many, if not most, are not—their promise will remain largely an unpaid debt. Both municipal attorneys and private practitioners alike must ensure that the promise does not go unfulfilled, for so long as it does, their clients will inevitably suffer from the want of guidance and reassurance that only these laws can provide.

SUMMARY OF KEY POINTS

- Municipal ethics laws promote integrity by seeking to prevent unethical conduct before it occurs, provide guidance to public officials and reassurance to the public, and encourage private citizens to take part in public service.
- The three pillars of local ethics are an ethics code, disclosure requirements, and administration.
- The ethics code should be clear and concise, with definitions that are easily understandable and that narrow, not expand, the scope of the ethics law. Common aspects of an ethics code include, among other things, conflict of interest provisions, waiver provisions, prohibitions on the use of public office for private gain, restrictions relating to moonlighting and gifts, pre- and postemployment rules, and whistleblower protections.
- Administration concerns the appointment and composition of the ethics board and its independence measures, to make sure the board is able to complete the duties and responsibilities of the board: training and educating public officials; enforcing the ethics code; waiving conflicts of interest provisions where appropriate; and collecting, reviewing, and maintaining disclosure forms.

NOTES

1. The views expressed in this chapter do not necessarily represent those of the New York City Conflicts of Interest Board.

2. The meaning of the terms "official," "officer," and "employee" varies according to the particular ethics law. In this chapter, unless otherwise specified, the term "municipal official" includes all elected and appointed public servants of the municipality.

3. *See generally* Mark Davies, *Ethics in Government and the Issue of Conflicts of Interest*, in GOVERNMENT ETHICS AND LAW ENFORCEMENT: TOWARD GLOBAL GUIDELINES (Yassin El-Ayouty, Kevin J. Ford, & Mark Davies eds. 2000); Mark Davies, *Governmental Ethics Laws: Myths and Mythos*, 40 N.Y.L. SCH. L. REV. 177 (1995); Mark Davies, *The Public Administrative Law Context of Ethics Requirements for West German and American Public Officials: A Comparative Analysis*, 18 GA. J. INT'L & COMP. L. 319 (1988); Mark Davies, *A Practical Approach to Establishing and Maintaining a Values-Based Conflicts of Interest Compliance System* (2012), http://www.nyc.gov/html/conflicts/downloads/pdf2/international/DaviesArticle_final.pdf (last visited Apr. 1, 2022).

4. 65 PA. CONS. STAT. ANN. § 1103(c); PHILADELPHIA, PA., CODE § 20-604; PHILADELPHIA HOME RULE CHARTER § 8-204; Executive Order No. 16-92, https://www.phila.gov/ExecutiveOrders/Executive%20Orders/16-92.pdf (last visited Apr. 1, 2020).

5. R.I. CONST. art. III, § 7.

6. R.I. CONST. art. III, § 8.

7. N.Y. CONST. art. VIII, § 1.

8. *See, e.g.*, Ala. Code §§ 36-25-1 through 36-25-30; Cal. Gov't Code §§ 82000–82054 (definitions), 83100–83124 (Fair Political Practices Commission), 87100–87505 (conflicts of interest), 89501–89503 (honoraria), 89506 (travel payments, advances, and reimbursements), 91000–91014 (enforcement); Mass. Gen. Laws ch. 268A (conduct of public officials and employees) and ch. 268B (state ethics commission; financial disclosure); N.Y. Gen. Mun. Law §§ 800–812; Ohio Rev. Code Ann. §§ 102.01–102.99; 53 Pa. Stat. Ann. § 551; 65 Pa. Cons. Stat. Ann. §§ 1101–1113; R.I. Gen. Laws §§ 36-14-1 through 36-14-21.

9. *See, e.g.*, Cal. Gov't Code §§ 82011 ("[c]ode reviewing body"), 82035 ("[j]urisdiction"), 82041 ("[l]ocal government agency"), 87300–87313 (conflict of interest code); N.Y. Gen. Mun. Law §§ 806 (local code of ethics), 808 (local ethics boards), 811 (financial disclosure forms); 65 Pa. Cons. Stat. Ann. § 1111 (supplemental provisions).

10. *See* Cal. Gov't Code §§ 82003, 87300.

11. *See id.* § 87100.

12. N.Y. Civ. Serv. Law § 107; N.Y. Gen. Mun. Law § 51.

13. N.Y.C., N.Y., Charter § 1126.

14. *See* Syracuse Police Benevolent Ass'n v. Young, 156 Misc. 2d 513, 593 N.Y.S.2d 718 (Sup. Ct., Onondaga Cnty. 1992); N.Y.C. Police Department Patrol Guide, *Guidelines for Acceptance of Gifts and Other Compensation by Members of the Service*, Procedure No. 203-16 (Jan. 1, 2000).

15. Municipal Code of Chicago § 2-156-450. *See also* San Francisco Campaign and Governmental Conduct Code §§ 3.216 (gifts), 3.218 (statement of incompatible activities).

16. For a collection of cases, see 56 Am. Jur. 2d, Municipal Corporations §§ 252–257; 63C Am. Jur. 2d, Public Officers and Employees §§ 65, 247–249, 251–259, 338, 343; 62 C.J.S., Municipal Corporations § 503.

17. Clarke v. Town of Russia, 283 N.Y. 272, 274, 28 N.E.2d 833, 835 (1940).

18. Pyatt v. Mayor & Council of Borough of Dunellen, 9 N.J. 548, 557, 89 A.2d 1, 5 (1952), *accord* Baker v. Marley, 8 N.Y.2d 365, 367, 170 N.E.2d 900, 901, 208 N.Y.S.2d 449, 450 (1960).

19. Zagoreos v. Conklin, 109 A.D.2d 281, 287, 491 N.Y.S.2d 358, 363 (2d Dep't 1985). *See also* Tuxedo Conservation & Taxpayers Ass'n v. Town Bd. of Town of Tuxedo, 96 Misc. 2d 1, 408 N.Y.S.2d 668 (Sup. Ct., Orange County, 1978), *aff'd*, 69 A.D.2d 320, 418 N.Y.S.2d 638 (2d Dep't 1979).

20. *See* Mark Davies, *How to Adopt a Municipal Conflicts of Interest Law: Contents* and *How to Adopt a Municipal Conflicts of Interest Law: Process, in* Municipal Ethics in New York: A Primer for Attorneys and Public Officials (Jeff Tremblay et al., eds., NYSBA 2016); Davies, *A Practical Approach to Establishing, supra* note 3, at 39–46.

21. State laws: Ala. Code §§ 36-25-1 through 36-25-30 (hereafter Ala.); Cal. Gov't Code §§ 82000–82055, 87000–87505 (hereafter Cal.); Mass. Gen. Laws ch. 268A–268B (hereafter Mass.); N.Y. Gen. Mun. Law § 800–812 (hereafter N.Y.S.); Ohio Rev. Code Ann. §§ 102.01–102.99 (hereafter Ohio); 53 Pa. Stat. Ann. §§ 551–553; 65 Pa. Cons. Stat. Ann. §§ 1101–1113 (hereafter Pa.); R.I. Const. art. III (hereafter R.I. Const.); R.I. Gen. Laws §§ 36-14-1 through 36-14-21 (hereafter R.I.).

Municipal laws: Anne Arundel Cnty., Md., Cnty. Code §§ 7-1-101 through 7-8-103 (hereafter Anne Arundel); Chi., Ill., Mun. Code §§ 2-156-005 through 2-156-530 (hereafter Chicago); Cook County, Ill., Code of Ordinances §§ 2-560 through 2-614 (hereafter Cook); D.C. Code §§ 1-1161.01 through 1-1171.07 (hereafter D.C.); Rev. Charter of Honolulu §§ 6-1112.2, 6-1112.3, 6-1112.6, 11-101 through 11-108 (hereafter Honolulu Charter); Honolulu, Haw., Rev. Ordinances §§ 3-6.1 through 3-6.12, 3-8.1 through 3-8.9 (hereafter Honolulu); Jacksonville, Fla., Code of Ordinances §§ 602.101–602.1213 (hereafter Jacksonville); King County, Wash., Code §§ 3.04.010–3.04.210 (hereafter King); L.A., Cal., City Charter §§ 700–712 (hereafter L.A. Charter); L.A., Cal., Mun. Code § 49.5.1–49.5.20 (hereafter L.A.); L.A., Cal., Ad. Code §§ 24.12–24.29 (hereafter L.A. Ad. Code); Maui Cnty., Haw., Charter §§ 10-1 through 10-5 (hereafter Maui); Miami-Dade Cnty., Fla., Code of Ordinances §§ 2-11.1 through 2-11.1.2, 2-1066 through 2-1076 (hereafter Miami); N.Y.C., N.Y., Charter §§ 2600–2607 (hereafter N.Y.C.); Philadelphia, Pa., Home Rule Charter §§ 3-806, 8-301, 10-100 through 10-111 (hereafter Philadelphia Charter); Philadelphia, Pa., Code §§ 20-601 through 20-615 (hereafter PHILADELPHIA); S.F., CAL., CHARTER §§ 15.100–15.107, app. C (hereafter S.F. CHARTER); S.F., CAL., CAMPAIGN & GOVERNMENTAL CONDUCT CODE §§ 3.1-100 through 3.1-510, 3.200-3.244, 3.300 (hereafter S.F.); SEATTLE, WASH., MUN. CODE §§ 3.70.010–3.70.200, 4.16.010-4.16.105 (hereafter SEATTLE); WESTCHESTER CNTY., N.Y., ADMIN. CODE §§ 883.01–883.111 (hereafter WESTCHESTER).

Proposed state law: Local Government Ethics Bill, *reproduced in* Temporary State Commission on Local Government Ethics, *Final Report*, 21 FORD. URB. L.J. 1 app. L at 26 (1993) (hereafter TSC BILL).

Model local law: Model Local Ethics Law, *reproduced in* Mark Davies, *Keeping the Faith: A Model Local Ethics Law—Content and Commentary*, 21 FORD. URB. L.J. 61 (1993) (hereafter DAVIES MODEL LAW). An updated and expanded model law, with section-by-section commentary, may be found in Appendix B to Mark Davies, *A Practical Approach to Establishing and Maintaining a Values-Based Conflicts of Interest Compliance System* (2012), http://www.nyc.gov/html/conflicts/downloads/pdf2/international/DaviesArticle_final.pdf (last visited April 4, 2022); although international in approach, that model law may easily be adopted to local government. *See also* Mark Davies, *Enacting a Local Ethics Law—Part I: Code of Ethics*, Mun. Law., Summer 2007, at 4 , http://www.nysba.org/workarea/DownloadAsset.aspx?id=1809 (last visited April 4, 2016). For websites setting forth the local laws cited in this chapter, as well as the TSC Bill and the Davies Model Law, see Appendix 9B annexed to this chapter.

22. *See, e.g.*, N.Y.S. § 800(3) ("[i]nterest"); PA. tit. 65, § 1102; ANNE ARUNDEL § 7-1-101(10), (15) ("[f]inancial interest," "[i]nterest"); CHICAGO § 2-156-010(*l*) ("[f]inancial interest"); COOK § 2-561 ("[f]inancial interest"); HONOLULU § 3-8.1 ("[c]ontrolling interest" and "[f]inancial interest"); N.Y.C. §§ 2601(4), (12), (16), (18) ("[a]ppear," "[i]nterest," "[o]wnership interest," "[p]osition"); WESTCHESTER § 883.11(f) ("[i]nterest"). *Compare* TSC Bill § 803; Davies Model Law § 105.

23. *See, e.g.*, N.Y.S. § 800(3); R.I. § 36-14-2(1), (3); D.C. § 1-1161.01(3) ("affiliated organization").

24. ANNE ARUNDEL § 7-1-101(3).

25. *See, e.g.*, TSC BILL § 801; DAVIES MODEL LAW § 102.

26. *See* N.Y.S. §§ 800(3), 801, 802.

27. *See* R.I. § 36-14-5(e)(1).

28. ANNE ARUNDEL §§ 7-2-107, 7-5-105(b).

29. D.C. § 1-1162.23(b).

30. N.Y.C. § 2604(e). For other examples of exceptions and waiver, see S.F. §§ 3.224(c), 3.226, 3.234(a)(1)(C); TSC BILL § 828; DAVIES MODEL LAW § 211.

31. For an example of an ethics code that grants waiver authority to legislative bodies, *see* WESTCHESTER § 883.21(h)(2). *Cf.* MIAMI § 2-11.1(c)(4), (c)(6).

32. N.Y.C. § 2604(e).

33. HONOLULU § 3-8.2(b). For examples of other restrictions based on employment position or ownership interest, *see* ALA. § 36-25-9(a); ANNE ARUNDEL § 7-5-102(a); KING § 3.04.030(B)(8); N.Y.C. § 2604(a); MIAMI § 2-11.1(*l*); SEATTLE § 4.16.070(A)(1).

34. CHICAGO § 2-156-110(a). *Cf.* ALA. § 36-25-11; MASS. ch. 268A, § 20; N.Y.S. § 801; 65 PA. CONS. STAT. ANN. § 1103(f); R.I. § 36-14-5(h); ANNE ARUNDEL § 7-5-102(a); COOK § 2-581(a); HONOLULU § 3-8.2(e); MIAMI § 2-11.1(c); PHILADELPHIA CHARTER §§ 10-100, 10-102; S.F. § 3.222(b).

35. For restrictions relating to legislation, *see* KING § 3.04.030(E)(1); PHILADELPHIA § 20-607. For a restriction relating to property, *see* KING § 3.04.030(F)(1). For a restriction regarding relatives, *see* KING § 3.04.30(B)(12).

36. MASS. ch. 268A, §§ 15A, 21A; PHILADELPHIA CHARTER § 8-301; S.F. § 3.220.

37. CAL. § 87100.

38. *Id.* § 87103.

39. ANNE ARUNDEL § 7-5-107(a). *See also* ALA. § 36-25-5(a); MASS. ch. 268A, §§ 13, 19, 23(b)(2)–(b)(3); OHIO § 102.03(D); 65 PA. CONS. STAT. ANN. §§ 1102 ("conflict of interest"), 1103(a); R.I. § 36-14-5(d); CHICAGO §§ 2-156-030, 2-156-080(a)–(b), 2-156-111; COOK §§ 2-572, 2-578(a); D.C. § 1-1162.23(a); HONOLULU CHARTER § 11-104; HONOLULU § 3-8-2(a), (e); JACKSONVILLE § 602.401; KING § 3.04.030(B)(1), (B)(3), (B)(5); L.A. § 49.5.5; MIAMI § 2-11.1(g), (n); N.Y.C. § 2604(b)(1), (b)(3);

PHILADELPHIA CHARTER §§ 10-100, 10-101, 10-104; S.F. §§ 3.210, 3.218, 3.226; SEATTLE § 4.16.070(B); TSC BILL § 800(1); DAVIES MODEL LAW § 100(1). *Cf.* MIAMI § 2-11.1(p) (prohibition on recommending services of any person to assist in any transaction involving the county).

40. KING § 3.04.020(A).

41. MAUI § 10-4(1)(d). *See also* ALA. §§ 36-25-5(c), (d); CHICAGO § 2-156-060; COOK § 2-576; L.A. § 49.5.5(B); S.F. §§ 3.218(c)(1), 3.232 (prohibition on use of public funds for printed greetings cards).

42. COOK § 2.586. *See also* D.C. § 1-1163.36 (prohibition on use of government resources at any time to support or oppose any candidate for elected office or any initiative, referendum, or recall measure); SEATTLE § 4.16.070(B)(2).

43. R.I. §§ 36-14-5(a), 36-14-7; ANNE ARUNDEL § 7-5-110(b); HONOLULU CHARTER § 11-102(c); JACKSONVILLE § 602.403(b); KING § 3.04.030(A)(9); MAUI § 10-4(1)(c); N.Y.C. § 2604(b)(2); SEATTLE § 4.16.070(1)(a); WESTCHESTER § 883.21(f), (g).

44. CHICAGO § 2-156-130; COOK § 2.582; HONOLULU CHARTER § 6-1112.6; S.F. § 3.212.

45. S.F. § 3.218.

46. ALA. § 36-25-9(c); 53 PA. STAT. ANN. § 551; ANNE ARUNDEL § 7-5-110(b)(2); CHICAGO § 2-156-080(a); MIAMI § 2-11.1(v).

47. *See* MASS. ch. 268A, § 23(b)(1); R.I. § 36-14-5(b); COOK § 2.573; JACKSONVILLE § 602.403; MIAMI §§ 2-11, 2-11.1(j)–(k).

48. *Compare* ANNE ARUNDEL §§ 7-5-102, 7-5-103 *with* WESTCHESTER § 883.21(g). *See also* KING §§ 3.04.030(B)(3), (B)(6), (B)(9), (C)(1)–(C)(2); L.A. § 49.5.7.

49. WESTCHESTER § 883.21(g).

50. KING § 3.04.030(C). *See also* JACKSONVILLE § 602.403.

51. HONOLULU CHARTER § 11-102(e). *See also* ALA. § 36-25-10 (notice to ethics commission but no prohibition); MASS. ch. 268A, §§ 11(a), (c), 17(a), (c); N.Y.S. § 805-a(1)(c); OHIO §§ 102.03(A)(1), 102.04(C), (D); R.I. §§ 36-14-5(e)(1) through 36-14-5(e)(3); ANNE ARUNDEL § 7-5-104; CHICAGO § 2-156-090; COOK § 2.579; HONOLULU § 3-8.2(c); JACKSONVILLE § 602.402; KING § 3.04.030(D); MAUI § 10-4(4); MIAMI § 2-11.1(m); N.Y.C. §§ 2604(b)(6)–(b)(8); PHILADELPHIA § 20-602; S.F. § 3.224; SEATTLE § 4.16.070(B)(3); WESTCHESTER § 883.21(c); TSC BILL §§ 800(4), (5), 801(7); DAVIES MODEL LAW §§ 100(4), (5), 102(7).

52. N.Y.S. § 805-a(1)(d); HONOLULU § 3-8.2(d); KING § 3.04.030(D); WESTCHESTER § 883.21(d).

53. ALA. §§ 36-25-5(e), 36-25-7; CAL. § 89503; MASS. ch. 268A, §§ 2–3; N.Y.S. § 805-a(1)(a); OHIO §§ 102.03(E), (F); 65 PA. CONS. STAT. ANN. § 1103(c); R.I. § 36-14-5(g); ANNE ARUNDEL § 7-5-106; CHICAGO § 2-156-142; COOK § 2-574; HONOLULU CHARTER § 11-102(a); HONOLULU §§ 3-8.7, 3-8.8; JACKSONVILLE §§ 602.701–602.703; KING §§ 3.04.020(C), (D), 3.04.030(B)(2)–(B)(4); L.A. 49.5.8; MAUI § 10-4(1)(a); MIAMI § 2-11.1(e); N.Y.C. § 2604(b)(5); PHILADELPHIA § 20-604; S.F. § 3.216; SEATTLE § 4.16.070(C); WESTCHESTER § 883.21(a); TSC Bill § 800(3); Davies Model Law § 100(3).

54. CAL. § 89502; OHIO § 102.03(H); 65 PA. CONS. STAT. ANN. § 1103(d); ANNE ARUNDEL § 7-5-106(d); CHICAGO § 2-156-142(b); COOK § 2.574(e); D.C. § 1-1162.26; JACKSONVILLE § 602.704.

55. CAL. § 89506; OHIO § 102.03(I); L.A. § 49.5.8(C)(5)(e); MIAMI § 2-11.1(w); S.F. § 3.216(d).

56. ANNE ARUNDEL § 7-5-106(b).

57. N.Y.S. § 805-a(1)(a) (held unconstitutionally vague in People v. Moore, 85 Misc. 2d 4, 377 N.Y.S.2d 1005 (Fulton Cnty. Ct. 1975)).

58. CAL. § 82028(b)(4); 65 PA. CONS. STAT. ANN. § 13A03; ANNE ARUNDEL § 7-1-101(11); CHICAGO § 2-156-142(d)(3); COOK § 2.574(b)(3); HONOLULU CHARTER § 11-102(a); JACKSONVILLE § 602.201(p)(2)(ii); KING §§ 3.04.017(I), 3.04.030(B)(4); MIAMI § 2-11.1(e)(2)(a); PHILADELPHIA § 20-601(10); SEATTLE § 4.16.070(C)(1); WESTCHESTER § 883.21(a); TSC BILL § 803(4); DAVIES MODEL LAW § 105(4).

59. CAL. §§ 84100–84511; COOK § 2.585; D.C. §§ 1-1163.01 through 1-1163.38; HONOLULU § 3-8.9; TSC BILL § 800(1)(f); DAVIES MODEL LAW § 100(1)(f).

60. HONOLULU CHARTER § 11-102(d). *See also* ALA. § 36-25-7(d); MASS. ch. 268A, § 3(b); D.C. § 1-1162.23(d)(1); N.Y.C. § 2604(b)(13); PHILADELPHIA CHARTER § 10-105. *Cf.* MIAMI §§ 2-11.1(e)(3), (k)(1).

61. *See, e.g.*, MASS. Ch. 268A, § 23(c); N.Y.S. § 805-a(1)(b); OHIO § 102.03(B); HONOLULU CHARTER § 11-102(1)(b); JACKSONVILLE § 602.401(b); KING § 3.04.020(F); L.A. § 49.5.3; MAUI § 10-4(1)(b); MIAMI § 2-11.1(h); WESTCHESTER § 883.21(b); TSC BILL § 800(6); DAVIES MODEL LAW § 100(6).

62. S.F. § 3.228. *See also* L.A. § 49.5.2 ("confidential information").

63. Philadelphia § 20-609.

64. *Id. See also* Ala. § 36-25-8; 65 Pa. Cons. Stat. Ann., §§ 1102 ("conflict of interest"), 1103(a); R.I. §§ 36-14-5(c), (d); Anne Arundel § 7-5-108.

65. Cook § 2.577; Seattle § 4.16.070(D)(1). *See also* Chicago § 2-156-070; N.Y.C. Ad. Code § 12-110(g)(3).

66. Cook § 2.577; N.Y.C. § 2604(b)(4). *See also* Anne Arundel § 7-5-108; S.F. § 3.228.

67. N.Y.C. §§ 2604(b)(9), (b)(11), (b)(12).

68. *Id.* § 2604(b)(15).

69. S.F. § 3.230. *See also* Chicago § 2-156-140; Cook § 2-583; D.C. § 1-1171.02; Honolulu Charter §§ 6-1112(2), 6-1112(3)(b)–(f); Honolulu §§ 3-8.6, 3-8.9; King § 3.04.020(E); L.A. § 49.5.5(B); Philadelphia Charter § 10-107; TSC Bill §§ 800(7), 803(16); Davies Model Law §§ 100(7), 105(11). *Cf.* Philadelphia Charter § 10-103 (prohibiting employees of political committees from interfering with members of uniformed services).

70. *See* 5 U.S.C. §§ 1501–1508 (Political Activity of Certain State and Local Employees). Information on the applicability of the Hatch Act to state and local employees may be obtained from the U.S. Office of Special Counsel, either through their web site, https://osc.gov/pages/hatchact-affectsme.aspx (last visited April 4, 2016), or by calling 800-854-2824. *See also* Philadelphia Charter § 10-107(5).

71. King § 3.04.030(B)(10).

72. Ala. § 36-25-5(e). *See also* N.Y.C. § 2604(b)(14). *Cf.* S.F. § 3.216(c) (gifts from subordinates).

73. King § 3.04.030(A)(7).

74. Seattle § 4.16.070(A)(2). *See also* Miami § 2-11.1(x); TSC Bill §§ 800(1)(d), 803(3); Davies Model Law §§ 100(1)(d), 105(2).

75. 65 Pa. Cons. Stat. Ann. § 1103(e).

76. N.Y.C. § 2604(b)(10). *See also* Honolulu Charter § 6-1112(3)(h); Philadelphia Charter § 10-108(2); S.F. § 3.208.

77. *See, e.g.*, Ala. § 36-25-13; Mass. ch. 268A, §§ 12, 18, 21A; Ohio §§ 102.03(A)–(B); 65 Pa. Cons. Stat. Ann. § 1103(g) (held unconstitutional as applied to former government employees who are also attorneys in Shaulis v. Pennsylvania State Ethics Comm'n, 574 Pa. 680, 833 A.2d 123 (2003)); R.I. § 36-14-5(e)(4); Anne Arundel § 7-5-105; Chicago § 2-156-100; Cook § 2.580; Honolulu Charter § 11-105; Honolulu § 3-8.3; Jacksonville § 602.412; King §§ 3.04.015(C), 3.04.030(A)(7), 3.04.035; L.A. § 49.5.13; Maui §§ 10-4(1)(f), 10-4(2); Miami § 2-11.1(q); N.Y.C. §§ 2604(d)–(e); Philadelphia § 20-603; S.F. § 3.234; Seattle § 4.16.075; Westchester § 883.21(h); TSC Bill §§ 800(8), 801(8); Davies Model Law §§ 100(8), 102(8).

78. *See, e.g.*, N.Y.C. § 2604(d)(6).

79. S.F. Charter § C3.699-13(d). *See also* Cal. § 83116.5; S.F. § 3.236; Rules of the City of New York, tit. 53, § 1-13(d), http://www.nyc.gov/html/conflicts/downloads/pdf2/books/red_book.pdf (last visited Apr. 4, 2016); TSC Bill § 800(10); Davies Model Law § 100(10). *Cf.* Honolulu § 3-8.2(f) (prohibiting city officers or employees from ordering any person to violate, or aiding or abetting any person in the violation of, certain charter provisions relating to the prohibition on political activities of persons in civil service); King § 3.04.030(B)(13) (prohibiting county employees from acting "as an accomplice in any act by an immediate family member which, if the act were performed by the employee, would be prohibited" by certain specified ethics provisions); L.A. § 49.5.5(C) (prohibiting any person from "induc[ing] or coerce[ing], or attempt[ing] to induce or coerce aother [sic] person to engage in any activity prohibited by Subsection . . . B [prohibiting city officials and employees from engaging in campaign-related activities]).

80. Westchester § 883.21(f). *See also* Miami § 2-11.1(o); TSC Bill § 800(9); Davies Model Law § 100(9). *Cf.* Miami § 2-11.1(u) (prohibition on business transactions with county contractors).

81. *See, e.g.*, Ala. § 36-25-24; Mass. ch. 268B, § 8; 65 Pa. Cons. Stat. Ann. § 1108(j); R.I. § 36-14-5(m); Anne Arundel § 7-4-109; Cook § 2.584; King §§ 3.04.017(M), 3.42.010–3.42.070; L.A. § 49.5.4; Philadelphia § 20-606(1)(j).

82. TSC Bill § 802. *See also* Davies Model Law § 103; L.A. Charter § 706; L.A. § 49.5.5(C).

83. ALA. § 36-25-5(d). *See also* CAL. § 83116.5 (prohibiting anyone from "purposely or negligently caus[ing] any other person to violate any provision of [the Act], or . . . aid[ing] and abet[ting] any other person in the violation of any provision of [the Act]," but then restricts the prohibition to persons who have filing or reporting obligations under the Act or who are compensated for services involving the planning, organizing, or directing of any activity regulated or required by the Act).

84. OHIO § 102.03(F). *See also* MASS. ch. 268A, § 3(a); 65 PA. CONS. STAT. ANN. § 1103(b); R.I. § 36-14-5(i); PHILADELPHIA § 20-604(2). *Cf.* R.I. § 36-14.1-2 (prohibiting state vendors from providing goods and services for less than fair market value for personal use of a procurement official of a state agency with which the vendor will be doing business in the succeeding 24 months or has done business in the previous 24 months).

85. MASS. ch. 268A, § 17(b). *See also* MASS. Ch. 268A, § 11(b).

86. COOK § 2.585(b).

87. N.Y.C. § 2604(a).

88. *Id.* § 2604(e).

89. MASS. ch. 268A, §§ 12(c)–(d), 18(c)–(d). *See also* R.I. § 36-14-5(f); JACKSONVILLE § 602.402(e); TSC BILL § 804; DAVIES MODEL LAW § 106.

90. *See* L.A. CHARTER § 707; L.A. § 49.5.6(E).

91. *See, e.g.*, N.Y. GEN. CONSTR. LAW § 41.

92. *See, e.g.*, COIB Ad. Op. No. 98-10, at 8.

93. *See, e.g.*, MASS. ch. 268A, §§ 6A, 13(b), 19(b); N.Y.S. § 803; OHIO §§ 102.04(D)–(E); 53 PA. STAT. ANN. § 551; 65 PA. CONS. STAT. ANN. § 1103(j); R.I. §§ 36-14-5(e), 36-14-6; ANNE ARUNDEL §§ 7-5-101, 7-5-109(c), 7-5-110, 7-5-111; CHICAGO §§ 2-156-080(b)–(c); COOK §§ 2.578(b)–(c); D.C. §§ 1-1162.23(b)–(c); HONOLULU CHARTER § 11-103; JACKSONVILLE § 602.406; KING § 3.04.037; MAUI § 10-4(1)(e); MIAMI §§ 2-11.1(c)(4), (e)(4), (f); N.Y.C. §§ 2604(a), (b)(1), 2605; PHILADELPHIA § 20-608; S.F. § 3.214; SEATTLE § 4.16.070(A); WESTCHESTER § 883.21(e); TSC BILL § 800(11); DAVIES MODEL LAW § 101.

94. *See, e.g.*, ALA. § 36-25-16; N.Y.S. § 809; R.I. § 36-14-5(f); KING § 3.04.120; MIAMI § 2-11.1(c)(4); TSC BILL § 806; DAVIES MODEL LAW §§ 108, 109. *Cf.* JACKSONVILLE § 602.406 (Public Official Bid and Contract Disclosure).

95. 65 PA. CONS. STAT. ANN. § 1103(h); R.I. § 36-14-5(j).

96. *See, e.g.*, ALA. §§ 36-25-14, 36-25-15; CAL. §§ 87200–87210; MASS. ch. 268B; N.Y.S. §§ 811–812; OHIO § 102.02; 65 PA. CONS. STAT. ANN. §§ 1104–1105; R.I. §§ 36-14-16 through 36-14-18; ANNE ARUNDEL §§ 7-6-101 through 7-6-107; CHICAGO §§ 2-156-150 through 2-156-200; COOK § 2-589; D.C. §§ 1-1162.24 through 1-1162.25; HONOLULU § 3-8.4; KING § 3.04.050; L.A. §§ 49.5.9, 49.5.10; MAUI § 10-3; MIAMI §§ 2-11.1(i), (k)(2); N.Y.C. § 2603(d); N.Y.C. AD. CODE § 12-110; PHILADELPHIA § 20-610; S.F. § 3.1-100 through 3.1-510; SEATTLE § 4.16.080; WESTCHESTER §§ 883.61–883.81; TSC BILL §§ 805, 812, 813, 824; DAVIES MODEL LAW §§ 107, 201, 202, 208.

97. N.Y.S. § 812(5).

98. *See* 65 PA. CONS. STAT. ANN. § 1103(h); R.I. § 36-14-5(j).

99. TSC BILL § 805(4). *Accord* DAVIES MODEL LAW § 107(4).

100. *See, e.g.*, ALA. § 36-25-3; CAL. §§ 83100–83110; MASS. ch. 268B, § 2; N.Y.S. § 808; OHIO § 102.05; R.I. § 36-14-8; ANNE ARUNDEL §§ 7-2-101 through 7-2-103; CHICAGO §§ 2-156-310 through 2-156-330; COOK § 2-591; HONOLULU CHARTER § 11-107; KING § 3.04.080; L.A. CHARTER §§ 700–701; MAUI § 10-2(1); MIAMI §§ 2-1066, 2-1069, 2-1071; N.Y.C. § 2602; PHILADELPHIA CHARTER §§ 3-100(e), 3-806; SEATTLE §§ 3.70.010–3.70.040, 3.70.110, 3.70.150, 3.70.170; TSC BILL §§ 814–820, 822; DAVIES MODEL LAW §§ 203–206.

101. *See, e.g.*, CAL. §§ 83101–83102 (prohibiting the governor's two appointees from being members of the same political party); 65 PA. CONS. STAT. ANN. § 1106(a) (prohibiting more than two of the Governor's appointees from being members of the same political party); HONOLULU § 3-6.4(a) (requiring the executive director of the ethics commission to be an attorney licensed to practice in the State of Hawaii); ANNE ARUNDEL § 7-2-103(a)(2) (requiring the executive director to be an attorney licensed to practice in the State of Maryland); JACKSONVILLE § 602.912(b) (listing various types of qualifications, including being an attorney, a

former judge, or a CPA with forensic audit experience); S.F. CHARTER §§ 15.100–15.101 (the appointee of the City Attorney must have a background in government ethics law; the appointee of the Assessor must have a background in campaign finance; and the executive director must have a background in campaign finance, public information, and public meetings and government ethics law).

102. *See, e.g.*, 65 PA. CONS. STAT. ANN. § 1106(d); R.I. § 36-14-8(f); HONOLULU § 3-6.9; L.A. CHARTER § 700(d); N.Y.C. § 2602(b); SEATTLE § 3.70.060.

103. MIAMI § 2-1069(e). *See also* S.F. CHARTER § 15.100 (prohibiting Ethics Commission members and employees from holding any other city or county office, being an officer of a political party, being, or being employed by, a registered lobbyist or campaign consultant, or participating in any campaign supporting or opposing a candidate for city elective office, a city ballot measure, or a city officer running for any elective office; prohibiting commission members from holding employment with the city and county and commission employees from holding any other city or county employment).

104. *See, e.g.*, CAL § 83105; CHICAGO §§ 2-156-310(b), 2-156-340; L.A. CHARTER § 700(e); N.Y.C. §§ 2602(c), (f); PHILADELPHIA CHARTER §§ 3-806(b), (f); SEATTLE § 3.70.030.

105. *See, e.g.*, ALA. § 36-25-3(a); N.Y.C. § 2602(c); PHILADELPHIA CHARTER § 3-806(d).

106. *See, e.g.*, ALA. § 36-25-3(d) ($50 per diem); COOK § 2-591(5) (no compensation); OHIO § 102.05 ($75 per meeting but capped at $1,800 in any fiscal year).

107. CHICAGO § 2-156-145(b). *See also* PALM BEACH COUNTY, FLA., CODE § 2-446 (mandating ethics training); CITY OF LONG BEACH, CAL., MUNICIPAL CODE § 2.07.020 (providing for automatic removal from office of any member of Charter commission or advisory body who fails to complete required ethics training).

108. *See, e.g.ci* ALA. § 36-25-4; MASS. ch. 268A, §§ 6A, 10; MASS. ch. 268B, §§ 3–5; N.Y.S. §§ 808, 811(1)(d); OHIO §§ 102.02, 102.06, 102.08, 102.09; 65 PA. CONS. STAT. ANN., §§ 1105(d), 1107, 1108; R.I. CONST. art. III, § 8; R.I. §§ 36-14-9 through 36-14-18; ANNE ARUNDEL §§ 7-2-104 through 7-2-107, 7-3-101 through 7-3-103, 7-4-101 through 7-4-108, 7-6-107, 7-8-101; CHICAGO §§ 2-156-145, 2-156-170 through 2-156-190, 2-156-210 through 2-156-290, 2-156-380 through 2-156-408; COOK §§ 2.587, 2-591(6)–(14), 2-592; D.C. §§ 1-1162.11 through 1-1162.22; HONOLULU CHARTER § 11-107; HONOLULU §§ 3-6.3, 3-6.5 through 3-6.7, 3-6.10, 3-8.4(d), (f), 3-8.5; JACKSONVILLE §§ 602.921, 602.931–602.941, 602.1001, 602.1101–602.1102; KING §§ 3.04.050, 3.04.057, 3.04.100–3.04.130; L.A. CHARTER §§ 702–711; L.A. §§ 49.5.4, 49.5.7, 49.5.9(C), 49.5.15, 49.5.16(E); L.A. AD. CODE §§ 24.12–24.14, 24.21–24.29; MAUI §§ 10-2(2) through 10-2(5); MIAMI §§ 2-11.1(r), (y), 2-1072, 2-1074(y); N.Y.C. §§ 2603, 2604(e), 2606; PHILADELPHIA CHARTER § 4-1100; PHILADELPHIA §§ 20-606, 20-608(1)(c), 20-610(4), 20-613; S.F. CHARTER §§ 15.100, 15.102, C3.699-10 through C3.699-14; SEATTLE §§ 3.70.100, 3.70.160, 4.16.080(A)–(B), 4.16.090; WESTCHESTER §§ 883.71(2), 883.81(6)–(7); TSC BILL §§ 821, 823–835; DAVIES MODEL LAW §§ 207–215. For a more extensive discussion of the administration of an ethics board, see Mark Davies, *A Practical Approach to Establishing and Maintaining a Values-Based Conflicts of Interest Compliance System*, 18–29 (2005), http://www.nyc.gov/html/conflicts/downloads/pdf2/international/DaviesArticle_final.pdf; Mark Davies, *Administering an Effective Ethics Law: The Nuts and Bolts* (2005), http://www.nyc.gov/html/conflicts/downloads/pdf2/international/nuts_and_bolts_speech_delivered_final.pdf.

109. *See, e.g.*, ALA. §§ 36-25-4(a)(11), 36-25-27(c); CAL. §§ 83115–83121, 91000–91014; MASS. ch. 268A, §§ 9, 15, 21, ch. 268B, § 4; N.Y.S. §§ 811(1)(c)–(1)(d), 812(6); OHIO § 102.06; 65 PA. CONS. STAT. ANN. §§ 1107(12)–(15), 1108, 1110; R.I. §§ 36-14-12 through 36-14-15; ANNE ARUNDEL §§ 7-4-101 through 7-4-107, 7-8-101 through 7-8-103; CHICAGO §§ 2-156-380 through 2-156-396; COOK §§ 2-591(6)–(9), 2-592; HONOLULU CHARTER §§ 11-107, 13-114, 13-115; HONOLULU §§ 3-6.3(b), (d), (e), (h), 3-6.5(e), 3-6.7; KING §§ 3.04.055, 3.04.057; L.A. CHARTER §§ 706–709; L.A. § 49.5.16; L.A. AD. CODE §§ 24.21–24.29; MAUI § 10-2; MIAMI §§ 2-1074, 2-1075; N.Y.C. §§ 2603(e)–(h), 2606; PHILADELPHIA §§ 20-606(1)(f)–(1)(k); S.F. CHARTER §§ 15.100, 15.105, C3.699-13; SEATTLE §§ 3.70.100(D)–(F), 3.70.160(A), (C), 4.16.090, 4.16.100, 4.16.105; TSC BILL §§ 825–827; DAVIES MODEL LAW §§ 209–210.

110. 65 PA. CONS. STAT. ANN. § 1110(a); R.I. § 36-14-5(k); MIAMI § 2-1074(t); PHILADELPHIA 20-606(1)(k); S.F. §§ 3.238, 3.240.

111. *See* N.Y.C. §§ 2603(e)(3), (g)(3), (h)(7); Seattle § 4.16.030 ("covered individual"). *Compare* Flynn v. State Ethics Commission, 87 N.Y.2d 199, 661 N.E.2d 991, 638 N.Y.S.3d 418 (1995) (holding under previous law that New York State Ethics Commission possessed no jurisdiction over former state officers and employees for acts committed while in state service), *statutorily overruled* by 2005 N.Y. Laws, ch. 165, codified as amended at N.Y. Exec. Law §§ 94(1), (11), 13(c) and N.Y. Leg. Law §§ 80(1), (8).

112. Cal. §§ 91004, 91005, 91009.

113. *See, e.g.*, Ala. § 36-25-27 (CF, F, M, R, T); Cal. §§ 83116, 91000–91014 (CF, DA, DG, DQ, I, M, Q, T, V); Mass. ch. 268A, §§ 2, 3, 9, 11–15, 17–21, 21B, 23, 25 (D, DA, DG, DQ, F, R, T, UF, V); N.Y.S. § 812(6) (CF, M); Ohio § 102.99 (M); 65 Pa. Cons. Stat. Ann. § 1109 (CF, DA, F, M, T); R.I. §§ 36-14-13(d), 36-14-14, 36-14-19 (CF, DA, DG, I, M); Anne Arundel §§ 7-4-104, 7-8-101 through 7-8-103 (CF, DA, I, V); Chicago §§ 2-156-465, 2-156-485 (D, DA, DG, T, UF, V); Cook §§ 2-601 through 2-603 (DA, M, UF, V); D.C. § 1-1162.21 (CF, T); Honolulu Charter § 11-106 (DA); Honolulu §§ 3-8.4(f), 3-8.5, 3-8.6(e), 3-8.7(e), 3-8.9(f) (CF, DA, DG, M, T, V); Jacksonville §§ 602.309, 602.1101, 602.1102, 602.1201, 602.1204, 602.1213 (DG, M, V); King § 3.04.060 (CF, DA, DR, M, V); L.A. Charter § 706(c) (CF, I, T); L.A. § 49.5.16 (CF, DA, I, M, Q, T); Maui § 10-5 (CF, DA); Miami §§ 2-11.1(c)(1), (cc) (DA, IN, R, UF, V, W); N.Y.C. § 2606 (CF, DA, DQ, M, V); Philadelphia Charter §§ 10-107(6), 10-108(4), 10-109 (CF, DA, DQ, M); Philadelphia §§ 20-612, 20-1301, 20-1302 (CF, V); S.F. Charter §§ 15.105, C3.699-13(c) (CF, DA,DQ, I, T); S.F. §§ 3.214(b), 3.242 (CF, DA, I, M, Q, V, W); Seattle § 4.16.100 (CF, D, DA, DG, R, T, V); Westchester §§ 883.71(3), 883.91 (CF, DA, M, UF); TSC Bill §§ 807–810 (CF, D, DA, DG, DR, F, I, M, T, V); Davies Model Law §§ 109–113 (CF, D, DA, DG, DR, I, M, T, V). CF = civil fines or administrative penalties; D = damages; DA = disciplinary action, such as suspension or removal; DG = disgorgement of ill-gotten gains; DR = debarment; DQ = disqualification from future office, including temporary disqualifications; F = felony; I = injunctive relief; IN = criminal infraction (less than misdemeanor); M = misdemeanor; Q = qui tam action; R = restitution; T = double or treble penalties, which may be subject to a cap; UF = fine (not specified as civil or criminal); V = voiding contract; W = warning or reprimand.

114. *See, e.g.*, Cal. §§ 81008, 83110; Mass. ch. 268B, §§ 4, 7; Ohio §§ 102.06(B), (F), (G), 102.07; 65 Pa. Cons. Stat. Ann. §§ 1104(e), 1107(10), 1108(a), (c), (g), (h); R.I. §§ 36-14-12(c)(3), (c)(6), 36-14-13(a)(5), (f); Anne Arundel §§ 7-2-107(c), 7-3-103, 7-4-106, 7-5-109(f), 7-5-111(e), 7-6-107; Chicago §§ 2-156-080(b), 2-156-180(d), 2-156-290, 2-156-400, 2-156-401; Cook § 2-592; Honolulu Charter § 11-107; Honolulu §§ 3-6.3(j), 3-6.5(c)–(e), 3-6.7 (e), 3-8.4(e); L.A. Charter §§ 705(a), 706(a)(2), (b), (c); L.A. § 49.5.4(C); L.A. Ad. Code §§ 24.1.1(e), 24.23(a)(4), 24.26(b)(2)–(b)(3); Miami §§ 2-1074(e), (n)(5), (p), (s); N.Y.C. §§ 2603(c)(3), (f), (h)(4)–(h)(5), (i), (k), 2604(e); N.Y.C. Ad. Code §§ 12-110(e), (g)(3); Philadelphia §§ 20-606(1)(d)(iii), (1)(f)(i), (1)(i), 20-608(1)(c), 20-610(4); S.F. Charter app. C, §§ C3.699-12(a), C3.699-13; Seattle § 4.16.90(H). *See also* TSC Bill § 836; Davies Model Law § 216.

115. Robert Service, The Cremation of Sam McGee stanza viii (1907), http://www.poetryfoundation.org/poem/174348 (last visited Apr. 4, 2022).

APPENDIX 9A

Municipal Ethics Boards and Enforcement Authority

Municipality	Ethics Board	Enforcement Authority	Investigative Authority	Citations
Albuquerque	Yes	Yes	Yes	Charter of the City of Albuquerque Art. XII, § 8 *ENF*, § 9 *INV* *IA* = Office of Internal Audit and Investigations (see Albuquerque Code of Ordinances § 2-10-4); Accountability in Government Oversight Committee (see Albuquerque Code of Ordinances § 2-10-5)
Anne Arundel County (MD)	Yes	Yes	Yes	Anne Arundel County (Annapolis, MD) Charter § 1001B(e) *INV*; § 1001(g) *RES*; County Code § 7-2-104(b)(3) *INV*, §§ 7-4-104, 7-8-101 to 7-8-103 *ENF*
Baltimore	Yes	Yes	Yes	Baltimore City Code Art. 8, § 9-4 *ENF*; Art. 8, § 3-5(d) *BUDG*; Art. 8, § 5-3 *INV* *IA* = Inspector General
Chicago	Yes	Yes	Yes	Mun. Code of Chicago § 2-156-380(b)-(c) *INV*; §§ 2-156-370, 2-156-380(j) *RES* *IA* = Inspector General (see Code § 2-56-030)
Cook County (IL)	Yes	Yes	Yes	Cook County, IL Code of Ordinances § 2-591(7), (8) *INV*; § 2-591(9) *ENF* *IA* = Inspector General (see Code § 2-283)
Detroit	Yes	Yes	Yes	Detroit City Charter § 2-106.9(2) *INV*; § 2-106.11 *ENF*; § 2-106.13 *BUDG*; Detroit Code of Ordinances § 2-6-91(a)(2) *INV*; § 2-6-95(a) *BUDG*; §§ 2-6-115(b)(4), (b)(5), (b)(7), (c) *ENF* *IA* = Ombudsman (see Charter §§ 7.5-407, 7.5-408)

Municipality	Ethics Board	Enforcement Authority	Investigative Authority	Citations
Honolulu	Yes	Yes	Yes	Rev. Charter of Honolulu §§ 11-107, 13-114 *INV*, *ENF*; Rev. Ordinance of City and County of Honolulu § 3-6.3(c)-(e) *INV*, *ENF*; § 3-6.4 *RES*
Indianapolis	Yes	Yes	Yes	Rev. Code of the Consolidated City and County Indianapolis/Marion, IN §§ 293-335(3) *INV*; § 293-339(b) *ENF* IA = Office of Audit and Performance (see Code § 202-303)
Jacksonville	Yes	Yes	Yes	Jacksonville Ordinance Code § 602.921(a) *INV*; § 602.921(d) *ENF*; § 602.611(b)(1) *BUDG* IA = Office of Ethics, Compliance, and Oversight (see Code § 602.621(k)–(l))
Los Angeles	Yes	Yes	Yes	Los Angeles City Charter § 706(a) *INV*, § 706(b), (c) *ENF*; § 711 *BUDG*; Los Angeles Administrative Code § 24.22 *INV*, § 24.25 *ENF*; Los Angeles Municipal Code § 49.5.16 *ENF* IA = City Ethics Comm'n, Director of Enforcement (see Administrative Code § 24.24)
Maui County (HI)	Yes	Yes	Yes	Maui County Charter §§ 10-2(2)(a), 10-2(3) *INV*; § 10-2(2)(b) *ENF*; § 10-2(6) *BUDG*
Miami-Dade County	Yes	Yes	Yes	Code of Miami-Dade County §§ 2-11.1(c)(4), 2-11.1(r), 2-11.1(s)(9), 2-11.1(y) *INV*; §§ 2-11.1(y), 2-11.1(cc)(1), 2-11.1.1(B) *ENF*; §§ 2-11.1(s)(2)(b), 2-11.1(s)(2)(d), 2-11.1.1(C)(3), 2-11.1.1(D)(3) *RES* IA = Inspector General (see Code § 2-8.1(i))
Milwaukee	Yes	Yes	Yes	Milwaukee City Code of Ordinances §§ 303-19(2), 303-21 *INV*; § 303-27(3) *ENF*; §§ 303-15(2), 303-17(3) *BUDG* IA = Dep't of Employee Relations, Code § 340-3(2)(d)

Municipal Ethics Boards and Enforcement Authority • 185

Municipality	Ethics Board	Enforcement Authority	Investigative Authority	Citations
Montgomery County (MD)	Yes	Yes	Yes	Montgomery County (MD) Code §§ 19A.06.01.01, 19A.17.01.03(B) *INV*; §§ 19A.06.01.04(E), 19A.06.02.04.12, 19A.06.02.05.2, 19A.06.02.06 *ENF*; § 19A-23 *RES*
New Orleans	Yes	Yes	Yes	New Orleans Code of Ordinances § 2-719(11) *INV*, § 2-719(1) *ENF*, § 2-719(1) *RES*; Charter of the City of New Orleans § 9-402 *ENF* *IA* = Civil Service Commission (see Code § 8-103(2)(f))
New York	Yes	Yes	No	NYC Charter §§ 2603(f)–(g) *INV*; §§ 2603(e), (g)–(h) *ENF* *IA* = Dep't of Investigation (see Charter § 803)
Oakland	Yes	Yes	Yes	Oakland Mun. Code § 2.24.030(A)–(B) *INV*; § 2.24.030(C) *ENF*; § 2.24.080 *RES* *IA* = City Auditor (See Charter § 403)
Philadelphia	Yes	Yes	Yes	Philadelphia Code §§ 20-606(1)(f)(ii)(2), 20-606(1)(g)(i) *INV*; §§ 20-606(1)(f), 20-606(1)(h) *ENF*; Philadelphia Home Rule Charter § 3-806(k) *BUDG* *IA* = Office of Inspector General (See Code § 20-606(1)(f)(ii)(5))
San Antonio	Yes	Yes	Yes	San Antonio, TX. Code of Ordinances § 2-82(a), (e)(6) *INV*, §§ 2-82 (e)(9), 2-87(f)(5) *ENF* *IA* = City council or city manager (see Charter § 48)
San Francisco	Yes	Yes	Yes	San Francisco Charter §§ 15.100, Charter Appendix § C3.699-13(a) *INV*; Charter Appendix § C3.699-13(c) *ENF*; Charter Appendix § C3.699-14 *RES* *IA* = Dep't of Human Resources (see Charter § 10.102), Civil Service Commission (see Employee Relations Ordinance § 16.204)

Municipality	Ethics Board	Enforcement Authority	Investigative Authority	Citations
Seattle	Yes	Yes	Yes	Seattle Mun. Code §§ 3.70.100(D), 3.70.160(C) INV; § 3.70.160(A) ENF; §§ 3.70.160 (D), 3.70.100(H) BUDG IA = Civil Service Commission (see Mun. Code § 4.04.250(L)(4))
Washington, D.C.	Yes	Yes	Yes	Cf. DC Code § 1-1162.02(4) INV; § 1-1162.21 ENF; § 1-1162.07 BUDG IA = Director of Government Ethics (see Code § 1-1162.11(3)), Office of the Inspector General (see Code § 1-301.115a(3)(d))
Denver	Yes	Limited	Yes	Denver Rev. Mun. Code § 2-58 INV; § 2-54(e) ENF; § 2-53(f) RES IA = Career service board (see Code § 18-2(a)(5))
Kansas City	Yes	Limited?	Yes	Kansas City Charter Art. XI § 1117(b), Kansas City Code of Ordinances §§ 2-2092, 2-2093(5), 2-2095 INV; Kansas City Charter Art. XI § 1117(a), Kansas City Code of Ordinances § 2-2098(b)(2) ENF Kansas City Code of Ordinances § 2-2097(b)–(d) RES IA = City Auditor's Office (see Charter Art. § 26(c)(3))
Tampa	Yes	Limited	Yes	Tampa Code of Ordinances §§ 2-658(b), 2-662 INV; §§ 2-657, 2-659 ENF
Austin	Yes	Limited?	Limited?	Austin City Code § 2-7-30 INV; §§ 2-7-26(3), 2-7-26(8), 2-7-41(C), (E) ENF; § 2-7-26 BUDG IA = Dep't of Human Resources, Employee Relations Division (see Austin City Charter, Art. 9 § 3)
Houston	Yes	No	Limited	Houston Code of Ordinances § 18.16(g),(h) INV; § 18.16(g),(h) ENF IA = Office of the Inspector General and other entities (see Code § 18.16(g))
Fort Worth	Yes	No	Yes	Fort Worth Code of Ordinances § 2-241(b)(10) INV; § 2-252 ENF; § 2-242 RES

Municipal Ethics Boards and Enforcement Authority • 187

Municipality	Ethics Board	Enforcement Authority	Investigative Authority	Citations
Memphis	Yes	No	Yes	*Cf.* Memphis Code of Ordinances § 2-10-10(B)(2) *INV*; §§ 2-4-12B, 2-10-13 *ENF* IA = Board of Commissioners (see Charter § 47)
Minneapolis	Yes	No	Limited	Minneapolis Code of Ordinances Art. 2 §§ 15.210(d), 15.210(e)(4), 15.230(a)(1) *INV*; §§ 15.210(e)(8), 15.240(b) *ENF*; § 15.220 *RES* IA = Dep't of Inspection (see Code §§ 28.40, 28.50)
Nashville-Davidson	Yes	No	Yes	Code of the Metropolitan Government of Nashville and Davidson Cnty., TN § 2.222.040(A)(5)(c) *INV*; § 2.222.040(C)(3)(a) *ENF* IA = Civil Service Commission (see Code § 2.222.060)
St. Paul	Yes	No	Yes	St. Paul, MN Code of Ordinances §§ 111.04(d), 111.04(i), 111.05 *INV*; § 111.05 *ENF*; 111.041 *RES*
Dallas	Yes	No	No	Dallas City Code §§ 12A-25(c), 12A-30 IA = City Auditor's Office (see Dallas City Charter Ch. IX § 2.3(2))
El Paso	Yes	No	No	El Paso Mun. Code § 2.92.030(E)(6) *INV*; §§ 2.92.030(E)(6), 2.92.090(I) *ENF*; § 2.92.030(D)(3) *RES*
Tulsa	Yes	No	No	City of Tulsa Rev. Ordinances Title 12, § 608 *INV*; § 609 *ENF*; § 610(F) *BUDG* IA = Human Resources Dep't, Police Dep't, City Auditor's Office, and/or City Attorney's Office (see Ordinances § 608)
Boston	No	—	—	*Cf.* Boston Mun. Code § 5-5.40 IA = City Council Committee on Post Audit and Oversight State: Mass. Gen. Laws c. 268A §§ 17-23

188 • Ethical Standards in the Public Sector

Municipality	Ethics Board	Enforcement Authority	Investigative Authority	Citations
Charlotte	No	—	—	Cf. Charter of the City of Charlotte § 8.101 ENF; Code of Ethics for the Mayor and City Council of the City of Charlotte, North Carolina § 7(a) INV; § 7(c) ENF IA = City Attorney (see Charter § 8.101, Code of Ethics § 7(a)) State: N. C. Gen. Stat. § 160A-86
Cleveland	No	—	—	Cf. City of Cleveland, Ohio Code of Ordinances § 155.02 Moral Claims Commission IA = Department of Finance, Division of Internal Auditing (see Code § 154.02) State: Ohio Admin. Code § 102-1-02
Columbus	No	—	—	[None] IA = Civil Service Commission (see Columbus City Charter § 154) State: Ohio Admin. Code § 102-1-02
Fresno	No	—	—	Cf. City of Fresno Mun. Code §§ 2-901, incorporating by ref. 2 Cal. Code of Regs. Section 18730 as the City Conflicts of Interest Code IA = Personnel Department State: 2 Cal. Code of Regs. § 18700, California Government Code § 83100 et seq.
Las Vegas	No	—	—	Cf. IA = Dep't of Detention and Enforcement under City Manager (see Las Vegas Mun. Code §§ 2.06.010, 2.09.020) IA = Audit Oversight Committee State: Nev. Rev. Stat. § 281A.010 et seq.
Long Beach	No	—	—	Cf. Long Beach Mun. Code § 2.07 IA = Civil Service Commission (see Long Beach City Charter § 1101), City Auditor (see Code § 803) State: 2 Cal. Code of Regs. § 18700, California Government Code § 83100 et seq.

Municipal Ethics Boards and Enforcement Authority • 189

Municipality	Ethics Board	Enforcement Authority	Investigative Authority	Citations
Mesa	No	—	—	*Cf.* Mesa City Charter §§ 206(B)(2)(a), 902(A)(4)–(6); Ad Hoc Ethics Committee IA = City Council (See Charter § 208) State: *Cf.* Ariz. Rev. Stat. §§ 38-501–511
Miami	No	—	—	*Cf.* Miami Code of Ordinances Art. V, §§ 2-611–619 IA = Mayor, City Commission (see Charter of the City of Miami § 14), Office of Independent Auditor General (see Charter § 48) State: Fla. Stat. § 112.320
Oklahoma City	No	—	—	[None] IA = City Manager (see Oklahoma City Charter, Art. IV § 3(f)) State: Okla. Stat. § 62
Omaha	No	—	—	[None] IA = City Mayor (see Omaha City Charter § 8.06), City Council (see Charter § 8.07) State: Nebr. Admin. Code, Title 4; Neb. Rev. Stat. § 49-14,105
Phoenix	No	—	—	*Cf.* Phoenix City Code §§ 2-52, 2-53 IA = City Auditor (See Code § 2-10) State: *Cf.* Arizona Revised Statutes §§ 38-501 to 38-511
Portland	No	—	—	*Cf.* Portland City Code, Ch. 1.03, § 1.03.040; Charter §§ 2-109, 2-403 INV, ENF IA = Office of Ombudsman, under City Auditor (see Code § 2-504) State: Or. Rev. Stat. § 244.250, Or. Admin. R. Chapter 199
Sacramento	No	—	—	*Cf.* Sacramento City Code, Chapter 2.16 IA = City Audit Office under City Manager (See Code § 61) State: 2 Cal. Code of Regs. § 18700, California Government Code § 83100 et seq.

Municipality	Ethics Board	Enforcement Authority	Investigative Authority	Citations
San Jose	No	—	—	Cf. San Jose City Charter § 805 IA = City Council (see Charter § 416) State: 2 Cal. Code of Regs. § 18700, California Government Code § 83100 et seq.
St. Louis	No	—	—	Cf. St. Louis City Rev. Code §§ 4.07.020, 4.07.040 IA = Director of Personnel (see Charter, Art. XVIII, § 25) State: Mo. Rev. Stat. § 105.955
Tucson	No	—	—	Cf. Tucson Charter Ch. X, §§ 1, 4 IA = Civil Service Commission (see Charter Ch. X, §§ 10-21) State: Cf. Ariz. Rev. Stat. §§ 38-501 to 38-511
Virginia Beach	No	—	—	Cf. Virginia Beach City Code §§ 2-80, 2-90 IA = City Council (see Code § 3-10) State: Code of Virginia §§ 2.2-3100 to 2.2-3131
Wichita	No	—	—	Cf. Wichita Mun. Code § 2.04.050 IA = City Manager (see Code § 2.04.400) State: Kan. Stat. Ann. § 75.4301a

Legend
INV = investigation provision
ENF = enforcement provision
IA = investigative authority (e.g., Department of Inspection, City Auditor's Office, etc.)
BUDG = budget provision
RES = provision ensuring resources or staff for ethics board, but not a formal budget

This chart was prepared by Leigh Warren while a third-year student at Columbia Law School and an intern at the New York City Conflicts of Interest Board.

APPENDIX 9B

Web Sites of Municipal Ethics Laws and Boards

Municipal laws can be hard to locate. Following are websites that provide the text of the municipal ethics laws cited in this chapter, as well as links to the corresponding ethics boards and to the model laws. Links to these websites, and to other helpful sites, may also be found on the website of the New York City Conflicts of Interest Board: http://www.nyc.gov/ethics, then "Ethics Links" in the left hand menu, then "U.S Municipal."

ANNE ARUNDEL COUNTY (MD.)

Ethics Commission: https://www.aacounty.org/boards-and-commissions/ethics-commission/index.html

Ethics Law (Anne Arundel County Code, Article 7): http://www.amlegal.comnxt/gateway.dll/Maryland/annearundelco_md/annearundelcountycode2005?f=templates$fn=default.htm$3.0$vid=amlegal:annearundelco_md

CHICAGO

Board of Ethics: http://www.cityofchicago.org/city/en/depts/ethics/auto_generated/ethics_mission.html

Ethics Law (Municipal Code Ch. 2-156): http://www.cityofchicago.org/city/en/depts/ethics/supp_info/governmental_ethicsordinance.html

COOK COUNTY (ILL.)

Board of Ethics: https://www.cookcountyil.gov/agency/board-ethics-1

Ethics Law (Cook County Code of Ordinances Art. VII): https://www.cookcountyil.gov/ethicsordinance

DISTRICT OF COLUMBIA

Board of Ethics: https://bega.dc.gov/

Ethics Law (District of Columbia Official Code § 1-1161.01): https://bega.dc.gov/service/ethics-manual

HONOLULU

Ethics Commission: http://www.honolulu.gov/ethics.html
Ethics Law (Revised Charter of Honolulu Art. XI): http://www.honolulu.gov/ethics/laws.html

JACKSONVILLE

Ethics Commission: http://www.coj.net/departments/ethics-commission.aspx
Ethics Law (Jacksonville, Fl. Code of Ordinances, Ch. 602): http://www.coj.net/departments/ethics-commission/duties-of-the-ethics-commission.aspx

KING COUNTY (WASH.)

Board of Ethics: http://www.kingcounty.gov/employees/ethics.aspx
Ethics Law (King County Code 3.04): http://www.kingcounty.gov/employees/ethics/ecomplete.aspx

LOS ANGELES

City Ethics Commission: http://ethics.lacity.org/About/about.cfm
Ethics Law (L.A. Mun. Code § 49.5.1): https://ethics.lacity.org/laws/

MAUI

Board of Ethics: http://www.co.maui.hi.us/boards/bDetail.php?BoardID=6
Ethics Law (Charter Art. 10): http://www.co.maui.hi.us/index.aspx?NID=162

MIAMI-DADE COUNTY

Commission on Ethics and Public Trust: http://www.miamidade.gov/ethics/
Ethics Law (Code of Miami-Dade County § 2-11.1): http://ethics.miamidade.gov/about.asp

NEW YORK CITY

Conflicts of Interest Board: http://www.nyc.gov/ethics
Ethics Law (New York City Charter Ch. 68): https://www1.nyc.gov/site/coib/the-law/chapter-68-of-the-new-york-city-charter.page

PHILADELPHIA

Board of Ethics: http://www.phila.gov/ethicsboard/
Ethics Law (Philadelphia Home Rule Charter Art. X, City Code Ch. 20-600): http://www.phila.gov/ethicsboard/PDF/Public%20Integrity%20Laws%2052411.pdf

SAN FRANCISCO

Ethics Commission: http://www.sfethics.org
Ethics Law (San Francisco Charter, Art. 15; Campaign & Governmental Conduct Code, Art. III): http://www.sfethics.org/ethics/2009/05/law-advice.html

SEATTLE

Ethics and Elections Commission: http://www.seattle.gov/ethics/
Ethics Law (Municipal Code Ch. 4.16): http://www.seattle.gov/ethics/etpub/et_code.htm

WESTCHESTER COUNTY (N.Y.)

Ethics Board: None
Ethics Law (County Code Ch. 883): https://www.municode.com/library/ny/westchester_county/codes/code_of_ordinances

NEW YORK STATE

S.6157/A.8637 (1991), proposed by the New York State Temporary State Commission on Local Government Ethics [TSC bill]: http://www.nyc.gov/html/conflicts/downloads/pdf2/municipal_ethics_laws_ny_state/temp_state_comm_lcl_govt_ethics_finl_rpt.pdf

MODEL LAW PROPOSED BY AUTHOR (DAVIES MODEL LAW)

http://www.nyc.gov/html/conflicts/downloads/pdf2/municipal_ethics_laws_ny_state/keep_faith_model_loc_ethics_law.pdf

INTERNATIONAL MODEL LAW PROPOSED BY AUTHOR

http://www.nyc.gov/html/conflicts/downloads/pdf2/international/DaviesArticle_final.pdf

CHAPTER 10

The Federal Inspectors General
The Honorable Mark Lee Greenblatt[1]

This chapter provides a description of the role, jurisdiction, and powers of federal inspectors general.

INTRODUCTION

Inspectors general serve a vital role in the federal government. They operate as independent and objective watchdogs within federal agencies and have the responsibility to combat waste, fraud, and abuse in those agencies and the programs they administer.

The positive impact of the inspectors general on the federal government's operations is considerable. Every year, IG reports and their recommendations identify billions of dollars that could be better spent by the federal government. For example, in fiscal year 2021 alone, federal IGs identified more than $62 billion that agency management could spend more effectively.[2] IGs further contribute to the operational integrity of the federal government by detecting misconduct and helping to bring the wrongdoers to justice. IG investigations facilitate the prosecution of thousands of such individuals and the recovery of billions of dollars each year.[3]

Following this introduction to the role of the IGs in the federal government, the second section of this chapter gives an overview of the federal inspectors general community and addresses the legal authorities that define its structure, how IGs are appointed and removed, and noteworthy distinctions among the individual IGs. The third section then discusses the unique dual-reporting obligation to which IGs are subject, as well as certain other features intended to ensure independence and objectivity in IG operations. The fourth section describes how IGs fulfill their oversight role, focusing, in particular, on the three main categories of activity in which they engage—audits, evaluations/inspections, and investigations—and the powers they may exercise in doing so. Finally, the fifth section addresses recent amendments to relevant legislation as well as ongoing proposals for change.[4]

OVERVIEW OF THE FEDERAL IG COMMUNITY: LEGAL FRAMEWORK AND STRUCTURE

While the inspector general concept is nearly as old as the United States itself, it existed only in the context of the military for much of our country's history. It was not until the latter half of the 20th century that the inspector general was introduced on a broad scale to the civilian side of the federal government through the enactment of the Inspector General Act of 1978 (IG Act).[5]

The IG Act established an office of inspector general (OIG) in 12 federal agencies by consolidating the internal auditing and investigative authority of each agency into these independent units. Under the IG Act, the express purpose of these new OIGs was to promote economy, efficiency, and effectiveness and to prevent and detect fraud, waste, and abuse in their agencies' programs.[6] Since the passage of the IG Act, the number of federal OIGs has steadily increased. Today, a total of 75 statutory inspectors general operate across different federal agencies, which is a sixfold increase in fewer than 40 years.[7]

Offices of inspector general share a number of common features. Under the IG Act, all inspectors general must be selected without regard to political affiliation and solely on the basis of integrity and demonstrated professional ability in any one of a number of fields, including accounting, auditing, financial analysis, law, management analysis, public administration, and investigations.[8] The offices they lead are typically permanent, nonpartisan, and independent units that conduct audits, investigations, and other evaluations of the programs and operations of the federal department or agency in which they are located.[9]

While the OIGs across government have much in common, there are certain distinctions among them. Among the OIGs established under the IG Act as amended, IGs can be grouped into two distinct groups: those located in "establishment" agencies and those in "designated federal entities" (DFE).[10] Whether an IG operates in an establishment agency or a DFE can affect the manner in which he or she is appointed, how an IG's office receives funding and resources, and even how the IG can be removed.[11] In addition, some distinctions between IGs are attributable to modifications made to the IG Act since 1978 and the enactment of separate legislation affecting specific OIGs.[12]

Another distinction within the IG community, and one of relatively recent provenance, is that between permanent, agency-based OIGs and "special" inspectors general established on a temporary basis to oversee specific government initiatives. The first of these short-term IGs, the Coalition Provisional Authority Office of Inspector General (CPA OIG), was established shortly after the 2003 invasion of Iraq to oversee the operations and programs of the Coalition Provisional Authority (CPA).[13] Upon the CPA's dissolution in 2004, its inspector general was converted into SIGIR, the Special Inspector General for Iraq Reconstruction.[14] Although SIGIR itself ceased operations in October 2013, other temporary inspectors general have been established to oversee and promote the integrity of other significant government initiatives. The Special Inspector General for Afghanistan Reconstruction (SIGAR) and the Special Inspector General for the Troubled Asset Relief Program (SIGTARP) were both established in 2008 under statutory authorities distinct from the IG Act, and both continue to carry out their targeted oversight mandates today.[15]

Separately, the IG Act itself has been amended to address one broad area of oversight. Under section 8L of the IG Act, a provision added to the statute by a 2013 amendment, the CIGIE Chair must name a "lead inspector general" for any overseas contingency operation that exceeds 60 days, selecting him or her from among the inspectors general for the Department of Defense, Department of State, and the United States Agency for International Development.[16] The designated lead inspector general has the responsibility for providing oversight and reporting over all aspects of the contingency operation and coordinating among the inspectors general at the other two agencies.[17] Thus, with respect to overseas military operations, section 8L provides an alternative to the ad hoc approach that Congress has taken in establishing special inspectors general.[18]

In addition, two oversight bodies were established to monitor, investigate, and provide transparency for the distribution of substantial domestic economic relief bills. The first was the Recovery Accountability and Transparency (RAT) Board, which was created under the American Recovery and Reinvestment Act of 2009, a roughly $830 billion stimulus package designed to address the economic downturn unfolding in 2008–2009.[19] The RAT board, which consisted of an IG chairperson and 12 other IGs, ended its operations in 2015. The second oversight committee—the Pandemic Response Accountability Committee (PRAC)—was established as part of the Coronavirus Aid, Relief, and Economic Security Act (CARES Act). The PRAC comprises a chair, vice chair, and 19 IG members and is a statutory committee within the Council of the Inspectors General on Integrity and Efficiency (CIGIE).[20] Similar to the RAT Board, PRAC's mission is to promote transparency and oversight of the coronavirus response funds provided in the CARES Act and three related pieces of legislation.[21] The CARES Act also established a Special Inspector General for Pandemic Recovery (SIGPR) to oversee and ensure the integrity of the distribution of the CARES Act funds.[22]

Regardless of the type of OIG (establishment, DFE, or special IG), the principles governing the removal of an Inspector General from office generally remain the same: the Inspector General Act permits the President (or the agency head for DFE IGs) to remove or transfer an Inspector General but also requires 30 days' written notice to Congress, including a reason for the removal.[23] This authority to remove IGs has been invoked rarely in the four decades since the enactment of the IG Act, and IGs have commonly served through multiple presidential administrations, including transitions between administrations of opposing political parties.[24] The issue of IG removals took on greater prominence following President Trump's removal of two IGs in 2020 under circumstances that raised concerns by stakeholders that the terminations may have been motivated by politically sensitive work or controversial decisions made by their offices.[25] These removals prompted some efforts in Congress to curtail or counter the President's removal authority, as discussed later in the chapter.[26]

ENSURING OIG INDEPENDENCE: DUAL-REPORTING AND OTHER MECHANISMS

In enacting the IG Act, Congress recognized that for the IGs to be truly effective in combating fraud, waste, and abuse within their agencies, they would need to be objective in their work. The key ingredient in ensuring objectivity is independence from agency management. With this in mind, Congress took a number of steps to ensure OIG operational independence from agency management, and one of the most prominent was the imposition of the so-called dual-reporting obligation.

Pursuant to the dual-reporting obligation, IGs are required to report about their oversight activities to both the head of their agency *and* Congress.[27] Specifically, an IG must keep both the relevant agency head and Congress "fully and currently informed" about the office's activities, disclosing any identified problems or deficiencies in the agency's administration of programs and operations, its recommendations for addressing those problems, and any progress made in pursuing corrective action.[28] The dual-reporting obligation promotes independence by ensuring the IG can provide effective oversight without undue pressure from the agency and by putting into place structural requirements for the IG to report outside of the agency itself.[29]

IGs satisfy this dual-reporting obligation—at least in part—through two types of reports. First, IGs provide Congress with a periodic snapshot of their oversight activities through semiannual reports.[30] These reports, which are commonly called SARs, provide information regarding the OIG's activities over the prior six months, including describing problems or deficiencies that the OIG identified during that period, summarizing current or unimplemented recommendations, and tallying prosecutorial referrals made to the Department of Justice or other law enforcement authorities during the period.[31]

A second type of report, the so-called seven-day letter, ensures that the IG can, if necessary, inform Congress of serious problems within the agency in relatively short order. Whenever an IG becomes aware of "particularly serious or flagrant problems, abuses, or deficiencies" relating to agency programs or operations, he or she is authorized to report such matters immediately to the agency head.[32] Within seven days of receipt, the agency head must transmit the IG's report, along with any comments of his or her own, to the appropriate congressional committees.[33] In practice, seven-day letters are rare.[34] One former IG called it the "nuclear weapon" of the IG world, as the issuance of such a letter may create substantial difficulties for the relevant agency head (such as public embarrassment and political repercussions from Congress) and therefore cause lasting damage to the relationship between the agency and its OIG.[35] As a result, issuing a seven-day letter is generally considered a tool of last resort among IGs.[36] To date, there is documentation of only three agencies that have issued a seven-day letter. Two agencies have publicly acknowledged transmitting such a letter. The Department of Treasury stated that the last seven-day letter it issued occurred in 2000.[37] The EPA has issued two seven-day letters, one in 2013 and another in 2019.[38] Despite the relative rarity of the seven-day letter, the existence of this option nevertheless provides IGs with considerable leverage vis-à-vis agency management in fulfilling their oversight duties. As one former inspector general described the seven-day letter, "Using it is not what you aspire to do . . . [b]ut having it there is a great deterrent and a force multiplier for getting things done."[39]

In addition to these reports, IGs often fulfill their dual-reporting obligation in many ways not expressly provided for under the IG Act. For instance, IGs regularly communicate with Members of Congress by submitting formal reports and letters and holding informal briefings. Some OIGs are required, pursuant to other legal authority, to submit agency or program-specific reports to Congress.[40] IGs also testify before congressional committees and meet with members and staff.[41]

Aside from the dual-reporting obligation, various other measures protect IG independence and objectivity. For instance, for several administrative purposes the IG is considered its own agency.[42] An OIG can have its own personnel office to effect recruitment, screening, selection, promotion, and discipline of its employees.[43] Larger OIGs may also have their own technology network separate from that of the agency.[44] All IGs must have access to legal advice by counsel reporting to the IG, another IG, or CIGIE;[45] that is, IGs do not rely on agency counsel. In addition, the IG Act specifically requires OIGs to report on "any attempt" to "interfere with the independence" of the OIG, including through "budget constraints designed to limit [its] capabilities" or through resistance or objection to oversight activities, including through restrictions on or significant delays to access to information.[46]

Further, the IG Act makes clear that OIGs operate with a great deal of discretion in setting priorities and engaging in oversight. For example, section 6 of the IG Act provides that IGs have the discretion to make such reports relating to the administration of their agency's programs and operations as are in their judgment "necessary or desirable."[47] Therefore, while IGs report to the head of their agency and function under its "general supervision,"[48] this supervision generally may not be used to limit the IG's operational discretion. In fact, the IG Act expressly states that the head of an agency is not permitted to exercise its supervisory authority to "prevent or prohibit the Inspector General from initiating, carrying out, or completing any audit or investigation, or from issuing any subpoena during the course of any audit or investigation."[49] Moreover, the head of an establishment agency cannot remove an IG; instead, only the President has this authority. While a DFE Agency Head may remove a DFE IG, there are conditions that must be met before removal.[50]

To ensure IGs remain separate and independent, they are prohibited from receiving "program operating responsibilities" from the agencies they oversee.[51] If an agency could transfer operational responsibilities to its OIG, the OIG might find itself in the position of having to review a program for which it has responsibility. By prohibiting such a transfer, Congress sought to ensure that IGs would not have a vested interest in agency policies or programs and would remain unbiased in their review of those programs.[52] As a result, however, OIGs must ultimately rely on agency management to take action when problems are identified, as they have no ability to implement corrective steps on their own.

OIG RESPONSIBILITIES AND RELATED POWERS

In pursuit of their mission to prevent and detect waste, fraud, and abuse, OIGs operate under a broad statutory mandate to "conduct audits and investigations relating to the programs and operations" of the agency they oversee and to "conduct . . . other activities . . . for the purpose of promoting economy and efficiency in the administration" of that agency.[53] This language in the IG Act refers to three categories of activity through which OIGs fulfill this mission: audits, inspections and evaluations, and investigations. Sometimes, OIGs will initiate work in response to requests from agency management or Congress.[54] In other cases, OIGs conduct work in response to media reports concerning their agency. IGs have a great deal of discretion in determining whether an inquiry is necessary at all and, if so, which of these options is most appropriate.

Audits are formal assessments of the effectiveness, economy, and integrity of agency programs and operations, including those performed by agency grantees and contractors. An OIG might initiate an audit for a host of reasons. Many audits are akin to a doctor's periodic check-up—routine matters planned months in advance—while others may be prompted by the perception that a program or agency operation is particularly high risk.[55] Certain audits are required by law, such as those mandated by the Geospatial Data Act of 2018[56] and the DATA Act.[57]

Regardless of the reasons behind its initiation, an OIG audit will always be a structured, formal process. OIG audits must be conducted in compliance with the Government Accountability Office's rigorous Government Auditing Standards—also known as the "Yellow Book"[58]—which require "auditors to plan and perform the audit to obtain sufficient, appropriate evidence to provide a reasonable basis for [their] findings and conclusions based on [their] audit objectives."[59]

The typical audit is conducted through a multistep process. First, in an engagement letter, the OIG notifies the agency of the audit, thereby alerting the relevant staff of upcoming fieldwork, defining the scope of the audit, and scheduling an entrance meeting. Next, at the entrance meeting with relevant agency staff, the auditors identify what they will need in order to complete the fieldwork—this may include access to files, computer systems, or the opportunity to interview employees about the subject of the audit. The auditors will then begin their fieldwork, which may include interviews with agency staff, agency contractors or grantees, and sometimes program beneficiaries. After the completion of fieldwork, some auditors may provide a discussion draft of the audit report that includes preliminary findings and recommendations for the auditees to review; the auditee may respond by providing additional information or documentation. Following the discussion draft, the OIG and auditees usually hold an exit conference with the audited unit's management and other stakeholders to discuss issues such as the accuracy of the discussion draft report. Management can also share its perspective and reactions to the findings and recommendations. Afterwards, a formal draft report is prepared and provided to unit management, which, in most cases, will have an opportunity to review the draft and provide comments or planned corrective actions. Lastly, the auditors prepare a final report, which may contain findings and recommendations to enhance management practices and procedures, offering better ways to spend agency funds, or questioning expenditures.[60]

Ultimately, agency management will either concur or reject the IG's findings and recommendations. If the agency concurs with the recommendations, it will generally prepare an action plan to correct any problems identified by the audit.[61] When agency management disagrees with an OIG recommendation and the parties cannot agree on a satisfactory result, OMB has established a process to prioritize such disputed recommendations and resolve the matter.[62] Specifically, after the auditee develops a final action plan for each recommendation, the OIG either agrees or disagrees in writing with the proposed actions. In the case of a disagreement, the auditor will attempt to informally resolve the matter with the auditee. If this is not successful, the matter is then referred to each agency's designated Audit Follow-up Official.[63]

Some OIGs also conduct inspections and evaluations, a flexible category of reviews that has long been used by oversight organizations as effective mechanisms to fulfill their mission.[64] CIGIE has described inspections and evaluations as "systematic and independent assessments of the design, implementation, and results of an Agency's operations, programs, or policies."[65] OIGs are expanding programs in inspections and evaluations. The majority of OIGs perform inspection and evaluation work in some capacity, and many have Inspection and Evaluation offices, commonly referred to as I & E units, with dedicated staff.[66]

Inspections and evaluations are subject to the requirements of CIGIE's Quality Standards for Inspection and Evaluation, which is called the "Blue Book,"[67] rather than to the standards of the Yellow Book.[68] However, in practice, there are many similarities, as inspections and evaluations also engage in fieldwork, develop findings and recommendations, and follow an analogous reporting process. The Blue Book guides the review through all of these phases as well as planning, data and evidence collection and analysis, and follow up.[69]

Because of the relative flexibility of many aspects of the Blue Book, OIG inspections and evaluations can cover a wide range of approaches and topics. For example, the U.S. Department of State OIG inspects more than 260 embassies, diplomatic posts, and international broadcasting installations throughout the world to assess a wide range of issues, including whether policy goals are being achieved and whether the interests of the United States are being represented and advanced effectively.[70] The Department of Defense evaluations component conducts independent reviews of its agency's operations and activities, including classified programs, space and missile programs, construction, safety, health care, and oversight of criminal investigations and audits conducted by other entities within the Department of Defense.[71] Some OIGs conduct inspections and evaluations to assess allegations of mismanagement that do not rise to the level of misconduct warranting criminal or administrative investigation.[72] Moreover, some I & E units produce reports concerning the potential misconduct of or concerns regarding a specific office or program.[73]

In contrast to audits, inspection and evaluation work, which are conducted to examine program or operational performance or financial management on a systemic level, OIG investigations are generally more targeted in scope. Investigations typically examine specific allegations concerning possible violations of law, regulation, or agency policy.[74] All OIGs investigate certain types of matters, such as allegations of fraud involving agency grants and contracts, improprieties in agency programs and operations, and allegations of employee misconduct.[75] Depending on the statutory responsibilities of their agencies, some OIGs also have unique investigative authority over other matters beyond the agencies' employees and recipients of grants and contracts. For example, the Department of Labor OIG investigates allegations of labor racketeering; the Social Security Administration OIG pursues fraud involving disability benefits and Social Security payments; and the Department of Health & Human Services OIG investigates cases of delinquent child-support payments and Medicare fraud.[76]

Much like OIG audits, investigations often proceed through a structured, multi-step process. OIG investigations must comply with CIGIE's Quality Standards for Investigation, which provide qualitative standards for planning investigations, executing investigations, reporting the information obtained in the course of an investigation, and managing investigative information.[77] Upon receiving a complaint or allegation, the threshold question for any OIG is whether the allegations warrant devoting a portion of its limited resources to an investigation. OIGs may adopt specified criteria to assist them in making this decision. After deciding to pursue an investigation, the OIG will create an investigative plan, which is intended to focus on the pertinent facts of an allegation or complaint and specify how best to obtain evidence that will either prove or disprove those allegations.[78] Having devised a plan, OIG staff will begin to accumulate evidence, examining documents—including files, contracts, reports, and internal memoranda—and interviewing witnesses, technical experts, and the subjects of the investigation.[79]

Once the investigation is complete, the OIG will generally produce a report based on the evidence gathered. After a final internal review of the report to ensure that its conclusions are fact-based, objective, and clear, the OIG will generally provide it to agency management, along with any recommendations for administrative action that the OIG believes will address the conduct at issue.[80] For example, after finding that an agency employee engaged in misconduct, an OIG may recommend that the agency consider taking personnel action (such as discipline or removal). If an OIG investigation identifies abuses by a government contractor, it may also refer the contractor to agency management for suspension or debarment, which are administrative remedies through which organizations and individuals are excluded from doing business with the federal government.[81] Similarly, an OIG may refer a matter to its agency for action under the Program Fraud Civil Remedies Act (or PFCRA), which allows agencies to administratively pursue false statements claims of $150,000 or less.[82] An investigation may also culminate in the referral of a matter to authorities outside the agency. For example, if OIG determines there is a credible complaint of a Hatch Act violation, the IG must refer the allegation to the Office of Special Counsel.[83] Whenever the IG uncovers "reasonable grounds" to believe that a violation of federal criminal law has occurred, it is obligated to promptly report the matter to the Department of Justice.[84] In the event that the OIG believes a violation of state criminal law has occurred or that evidence uncovered in the course of an investigation warrants civil action, the OIG has discretion to refer the matter to the relevant law enforcement authority.[85]

Following are examples of several recent OIG matters that illustrate the wide variety of OIG efforts:

- The Department of State (State) OIG conducted an audit of the armored vehicle program and found that the Bureau of Diplomatic Security (DS) did not effectively administer the program in accordance with department policies and guidelines because DS had not developed appropriate procedures, guidance, or processes. Among other findings, this audit concluded that DS had incurred an impairment loss of $24.9 million for 259 armored vehicles that were unused for more than one year, and, to reduce inventory, DS transferred 200 unused armored vehicles, valued at $26.4 million, to other U.S. government agencies without cost reimbursement. OIG questioned a total of $51.3 million and made 38 recommendations to three department bureaus and three overseas posts to address the deficiencies.[86]
- In May 2013, the Department of Justice OIG issued an interim report during an ongoing audit of the U.S. Marshals Service's Witness Security Program; this interim report revealed that known or suspected terrorists who were participating in the federal witness protection program could not be identified. Moreover, the DOJ OIG interim report found that program officials had provided approval for some witness protection participants who were on the federal No Fly list to fly on commercial flights and that these individuals

could have flown on their own accord (i.e., without the officials' knowledge and specific approval).[87]

- The SBA OIG evaluated SBA's grant programs for fiscal years 2014 through 2018; it issued nine audit and evaluation reports reviewing SBA's management of its grant programs and grant recipients' compliance with grant requirements. These nine reviews covered $63.4 million of grant awards to support entrepreneurial development programs. SBA OIG identified systemic issues with SBA's financial and performance oversight across multiple grant programs, including ineffective grant monitoring and financial reporting requirements. As a result, OIG determined that SBA's grant programs are at risk of funds not being used for their intended purpose and of not achieving program goals and objectives.[88]

- A Department of the Interior (DOI) OIG evaluation determined that the DOI did not deploy and operate a secure wireless network infrastructure, as required by National Institute of Standards and Technology (NIST) guidance and industry best practices. The OIG conducted reconnaissance and penetration testing of wireless networks representing each bureau and office and stimulated attack techniques of malicious actors attempting to break into departmental wireless networks. The report concluded that the identified deficiencies occurred because the Office of the Chief Information Officer (OCIO) did not provide effective leadership and guidance to the department and failed to establish and enforce best practices. The OIG made 14 recommendations to strengthen the department's wireless network security to prevent potential security breaches.[89]

- DOT OIG assessed the effectiveness of the Federal Aviation Administration's inspection program—the Drug Abatement Program (DAP). The DAP is responsible for the development, implementation, administration, and compliance monitoring of the aviation industry drug and alcohol testing programs. OIG found that the system FAA uses to develop inspection schedules does not assign risk levels to companies or prioritize inspections based on risk, an approach that is contrary to FAA's Safety Risk Management Policy, which was implemented to identify hazards, analyze and assess safety risk, and develop controls. OIG made two recommendations to improve the effectiveness of the DPA.[90]

- On April 20, 2010, BP's Deepwater Horizon Mobile Offshore Drilling Unit exploded in the Gulf of Mexico, claiming 11 lives and discharging an estimated 4.9 million barrels of oil in the largest environmental disaster in U.S. history. Between June 2010 and February 2016, the DOI OIG led the investigative efforts of the Deepwater Horizon Task Force and played a critical role in the success of this historic investigation. As a result of this investigation, multiple companies pleaded guilty to federal offenses and paid more than $6 billion in criminal fines and penalties. Halliburton Energy Services,

Inc. pleaded guilty to destroying evidence and agreed to pay $55 million to the National Fish and Wildlife Foundation.[91]
- In 2018, VA OIG substantiated that the VA Secretary misused VA funds by taking an official July 2017 trip to Europe for personal activities. The 11-day trip included two extensive travel days and three-and-half days of official events costing the VA at least $122,334. OIG determined that the Chief of Staff made misrepresentations to ethics officials and that the Secretary improperly accepted a gift (Wimbledon tickets); the report also identified misuse of employees' time and inadequate documentation of the trip's full cost. The investigation resulted in leadership changes, employee retraining, and recovery of taxpayer dollars.[92]
- GSA OIG found that many of the expenditures at the GSA Western Regions Conference were excessive and wasteful and that, in many instances, GSA followed neither federal procurement laws nor its own policy on conference spending. Conference costs included eight off-site planning meetings and significant food and beverage costs. Specifically, GSA incurred excessive and impermissible costs for food totaling $146,427.05 that included $5,600 for three semi-private catered in-room parties and $44 per person daily breakfasts. Additionally, GSA incurred impermissible expenses, including mementos for attendees and clothing purchases by employees. The total cost of the conference was more than $820,000 for approximately 300 attendees.[93]
- An Amtrak OIG investigation uncovered a complex fraud scheme involving the purchase and sale of more than $540,000 in fraudulent Amtrak tickets and e-vouchers using stolen information from more than 1,100 credit cards. Review of seized digital evidence revealed that the perpetrator had memorialized intentions to kill police officers. Additionally, the search revealed two loaded assault rifles, 11 improvised explosive devices, two pipe bombs, other forms of contraband, and other deadly weapons. The seizure and other key evidence led to an indictment and guilty plea.[94]

When engaging in these three primary categories of oversight activities, OIGs have powerful tools at their disposal. Given that gathering evidence is crucial to effectively performing any of these functions, some of the OIGs' broadest statutory powers are related to the manner in which they can acquire information. The first of these information-gathering powers pertains to the records of the agency in which an OIG is located. Section 6(a)(1) of the IG Act provides that each IG is authorized to have access to "all records" available to the agency that relate to the programs and operations the IG oversees.[95] If an agency employee refuses or fails to provide records that an IG has requested pursuant to this authority, the IG must report the circumstances to agency management without delay and include the incident in the OIG's semiannual report.[96]

In addition to the authority IGs have under section 6(a)(1) to access internal agency records, OIGs can obtain information from external sources in two ways. First, IGs have the authority provided under the IG Act to request information or assistance from federal agencies other than their own.[97] Agency heads must comply with such requests for information or assistance "insofar as is practicable" and to the extent that the request would not violate some other statute or regulation applicable to the agency.[98] As with requests for internal agency information, an IG who requests information or assistance from another federal agency must report any "unreasonabl[e]" refusal of such a request to the head of the agency involved "without delay" and may include the incident in its semiannual report.[99]

Second, IGs have broad authority to subpoena any information—whether in the form of documents, reports, answers, records, accounts, papers, data in any medium (including electronically stored information), or a tangible thing—that is necessary to the performance of their responsibilities under the IG Act.[100] Subpoenas, which are enforceable in federal district court, enable IGs to compel the production of evidence from sources outside the federal government.

While all OIGs operating under the provisions of the IG Act have broad powers to further their oversight activities, certain IGs are permitted to exercise law enforcement authority as well. Thirty-nine OIGs are authorized to employ special agents who can (1) carry a firearm, (2) make an arrest without a warrant for any federal offense committed in their presence or which they have reasonable grounds to believe was committed, and (3) seek and execute warrants for arrest, search of a premises, or seizure of evidence under the authority of the United States.[101] Those OIGs that are permitted to exercise law enforcement authority must do so in accordance with guidelines promulgated by the attorney general.[102]

Notwithstanding the OIGs' significant powers and broad mandate, the OIGs' ability to fulfill their missions free of interference has become an occasional flashpoint in recent years. In August 2014, 47 inspectors general signed a letter to congressional oversight committees expressing concerns that leadership at three federal agencies (the Department of Justice, the Peace Corps, and the Chemical Safety and Hazard Investigation Board) had impeded the work of their respective OIGs by limiting or delaying their access to agency records.[103] In each case, agency lawyers had construed statutes other than the IG Act or attorney-client privilege as overriding section 6(a)(1)'s broad information-gathering authority.[104]

Following the IGs' letter and related congressional hearings, Members of Congress introduced legislation that would have expanded IGs' authority significantly.[105] For instance, the proposals provided clear language in support of OIG access to all agency materials and would have expanded IGs' authority to authorize testimonial subpoenas, which would have empowered IGs to require testimony from former federal employees as well as contractors (albeit not current or former employees of contractors). Although Congress ultimately did not authorize this testimonial subpoena power for OIGs, the reform efforts did result in the enactment of the Inspector General Empowerment Act (IGEA) in December 2016, discussed in more detail next.

THE INSPECTOR GENERAL EMPOWERMENT ACT OF 2016 AND OTHER PROPOSALS FOR CHANGE

The IGEA expanded IGs' authority in various ways, including by partially addressing the disputes over agency limitations to OIG access.[106] In particular, the IGEA amended the IG Act to "guarantee[] that federal IGs have access to agency records . . . and allow IGs to match data across agencies to help uncover wasteful spending."[107] The act did so through provisions authorizing IGs to access all records (i.e., agency materials) and exempting them from procedural requirements and information privacy protections under certain legislation (namely, the Computer Matching and Privacy Protection Act of 1988 and the Paperwork Reduction Act).[108] The exemption from the Computer Matching and Privacy Protection Act streamlined the IGs' ability to analyze multiple sets of data in furtherance of their oversight mission.[109] The IGEA also exempted OIGs from the Paperwork Reduction Act, which requires that a government agency receive approval from the Office of Management and Budget (OMB) before requesting certain information from the public.[110] These statutory changes permit OIGs to conduct investigations without the need to obtain approvals from other agencies, a potentially time-consuming process.[111]

The IGEA also imposed additional reporting and internal oversight requirements. Some of these requirements pertained specifically to CIGIE. For example, after passage of the IGEA, CIGIE was required to submit annual reports to Congress (which were previously only submitted to the President), and it clarified CIGIE's duty to report to Congress any "critical issues that involve the jurisdiction of more than one IG."[112] In addition, some provisions were intended to promote accountability and fairness in CIGIE investigations.[113]

Other reporting requirements apply directly to individual IGs, including a number of provisions pertaining to the semiannual report to Congress.[114] For example, IGs were required to include additional information on the number and nature of investigations relating to senior government officials, instances of whistleblower retaliation, information on efforts to constrain the office's ability to perform its work, and "closed" audits, evaluations, and inspections that were not disclosed to the public.[115] The IGEA also included additional public reporting requirements.[116] In particular, IGs must generally submit any documents containing "recommendation[s] for corrective action" to agency heads and congressional committees of jurisdiction as well as to any Member of Congress or other individuals upon request.[117]

The IGEA also attempted to address the concern over IG vacancies. To examine this issue, the act required the GAO to perform a onetime study to evaluate the vacancies and determine the best course of action in addressing them.[118] In 2018, GAO completed this report.[119] Since this report was issued the concern over vacancies has grown,[120] and potential reforms are discussed here.

In the years since the enactment of the IGEA, new issues have emerged regarding the IG community, prompting calls for further reform efforts. As noted briefly earlier, President Trump's removal of two IGs in 2020 led to proposals that would affect a president's ability to take similar actions in the future. For instance, one proposal would require that the president or agency head provide Congress with a substantive rationale—as opposed to mere notice—when an IG is removed, transferred, or placed under nonduty status under sections 3(b) and 8G(e) of the IG Act.

An emerging issue related to the removal of IGs is the temporary appointment of officials currently serving in the presidential administration to vacant IG positions. The appointment or publicly contemplated appointment of administration officials into vacant IG positions, including officials who maintain their existing positions at the same time, raised concerns among some stakeholders about potential conflicts of interest. In particular, these appointments and potential appointments raised questions regarding whether an official serving in a managerial or political role and simultaneously as acting IG would inherently face a real or apparent conflict that would compromise the ability to exercise independent and objective oversight.[121] With those concerns in mind, several stakeholders, including some Members of Congress, have explored limitations on a president's ability to appoint officials to vacant IG positions.[122] For instance, one proposal would amend the Federal Vacancies Reform Act (FVRA) to require the president to choose acting IGs from the ranks of senior officials then serving in an OIG.[123]

The issue of filling IG vacancies has itself been a focal point for reform efforts. Vacancies have been widespread and persistent in the IG community throughout multiple presidential administrations, with some positions going unfilled for several years. Causes include the failure of numerous administrations to nominate candidates, the Senate's failure to confirm nominees, and, for DFE IGs, inaction by agency heads. There has been recent progress in filling vacancies, and as of March 29, 2022, there were eight vacant IG positions.[124] The lack of permanent IGs has been more pronounced in the "establishment" agencies, where there have been more vacancies that have extended for longer periods.[125] Out of the eight vacancies existing in March 2022, seven are establishment IGs, and three of those are from Cabinet-level executive agencies.[126] Several stakeholders and Members of Congress have suggested potential reforms, such as requiring the president to submit a report on vacancies that last longer than 210 days[127] and encouraging the White House Office of Presidential Personnel and agency leaders to request from CIGIE lists of qualified potential candidates to expedite filling vacant IG positions.[128]

Finally, the IG community has a strong interest in several other legislative proposals that could further IG independence and the ability to exercise effective oversight. These proposals include expanding the authorization to use testimonial subpoena authority throughout the IG community, reformation of the Program Fraud Civil Remedies Act, improving cybersecurity protections of vulnerable information, and implementing protections against reprisal for federal subgrantee employees.[129]

SUMMARY OF KEY POINTS

- The IG Act established Inspectors General to promote economy, efficiency, and effectiveness and to prevent and detect fraud, waste, and waste in their agencies' programs; today there are 75 statutorily created OIGs.
- IGs must be selected on the basis of integrity and professional ability, without regard to political affiliation.
- The independence safeguards of Inspectors General include dual reporting requirements to the IG's agency head and Congress.
- The responsibilities of IGs include audits, inspections and evaluations, and investigations.
- OIGs have powerful tools including the right to access all agency records, subpoena power, and law enforcement authority.
- IGs have amassed an impressive record of accomplishments, including—in Fiscal Year 2021 alone—nearly $62.7 billion in potential savings from audit recommendations;
  - $12 billion in investigative recoveries;
  - 4,297 indictments and criminal informations;
  - 1,058 successful civil actions; and
  - 2,436 suspensions and debarments.[130]
- Members of Congress have recently proposed legislation to strengthen the independence and powers of Inspectors General.

NOTES

1. The author is the Inspector General for the U.S. Department of the Interior and the Vice Chair for the Council of the Inspectors General on Integrity and Efficiency (CIGIE). He has been in the federal oversight community since 2003 and served with CIGIE as its Executive Director; the U.S. Department of Commerce Office of Inspector General as the Assistant Inspector General for Investigations, Deputy Assistant Inspector General for Compliance & Ethics, and Director of Special Investigations; U.S. Department of Justice Office of Inspector General as an Investigative Counsel in the special investigations unit; and the U.S. Senate Permanent Subcommittee on Investigations as Minority Staff Director and Chief Counsel, Deputy Chief Counsel, and Investigative Counsel. The author thanks L. Browning VanMeter Jr., Michael Thomas Wasenius, Sidrah Miraaj-Raza, Lorraine A. Luciano, and Jill Baisinger for their contributions to this chapter, including conducting research and drafting text. *Any reference to any organization, products, or services does not constitute or imply the endorsement, recommendation, or favoring by the U.S. government, CIGIE, or the DOI OIG.* This chapter is available to the public at https://www.doioig.gov/ and https://www.ignet.gov/content/aba-law-journal-chapter-ethical-standards-public-sector-3rd-edition.

2. COUNCIL OF THE INSPECTORS GENERAL ON INTEGRITY AND EFFICIENCY, PROGRESS REPORT TO THE PRESIDENT AND CONGRESS, FISCAL YEAR 2021, 1 (2021), https://www.ignet.gov/sites/default/files/files/992-011CIGIEAnnualReport-Full508.pdf (hereinafter 2021 CIGIE REPORT).

3. *E.g., id.* at 24–26.

4. This chapter describes Inspectors General in our federal system. Many states and some municipal governments also have Inspectors General that perform similar oversight functions. To learn more about IGs on the state and local level, *see* Frank Anechiarico &

Rose Gill Hearn, *Who Is the Inspector General?* Hamilton Digital Commons (Fall 2010), https://digitalcommons.hamilton.edu/articles/147; Phillip Zisman, *The People's Watchdog: Inspectors General Foster Accountability, Transparency*, Capitol Ideas (2017), https://issuu.com/csg.publications/docs/marapril2013; Brian Peteritas, *States and Localities Realize the Importance of Inspectors General*, Governing (June 27, 2013), https://www.governing.com/archive/col-states-localities-realize-importance-of-inspectors-general.html.

5. Council of the Inspectors General on Integrity and Efficiency, The Inspectors General 1 (2014), https://www.ignet.gov/sites/default/files/files/IG_Authorities_Paper_-_Final_6-11-14.pdf [hereinafter CIGIE IG Summary]. Before CIGIE was established as a stand-alone federal agency, two previous commissions performed similar functions. In 1981, The President's Council on Integrity and Efficiency (PCIE) was created by Executive Order (EO) 12301, to coordinate and enhance governmental efforts to promote integrity and efficiency and to detect and prevent fraud, waste, and abuse in federal programs. In 1992, EO 12805, created the Council on Integrity and Efficiency (ECIE) to perform this same mission among the agency-head appointed IGs. This 1992 Executive Order also updated the responsibilities of the PCIE. Subsequently, in 1996, EO 12993 instituted a special Integrity Committee to independently investigate allegations of wrongdoing by individual inspectors general. In 2008, the IG Reform Act consolidated the PCIE and ECIE into CIGIE as a unified council of all statutory Federal IGs. Exec. Order No. 12301, (46 Fed. Reg. 19211, March 30, 1981); Exec. Order No. 12805 (57 Fed. Reg. 20627, May 14, 1992); Exec. Order No. 12993 (61 FR 13043, Mar. 21,1996). *See generally* An Introduction to the Inspector General Community, (last accessed Feb. 19, 2021), https://www.ignet.gov/sites/default/files/files/igbrochure04.pdf; *see also* Office of the Inspector General U.S. Department of Transportation, OIG History, https://www.oig.dot.gov/about-oig/oig-history (last accessed Feb. 19, 2021).

6. *Id.*

7. *Id.* This expansion of OIGs is attributable to two legislative developments since 1978. First, amendments to the original IG Act—particularly those made in 1988—broadened the IG concept beyond the original 12 agencies, creating OIGs in most executive branch agencies. *See* 2021 CIGIE Report at 1. Second, several subsequent pieces of legislation, distinct from the IG Act, have instituted inspectors general in the legislative branch and intelligence agencies and established a number of temporary inspectors general to oversee specific federal government initiatives. *See* CIGIE IG Summary at 14. Currently, 65 OIGs were created by, derive their authority from, and operate pursuant to the provisions of the IG Act. *See id.* at 13 and Congressional Research Service, Statutory Inspectors General in the Federal Government: A Primer 4 (2019), https://fas.org/sgp/crs/misc/R45450.pdf. The remaining nine are governed by the statutes establishing those offices; however, most are subject to various provisions of the IG Act as well. *Id.* at 14. These statutorily created OIGs are discussed in greater detail later.

8. Inspector General Act (IG Act) Section 3 "Appointment of Inspector General..." 5 U.S.C. App. 3 § 3(a) and Section 8 "Additional provisions... to the Inspector General of the Department of Defense" 5 U.S.C. App. 3 § 8G(c).

9. Wendy Ginsberg & Michael Greene, Congressional Research Service, Federal Inspectors General: History, Characteristics, and Recent Congressional Actions (2016), http://www.fas.org/sgp/crs/misc/R43814.pdf [hereinafter CRS Report 2016].

10. *See* CIGIE IG Summary at 2.

11. *See* CRS Report 2016 at 3; *see also* U.S. Gov't Accountability Office, GAO-09-270, Survey of Governance Practices and the Inspectors General Role 40-41 (April 2009), https://www.gao.gov/new.items/d09270.pdf.

12. *See* CIGIE IG Summary at 2.

13. Pub. L. 110-181.

14. Pub. L. 108-375.

15. National Defense Authorization Act for Fiscal Year 2008, Pub. L. No. 110-181, 122 Stat. 378-85; Emergency Economic Stabilization Act of 2008, Pub. L. No. 110-343; CRS Report at 4. Kathy A. Buller, *Overseeing the Overseers:* The Council of the Inspectors General on Integrity

AND EFFICIENCY (last accessed Sept. 18, 2019), https://www.ignet.gov/sites/default/files/files/Buller_Peace_Corps_OIG_Testimony_Sep_18_2019_for%20web.pdf.

16. IG Act Section 8 "Additional provisions . . . to the Inspector General of the Department of Defense" 5 U.S.C. App. 3 § 8L (2014).

17. *Id.*

18. Section 8L was put to use for the first time in December 2014 when the CIGIE Chair named Jon T. Rymer, Inspector General for the Department of Defense as the Lead Inspector General for Operation Inherent Resolve, the United States military's official designation for ongoing operations against the Islamic State of Iraq and Syria. Press Release, Council of the Inspectors General on Integrity and Efficiency, Designation of Lead Inspector General for Overseas Contingency Operation, Operation Inherent Resolve (Dec. 19, 2014), https://www.ignet.gov/sites/default/files/files/CIGIE%20Press%20Release%20-%2012-19-14.pdf. It obviated the need for future legislation outside of the IG Act to establish special inspectors general, at least with respect to certain specified overseas contingency operations. Since the amendment passed, there have been more than five Lead IG Appointments for Military Overseas Operations. *See* DEPARTMENT OF DEFENSE OFFICE OF INSPECTOR GENERAL, LEAD INSPECTOR GENERAL REPORTS (last accessed Oct. 26, 2020), https://www.dodig.mil/Reports/Lead-Inspector-General-Reports/.

19. The Recovery Accountability and Transparency (RAT) Board was established as an independent Federal Board that had mandates similar to those of the PRAC. Pub. L. No. 111-5, 123 Stat. 115 (2009). *See also* COUNCIL OF THE INSPECTORS GENERAL ON INTEGRITY AND EFFICIENCY, IG ACT HISTORY, https://www.ignet.gov/content/ig-act-history (last accessed Oct. 26, 2020); Michael Wood, RECOVERY ACCOUNTABILITY AND TRANSPARENCY BOARD (OCT. 14, 2011), https://www.nsf.gov/oig/_pdf/presentations/SD2011/5.pdf.

20. PANDEMIC RESPONSE ACCOUNTABILITY COMMITTEE, Top Challenges Facing Federal Agencies: COVID-19 Emergency Relief and Response Efforts (June 2020), https://www.oversight.gov/sites/default/files/oig-reports/Top%20Challenges%20Facing%20Federal%20Agencies%20-%20COVID-19%20Emergency%20Relief%20and%20Response%20Efforts_1.pdf.

21. PANDEMIC OVERSIGHT, ABOUT THIS WEBSITE, https://www.pandemicoversight.gov/our-mission/about-this-website (last accessed Oct. 26, 2020); PANDEMIC OVERSIGHT, PRAC MEMBERS, https://www.pandemicoversight.gov/our-mission/prac-members (last accessed Oct. 26, 2020).

22. SPECIAL INSPECTOR GENERAL FOR PANDEMIC RECOVERY, ABOUT SIGPR, https://www.sigpr.gov/about-sigpr/sigpr-overview.

23. IG Act Section 3 "Appointment of Inspector General..." 5 U.S.C. App. 3 § 3(b) and Section 8 "Additional provisions . . . to the Inspector General of the Department of Defense" 5 U.S.C. App. 3 § 8G(e) (2016). DFEs may have an additional requirement when a "board, chairman of a committee, or commission is the head of the designated Federal entity, as a removal under this subsection may only be made upon the written concurrence of a two-thirds majority of the board, committee, or commission"; the agency head must then provide 30 days' written notice to both Houses of Congress. *Id* § 8G(e)(1) (2016).

24. After the first presidential transition following the enactment of the 1978 IG Act, President Ronald Reagan removed all of the 15 IGs in office early in his first term but faced a bipartisan backlash in Congress and ultimately rehired several of those IGs. CONGRESSIONAL RESEARCH SERVICE, REMOVAL OF INSPECTORS GENERAL: RULES, PRACTICE, AND CONSIDERATION FOR CONGRESS (2020), https://crsreports.congress.gov/product/pdf/IF/IF11546. Since then, no president has entered office and attempted to remove large numbers of IGs appointed by his predecessors.

25. Todd Garvey, CONGRESSIONAL RESEARCH SERVICE, PRESIDENTIAL REMOVAL OF IGS UNDER THE INSPECTOR GENERAL ACT (May 22, 2020), https://crsreports.congress.gov/product/pdf/LSB/LSB10476.

26. *See also* U.S. GOV'T ACCOUNTABILITY OFFICE, GAO-11-770, INSPECTORS GENERAL: REPORTING ON INDEPENDENCE, EFFECTIVENESS, AND EXPERTISE 8-9 (Sept. 2011), http://www.gao.gov/assets/330/323642.pdf.

27. IG Act Section 4 "Duties and Responsibilities..." 5 U.S.C. App. 3 § 4(a)(5).

28. *Id.*

29. *See* Congressional Research Service, Statutory Inspectors General in the Federal Government: A Primer 22 (2019), https://fas.org/sgp/crs/misc/R45450.pdf. *See also* Partnership for Public Service, Walking the Line, Inspectors General Balancing Independence and Impact (Sept. 2016), https://www.ourpublicservice.org/wp-content/uploads/2016/09/0bd2a00052bc1e7c216c5ee89fc4b457-1491000841.pdf (Partnership for Public Service is a nonprofit and nonpartisan organization).

30. *See* IG Act Section 5 "Semiannual Reports . . ." 5 U.S.C. App. 3 § 5(a).

31. *Id.*; *see also* CIGIE IG Summary at 5.

32. *See* IG Act Section 5 "Semiannual Reports..." 5 U.S.C. App. 3 § 5(d).

33. *Id.*

34. U.S. Gov't Accountability Office, GAO-11-770, Inspectors General: Reporting on Independence, Effectiveness, and Expertise 8–9 (2011), http://www.gao.gov/assets/330/323642.pdf (explaining that, during fiscal years 2008, 2009, and 2010, only one out of 62 IGs surveyed had issued a seven-day letter) ("GAO-11-770").

35. Kevin Bogardus, *Watchdogs Reluctant to Use "Nuclear Weapon," an Alert to Congress*, Greenwire (Sept. 24, 2014), http://www.eenews.net/greenwire/stories/1060006382 (quoting Earl Devaney, former Inspector General for the Department of the Interior).

36. *See* GAO-11-770.

37. *Id.* at 8.

38. Environmental Protection Agency, Seven Day Letter Refusals to Fully Cooperate and Provide Information for Audit and Investigation (Oct. 29, 2019), https://www.epa.gov/sites/production/files/2019-11/documents/_epaoig_7dayletter_11-6-19.pdf.

39. Bogardus, *supra* note 35 (quoting Earl Devaney, former Inspector General for the Department of the Interior).

40. *See* CIGIE IG Summary at 5.

41. *Id.*

42. Council of the Inspectors General on Integrity and Efficiency, Presidential Transition Handbook: The Role of Inspectors General and the Transition to a New Administration 3 (Dec. 2020), https://ignet.gov/sites/default/files/files/CIGIE-Presidential-Transition-Handbook.pdf ("CIGIE Transitional Handbook").

43. *Id.*

44. *Id.*

45. IG Act Section 3 "Appointment of Inspector General..." 5 U.S.C. App. 3 § 3(g) and IG Act Section 8 "Additional provisions... to the Inspector General of the Department of Defense" 5 U.S.C. App. § 8G(g)(4). Pursuant to 8G(g)(4)(C), the services obtained from another IG or CIGIE are reimbursable.

46. IG Act Section 5 "Semiannual Reports..." 5 U.S.C. App. 3 § 5(a)(21)(B).

47. IG Act Section 6 "Authority of Inspector General..." 5 U.S.C. App. 3 § 6(a)(2). *See also* U.S. Nuclear Regulatory Comm'n, Wash., D.C. v. Fed. Labor Relations Auth., 25 F.3d 229, 235 (4th Cir. 1994) (referring to the supervisory authority exercised by agency heads over IGs as "nominal").

48. IG Act Section 3 "Appointment of Inspector General..." 5 U.S.C. App. 3 § 3(a) and IG Act Section 8 "Additional provisions... to the Inspector General of the Department of Defense" 5 U.S.C. App. § 8G(d).

49. IG Act Section 3 "Appointment of Inspector General..." 5 U.S.C. App. 3 § 3(a) and IG Act Section 8 "Additional provisions... to the Inspector General of the Department of Defense" 5 U.S.C. App. 3 §§ 8, 8A, 8D, 8E, 8G(d). This prohibition is subject to one narrow exception: the heads of seven agencies—the Department of Defense, Department of Homeland Security, Department of Justice, Treasury Department, Federal Reserve Board, Consumer Financial Protection Bureau, and Postal Service—may prevent their IGs from engaging in these activities but only on the basis of a permissible reason specified under the IG Act. *See* CIGIE IG Summary at 4. Although the permissible reasons vary for each agency, they might include, among others, the preservation of national security, protecting ongoing criminal prosecutions, or that the information would significantly influence the economy or market behavior. *Id.* In order to promote accountability in the use of this power, an agency head invoking it must

send an explanatory note to the relevant IG, identifying the reason for its exercise, and within 30 days, the IG must transmit the note to the appropriate congressional committees. *Id.* at 5.

50. IG Act Section 3 "Appointment of Inspector General..." 5 U.S.C. App. 3 § 3(b) and IG Act Section 8 "Additional provisions... to the Inspector General of the Department of Defense" 5 U.S.C. App. 3 § 8G(e); *See also infra* section 5.

51. IG Act Section 8 "Additional provisions... to the Inspector General of the Department of Defense" 5 U.S.C. App. 3 § 8G(b) and IG Act Section 9 "Transfer of Functions" 5 U.S.C. App. 3 § 9(a)(2) (2016). *See also* Burlington Northern R. Co. v. Office of Inspector Gen. R.R. Retirement Bd., 983 F.2d 631, 635 (5th Cir. 1993) (explaining that Congress expressed an intent that Inspectors General not be allowed to conduct an agency's program operating responsibilities).

52. *See* CIGIE IG Summary at 11.

53. IG Act Section 4 "Duties and Responsibilities..." 5 U.S.C. App. 3 §§ 4(a)(1), (a)(3) (2016).

54. Jonathan D. Shaffer & Nora Brent, Federal Grant Practice § 6:18 (2020 ed.) [hereinafter Federal Grant Practice].

55. *Id.* § 6:18.

56. Federal Aviation Administration Reauthorization Act of 2018 [P.L. 115-254]. The act requires the Inspector General of each covered agency (or the senior ethics official of a covered agency without an Inspector General) to submit to Congress an audit not less than once every two years of the collection, production, acquisition, maintenance, distribution, use, and preservation of geospatial data by the covered agency.

57. Pub. L. No. 113-101, 128 Stat. 1146 (2014). *See also* U.S. Gov't Accountability Office, GAO-20-540, DATA ACT OIGs Reported That Quality of Agency Submitted Data Varied, and Most Recommended Improvements (July 2020), https://www.gao.gov/assets/gao-20-540.pdf. The act requires each Office of Inspector General (OIG) to issue reports on the quality of agency spending data. The OIGs determine quality based on the rate of data errors. In FY 2019, the Government Accounting Office issued a report concluding that out of 51 federal agencies, 37 OIGs reported that agency data submissions for the first quarter of FY 2019 had an error rate of less than 20%, but 10 of those submissions were missing data; 37 OIGs reported that agencies correctly used data standards; and 44 OIGs made recommendations to improve data quality at the agencies.

58. 2021 CIGIE Report at 11; U.S. Government Accountability Office, The Yellow Book, https://www.gao.gov/yellowbook/overview#t=0 (last accessed Nov. 24, 2020) [hereinafter Yellow Book].

59. Comptroller General of the U.S., Government Auditing Standards 124, 141, 207 (2018). *See also* Federal Grant Practice at § 48:18.

60. *E.g.*, Federal Grant Practice at § 6:18; Office of Inspector General, Smithsonian Institution, Understanding the OIG Audit Process, http://www.si.edu/Content/OIG/Misc/Understanding Audits.pdf.

61. Federal Grant Practice at § 6:18.

62. Office of Management and Budget, Circular No. A-50 Revised, Sept. 29, 1982, https://www.whitehouse.gov/omb/circulars_a050 (last accessed Oct. 13, 2020) [hereinafter Circular No. A-50 Revised].

63. *See* Circular No. A-50 Revised.

64. *See* CIGIE IG Summary at 9, Council of the Inspectors General on Integrity and Efficiency, Quality Standards for Inspection and Evaluation at 1 (2020), https://www.ignet.gov/sites/default/files/files/QualityStandardsforInspectionandEvaluation-2020.pdf [hereinafter Blue Book].

65. *Id.* at 1.

66. Council of the Inspectors General on Integrity and Efficiency, Growth and Development of the Inspection and Evaluation Community: 2010 Survey Results at 6 (2011), https://www.ignet.gov/sites/default/files/files/ie2011survey.pdf [hereinafter CIGIE I & E Community].

67. CIGIE IG Summary at 7. *See also* Inspector General Act of 1978, 5 U.S.C. App. 3 § 11(c)(2)(A) (2014).

68. Blue Book; Yellow Book.

69. *See* Blue Book at 8-18.

70. U.S. Dep't of State Office of the Inspector General, https://www.stateoig.gov/about (last accessed Dec. 4, 2020).

71. Inspector General, U.S. Dep't of Defense, *Semiannual Report to Congress* 43 (Sept. 30, 2020), https://media.defense.gov/2020/Nov/30/2002542685/-1/-1/1/DOD%20OIG%20SEMIANNUAL%20REPORT%20TO%20THE%20CONGRESS%20APRIL%201,%202020%20TO%20SEPTEMBER%2030,%202020.PDF.

72. CIGIE IG Summary at 9.

73. CIGIE I & E Community at 30.

74. *E.g.*, Office of Inspector General, Fed. Housing Finance Agency, *What We Do* (last accessed Oct. 19, 2020), https://www.fhfaoig.gov/About/WhatWeDo.

75. *Id.*

76. Federal Grant Practice at § 6:19; Office of Inspector General, U.S. Dep't of Labor, *Office of Inspector General*, https://www.oig.dol.gov/about.htm (last accessed Oct. 19, 2020); Office of Inspector General, Social Security Administration, *What Do We Investigate?* (last accessed Oct. 13, 2020), https://oig.ssa.gov/fraud-reporting/what-can-oig-investigate/; Office of Inspector General, U.S. Dep't of Health & Human Services, *Fraud*, http://oig.hhs.gov/fraud/ (last accessed Oct. 13, 2020).

77. *See generally* Council of the Inspectors General on Integrity and Efficiency, Quality Standards for Investigations (2011), https://www.ignet.gov/sites/default/files/files/committees/investigation/invprg1211appi.pdf [hereinafter CIGIE Investigative Standards].

78. *See* CIGIE Investigative Standards at 10.

79. CIGIE Investigative Standards at 12.

80. Office of Inspector General, U.S. Dep't of the Interior, Office of Investigations, https://www.doioig.gov/about/oig-offices/office-investigations (last accessed Oct. 16, 2020).

81. Council of the Inspectors General on Integrity and Efficiency, Looking Inside the Accountability Toolbox: An Update from the CIGIE Suspension and Debarment Working Group 1 (2013), https://www.ignet.gov/sites/default/files/files/Suspension%20and%20Debarment%20Working%20Group%20Report%20-%2011-19-13.pdf.

82. *Id.* at 7. Since the PFCRA allows agencies to pursue claims based on false statements that did not result in the payment of any funds by the agency, it provides agencies with an administrative avenue for taking action against those who unsuccessfully attempt to obtain federal grant funds under false pretenses. *Id.*

83. 5 C.F.R.§ 734.102. The United States Office of Special Counsel has exclusive authority to investigate allegations of political activity prohibited by the Hatch Act Reform Amendments of 1993.

84. IG Act Section 4 "Duties and Responsibilities…" 5 U.S.C. App. 3 § 4(d) (2016).

85. *E.g.*, Office of Inspector General, U.S. Dep't of the Interior, *Complaint Hotline—Additional Information* (last accessed Mar. 29, 2022), https://www.doioig.gov/complaints-requests/complaint-hotline/complaint-hotline-additional-information.

86. Office of the Inspector General, U.S. Dep't of State, *Semiannual Report to Congress* (Mar. 31, 2017), https://www.stateoig.gov/system/files/oig_spring_2017_sar_508_0.pdf.

87. U.S. Dep't of Justice Office of the Inspector General, *Interim Report on the Department of Justice's Handling of Known or Suspected Terrorists Admitted into the Federal Witness Security Program*, May 2013, http://www.justice.gov/oig/reports/2013/a1323.pdf.

88. Small Business Administration Office of Inspector General, *Consolidated Findings of the Office of Inspector General Reports on SBA's Grant Programs, Fiscal Years 2014–2018*, Report No. 19-02, Nov. 8, 2018, https://www.oversight.gov/report/sba/consolidated-findings-oig-reports-sbas-grant-programs-fys-2014-2018.

89. U.S. Dep't of the Interior Office of the Inspector General, *Evil Twins, Eavesdropping & Password Cracking: How OIG Successfully Attacked DOI's Wireless Networks* (Sept. 16, 2020), https://www.doioig.gov/reports/audit/evil-twins-eavesdropping-password-cracking-how-oig-successfully-attacked-dois.

90. U.S. Dep't of Transportation Office of the Inspector General, *Semiannual Report to Congress* at 31 (Sept. 30, 2019), https://www.oig.dot.gov/sites/default/files/DOT%20OIG%20Semi annual%20Report%20to%20Congress%5EApril%202019%20-%20September%202019.pdf.

91. U.S. Dep't of the Interior Office of the Inspector General, *Semiannual Report to Congress* at 14, April 2014, https://www.doioig.gov/reports/semiannual-report/april-2014-semi annual-report-congress.

92. U.S. Dep't of Veterans Affairs Office of the Inspector General, *Semiannual Report to Congress* at 53, Sept. 30, 2018, https://www.va.gov/oig/pubs/sars/vaoig-sar-2018-2.pdf.

93. Office of the Inspector General U.S. General Services Administration, *Management Deficiency Report*, Apr. 2, 2012, https://www.gsaig.gov/sites/default/files/news/Final%20Manage ment%20Deficiency%20Report_WRC_2012%20April%202%20%28508%20compliant%29.pdf.

94. Council of the Inspectors General on Integrity and Efficiency at 15, *Annual Report to the President and Congress*, 2019, https://www.ignet.gov/sites/default/files/files/FY19_Annual _Report_to_the_President_and_Congress.pdf.

95. IG Act Section 6 "Authority of Inspector General..." 5 U.S.C. App. 3 § 6(a)(1) (2016).

96. IG Act Section 6 "Authority of Inspector General..." 5 U.S.C. App. 3 § 6(c)(2) and IG Act Section 5 "Semiannual Reports..." 5 U.S.C. App. 3 § 5(a)(5) (2016).

97. IG Act Section 6 "Authority of Inspector General..." 5 U.S.C. App. 3 §6(a)(3).

98. IG Act Section 6 "Authority of Inspector General..." 5 U.S.C. App. 3 §6(c)(1).

99. IG Act Section 6 "Authority of Inspector General..." 5 U.S.C. App. 3 §6(c)(2).

100. IG Act Section 6 "Authority of Inspector General..." 5 U.S.C. App. 3 §6(a)(4). *See also Report to Congress on the Use of Administrative Subpoena Authorities by Executive Branch Agencies and Entities*, U.S. Dep't of Justice Office of Legal Policy (Dec. 2002), http://www .justice.gov/archive/olp/rpt_to_congress.htm#2b.

101. IG Act Section 6 "Authority of Inspector General..." 5 U.S.C. App. 3 § 6(f)(1). Twenty-five of these IGs are authorized law enforcement authority by § 6(f)(3). Others have either been conferred such authority by the Attorney General in accordance with § 6(f)(2) or derive their law enforcement authority from legislation other than the IG Act.

102. IG Act Section 6 "Authority of Inspector General..." 5 U.S.C. App. 3 §6(f)(4); Office of the Attorney General, Attorney General Guidelines for Offices of Inspector General with Statutory Law Enforcement Authority (2003), https://www.ignet.gov/sites/default/files/files /agleguidelines.pdf.

103. Letter from Forty-Seven Inspectors General to Hon. Darrell Issa, Chairman, House Committee on Oversight and Government Reform, et al. (Aug. 5, 2014), https://www.govinfo .gov/content/pkg/CHRG-113hhrg91650/pdf/CHRG-113hhrg91650.pdf, at 61.

104. *Id.*

105. *E.g.*, Inspector General Empowerment Act of 2014 (HR 5492); Inspector General Empowerment Act of 2015 (S. 579, 114th Cong., 1st Sess.).

106. Inspector General Empowerment Act of 2016, Pub. L. No. 114-317, 130 Stat. 1595 (2016) (IGEA).

107. U.S. Dep't of Justice Office of the Inspector General, *House Passes IG Empowerment Act* (June 21, 2016), https://oig.justice.gov/news/house-passes-ig-empowerment-act.

108. Privacy Protection Act, 5 U.S.C. § 552a; Computer Matching and Privacy Protection Act of 1988, Pub. L. No. 100-503. The Computer Matching and Privacy Protection Act allows for improved identification of improper and duplicative government expenditures, in part by requiring Federal agencies to enter into written agreements with other agencies or non-federal entities before disclosing records for use in computer matching programs.

109. IGEA, § 2 (amending Inspector General Act of 1978, 5 USCA App. 3 § 6, to expressly exempt Inspectors General from the information sharing and matching requirements of the Privacy Protection Act and expressly exempting Inspectors General from the Paperwork Reduction Act).

110. Paperwork Reduction Act, PL 104–13, 109 Stat. 163 (1995).

111. IGEA § 2.

112. Pub. L. No. 114-317; *see also* IGEA § 4(b).

113. IGEA §§ 4, 11. Section 11 is intended to improve the Integrity Committee, which is responsible for receiving, reviewing, and referring investigations, if deemed appropriate, regarding allegations of wrongdoing made against senior IG employees. Before implementation of the IGEA, this process was managed by the FBI. The Integrity Committee is now managed by CIGIE. CIGIE also launched Oversight.gov following enactment of the IGEA to enhance the public's access to information. This is a website that enables the public to follow the oversight work of all federal IGs that release public reports. *See* U.S. DEP'T OF JUSTICE OFFICE OF THE INSPECTOR GENERAL, *Statement of Michael E. Horowitz Chair* (Sept. 18, 2019), https://oig.justice.gov/sites/default/files/2019-12/t190918_0.pdf. *See also* COUNCIL OF THE INSPECTORS GENERAL ON INTEGRITY AND EFFICIENCY, *Annual Report to the President and Congress*, 2017, https://www.ignet.gov/sites/default/files/files/FY17_Annual_Report_to_the_President_and_Congress.pdf.

114. *Id.*

115. IGEA § 5(a)(19)-(22).

116. *Id.* IG Act Section 4 "Duties and Responsibilities…" 5 U.S.C. App. 3 § 4(e)(1)(C) (requiring certain recommendations be made public and setting out procedures for certain public disclosures not later than three days after the recommendation for corrective action is submitted in final form to the head of the establishment).

117. CONGRESSIONAL RESEARCH SERVICE, STATUTORY INSPECTORS GENERAL IN THE FEDERAL GOVERNMENT: A PRIMER 4 (Jan. 3, 2019), https://fas.org/sgp/crs/misc/R45450.pdf.

118. IGEA § 4. *See also* U.S. GOV'T ACCOUNTABILITY OFFICE, GAO-18-270, INSPECTORS GENERAL: INFORMATION ON VACANCIES AND IG COMMUNITY VIEWS ON THEIR IMPACT (2018), http://www.gao.gov/assets/700/690561.pdf.

119. *Id.* at 32. The report surveyed nine acting IGs and a random sample of OIG employees working under the acting IGs. GAO concluded that, overall, the vacant IG positions did not impact the "OIGs' ability to carry out their duties and responsibilities." However, most OIG employees who were polled expressed the opinion that an acting IG may *appear* to have less independence.

120. COUNCIL OF THE INSPECTORS GENERAL ON INTEGRITY AND EFFICIENCY (Oct. 8, 2020), https://www.ignet.gov/sites/default/files/files/CIGIE-Views-Letter-House-NDAA-HR-6395-Sec1115_10082020.pdf.

121. *E.g.*, COUNCIL OF THE INSPECTORS GENERAL ON INTEGRITY AND EFFICIENCY (July 8, 2020), https://www.ignet.gov/sites/default/files/files/S3994_CIGIE_Views_letter_07082020.pdf [hereinafter CIGIE Views Letter].

122. *See id.*

123. COUNCIL OF THE INSPECTORS GENERAL ON INTEGRITY AND EFFICIENCY, *supra* note 120.

124. *See* CIGIE Transition Handbook, 17; *see also* ALL FEDERAL INSPECTORS GENERAL REPORTS IN ONE PLACE, INSPECTOR GENERAL VACANCIES, https://www.oversight.gov/ig-vacancies (last accessed Nov. 12, 2020).

125. COUNCIL OF THE INSPECTORS GENERAL ON INTEGRITY AND EFFICIENCY, *Inspectors General Directory*, https://ignet.gov/content/inspectors-general-directory (last visited Oct. 26, 2020).

126. THE WHITE HOUSE, *The Cabinet*, https://www.whitehouse.gov/administration/cabinet/ (last accessed Mar. 29, 2022). In order of the number of days vacant, these vacancies are Department of Defense, Department of the Treasury, and Department of State, https://www.oversight.gov/ig-vacancies.

127. Courtney Buble, *Inspector General Vacancies Continue to Jeopardize Oversight and Investigations*, GOV'T EXECUTIVE (Sept. 18, 2019), https://www.govexec.com/oversight/2019/09/inspector-general-vacancies-continue-jeopardize-oversight-and-investigations/159978/.

128. BIPARTISAN POLICY CENTER, OVERSIGHT MATTERS: WHAT'S NEXT FOR INSPECTORS GENERAL (July 2018), https://bipartisanpolicy.org/wp-content/uploads/2019/03/Oversight-Matters-Whats-Next-for-Inspectors-General.pdf.

129. COUNCIL OF THE INSPECTORS GENERAL ON INTEGRITY AND EFFICIENCY (Jan. 28, 2021), https://www.ignet.gov/sites/default/files/untracked/CIGIE_Legislative_Priorities_117th_Congress.pdf.

130. 2021 CIGIE Report, 1.

CHAPTER 11

Whistleblower Law and Ethics

Thomas Devine, Janet Arnott[1]

This is a revision of a chapter originally prepared by Robert Begg.

> This chapter focuses on issues relating to whistleblowing, including the statutory erosion of the at-will employment doctrine, federal and state whistleblower statutes and their underlying purposes, statutory financial incentives meant to encourage whistleblowing, common-law exceptions to the at-will doctrine, and an analysis of special issues encountered by in-house counsel and government lawyers who are placed in the role of whistleblower.

To whistle is "to utter a clear shrill sound, note, or song, as various birds . . . ; also formerly, to hiss, as a serpent."[2] As will be seen, this definition of the verb "whistle" rather nicely illustrates the role of a whistleblower in our society. Whistleblowers exercise free speech rights to challenge abuses of power that betray the public trust. A whistleblower is usually "an employee who refuses to engage in and/or reports illegal or wrongful activities of his employer or fellow employees."[3] As a legal doctrine, whistleblowing is modern enough to justify having a number of web pages devoted to it,[4] yet old enough to have been recognized by statute during the Civil War era.[5] It is now strongly entrenched in federal and most states' statutory or common law. Globally, 48 nations have adopted whistleblower laws, swelling to 62 with nations covered by the 2020 European Union Whistleblower Directive, as well as intergovernmental organizations such as the United Nations and World Bank.[6]

Whistleblowing is analyzed herein in its broadest sense, that in which individuals, virtually always employees, have the right to lawfully reveal wrongdoing for the public good and are protected from retaliation for doing so. At times there is a necessary overlap between two interrelated but distinct bodies of law. One is the law of retaliatory or wrongful discharge, which is concerned with a wide spectrum of causes for unjust dismissal, including dismissal for whistleblowing. The other is the law of whistleblowing, which is directed at many different forms of retaliation, including, but not limited to, discharge. Whistleblower law is also distinct in that it seeks to encourage employees to come forward by providing protection against retaliation, and also by providing financial incentives in some instances.

Distinctions will also be drawn between active whistleblowing, which entails voluntarily coming forward to report wrongdoing, and passive whistleblowing, in which the employee does nothing more than respond to a lawful request for information from a public entity or refuse to carry out an illegal instruction.[7]

THE CONTROVERSIAL NATURE OF WHISTLEBLOWING

The act of whistleblowing has always tended to be controversial. Indeed, individual whistleblowers are frequently viewed in stark contrast as either heroes or villains, or, as the definition quoted at the beginning of the chapter suggests, as benevolent songbirds or venomous snakes. It all depends on one's perspective. Whether the whistleblower is perceived as a saint or sinner generally is tied to the speech's impact on the beholder. Even though the general public, especially politicians and the media, may laud and wish to encourage corporate or governmental employees to come forward with information about threats to the public safety, gross waste, or illegal activities, those exposed by the disclosure will almost surely have an opposite reaction.[8] Managers of corporations or government agencies, coworkers, and even friends and neighbors often view whistleblowers as disloyal and treacherous spies, squealers, stool pigeons, or threats to their communities, rather than as heroes.

Although retaliation is not always the response to whistleblowing,[9] the instinctive reaction of some managers has been to retaliate against whistleblowers through dismissals, demotions, or other forms of harassment. Whistleblowers know that speaking out can be a threat to job security or can result in their being shunned as outcasts by coworkers, and even, in extreme cases, that it can be hazardous to their personal safety.[10] Whistleblowing often has a long-term impact on one's career because bureaucracies supposedly never forget.[11] Therefore, it is not surprising that employees are reluctant to report improprieties either in house or publicly because they can anticipate both immediate and long-term negative consequences.

Normally, the decision to blow the whistle on improper activities is a voluntary and intensely personal one.[12] Except in very narrow circumstances, an employee is usually not required by law to report the improper or even illegal activities of an employer, although citizens are generally encouraged to do so.[13] Thus, employees who blow the whistle are voluntarily placing what they perceive to be the public interest or a matter of conscience ahead of the interests of their employing business or institution.

The employer may respond by viewing the whistleblower's disclosure as a breach of one or more fundamental expectations inherent in their employment relationship. Both employers and employees have well-established expectations of the others' conduct and responsibilities. Employers have the right to expect their employees to perform their assigned work competently, to obey orders, to be loyal and avoid conflicts of interest, and to maintain appropriate confidences of the employer.[14] Employees in return expect compensation, a minimal degree of job security if they do their jobs well, and assurance that any job responsibilities or orders are not illegal or unethical.[15] Within these strictures employees still have rights and obligations as citizens, and moral, religious, or political motivations may have an impact on how they interpret or respond to the policies of their employer.[16] Thus, a decision to expose improper conduct is a difficult one, which can be fraught with conflicting values, responsibilities, and loyalties.

Unfortunately, too often there is no bright-line rule that tells employees when they have a duty to blow the whistle or when doing so would be an inappropriate course of action. Whistleblowing is at the intersection of valid, but conflicting values. We appreciate team players and dislike naysayers, but we disrespect those who just go along with the crowd while admiring rugged individualists who are true to themselves. We scorn squealers and tattletales as rats, but we feel the same about those who don't want to get involved or who cover up the truth. We value both personal privacy and the public's right to know. Whistleblowers must choose whether their ultimate loyalty is to their employer (perhaps better viewed as a means to support their family), versus loyalty to the law and the public. These choices create an ethical conundrum involving a confrontation between the whistleblower's self-interests and the consequences of remaining silent in an environment with few absolutely clear lines of demarcation.[17]

Views on how one should react in a given situation vary considerably. On one hand, virtually all will agree that an employee's refusal to obey an order to commit a criminal act is appropriate. Conversely, many might feel that it would be inappropriate to report this information to the news media or even to a law enforcement agency. In some instances, an employee may have a fair degree of discretion as to an appropriate course of action; however, in others, the employee may have no option, such as when a code of professional responsibility mandates revelation of confidential employer information.[18] Often whistleblowing is involuntary, such as when an inspector or investigator reports politically unpopular findings of illegality.

Like all freedom of expression, this right is vulnerable to abuse. It is not unheard of for an employee to blow the whistle on relatively minor or trivial violations of law or regulations in order to use whistleblower protection provisions as a bar to legitimate negative personnel actions or to exact revenge on a coworker or supervisor.[19] So, even though ethical issues and quandaries may exist for potential whistleblowers, difficulties also arise for employers who must at times deal with employees who are using the whistleblower protection mechanisms improperly to serve their own self-interests or political, moral, or religious agendas. Thus, the employer's interest in being able "to manage his work force free from false or spurious claims of reprisal" is another factor to be included in the whistleblower protection calculus.[20]

Within this quagmire, lawmakers have been required to determine the nature and scope of protection for whistleblowers by determining which employees are protected and which are not, and which types of activities are encouraged and which are not. As will be seen, public policies underlying protection for public- and private-sector employees can differ significantly. For example, the law may protect a public-sector employee from reprisal for revealing gross mismanagement or waste of public funds, whereas a private-sector employee may not be protected for reporting an equivalent waste of resources unless it would materially affect investment values. This is especially true if that employee is not covered by the Sarbanes-Oxley Act, which applies only to publicly traded corporations. In nearly all cases, U.S. private sector whistleblower laws are enforcement provisions of remedial statutes for public health or safety, regulation of the financial industry, or oversight of government contracts.[21] As a result, protection for private-sector employees tends to be provided only when the shareholder or public interest is directly affected.

The law in this area reflects a conflict between two public policies. The first public policy supports an employer's contractual right to hire, fire, and discipline employees. A second, competing public policy encourages whistleblowers to come forward for the good of society to protect the public from harm, or to protect statutory rights. This second public policy is reflected in the common law and statutes that seek to prevent retaliation against whistleblowers in the first instance, or to provide a remedy when retaliation has taken place. Such anti-retaliation policies, however, constitute an erosion of the long-standing doctrine of employment at will. An appreciation of the at-will employment doctrine is essential to an understanding of the law of unjust dismissal and specifically the law of retaliation for whistleblowing.

THE AT-WILL EMPLOYMENT DOCTRINE

The at-will employment doctrine creates a presumption that applies when an employment contract fails to state a definite duration for the contract or specifically states that the employment is at will.[22] If no term or length of employment is stated or agreed to, the contract is presumed to be at will, and either the employer or the employee may terminate the employment agreement at any time, for any reason or for no reason.[23] The at-will doctrine, which assumes equal bargaining power between employer and employee, is premised on the freedom of contract and reflects the pro-business, laissez-faire economic attitudes of the late 19th and early 20th centuries.[24]

The at-will doctrine is a uniquely American rule, having been articulated for the first time in an early treatise on master and servant law.[25] The rule represents a clear departure from the English common law rule that, when dealing with employment contracts for an indefinite term, assumes that the term is for one year.[26]

Most other major industrialized economies have rules that provide greater protection for employees under contracts of indefinite duration than does the American rule.[27] The at-will doctrine developed during the late 1800s and was eventually adopted as a principle of common law by all American jurisdictions. Business and industry were strong supporters of the doctrine since it was easy to terminate workers in response to the business cycle or to dampen union activity. The impact on employees, however, was quite harsh.

Congress, state legislatures, and the courts attempted to mitigate the harshness of the rule by creating a number of exceptions premised on various public policy considerations. Public-sector employees were the first to benefit from an exception to the at-will doctrine.[28] Most government employees at the state and federal levels are now protected from arbitrary dismissal by civil service statutes that require a "just cause" for firings. Public-sector employees may also be protected from dismissal in certain circumstances by provisions of the United States Constitution. Freedoms of speech and association under the First Amendment have protected public employees from dismissal for public statements directly concerning matters of legitimate public concern.[29]

The first major exception to the at-will employment doctrine for private-sector employees was the National Labor Relations Act, which guaranteed employees the right to organize and bargain collectively.[30] This allowed labor unions to negotiate for "just cause" provisions in their contracts, providing union members with far greater job security than non-union employees, who are still subject to the at-will doctrine. A third wave of legislation limiting employers' right to fire at will consisted of federal and state civil rights initiatives prohibiting improper discrimination in the hiring and firing of employees. Discriminatory dismissals based on race, sex, color, religion, national origin, age, or disability are now prohibited.[31]

Paralleling the civil rights movement was an expansion of federal regulation of business conduct in the general areas of environmental protection, consumer protection, workplace safety, and public health.[32] These business conduct statutes were aimed at protecting individuals, society, or the environment from specific enumerated harms,[33] but the statutes were also clearly needed to protect employees who were seeking to exercise their statutory rights in furtherance of the policy aims of Congress. Most of these statutes therefore contain provisions that protect employees from retaliation for exercising rights under the statute, for testifying in investigations, or for filing charges against an employer for violation of the statute.[34]

Despite this erosion of the common-law at-will employment doctrine, today 49 of the 50 states still retain either a common law or statutory version of the rule. The state of Montana has abrogated the rule with a just-cause statute,[35] and the statutory and court-made exceptions to the rule in many jurisdictions have greatly reduced management's unbridled discretion to fire employees for any or no reason.

STATUTORY PROTECTION FOR PUBLIC-SECTOR WHISTLEBLOWERS—WHY IS THERE A NEED FOR WHISTLEBLOWER PROTECTION IN THE PUBLIC SECTOR?

Government in its many forms collects and spends vast amounts of money and employs millions of citizens in capacities ranging from garbage collectors to physicists to the president.[36] It is society's ultimate arbiter of power, and official guardian for the rule of law. Corresponding to the magnitude of the enterprise of government is the opportunity for government employees to take advantage of their positions of public trust by making improper use of governmental resources, information, or authority. Taking note of this phenomenon in an earlier era, Benjamin Franklin said, "There is no kind of dishonesty into which otherwise good people more easily and frequently fall than that of defrauding the government."[37]

The free flow of information from individuals free to bear witness is the life blood for informed, responsible institutional decisions, organizational checks and balances, and law enforcement. It is clearly in the public interest to prevent criminal acts by public employees, including theft, fraud, corruption, and self-dealing. But it is also important to prevent damage to the public weal from acts, such as waste of public resources, gross mismanagement, favoritism, or unethical conduct that might not reach to the criminal level but are damaging nonetheless. To prevent improper activities by public employees, there is a panoply of institutional mechanisms and agencies charged with the formal responsibility of ferreting out governmental crime and corruption. These agencies conduct formal audits, inventories, and investigations in hopes of deterring, detecting, or remedying improper activities. One of the most important sources of information for these agencies is derived from public-sector employees who become aware of improper activities.[38] As a rule, investigations cannot succeed without testimony from witnesses. Whistleblowers, in essence, are "an additional check and balance that ensures government integrity and prevents government corruption."[39]

Information concerning improper acts comes to the attention of investigative agencies primarily in three ways. In the first instance, an honest employee learns of an impropriety and voluntarily comes forward with information that results in the initiation of an investigation. This can be viewed as active whistleblowing and is often the only way in which a particular improper activity would ever be brought to light.[40] Unfortunately, it is still relatively rare for a public-sector employee to come forward voluntarily to incriminate a supervisor or coworker because "squealing" continues to be frowned upon by many within our society.[41] Also, other factors, such as the wish not to stir up trouble, the desire to just do one's job and not get involved, and the fear of retaliation if an employee does come forward, militate against voluntarily speaking out. Most public employees know the costs and risks associated with whistleblowing and are not comforted by the formal legal protections that are in place to protect them. The enormous institutional hostility targeted at those who betray organizational norms cannot be eliminated by formal legislative language.[42]

The second way investigators learn of wrongdoing involves passive whistleblowing, which may be involuntary. Here, a public-sector employee provides information concerning improper conduct when the employee is questioned during the course of an investigation. Although the employee may not have initiated the inquiry, he or she may have provided pertinent information that has incriminated or embarrassed a supervisor, co-employee, or other person with strong political connections. Such information could surface in a routine investigative interview or under oath pursuant to a subpoena. It is in the public interest for public-sector employees to be encouraged to cooperate with investigating agencies and to testify fully and honestly under oath.[43]

A third form of whistleblowing may be the most common—the "duty speech." This occurs when an inspector, investigator, auditor, accountant or similar professional makes controversial disclosures within a report or official findings. Again, it is involuntary if the employee is loyal to the rule of law. To misrepresent the record would be a false statement, and a criminal offense.[44] Emphasizing the importance of whistleblower statutes, since 2006 duty speech by government workers has not enjoyed constitutional protection under the First Amendment.[45]

Clearly, society benefits when public employees are willing to come forward and to speak freely about inappropriate activities. It has long been recognized that it is in the public interest to provide protection from retaliation for public-sector employees for doing so. Therefore, the federal government, many states, and even some local governments[46] have attempted to provide statutory protection for public employees to further this public interest.

FEDERAL STATUTORY PROTECTIONS FOR WHISTLEBLOWERS

Although federal employees long enjoyed the protection of civil service statutes requiring "just cause" for dismissal, until 1978 there was no provision specifically applicable to federal employee whistleblowers. In that year, Congress dramatically reformed the federal civil service laws. The Civil Service Reform Act of 1978 (CSRA) includes specific statutory protection for whistleblowing, making it a "prohibited personnel practice" to act in retaliation for a lawful disclosure which the employee reasonably believes is evidence of illegality, gross waste, gross mismanagement, abuse of authority or a substantial and specific danger to public health or safety.[47]

In addition to banning retaliation for bona fide whistleblowing, the CSRA created new government bodies to deal with employment issues relating to federal employees. These include the Office of Personnel Management, the Merit System Protection Board (MSPB), and the Office of Special Counsel (OSC).

Each of these bodies has specialized functions. The Office of Personnel Management executes, administers, and enforces rules for day-to-day personnel management and serves an advisory function to the agencies and the president.[48] The Merit System Protection Board is charged with ensuring adherence to merit system principles and with reviewing appealable agency actions affecting the merit system.[49] The Office of Special Counsel is required to protect employees from prohibited personnel practices, to file complaints for disciplinary action against those who commit prohibited personnel practices, and to protect whistleblowers.[50] It also has authority to order and oversee agency investigations and corrective action on whistleblowing disclosures.[51]

Despite the clearly expressed intent of Congress to protect whistleblowers, the promise of the CSRA was not fulfilled initially. Whistleblowers learned to their dismay that they were not adequately protected in those instances when they had come forward.[52] Congress had intended the OSC to play an activist role in protecting whistleblowers, but the reality was that the OSC's performance at best was uninspired and ineffectual. At times it functioned in practice as a legalized "Plumbers Unit," counseling managers on how to fire whistleblowers, while funneling employees' confidential evidence back to the agencies charged with retaliation.[53]

Congress attempted to strengthen protection through the enactment of the Whistleblower Protection Act of 1989 (WPA),[54] which significantly amended and expanded the CSRA. The WPA mandated that the OSC protect employees from prohibited personnel practices, especially retaliation for whistleblowing, as its paramount function, and that the OSC did not have authority to undermine the rights of those seeking assistance.[55] It eliminated the requirement to prove animus by only requiring a causal link with protected activity, instead of retaliation as in the 1978 law.[56] Perhaps most significant, it overhauled unrealistic legal burdens of proof for employees to prevail when asserting their rights. In the 1978 law, in order to establish a *prima facie* case the employee had to prove that protected activity was a "predominant motivating factor" for the challenged personnel action. This was based on the burden of proof from a 1977 Supreme Court First Amendment case, *Mt. Healthy v. Doyle School District.*[57] At that time, the agency could prevail by proving with a preponderance of the evidence that it would have taken the same action for independent reasons in the absence of protected speech. The WPA significantly lowered the bar. Now an employee establishes a prima facie case merely by demonstrating that protected activity is a "contributing factor to the agency's action."[58] This basically is a relevance standard, defined in legislative history as "any factor, which alone or in combination with other factors, tends to affect in any way the outcome."[59] At the same time, the agency's burden was increased. It must have clear and convincing evidence to establish it would have acted independently, not a mere preponderance.[60] Virtually all federal whistleblower laws since 1989 have adopted the WPA legal burdens of proof to govern how cases are decided.[61]

Enactment of the WPA and its enhanced protections for whistleblowers led to a marked increase in the number of new complaints received by the OSC.[62] Surveys of federal employees who had requested assistance from the OSC suggested, however, that the OSC continued to be viewed as relatively ineffective in protecting whistleblowers from retaliation.[63] This led to significant amendments to the CSRA and WPA in 1994.[64]

The same frustration extended to the law's due process reforms. When enacted, the WPA was hailed as the strongest free speech law in history. Unfortunately, a monopoly on judicial review by a hostile court, the Federal Circuit Court of Appeals, proved the reform's structural Achilles' heel. The Court's precedents canceled protection in nearly all relevant circumstances, such as when disclosures are made to supervisors, disclosures made to possible wrongdoers, disclosures connected with one's job duties, and indeed disclosures of any misconduct that had been previously disclosed by another employee.[65] Further, the Court held that to have reasonable belief that a disclosure constitutes evidence of misconduct, the employee first must overcome the presumption that the government acts "correctly, fairly, in good faith, and in accordance with the law and governing regulations" by "irrefragable proof."[66] "Irrefragable" means "irrefutable, undeniable, incontrovertible, or incapable of being overthrown."[67] Even if a whistleblower survived this gauntlet of loopholes, the standard to qualify for protection became far higher than that necessary to incarcerate a criminal.

The WPA became a symbol of whistleblowers' inability to fairly challenge retaliation, and in fact was counterproductive. By exercising these rights, whistleblowers routinely spent years of further effort and tens or hundreds of thousands of dollars to earn an inevitable ruling that they deserved whatever action had been challenged. Whistleblower support organizations like the Government Accountability Project warned employees that filing suit could be hammering the final nail in their own professional coffins.

A 13-year process developing this record of failure led to unanimous passage of the Whistleblower Protection Enhancement Act of 2012 (WPEA).[68] In addition to a pilot program expanding appellate review for five years, the law statutorily overturned nearly all Federal Circuit judicial precedents hostile to protecting whistleblowers.[69] It also expanded the scope of protection,[70] strengthened due process rights against agency restraints on speech,[71] and made it easier for the special counsel to seek discipline against retaliation.[72]

Currently, basic protection for whistleblower activities for most federal employees is provided by provisions of the CSRA as amended and expanded by the WPA, 1994 amendments and the WPEA. Fundamental to the federal civil service is the concept of employment protection premised on a merit system in which employees are protected from eleven "prohibited personnel practices." It is a merit system principle that federal employees be protected from reprisal for bona fide whistleblower activities and that retaliation for whistleblowing is a prohibited personnel practice.[73] Persons in a position to influence a personnel action shall not "take or fail to take, or threaten to take or fail to take, a personnel action with respect to any employee or applicant for employment" due to whistleblower activities.[74]

Whistleblower activities for purposes of these statutes are defined in section 2302(b)(8)(A)(B) as disclosures of information that the employee reasonably believes evidence "a violation of any law, rule or regulation, or gross mismanagement, a gross waste of funds, an abuse of authority, or a substantial and specific danger to public health or safety." Any such disclosures can be made to the special counsel, to the inspector general of an agency, or to other employees designated to receive such disclosures within an agency.[75] Such disclosures can be made to others, but only if doing so is not specifically prohibited by law or by an executive order that requires disclosures to be kept secret in the interest of national defense or the conduct of foreign affairs.[76]

An employee, applicant, or former employee also can seek to make a difference through investigation and corrective action on alleged misconduct evidenced by the disclosure. Upon receipt of an allegation of improper conduct by a whistleblower, if requested the OSC must determine within 15 days whether there is a substantial likelihood that the alleged agency misconduct actually occurred.[77] If there is a positive determination, the OSC informs the agency head, who must then conduct an investigation and submit a written report of findings to the special counsel that includes a summary of the whistleblower's evidence, a review of evidence obtained by the investigation, relevant findings of fact and conclusions of law, and any corrective action commitments. The whistleblower then has an opportunity to comment on the report's adequacy, after which the OSC grades it for accuracy and completeness. The entire package then is submitted to the President, relevant congressional audiences and placed in a public file.[78] If the disclosure evidences a reasonable belief of relevant evidence, the Special Counsel must forward it to the agency head to provide notice but there is no requirement for further action.[79] If there is no positive determination, the OSC may still pass on the information to the agency head with the consent of the whistleblower. If it is not transmitted to the agency head, the OSC shall return any documentation to the whistleblower, inform him or her why the disclosure is not being pursued, and also specify what other options are available should the individual wish to pursue the matter further.[80] The whistleblower's identity may not be disclosed by the special counsel without consent unless revealing it is necessary to prevent "imminent danger to public health or safety or imminent violation of any criminal law."[81]

If a personnel action is taken against the whistleblower for a protected disclosure, the retaliation constitutes a prohibited personnel practice and the whistleblower may seek protection from the OSC. If permitted under law, rule, or regulations such as disciplinary actions causing greater than a two week suspension,[82] the whistleblower may seek corrective action directly from the MSPB, rather than from the special counsel.[83] Since the OSC's paramount responsibility is the protection of federal employee whistleblowers, during an OSC investigation no disciplinary action can be taken against the employee for the activity under investigation without approval of the special counsel.[84] Protection is also provided by the OSC's ability to request a stay of a personnel action from any member of the MSPB if there "are reasonable grounds to believe that the personnel action was taken as a result of a prohibited personnel practice."[85] There are detailed OSC guidelines in place for keeping the whistleblower informed, for completing the investigation in a timely fashion, and for maintaining confidentiality. If the OSC is unable to achieve a correction of the prohibited personnel practice, or the employee's agency has not acted, after 120 days the OSC may petition the MSPB for corrective action.[86] Judicial review is available in the case of an adverse order or decision of the MSPB.[87] While previously limited to the Federal Circuit Court of Appeals, under the WPEA appeals can now be brought to the regional federal appellate court.[88]

To prove a prima facie case for whistleblower retaliation, the OSC or the whistleblower must prove by a preponderance of the evidence four elements of the case.[89]

1. *"That the employee engaged in protected conduct."* This would be disclosure of information under 5 U.S.C. section 2302(b)(8)(A) or (B) as noted previously. The disclosure may be based on the employee's reasonable belief that there was improper activity or wrongdoing, even though the disclosures may ultimately be proven to be incorrect.[90]

2. *"That an official in an appropriate capacity knew about the whistleblower disclosures."* This may be either actual or constructive knowledge of the disclosure and can be proved by circumstantial evidence, such as if "the personnel action occurred within a period of time such that a reasonable person could conclude that the disclosure was a contributing factor in the personnel action."[91]

3. *"That a personnel action was taken or failed to be taken or that a threat was made to take or fail to take a personnel action in retaliation for disclosure."* Section 2302(a)(2)(A) defines personnel action in some detail, including "any other significant change in duties, responsibilities, or working conditions." Thus both formal and informal forms of retaliation against a whistleblower are viewed as personnel actions.[92]

4. *"That there was a causal connection between the protected activity and the adverse personnel action."* As discussed earlier, the whistleblower must prove that the disclosure was "a contributing factor" in the decision to take the personnel action.[93] The agency then has an affirmative defense if it can prove by "clear and convincing evidence" that it would have taken the same personnel action even without the disclosure, that is, that there was a legitimate managerial reason for the agency action.[94] If the agency cannot meet the burden of proof on its affirmative defense, the MSPB shall order appropriate corrective action.[95]

Corrective action by the MSPB may include placing the whistleblowing employee, "as nearly as possible," in the position the employee would have been in had the retaliation for disclosure not occurred.[96] For example, a whistleblower may be granted reinstatement or a preference in receiving a transfer within the same or another agency to a position with comparable tenure and status to the employee's original position, assuming the employee is otherwise qualified.[97] Corrective actions may "include reimbursement for attorney's fees, back pay and related benefits, medical costs incurred, travel expenses, and any other reasonable and foreseeable consequential damages."[98] The WPEA added the availability of compensatory damages.[99] [100]

In enacting the CSRA, Congress intended "to channel grievances and disputes arising out of government employment into a single system of administrative procedures and remedies, subject to judicial review."[101] A line of judicial precedents emphasized that remedies under the CSRA were exclusive and that other remedies such as actions under the Federal Tort Claims Act,[102] constitutional claims,[103] and suits for back pay under the Tucker Act,[104] were precluded by the CSRA.[105]

The WPA, by contrast, specifically provides at 5 U.S.C. section 1222 (2000), that, except as provided in the individual right of action provisions of section 1221(i), nothing in chapters 12 (Office of Special Counsel) or 23 (Merit System Principles) "shall be construed to limit any right or remedy available under a provision of statute which is outside of both this chapter and chapter 23." The legislative history states the position, however, that "§ 1222 is not intended to create a cause of action where none now exists or to reverse any court decision. Rather § 1222 says it is not the intent of Congress that the procedures under these chapters of title 5, United States Code, are meant to be exclusive."[106] The courts, relying on the legislative history, have held, therefore, that remedies not available prior to the WPA are also not available under section 1222, and that the exclusivity of remedies under the CSRA as established by earlier precedents is still valid and controlling.[107] It was the intent of Congress to expand and enhance appeal rights available in other statutes rather than to create any new cause of action against the government.[108] Thus, the preference for exclusivity of remedies under the CSRA remains, apparently, until Congress specifically creates new remedies outside the scope of the CSRA.

FEDERAL WHISTLEBLOWER AND ANTI-RETALIATION PROVISIONS OUTSIDE THE MERIT SYSTEM

The CSRA and WPA provide significant protections and remedies for most federal employee whistleblowers. But what of federal employees not covered by these enactments, or nonfederal employees in the public and private sectors, or employees who are retaliated against for activities that combine whistleblower and non-whistleblower motivations?

The answer to some of these questions requires an examination of the broader federal regulatory structure. Over the past several decades, the federal government has expanded its role in regulating employment practices, workplace safety, consumer protection, financial institutions, corporate wrongdoing, transportation, and threats to the environment, as indicated later in the chapter. Congressional intent in enacting legislation in these areas was primarily to protect the public against unfair or dangerous business or governmental practices or conditions. It became apparent, however, that enforcement of these statutes and regulations was difficult, if not impossible, without the cooperation of employees of the businesses or governmental agencies who were aware of such violations. Employees knew that in an at-will employment environment, coming forward with incriminating information concerning their employers could result in retaliation. Congress responded by promulgating witness protection provisions in a large number of federal statutes. Many of these statutes protect active whistleblowers; however, others are meant to protect employees in the exercise of certain professional duties or civic rights and responsibilities or in the enforcement of personal rights under a statute.

The following chart illustrates the range of over 60 federal statutes that provide whistleblower and anti-retaliation protection for public and/or private-sector employees. Although it is recognized that not all of these statutes are purely whistleblower in nature, an all-inclusive chart may be more useful than one that attempts to define too narrowly whistleblower protection. The chart lists the name of the provision, its citation, and whether it is targeted at public- or private-sector employees or both. The chart is divided into sections based on the nature of the subject matter dealt with in the statute.

Military		
Armed Forces Members' Communication with Congress and Inspector General	10 U.S.C. § 1034(b)	Public sector
Armed Services Contractor's Employees Protection	10 U.S.C. § 2409(a)	Private sector
Civilian Employees of the Armed Forces	10 U.S.C. § 1587(b)	Private sector
False Claims Act	31 U.S.C. § 3730	Both
Veterans Affairs Office of Employment Discrimination Complaint Adjudication	38 U.S.C. § 319	Public Sector
Intelligence Community Whistleblower Protection Act	50 U.S.C. § 403q(d)(5)	Both

230 • Ethical Standards in the Public Sector

Environment		
Toxic Substances Control Act	15 U.S.C. § 2622(a)	Private sector
Asbestos Hazard Emergency Response Act	15 U.S.C. § 2651	Both
Asbestos School Hazard Detection and Control Act of 1980	20 U.S.C. § 3608	Public sector
Federal Water Pollution Control Act	33 U.S.C. § 1367(a)	Private sector
Safe Drinking Water Amendments	42 U.S.C. § 300j-9(i)	Both
Solid Waste Disposal Act	42 U.S.C. § 6971(a)	Both
Clean Air Act	42 U.S.C. § 7622(a)	Both
Comprehensive Environment Response, Compensation, and Liability Act of 1980; hazardous substances releases	42 U.S.C. § 9610	Private sector
Pipeline Safety Improvement Act of 2002	49 U.S.C. § 60129	Private sector
Citizens' Rights and Responsibilities		
Bankruptcy Reform Act	11 U.S.C. § 525	Both
Racketeering Influenced and Corrupt Organization Act (indirect application)	18 U.S.C. § 1964(c)	Private sector
Jury Systems Improvement Act	28 U.S.C. § 1875(a)	Both
Age Discrimination	29 U.S.C. § 623(d)	Both
Employee Polygraph Protection Act	29 U.S.C. § 2002(3), (4)	Private sector
Family and Medical Leave Act of 1993	29 U.S.C. § 2615	Both
Public Health Service Act	42 U.S.C. § 300a-7(c)	Private sector
Emergency Health Care	42 U.S.C. § 1395dd(i)	Employees of participating hospitals
Civil Rights of Institutionalized Persons Act	42 U.S.C. § 1997d	Both
Title VII	42 U.S.C. § 2000e-3	Both
State Long Term Care Ombudsman Program	42 U.S.C. § 3058g(j)(2)–(3)	Private sector
Americans with Disabilities Act	42 U.S.C. § 12203	Both
Labor and Workplace Safety		
Whistleblower Protection Act	5 U.S.C. § 2302(8)	Public sector
Federal Labor Relations–Unfair Labor Practices	5 U.S.C. § 7116(a)(4)	Public sector
National Labor Relations Act	29 U.S.C. § 158(a)(1), (3), (4)	Private sector
Fair Labor Standards Act	29 U.S.C. § 215(a)(3)	Both
Occupational Safety and Health Act	29 U.S.C. § 660(c)(1)	Private sector

Migrant Seasonal and Agricultural Protection Act	29 U.S.C. § 1855(a)	Private sector
Taxpayer First Act	26 U.S.C. § 7623(d)	Private sector
Transportation		
Longshore and Harbor Workers Compensation Act	33 U.S.C. § 948a	Private sector
Federal Employers' Liability Act (Railroads)	45 U.S.C. § 60	Private sector
Railway Labor Act	45 U.S.C. § 152	Private sector
Vessels and Seamen Laws	46 U.S.C. § 2114	Private sector
Safe Containers for International Cargo Act	46 U.S.C. § 80507	Private sector
Surface Transportation Assistance Act	49 U.S.C. § 31105(a)	Private sector
Protection of Employees Providing Air Safety Information	49 U.S.C. § 42121	Private sector
Hazardous Industries		
Federal Mine Safety and Health Act	30 U.S.C. § 815(c)	Private sector
Surface Mining Control and Reclamation Act of 1977	30 U.S.C. § 1293(a)	Private sector
Energy Reorganization Act	42 U.S.C. § 5851(a)	Private sector
Financial Institutions		
Corporate Transparency Act	31 U.S.C. § 5328	Private sector
Dodd Frank Act	15 U.S.C. § 78u-6, 7 U.S.C. § 26	Private sector
Resolution Trust Corporation Whistleblower Act	12 U.S.C. § 1441a(q)	Public sector
Federally Insured Credit Union Employees	12 U.S.C. § 1790b(a)	Private sector
Financial Institutions Reform, Recovery, and Enforcement Act of 1989	12 U.S.C. § 1831j	Private sector
Criminal Anti-Trust Retaliation Act	15 U.S.C. § 7a-3	Private sector
Anti-Money Laundering Act	31 U.S.C. § 5323(g) and (j)	Private sector
Consumer Protection		
Consumer Credit Protection Act	15 U.S.C. § 1674	Both
Employee Retirement Income Security Act	29 U.S.C. § 1140	Private sector
Intergovernmental Communications		
Congressional Accountability Act of 1995	2 U.S.C. § 1317(a)	Public sector
Federal Employees' Right to Petition Congress	5 U.S.C. § 7211	Public sector

Sarbanes-Oxley Act		
Enforcement	15 U.S.C. § 7202(b)(1)	Private sector
Rules of Professional Responsibility for Attorneys Appearing Before the Securities and Exchange Commission	15 U.S.C. § 7245	Private sector
Retaliating Against a Witness, Victim, or an Informant	18 U.S.C. § 1513(e)	Private sector
Whistleblower Protection for Employees of Publicly Traded Companies	18 U.S.C. § 1514A	Private sector
Miscellaneous		
Major Fraud Act	18 U.S.C. § 1031(h)	Both
Federal Acquisition Streamlining Act of 1994	41 U.S.C. § 265	Private sector
Department of Energy Whistleblower Protection Program	50 U.S.C. § 2702	Public sector

The impact of these federal whistleblower protection and anti-retaliation statutes is significant. They encourage both public- and private-sector employees to come forward to protect their own personal interests in some cases, but more frequently to protect the public interest. The underlying public policies and justifications for whistleblower protection at the federal level have also been compelling at the state level. Many states have enacted whistleblower protection statutes in response to concerns of fraud and corruption in government and threats to the public health or safety by business enterprises and government.

STATUTORY WHISTLEBLOWER PROTECTION AT THE STATE LEVEL

Generally

In addition to the protection given to whistleblowers through exceptions to the at-will doctrine, all states have enacted whistleblowing statutes.[109] Although many state whistleblower statutes are modeled after the federal Civil Service Reform Act,[110] as a rule they are far weaker and vary considerably in the scope of who is covered under the statute and in the nature of the conduct protected or encouraged. Public policy in some states seeks to provide comprehensive coverage to a broad pool of potential whistleblowers, whereas other states have carefully refined and targeted their protections. Public-sector employees are generally more likely to be protected by whistleblower statutes and to have a much broader range of protected conduct than are private-sector employees or individuals.[111] Thirty states and the District of Columbia also have False Claims Act whistleblower laws, echoing the federal statute by allowing and protecting "relators" in challenges to fraud in government contracts.[112]

Making generalizations about these statutes can be useful for a broad understanding of state whistleblower protection, but it is also dangerous relative to any specific state. For example, some states exclude legislative or judicial employees from the definition of "state employee."[113] On the other hand, many states have adopted some common provisions to prevent retaliation against employees for exercising rights under specific statutes such as workers' compensation, civil rights, or occupational safety and health, or for service on juries or in the National Guard. General "just cause" civil service provisions also provide protection to public employees in some circumstances, but they will not be considered in this chapter due to their distinct nature.[114]

State whistleblower statutes are premised on public policy concerns and public interests sufficient to override the at-will employment doctrine.[115] The purpose of these statutes is to encourage specified employees, and in some cases non-employee individuals, to report or disclose certain types of information or to refrain from committing certain types of acts. This encouragement is provided in three distinct ways: (1) the statutes prohibit retaliation and provide remedies for whistleblowers who are retaliated against; (2) some statutes provide financial incentives either in the form of a remedy for retaliation (treble damages or punitive damages) or as pure financial rewards under false claims acts; and (3) punishments, ranging from criminal sanction to dismissal from supervisory positions and fines, are established for those who retaliate against whistleblowers in many states.

Protected Conduct

The most common type of protected conduct is reporting, or threatening to report, a violation of a federal, state, or local law, rule, or regulation. Also frequently protected is disclosure of a substantial and specific threat or danger to the public health or safety. Such strong public policies support the enforcement of laws and the prevention of serious harm to the public. Virtually all of the state whistleblower statutes provide protection to state and some other public-sector employees for such disclosures, as do most of the statutes covering private-sector employees.

Public policy also strongly favors ferreting out "gross" mismanagement and "gross" waste or abuse of authority in governmental operations. Although public-sector employees are usually protected for reporting such abuses in their employment, private-sector employees often are not, since the waste of private or corporate assets is not viewed as being on par with the waste of public resources.[116]

Beyond these broad categories, various states have identified other conduct that it is believed to be in the public interest specifically to protect. Examples include an employee's refusal to obey an illegal directive[117] or to expose oneself or others to a hazardous condition.[118] Many states have also adopted protections for workers in certain professions to encourage reporting, as in the case of health care providers[119] and those dealing with abused children.[120] Such workers may be required by law to report abuses, so corresponding whistleblower protections have been enacted. Some states have chosen to target public utilities workers[121] and those who report threats to the environment for special protection.[122]

In adopting whistleblower protection statutes, state legislatures felt compelled to distinguish between the types of information that should be disclosed in the public interest and the types of information the revelation of which should be discouraged or prohibited. Thus, many statutes specifically exclude from protection the reporting of information that is prohibited from disclosure by law.

Legislators were also very concerned about abuse by disgruntled, overzealous, or misinformed employees or by those seeking to use the statutes for their own personal interests rather than the public interest.[123] Concerns about false or unfounded reporting led to the requirement in many statutes that disclosures must be made "in good faith" or "truthfully" and be based on a reasonable belief that the disclosure evidences an improper activity.[124] It is also common for the statutes to discourage the reporting of merely technical or minimal violations of law or rules. Disclosures of waste, mismanagement, or abuse of authority usually must be "gross" in nature before meriting protection in most states. Although some of these provisions are targeted at the overzealous employee who reports minor rules violations or insignificant amounts of waste, there is also a desire to prevent unscrupulous employees from using technical or minor violations as a ruse to gain protection of the whistleblower statutes as a shield to prevent discipline for legitimate reasons.[125] On balance, the impact is that limitations on protection can be very subjective, with no clear guidance for a would-be whistleblower.

Communications

Whistleblower statutes at their most basic level are concerned with communications from a person having knowledge of wrongdoing to a person in authority who can act upon that information. Just as state statutes vary in their coverage as to who may be a protected party in communicating information, they also have variations as to the parties or institutions to whom disclosures may or should be made and when.

Reflecting concerns about premature or misinformed reporting, some statutes require a potential whistleblower first to exhaust internal remedies or to seek internal corrections of wrongdoing or statutory violations before proceeding with a disclosure to outside authorities.[126] Giving notice to the appropriate supervisor about an employee's concerns provides an opportunity for an agency or for the department of a business, acting in good faith, to attempt to correct a violation or hazard. Potential complaints based on misinformation or false information can be nipped in the bud, while legitimate complaints can be addressed without external involvement that could prove harmful or embarrassing to an institution.[127] Most employers expect that an employee's duty of loyalty mandates trying to resolve a matter internally to avoid harming the employer by an inaccurate, inappropriate, or needless disclosure.[128] Even in states without the internal disclosure mandate, it would seem wise for employees to exhaust internal remedies before going public to prevent suspicions that they are motivated by a desire to intentionally inflict harm on the institution or to serve their own personal interests, at the expense of the institution.[129] Failure to exhaust internal remedies may be justified in circumstances where exhaustion of remedies is clearly futile or where there is a hazardous condition posing an imminent risk of death or serious injury and insufficient time to seek corrective action by the employer.[130]

After exhausting appropriate internal procedures, if required, an employee may still reasonably believe it is necessary to disclose information covered by the statute, but it must be reported to the appropriate body or authority. In some instances this is the legislature, a legislative committee, or an agency having oversight authority over particular public agencies or institutions. There is a strong public interest in the legislature being well informed about what is occurring throughout state government, so persons speaking to legislators or testifying before legislative committees often receive special protection.[131] The legislature or executive bodies with oversight responsibilities are particularly concerned about complaints or disclosures relating to waste, abuse of authority, political abuse, or mismanagement.[132] Although violations of law may usually be reported to any appropriate law enforcement authority, some statutes are very specific about reporting requirements, designating that disclosures be made to certain officials such as the attorney general[133] or the state auditor.[134] Other statutes are drafted very broadly, protecting all kinds of reports made to state or federal agencies or appropriate authorities, and in some cases, complaints made to "any persons."[135] Several states protect participation in investigations, hearings, or inquiries held by public bodies or court actions.[136]

To ensure that employees are aware of their rights under the whistleblower statutes, a number of state laws require that notices of employee rights be posted.[137] Some states have developed whistleblower hotlines to encourage whistleblowers to come forward,[138] and a number of states have adopted provisions in their statutes to protect confidentiality.[139]

Retaliation and Remedies

The forms of retaliation against whistleblowers are limited only by the imagination. One extreme consists of mild harassment, as when coworkers give the whistleblower "the cold shoulder" or an anonymous note refers to him or her in derogatory terms. The other extreme is much less subtle, such as being summarily discharged or finding the locks to one's office changed and a security guard posted at the door (which of course prevents access to personal files and any evidence carelessly left in the office).[140]

Some legislatures have attempted to define in detail the types of retaliatory actions or inactions that are prohibited.[141] This has the merit of specificity and also allows the statute to exclude trivial complaints of retaliation.[142] Other statutes do not define the term "retaliation," which leaves the matter up to the courts or administrative apparatus to define.[143]

The most obvious and severe type of retaliatory action is dismissal. Being fired, when coupled with negative job references or no references, can literally drive a person out of a profession or occupation.[144] Dismissal of a perceived troublemaker can be disguised as a reduction in force or based on other seemingly legitimate job-ending rationales that the whistleblower has the burden of exposing. Equivalent to dismissal is the refusal to appoint a person to a position in the first instance because of whistleblower activities, so several jurisdictions provide whistleblower protection for job applicants as well as current employees.[145]

Other formal retaliatory actions can include unwanted transfers or reassignments, reprimand, admonishment, or just the warning of a possible dismissal. Some retaliatory actions, such as salary reduction, failure to receive appropriate increases in wages and benefits, or failure to be considered for special financial awards or bonuses, hit the pocketbook. Financial and psychological damage can accompany negative or even neutral performance evaluations, which can eventually lead to demotions or to failure to receive an appropriate promotion or tenure. Subtle forms of harassment, such as informal lessening of job responsibilities, authority, or status, or even the withholding of work, can damage a career. Finding one's office moved to the basement, having all one's classes scheduled at what are perceived to be bad times, or being asked to undergo a psychiatric examination sends a strong message to a whistleblower.[146] Working conditions have been made so intolerable in some instances that the employee has resigned and has, in effect, been constructively discharged.[147]

Although whistleblowing is virtually always confined to the employment context, in certain circumstances non-employees may be subject to retaliation also. Non-employee whistleblowers may find themselves at a disadvantage when bidding for government contracts or privileges.[148] Whistleblowers who report problems in nursing homes, health care facilities, or other institutions may be concerned about retaliation against themselves or their relatives who may be housed there.[149]

Whistleblower protection statutes provide remedies for many of these forms of retaliation. In general, the remedies seek to make the whistleblower whole in an economic sense or seek to punish the violator, which may provide psychological relief in that somehow justice has been served. Violators may be subject to criminal or administrative sanctions, or fines.

The statutes, while again varying widely, generally require the whistleblower first to exhaust administrative remedies before seeking judicial review. Usually, provision is made for a civil action that can provide appropriate injunctive relief or, in some states, actual damages or both. Typical remedies include reinstatement to the same or an equivalent position, back wages, reinstatement of fringe benefits and seniority rights, and costs of litigation including lawyers' fees and witnesses' fees. It is important to note that some states specifically provide for exemplary or punitive damages[150] or triple damages[151] and that a small number of states place limitations on certain types of damages.[152]

FINANCIAL INCENTIVES FOR WHISTLEBLOWING

Whistleblowers come forward for a variety of reasons. Some are motivated by altruism: the desire to do the right thing, to be a good citizen, or to prevent harm to others; whereas others come forward because there may be a chance to profit from blowing the whistle. As one commentator has noted: "Virtue may be its own reward, but for many, money is more gratifying."[153]

To this point, the analysis of whistleblowing has focused on the most common approach to encouraging disclosures of wrongdoing—extending remedies such as reinstatement, lost wages, or damages to whistleblowers who have suffered from retaliation. The federal government and a few states, in addition to the traditional approach of providing remedies, opt to entice whistleblowers to come forward by providing financial incentives as a form of encouragement.[154]

Preeminent among these statutes is the federal False Claims Act,[155] which was enacted in 1863 to deal with rampant fraud during the Civil War era. The original act allowed private persons, or "relators," who brought a qui tam action[156] against persons making false monetary claims against the federal government and prosecuted the case to final judgment to receive half of the damages and forfeitures recovered and collected, plus costs.[157] The current act is targeted at false or fraudulent claims, usually for goods or services that were not provided as claimed to the U.S. armed forces or government.[158] The qui tam plaintiff is usually an employee of a government contractor, who brings a civil action for violation of section 3729. The action is brought for both the person and the U.S. government, but in the name of the government.[159] The statute requires that the government be served with a copy of the complaint and a written disclosure of substantially all material evidence and information,[160] thus alerting the government to the action. If successful, a qui tam plaintiff receives a percentage of the recovery from 15 to 13 percent of treble damages. The amount of the award may vary, depending on whether the government assumes control of the action[161] or not,[162] and it may also vary based on the source of the disclosure of information.[163]

Awards can be significant, and they have successfully attracted the attention of whistleblowers and law firms alike.[164] In fact, it is not uncommon to have several law firms band together in a qui tam action to share resources and expertise and to spread the costs, especially when the case has been turned down by the government. Fraud against the Department of Defense had traditionally been the main subject of qui tam litigation under the False Claims Act; however, this has now been surpassed by fraud in the health care field, especially in the Medicare and Medicaid programs.[165] The False Claims Act is applicable to the entire array of federal programs, so the potential for uncovering wrongdoing is enormous, as is the potential for recovery by individuals and law firms in qui tam litigation in the future. On balance, the act has been remarkably effective. In 1985, before it was modernized, the Justice Department collected only $26 million in recoveries.[166] Since the 1986 amendments that modernized the original Civil War-era law, the False Claims Act has recovered some $62 billion, including $5.69 billion in FY 2014.[167]

Ironically, financial incentives under the False Claims Act can create a conflict of interest for an employee who works for a company with internal whistleblower procedures. The employee may have a significant financial incentive to go outside the organization with information concerning a false claim, rather than to report the impropriety internally, which would be in the best interest of the organization.[168] In practice, however, those fears have proven unfounded. As a 2010 Ethics Resource Center study reported, 96 percent of corporate employees who blow the whistle do not break organizational ranks, instead making their disclosures make their disclosures within the company.[169]

In addition to the financial incentives, whistleblowers are provided with specific protection against retaliation for involvement in an action under the False Claims Act. Remedies include any relief necessary to make the employee whole, plus two times back pay, interest, and compensation for any special damages.[170]

The False Claims Act requires whistleblowers to fight and win a legal war on behalf of taxpayers to receive financial rewards. An increasing new phenomenon, however, is "bounty" statutes that pay whistleblowers if their evidence contributes to a significant government recovery. The best known provisions are for IRS whistleblowers,[171] and provisions in the Dodd Frank Act for whistleblowers to the Securities and Exchange Commission[172] and the Commodities Futures Trading Commission.[173] The most well-known is the SEC program, which provides financial rewards of 10 to 30 percent for recoveries of greater than a million dollars. The SEC Whistleblower Office's FY 2019 Annual Report notes that in FY 2019 alone there were 5,200 disclosures of alleged securities violations from whistleblowers in 71 countries, and that the program has recovered more than $2 billion since its inception. In that time, the commission also noted payments of $372 million to 67 whistleblowers.[174] The SEC regulations make prior internal reporting normally a prerequisite for those with duty speech responsibilities, such as auditors, accountants, or compliance officers whose job is to find and report errors or misconduct, and specify that there is no loss of reward for disclosing the SEC violation internally as a prelude for voluntary corporate corrective action.[175]

Several states have also adopted statutes that provide financial incentives for whistleblowers. California, Florida, and Illinois have enacted false claims statutes very similar to the federal False Claims Act, providing for qui tam actions by individuals with awards for success similar to those provided by the federal statute.[176] Several other states have enacted false claims acts specifically relating to health care.[177] Also, several states' general whistleblower provisions provide cash incentives. For example, in South Carolina, if a whistleblowing employee's report results in a savings of public money from the elimination of abuses, the employee is awarded 25 percent of the estimated net savings but not in excess of $2,000.[178]

By contrast, some states are reluctant to provide whistleblower protection to employees who might benefit financially from their disclosures.[179] Wisconsin seems a bit schizophrenic in that it does not allow employees to receive anything of value for reporting, unless it is in pursuit of an award offered by a governmental unit for information to improve government administration or operations.[180]

COMMON-LAW PROTECTIONS FOR WHISTLEBLOWERS

The statutory exceptions to the at-will employment doctrine, which have just been examined, are premised on public policies that seek to mitigate the harshness of a rule that allows for arbitrary or unreasonable dismissal of employees. In the absence of specific statutory protections, or in furtherance of public policies expressed in statutes not necessarily related to labor law, the courts have encroached on the at-will doctrine by providing common-law remedies for improper dismissals in certain circumstances, including whistleblowing.

Three major common-law exceptions to the at-will doctrine have evolved. Remedies have been provided for dismissed employees based on implied-in-fact contracts, implied-in-law or quasi-contracts, and the public policy exception to the at-will doctrine.

A majority of jurisdictions recognize wrongful dismissal claims premised on an employer's breach of an implied-in-fact contract.[181] The employee must show that the employer made representations orally or in writing that the employee would not be discharged, except for good cause.[182] Written representations set forth in employee handbooks or other such policy guides or manuals may imply that the parties intended to extend contractual rights, such as job security, during periods of good job performance, even though not expressly stated in the employment contract.[183] Such representations have also been found in an employer's course of conduct concerning pensions, sales commissions, or other benefits.[184] The doctrine of promissory estoppel may also be applied to provide relief for persons who have resigned from their employment in reliance on an offer of a new position with a second employer, which offer is then withdrawn before the person has begun work.[185]

In a minority of jurisdictions, in circumstances where an employee cannot prove that a promise of job security was implied in fact, it may be possible to show that the employer has breached an implied covenant of good faith and fair dealing.[186] Implied-in-law contracts usually are brought as contract actions but may be sounded in tort law or in both contract and tort. Generally, it is not enough that an employee shows an absence of just cause or good faith, but rather the employee must prove bad faith or unfairness, and in some states, he or she must present evidence of a violation of public policy to prove a breach of the covenant.[187]

The public policy exception to the at-will doctrine is the primary vehicle for common-law remedies for whistleblowers. In some circumstances, courts have held that public policy allows an exception to the at-will rule. The common-law erosion of the at-will doctrine began in 1959 with the landmark California case *Petermann v. Teamsters*,[188] where an employee was fired for refusing to commit perjury before a state legislative committee. The court of appeals, after taking note of the at-will rule, stated that the right to discharge an employee under an employment contract of indefinite duration "may be limited by statute . . . or by considerations of public policy."[189] While recognizing that "the term 'public policy' is inherently not subject to precise definition," the court noted that perjury is a crime and that false testimony interferes with the administration of justice.[190] "It would be obnoxious to the interest of the state and contrary to public policy and sound morality to allow an employer to discharge any employee . . . on the ground that the employee declined to commit perjury."[191] To effectuate fully the state's policy against perjury, the court held that the employer may be denied dismissal rights under the at-will rule and that the employee may be entitled to civil relief.[192]

It was not until the mid-1970s that the public policy exception began to be adopted in other jurisdictions. Today a large majority of states have some form of public policy exception to the at-will rule for wrongful or retaliatory discharge, although the existence of statutory options in some cases has meant cancelation of jurisdiction for tort actions.[193] This can be a net disadvantage for whistleblowers, since tort actions mean jury trials and statutory remedies generally are limited to administrative boards with little judicial independence. Even though the exception originated as a contract action, the action now usually sounds in tort or in both contract and tort in some jurisdictions, which may allow for damages for emotional distress or punitive damages.

The fundamental problem relating to the public policy exception has always been the difficulty of defining public policy, or determining what activities are in the public interest to protect.[194] The wide variations in protected conduct that were seen in the state whistleblower protection statutes are also evident in the common law, as the judiciary struggled to provide remedies when appropriate but not to destroy completely the at-will employment rule. Some state courts have chosen to defer to the legislature for a determination of public policy, rather than to create a broad common-law public policy exception to the at-will doctrine.[195]

The public policy exceptions that have been recognized vary considerably in tone and content, but they have certain common characteristics. Normally, the underlying public policy must be one that enhances public interests, rather than merely private concerns; the public policy must be clearly expressed by a law, regulation, or constitutional provision; and the public policy exception is applied only when there is a dismissal from employment rather than lesser forms of retaliation.[196] The four categories in which employees are most frequently protected from discharge under the public policy exception concern refusal to commit an unlawful act, exercise of a legal right or privilege, performance of a civic obligation, and active whistleblower disclosures.[197]

The definition of whistleblower in the introduction to this chapter suggested that whistleblowing can be either passive in nature, that is, a refusal to engage in wrongful activities of an employer, or active, in that the employee reports illegal or wrongful activities of the employer or coworkers to proper authorities. The first three categories noted in the preceding paragraph reflect passive whistleblowing in that the employee is discharged not for actively communicating employer wrongdoing, but for refusing to comply with an order to commit an improper or illegal act, for exercising a statutory right, or for performing a civic duty. The employer in effect has forced the employee to choose between his job and possibly going to jail, or forfeiting a worker's compensation claim, or failing to serve on a jury. Forcing these choices on the employee clearly defies the public policies in question. The public policy exception to the at-will doctrine thus seeks "to protect whistleblowers under either the rubric of one of these three general categories, or as an extension of these general categories."[198] While many jurisdictions seek to protect passive whistleblowers in this sense, protection for active whistleblowers under the public policy exception has varied from state to state.[199]

Active whistleblowing entails reporting by an employee of information concerning improper activities occurring or threatening to occur within an organization. This reporting can be made either internally within the organization, or externally to appropriate public authorities. Since public-sector employees generally have greater statutory whistleblower protection in such circumstances than private-sector employees have, private-sector employees tend to be involved in most public policy exception whistleblower cases.[200]

Generally speaking, the courts have been willing to protect active whistleblowers under the public policy exception both for disclosures of criminal activities and for violations of noncriminal statutes.[201] Constitutional provisions may also provide a public policy basis for an action in some states; but whatever the source, the public policy must be clearly expressed before it can serve as a basis for the public policy exception.[202] Since nothing is more basic than a state's enforcement of its criminal code, reporting of a violation of criminal law is a very compelling case for protecting a whistleblower.[203] Public policy clearly favors "citizen crime fighters,"[204] so whistleblower protection for refusal to commit or for reporting a criminal act is commonly provided by both statutes and the common law. Thus, public policy clearly favors resolving the employee's conflict between obeying an employer's illegal orders or ignoring criminal activity, and the loss of one's job, in favor of the whistleblower. Civil statutes may also provide the clear public policy mandate required for the exception, as, for example, in the case of providing protection for health care professionals who may be required by statute to report certain types of patient abuse.

Once one gets past the public policies established by statute, finding a clearly mandated source of public policy to support the public policy exception becomes much more difficult, if not impossible, in some states. Several courts, for example, have ruled that without a violation of some specific law or regulation, employee complaints about product safety are usually not protected.[205] In addition, complaints about company mismanagement, policy disagreements with employers, or private concerns are not covered by the exception.[206] Also, judges, like legislators, are concerned about abuse of whistleblower protection provisions. Therefore, whistleblower disclosures that are made in bad faith, or where the employee does not have direct personal knowledge of the illegal activity, or where the whistleblower participated personally in the crime that is disclosed, or when the whistleblower has failed to exhaust internal channels before going public, may not be protected by the public policy exception.[207]

A retaliatory discharge for whistleblowing may give rise to overlapping statutory and common-law claims. It is quite possible that an employee who is a member of a union with a "just cause" contract could have potential remedies available under the contract, under a whistleblower protection statute, and under the common-law public policy exception in tort. Remedies could vary significantly, depending on which claim is pursued. A whistleblower may not have an option as to which claim will prevail, however, due to the doctrine of preemption. Preemption "arises when a statutory remedy and a common law remedy exist for the same conduct, in circumstance implying a legislative intent to supplant common law."[208] Generally, there is a preference for a pervasive statutory scheme of regulation over a common-law remedy; therefore, most state whistleblower statutes will preempt a common-law public policy exception.[209] Overlapping federal and state statutory claims can also lead to preemption. Federal statutes will preempt state law under the Supremacy Clause of the U.S. Constitution when they conflict.[210] Thus, for example, federal labor law will preempt state labor statutes when an employee asserts a state wrongful discharge claim that is also an unfair labor practice under federal law.[211]

PROFESSIONAL ETHICS CODES AS SOURCES OF PUBLIC POLICY

Remedies for whistleblowers are provided by statute or by some other clearly mandated source that will support the public policy exception in a tort or contract action for wrongful discharge. Frequently, professionals will complain that they were wrongfully discharged because they insisted on adhering to a professional code of ethics that mandated their actions. They argue that violation of a code of ethics is equivalent in a public policy sense to violation of criminal statute because such a violation can subject them to professional discipline. Here the professional is faced with the classic whistleblower conflict: the choice between violating one's ethical code, which can potentially result in sanctions, and losing one's job. Some states have recognized the problem and specifically provide protection in their whistleblower statutes for reporting of wrongdoing that is a violation of a code of conduct or code of ethics or for refusing an order to violate the ethics code.[212] Other jurisdictions provide statutory protection for reporting unethical practices in a state agency or department.[213]

Still, the vast majority of jurisdictions do not specifically deal with ethical codes in their whistleblower statutes. The courts have widely disparate views on whether professional codes of ethics are sufficiently clear examples of such strong public policy that they will warrant protection for wrongful discharge in defiance of the at-will doctrine.[214] As a source of public policy, ethical codes vary in status: some may be endorsed by the legislature,[215] others may have judicial involvement in their content,[216] while still other codes are merely the products of the professional organizations themselves[217] and may not be infused with the public interest or have any form of official state imprimatur.

The cases that have dealt with retaliatory discharge for reporting ethical violations or for refusing to violate professional ethics codes fall into two categories.[218] The first category includes those cases that reject outright any non-legislative sources of public policy. These cases hold that only statutes or constitutions can evidence a clear public policy mandate sufficient to support the public policy exception in those jurisdictions.[219]

The second category of cases recognizes professional ethics codes as sources of public policy, but recognizes only those provisions of the code that clearly serve public interests, rather than just the interests of a particular profession, as sources of public policy. Usually the provision must also mandate that the professional act or not act in a designated way in a particular situation.[220] The public policy exception has been analyzed in these circumstances in wrongful discharge cases concerning ethical codes for accountants,[221] physicians,[222] pharmacists,[223] securities dealers,[224] and lawyers.[225] The courts find clearly mandated public interests in some ethical violations but not in others, and they have been very reluctant to protect professional employees when there are merely differences of professional opinion within an organization or where the employee has violated ethical obligations to a specific client or patient.[226]

SPECIAL ISSUES ENCOUNTERED BY LAWYERS

Perhaps more so than any other professional group, lawyers gain information about improper or illegal client conduct whether employed in the public or private sector. Knowledge of client misconduct is usually gained after the fact, as when a lawyer is retained to represent a client who has been arrested for a crime, and the client then confides his guilt to the lawyer. Occasionally, a lawyer learns in advance of a client's intent to commit a criminal act. The lawyers' codes of ethics have long recognized that a lawyer can be placed in a position of knowing of client wrongdoing, and several rules attempt to provide guidance, especially the rules concerning confidentiality and those concerning entity representation.

Most information gained through the lawyer–client relationship is sacrosanct, including revelations of past criminal acts.[227] There are, however, limits and exceptions to the confidentiality rules. Lawyers may in certain circumstances reveal their client's intent to commit a future criminal act[228] and must, in some instances, reveal a client's perjury.[229] Also, the confidentiality rules do not protect a client who has sought out a lawyer for aid in perpetrating a crime or a fraudulent scheme.[230] Generally, lawyers may not actively participate in or further the illegal acts of their clients, nor is it permissible for a lawyer to violate or attempt to violate the rules of professional conduct.[231] Under these standards, a lawyer must refuse to accept certain cases or, in other situations, may or must withdraw from a representation.[232] When a lawyer is representing a specific personal client under a retainer, as opposed to a corporate entity, the rules relating to revelation of client wrongdoing are generally well understood and work reasonably well.

Also well understood is a lawyer's status vis-à-vis an individual personal client. Although lawyers in private practice usually do not view themselves as employees of their clients, the lawyer–client relationship is a contractual, fiduciary relationship that is nevertheless subject to the employment at-will doctrine.[233] Except in certain limited circumstances, clients can fire their lawyers for any reason, or no reason, and the lawyer must withdraw, with the only recourse being a suit in quantum merit for the fair value of services rendered.[234] Conversely, subject to certain exceptions, a lawyer is under no obligation to accept a person as a client initially and may withdraw from a representation if the withdrawal can be accomplished without material adverse effect on the client.[235] The employment relationship differs, however, for lawyers who are hired as in-house counsel or in other capacities within a corporate entity. Such lawyers are usually hired on a salaried basis with an expectation of continuing employment and clearly view themselves as employees of the organization. Despite the differences between retained lawyers and salaried in-house counsel, both are subject to the employment at-will doctrine.

THE IN-HOUSE COUNSEL'S DILEMMA

In-house counsel, due to their role in the organization, often find themselves privy to confidential corporate information and may at times become aware of various types of wrongdoing by corporate officers or employees that could be detrimental to the organization. Such wrongdoing can range from waste of corporate assets to violations of law that could potentially result in legal actions being brought against the corporation and losses to shareholders.

In-house counsel who become aware of wrongdoing by corporate insiders may find themselves in a difficult position. The persons committing or threatening to commit improper or illegal acts may be corporate officers, directors, or others in positions of authority, potentially positions senior to that of corporate counsel. Thus, in-house counsel will have to determine who is the appropriate person to whom he or she should report instances of misconduct and who has final say as to whether an action is improper or merely questionable business judgment. But after reporting wrongdoing internally, what must or should in-house counsel do when corporate officers continue to follow what counsel views as an illegal path, or one that will financially harm the corporation, or one that could harm innocent people? In-house counsel can thus easily be placed in the role of internal whistleblower, defending the interests of the corporation against insider wrongdoers; or potentially, in extreme cases, in-house counsel may have to determine whether it is proper to report information concerning illegal activities to public officials outside the organization. Lawyers' ethics codes attempt to aid in-house counsel in resolving some of these issues.

The ABA Model Rules of Professional Conduct provide some guidance for lawyers who discover wrongdoing in the corporate context by first making it clear that lawyers, whether employed or retained, represent the organization as a legal entity.[236] Since the legal entity is the client, lawyers are instructed that they must always act in the best interests of the entity, rather than in the interests of individuals who make up the constituent parts of the organization, although it is obvious that a lawyer must act through the organization's duly authorized representatives.[237] Difficulties can arise for counsel, however, when authorized corporate agents are involved in wrongdoing that can potentially harm the organization.

Model Rule 1.13(b) provides that when a lawyer gains knowledge "that an officer, employee or other person associated with the organization is engaged in action, intends to act or refuses to act in a matter related to the representation that is a violation of a legal obligation to the organization, or a violation of law that reasonably might be imputed to the organization, and that is likely to result in substantial injury to the organization, then the lawyer shall proceed as is reasonably necessary in the best interest of the organization." As explained in the New York Rules which in April 2009 adopted the Model Rule," the lawyer shall explain that the lawyer is the lawyer for the organization and not for any of the constituents." Among the factors that the lawyer must consider in determining the manner of response to the wrongdoing are the seriousness of the violation and its consequences, the role the lawyer plays in the representation and in the organization, the motivation of the persons involved, and organizational policies regarding such matters.[238]

The lawyer, when determining the proper measures to take in dealing with a threat to the organization, must "proceed as is reasonably necessary in the best interests of the organization."[239] Among the options available to the lawyer when corporate agents are engaged in improper activities and refuse to heed counsel's advice are asking for reconsideration of the matter and referring the matter to higher authority, even to the highest authority that can act on the matter if necessary.[240] If the lawyer is unsuccessful in preventing the organization from acting or failing to act in a matter that would be a clear violation of law and would be likely to cause substantial injury to the organization, the lawyer may remain silent, resign in compliance with the withdrawal provisions of Model Rule 1.16, or disclose the violation—to the extent the lawyer reasonably believes necessary to prevent substantial injury to the organization—to outside authorities.

Until 2003, Model Rule 1.13 expressed a clear preference for confidentiality over revelation of illegal conduct. In-house counsel could not reveal confidential knowledge of a clear violation of law even though the wrongdoing had been condoned by the highest authority within the organization. Rather than being able to go to external authorities with the information, counsel could only resign or remain silent. The rule's tacit assumption was therefore that, in instances when internal remedies for unlawful insider conduct were unsuccessful, silence should always be considered preferable to the alternative of allowing the company's lawyer to alert authorities outside the entity.[241] This proved to be an undesirable rule, and scandals like Enron and WorldCom prompted the ABA to reexamine its premises and eventually to amend the Rule to permit outside disclosure.[242] Under the current version of Rule 1.13, a corporate lawyer may disclose wrongdoing to third parties "if (1) despite the lawyer's efforts ... the highest authority that can act on behalf of the organization insists upon or fails to address in a timely and appropriate manner an action, or a refusal to act, that is clearly a violation of law, and (2) the lawyer reasonably believes that the violation is reasonably certain to result in substantial injury to the organization[.]"[243] Once these conditions are met, the lawyer may disclose information to outside sources regardless of whether or not the information would otherwise be confidential, "but only if and to the extent the lawyer reasonably believes necessary to prevent substantial injury to the organization."[244] In other words, if, after going "to the highest authority in an organization ... that authority itself turns a blind eye to a violation of law that the lawyer reasonably believes will result in substantial injury to the organization—not to third parties—then the lawyers may finally go outside the organization to make disclosure."[245]

Accordingly, disclosure to external authorities is now permitted under the model rules, but it is not mandatory. There will likely be some in-house counsel who view outside disclosure as disloyal to the corporation or to coworkers. Some attorneys may believe that disclosure to outside sources will cause more harm than good to the corporation; others may doubt whether any external entities exist that could adequately protect the corporation's interests upon disclosure.[246] These lawyers will have difficult choices to make. Although resignation is no longer explicitly provided as an option under Model Rule 1.13, it may still be a possible choice under Model Rule 1.16 for in-house counsel who do not wish to make external disclosures.[247] However, even though resignation does provide a solution, it comes at a very high cost to the lawyer and in the final analysis does not resolve the lawyer's underlying concern about the wrongdoing. Depending on the circumstances, an in-house lawyer may not have the financial resources or other job opportunities necessary to make resignation a viable option. As an alternative to external disclosure or resignation, many lawyers, after exhausting all available in-house options to protect the best interests of the organization, will choose to keep silent and try to go on with their careers. Not only does this put lawyers in a precarious professional position—as their employers may not wish to retain the services of employees seen as troublemakers—the choice to forego external disclosure may in fact be a disservice to the lawyers' true clients, the corporate entities. For this reason, some commentators point out that although couched in optional language, the new Model Rule 1.13 should be understood as seriously recommending outside disclosure as a solution to the in-house whistleblower.[248]

This position is reinforced by the report produced by the ABA Task Force on Corporate Responsibility, which, in recommending the 2003 changes to Model Rule 1.13, explained that

> [t]he second substantive change to Rule 1.13(b) recommended by the Task Force addresses the lawyer's obligation to report wrongdoing to higher authority in the organizational client. Currently, that rule identifies "reporting up" as a potential course of action when the lawyer has discerned an actual or threatened violation of law or violation of legal obligation to the organization, but the Rule imposes no clear obligation to pursue that course of action. The Task Force believes, however, that the Rule should more actively encourage such action, by requiring that the lawyer refer the matter to higher authority in the organization—including, if warranted, the organization's highest authority—unless the lawyer reasonably believes that it is not necessary to do so.[249]

The same point of view was reflected in the Task Force's explanation of why it recommended the adoption of Rule 1.13(e), which provides that a lawyer who reasonably believes she has been retaliated against for reporting violations must alert the corporation's highest authority of the reasons why he or she was discharged. The rule also requires a lawyer to alert the corporation's highest authority if the lawyer resigns from representation rather than using the reporting provisions of the Rule. As the Task Force explained:

> The Task Force also recommends that Rule 1.13 be amended to include a new provision to assure that the organization's highest authority is made aware that a lawyer for the organization has withdrawn or is discharged in circumstances addressed by the Rule. In some instances, the actions of the lawyer within the organization, pursuant to Rule 1.13(b), may fail to prevent or avoid action that seriously threatens the interest of the organization. Current Rule 1.13(c) provides that a lawyer, in this circumstance, may choose to withdraw. In that event, or if the organizational client discharges the lawyer because of the lawyer's actions under

> Rule 1.13(b) in reporting to higher authority, the lawyer's professional obligations to act in the best interest of the organization should require the lawyer to take reasonable steps to assure that the organization's highest authority is aware of the withdrawal or discharge, and the lawyer's understanding of the circumstances that brought it about.[250]

Accordingly, although subsection (e) does not require a lawyer who chooses to resign in response to corporate wrongdoing to disclose the reason for his or her withdrawal to outside authorities, it does not permit the lawyer to walk away from the corporation without alerting the corporation to the problem. This is equally true for the lawyer who resigns because the highest authority of the corporation will not respond to his or her complaints as it is for the lawyer who wants to resign in order to avoid stirring up controversy within the organization. And this is as it should be; the lawyer's client, after all, is the corporation, and the lawyer must protect the client's interests during the course of withdrawal.[251] Moreover, the rule reinforces the role of the in-house lawyer in the system of corporate governance.[252]

Regardless of whether a state's particular adoption of the model rules permits an in-house lawyer to go outside the corporation to report wrongdoing, the whistleblowing corporate attorney will still face the specter of retaliatory discharge. For lawyers operating under a version of the old rule, the disclosure of confidential information will likely cause problems. Any privilege relating to the information concerning corporate wrongdoing belongs to the organization as a legal entity, not to the in-house counsel.[253] It is highly unlikely that the organization's representatives would choose to waive the privilege since, in doing so, they would be revealing illegal conduct by corporate employees that could result in substantial injury to the organization. Also, it is unlikely that the organization would waive confidentiality since the highest authority in the organization has already refused to act. Although it is possible that the future criminal act exception to the confidentiality rule may allow in-house counsel to reveal the wrongdoing, this exception is quite limited and depends on the nature of the illegal act being contemplated by the corporate insiders.[254] Yet the prospect of the terminated in-house counsel disclosing the organizational client's confidential, and probably incriminating, communications during a lawsuit for damages may well seem abhorrent to some courts, striking as it would at such fundamental precepts of the profession as confidentiality and loyalty.[255] Surely, some would argue, a lawyer has a higher level of duty to a client, even if it is a corporate entity, than does a typical corporate employee and thus should not be allowed to breach a client's confidences or expectations of loyalty to recover in a wrongful discharge action.

The countervailing argument in favor of allowing a remedy for in-house counsel is premised on justice and fairness. If a non-lawyer employee would have a remedy under a whistleblower statute or a court-made exception to the at-will rule for a particular action, is it fair to deny the remedy to a lawyer for the same action?[256] If an in-house counsel follows the rules of the profession and is loyal to the employer in seeking to prevent harm to the organization, should public policy condone his or her being fired for doing so? Does public policy condone a lawyer's being fired for disclosing illegal activity to public authorities concerning a significant, clear threat or danger to the public health and safety when a non-lawyer would be protected?

The following cases present contrary views as to whether lawyers, because of the fiduciary nature of their profession, should enjoy the same degree of protection as do other private-sector employees or whether such protections should be denied or limited in some fashion.

The first of this type of case to reach a state's highest court, *Balla v. Gambro, Inc.*,[257] is a classic example of an in-house counsel being fired for whistleblowing. The plaintiff, the general counsel of an Illinois distributor of dialysis equipment, learned that defective machines had been shipped to his employer for distribution. He informed his superiors in the corporation that the machines posed a serious risk to health, were not in compliance with Food and Drug Administration regulations, and should be rejected. Upon learning that the company planned to sell the equipment anyway, he confronted the company president and told him that he would do anything necessary to stop the sale. Two weeks later the plaintiff was abruptly fired. In response, he brought a tort action for retaliatory discharge, alleging that he was discharged for reasons that contravened fundamental public policy.

The Illinois Supreme Court, while noting its adherence to the at-will employment doctrine, recognized that there was a limited and narrow tort-action exception for retaliatory discharge based on contravention of a clearly mandated public policy.[258] The court agreed that the plaintiff's discharge contravened the clearly mandated public policy of protecting the lives and property of the state's citizens, but it refused to allow him to maintain the retaliatory discharge action because of his role as general counsel for the defendant corporation.[259] The court had two reasons for rejecting his suit. First, the public policy to be protected, saving citizen's lives, was already adequately protected in this case. The plaintiff was obliged to reveal the information under the Illinois Rules of Professional Conduct, which require that a lawyer "shall reveal information about a client to the extent it appears necessary to prevent the client from committing an act that would result in death or serious bodily harm."[260] Unlike other non-lawyer corporate employees who have a choice as to their actions, in-house counsel under this rule do not have a choice of whether to follow their ethical obligations or to "follow the illegal and unethical demands of their clients."[261] Thus, a tort remedy was redundant, since counsel's duty is mandated by the ethical rules and public policy is served.

The second reason asserted by the court for not extending the retaliatory discharge tort to in-house counsel was its undesirable effect on the lawyer–client relationship. Since the relationship is based on trust and confidentiality, granting the right to sue for retaliatory discharge might make employers "less willing to be forthright and candid with their in-house counsel," and less likely to turn to in-house counsel for advice regarding potentially questionable corporate conduct.[262] Thus, lawyers were found to be different from other employees because of the fiduciary qualities that pervade the lawyer–client relationship.

The Illinois Supreme Court was not alone in declining to provide a tort remedy for in-house counsel in these circumstances. Until 1994, all other courts that considered the issue had refused to allow tort recovery for wrongful discharge of in-house counsel,[263] although some had allowed for damages under implied contract exceptions to the at-will doctrine.[264] For example, the Supreme Court of Minnesota in *Nordling v. Northern States Power Co.*[265] held "that in-house counsel should not be precluded from maintaining an action for breach of a contractual provision in an employee handbook, provided, however, that the essentials of the attorney-client relationship are not compromised." The threat to the lawyer–client relationship was not viewed as significant in the case of a breach of an implied contract as it is in a tort action for retaliatory discharge.

At the opposite extreme from the *Balla* decision is the 1994 California Supreme Court's opinion in *General Dynamics Corporation v. Superior Court*.[266] There, in-house counsel Rose was fired because he investigated employee drug use, protested electronic bugging of the chief of security's office, and pointed out possible violations of federal law. He alleged in his complaint that General Dynamics "had by its conduct and other assurances impliedly represented to Rose over the years that he was subject to discharge only for 'good cause,'" which was not present in this firing, and that he was also fired for reasons "which violated fundamental public policies."[267] General Dynamics responded with the argument that they could fire their in-house lawyer "for any reason or for no reason."[268]

The court reaffirmed the rule that a client could unilaterally discharge his or her lawyer but noted that "there is a cost to be paid for such an action under the circumstances alleged in the complaint—either in lost wages and related damages in the case of the implied-in-fact contract claim, or as tort damages in the case of the public policy tort claim."[269] Thus, in-house counsel may pursue a wrongful discharge claim for damages, even though reinstatement will never be available as a remedy.[270] The court held that an implied-in-fact contract action could lie for in-house counsel, since it would not be "likely to present issues implicating the distinctive values subserved by the attorney-client relationship."[271] These cases should therefore be treated the same as implied-in-fact actions brought by non-lawyer employees.

The court then examined the public policy wrongful discharge tort claim, noting that it arises out of duties implied in law. Such duties require employers to conduct their businesses in compliance with public policy. A tort action can therefore be viewed as a means to vindicate the public policy interest itself, while at the same time compensating the individual for the loss of employment.[272] After recognizing that some professional norms incorporate important public values, the court held that the case for protecting in-house lawyers from retaliation for insisting on adherence to mandatory ethical norms or for refusing to violate those ethical norms is clear, and in fact even more powerful than the claim of a similarly situated nonprofessional employee.[273]

After observing that the *Balla* decision had been criticized by commentators as a bizarre and anachronistic view of the lawyer's role, the court stated that it is precisely because of the unique role that lawyers play in our society that they should be accorded a retaliatory discharge remedy. When "*mandatory ethical norms . . . collide with illegitimate demands of the employer* and the attorney insists on *adhering to his or her clear professional duty*[,]"[274] the lawyer is entitled to a judicial remedy. Such a remedy will help to mitigate the economic and cultural pressures that can force an individual employee to conform to organizational misconduct without protest, particularly in view of the "illusory" remedy of the in-house lawyer's duty of withdrawal, "a course fraught with the possibility of economic catastrophe and professional banishment."[275]

This holding that in-house counsel may bring a tort action for wrongful discharge was limited in two ways. First, the court distinguished between retaliatory discharge resulting from in-house counsel's following of an ethical obligation mandated by ethical rule or statute and where the lawyer's conduct "is merely ethically *permissible* but not *required* by statute or ethical code[.]"[276] When merely permissible conduct is involved, two additional questions must be answered. First, would a non-lawyer employee have a retaliatory discharge cause of action for the same conduct, and second, does the statute or ethical rule "specifically permit the attorney to depart from the usual requirement of confidentiality with respect to the client-employer and engage in the 'nonfiduciary' conduct for which he was terminated?"[277]

The second limitation placed on the retaliatory discharge tort for in-house counsel reflects the concerns expressed in *Balla* relating to the fiduciary aspects of the lawyer–client relationship. The court expressed a desire to protect the fiduciary qualities of mutual trust and confidence that are inherent in the relationship. Therefore, only in the instances where a disclosure is explicitly permitted or mandated by an ethics code or statute may an in-house counsel expose the client's secrets. If the elements of a wrongful discharge claim cannot be established without breaching the attorney–client privilege, the suit must be dismissed.[278] Thus, the court expressed a preference for confidentiality over the remedy for wrongful discharge, and an insistence that the statutory attorney–client privilege must continue to be strictly observed.[279] Finally, the court indicated that trial courts can and should apply ad hoc equitable remedies, such as sealing and protective orders, to allow in-house counsel to meet their burden of proof while still protecting privileged confidences.[280]

General Dynamics' significance lies in the fact that it was the first case to allow a public policy exception tort action to be brought for the retaliatory dismissal of an in-house counsel.[281] The court's opinion is tailored in a way that recognizes the current economic realities of practice as an in-house counsel, while attempting to preserve the employer/client's traditional rights of confidentiality and the right to fire one's lawyer. The court thus provided in-house counsel with meaningful potential tort and implied-in-fact contract remedies compared with the illusory non-remedy of withdrawal from employment that was contemplated in *Balla*. The majority of courts to consider the question have agreed with *General Dynamics*, permitting in-house counsel to maintain suits for retaliatory discharge.[282] *Balla* seems to have been soundly disaffirmed; one court went so far as to refer to its "tortured logic."[283]

THE LAW FIRM COROLLARY TO THE IN-HOUSE COUNSEL DILEMMA

The California Supreme Court recognized the dilemma faced by in-house counsel who function in a one-client environment, which can lead to total economic dependence on that client/employer. Such dependency limits the number of realistic options available to in-house counsel upon learning of corporate wrongdoing, since, as was seen, a duty to withdraw from corporate employment or to blow the whistle can be no less than an order to commit economic suicide and, as such, hardly a satisfactory option.

A corollary to this dilemma is encountered by lawyer-employees of law firms, who may discover wrongdoing committed by other lawyers in the firm. Associates and even partners in law firms may have economic dependency on their firms, equivalent to that which in-house counsel have on their corporate employers. They also have mandated ethical rules of conduct to which they must adhere or be subject to sanction. As members of a self-policing profession, individual lawyers have mandatory whistleblower responsibilities vis-à-vis other lawyers in certain circumstances. For example, ABA Model Rule of professional Conduct 8.3 requires that a lawyer who has knowledge of another lawyer's violation of an ethical rule that raises a substantial question as to that lawyer's honesty, trustworthiness, or fitness as a lawyer shall inform the appropriate professional authorities, unless the information is confidential or it was information gained while participating in an approved lawyer assistance program.[284] Also, a law firm's senior managers and any other lawyers in a supervisory capacity have distinct obligations to ensure that lawyers within the firm conform to ethical standards.[285] As in the corporate environment, where Model Rule 1.13 suggests that a lawyer initially should try to resolve concerns about wrongdoing internally, it also is viewed as the best policy when an associate or partner in a law firm learns of unethical behavior within the firm.[286]

The first step in such cases is usually to confront the lawyer believed to be in violation of the rule. This allows the associate to determine the other lawyer's motivation and understanding of the ethical violation in an attempt to resolve the issue.[287] If this is not possible, or if confronting the rule violator is of no avail, it is next appropriate to consult others within the firm. Consultation with senior partners, department heads, or firm ethics committees, if available, may lead to peer pressure or to formal demands upon the rule violator to reform.[288] At this point, the improper actions may be stopped before damage has been done or perhaps when damages can still be mitigated. There may be instances, however, where other lawyers in the firm do not believe a rule violation has occurred or where an ethical violation is merely arguable, in which case the associate may wish to reconsider his or her position on the potential rule violation.[289] Although it is viewed as highly unlikely that any firm would consciously allow a partner or associate to be in violation of the ethics rules, in the last analysis, an associate who is convinced that there is a substantial violation of the rules shall inform the appropriate authorities under Model Rule 8.3(a).[290]

These rules can result in an associate being placed in the classic whistleblower dilemma.[291] If an associate learns of a substantial ethics rule violation by a firm lawyer and reports that violation internally within the firm, and the partners refuse to act, the associate must then blow the whistle externally. If the associate is then fired for insisting on a course of conduct mandated by the lawyer's ethics rules, is there any recourse available for the associate in a state that adheres to the at-will employment doctrine? Such recourse will lie only if there is specific protection provided by the state's whistleblower statute[292] or if the state's courts have adopted common-law exceptions to the at-will employment rule.

Just such a dilemma arose in the New York case of *Wieder v. Skala*.[293] In *Wieder*, an associate in a law firm became aware of conduct of another of the firm's lawyers that raised substantial questions about that lawyer's honesty and fitness as a lawyer. Wieder reported his concerns to two of the firm's partners, who conceded that the other lawyer was a pathological liar who had lied to other members of the firm regarding the status of legal matters. Wieder asked the partners to report the misconduct to the appropriate authorities under Disciplinary Rule 1-103, the New York equivalent to Model Rule 8.3, but they declined to act and in fact attempted to dissuade Wieder from reporting the matter himself, even to the extent of threatening him with dismissal. Eventually the firm did report the misconduct but thereafter continuously berated Wieder for forcing them to do so. Not long after, Wieder was fired. Wieder then brought a suit for wrongful discharge, alleging breach of contract and a violation of public policy sufficient to allow a tort action for compensatory and punitive damages.

Historically, the New York Court of Appeals has not been receptive to arguments that it should adopt breach-of-implied contract or wrongful discharge tort exceptions to the at-will employment doctrine; rather, the court usually defers to the legislature for an appropriate statutory remedy.[294] In this case, after noting the lower court's holding that the state's whistleblower law was not applicable because there was no danger to the public health or welfare, the court of appeals examined the breach of contract claim.[295]

Since there were no allegations of express contractual limitations in the case,[296] the court had to determine if there were any implied duties that distinguished the case from earlier precedents. The court was able to find an implied-in-law obligation, stating "that in any hiring of an attorney as an associate to practice law with a firm there is implied an understanding so fundamental to the relationship and essential to its purpose as to require no expression: that both the associate and the firm in conducting the practice will do so in accordance with the ethical standards of the profession."[297] The court stressed the importance of Disciplinary Rule 1-103 as being critical to the self-regulation of the legal profession and noted that a lawyer who fails to comply with the reporting requirement can be disciplined.[298] Thus, by insisting that Wieder disregard the rule, the firm's partners were not only making it impossible for him to perform his ethical obligations but also forcing him "to choose between continued employment and his own potential suspension and disbarment."[299] It is this unique characteristic of the profession, relating to this "core" disciplinary rule, that makes the relationship of an associate in a law firm to his employers intrinsically different from the non-lawyer employees of corporations whose claims for at-will exceptions were rejected in earlier New York cases.[300]

Even though the court held that Wieder had stated a claim for breach of an implied-in-law contractual obligation, the public policy tort claim was summarily dismissed, even though the court felt that the arguments were persuasive and the circumstances compelling. Although noting that the state's whistleblower statute had been criticized for failing to afford sufficient safeguards against retaliatory discharge, the court was determined to follow its pattern of leaving the problem to the legislature.[301]

Wieder was a significant departure from prior New York case law, but the opinion "is so replete with language of limitation and qualification" that its application will probably only encompass law firm associates in a situation precisely similar to Wieder's.[302] One court has suggested that "*Wieder* goes to substantial lengths to confine its reach primarily and possibly exclusively to cases involving legal ethics."[303] Even then, one must ask which rules other than Disciplinary Rule 1-103 will qualify as "core" provisions of the Code of Professional Responsibility for purposes of the implied-in-law exception to the at-will doctrine. Surely, "core" provisions will be only those that are meant to safeguard the public or to protect the integrity and efficiency of the judicial process, compared with those rules having as their primary purpose the protection of "the exclusivity or economic welfare of the legal profession."[304]

Corporate Whistleblower Statutes and Lawyers

Corporate whistleblower statutes do little to clarify the boundaries. The eligibility of corporate counsel for Dodd Frank bounty awards depends on state bar rules, unless outside disclosure is necessary to prevent illegality or significant adverse consequences.[305] Corporate counsel have been protected under the Sarbanes Oxley law from retaliation despite the attorney client privilege.[306] In fact, that law requires them to make internal disclosures of the misconduct to corporate authorities, including the board of directors.[307] It should be cautioned, however, that the remedies are limited to employment actions and may not shield an attorney from independent liability.

WHISTLEBLOWING AND THE FEDERAL GOVERNMENT LAWYER

The final section of this chapter examines special issues encountered by government-employed lawyers relating to whistleblowing. Although many of these issues could potentially arise at any level of government, for purposes of analysis the focus will be on federal government lawyers. Just as the "triangular relationship among a corporate lawyer, the client's agents, and the client itself accounts for many of the ethical complications in corporate representation,"[308] a comparable relationship exists among a governmental entity, its agents, and the lawyers employed by the entity, resulting in similar ethical complications. These complications are most likely to develop when differing or incompatible interests arise within the relationship,[309] as when a government lawyer learns of illegal conduct by other agency employees.

As in the corporate setting, the threshold question when representing a governmental entity is: "Who is the client?" The response is the same as in the corporate setting—the lawyer represents the entity acting through its duly authorized agents. But government at all levels can be incredibly complex, and determining "who is the client" relative to a government lawyer's actions is not always immediately apparent and has been a source of controversy. One commentator has suggested that the appropriate response to the question of the client's identity should be that "it depends" on why you are asking![310] For day-to-day purposes, it may be most practical to view officials within the employing agency as the client of the government lawyer, but this may not resolve the issue in all circumstances, and it may be necessary to view the "government as a whole" or other alternative officials as the client in other situations.[311]

Being a federal government lawyer differs from being a private-sector lawyer in a number of significant ways. As a federal government employee, the lawyer faces a federal ethics regulatory structure (including statutes, regulations, executive orders, ethics codes, and general codes of conduct) that is highly detailed and complex.[312] This structure is in addition to the regulatory apparatus in place in the jurisdiction where the lawyer was admitted to the bar. With so much overlapping regulation, it is not surprising that ethical mandates can sometimes conflict. Also, "[a] government lawyer serves the interests of many different entities: his supervisor in the department or agency, the agency itself, the statutory mission of the agency, the entire government of which that agency is part, and the public interest."[313] All of this regulation occurs in a governmental environment subject to a system of separation of powers with built-in checks and balances.[314] Furthermore, as will be seen, government employees may have affirmative duties to report crime in certain situations that may not be applicable to a private-sector lawyer. Also, because of the nature and vast scope of government operations, a government lawyer may have different obligations concerning certain types of client information than would a private-sector lawyer.[315] For example, under the Freedom of Information Act, a government lawyer may be required by law to disclose documentary information that a private-sector lawyer's client would deem confidential.[316] Congress, by statutorily consenting to disclosure, has in essence waived governmental confidentiality relative to such documents. On the other hand, contrary to open-access laws, some federal statutes specifically prohibit the revelation of certain types of secret or confidential government information concerning individuals, military secrets, or trade secrets.[317] Such statutes subject a government lawyer who violates them to criminal liability above and beyond professional sanction for violating confidentiality.[318] In a more positive vein, federal government lawyers, who are covered by the Civil Service Reform Act, may have greater job security than private-sector lawyers who are subject to the harshness of the at-will employment doctrine.[319] There is no attorney client exception in the Whistleblower Protection Act's rights against retaliation for public disclosures.

At the most fundamental level, a government lawyer remains a fiduciary who is required to be loyal, to avoid conflicts of interest, and to maintain the confidences of his client, usually viewed as the agency. These duties may be put to the test when the lawyer learns of wrongdoing within the agency. Under what circumstances must the government lawyer blow the whistle? What wrongdoing must be reported in light of the confidentiality and conflict of interest rules? Does the fiduciary duty of loyalty ever play a role?

Government lawyers are encouraged to come forward with information about criminal activities in certain circumstances. By executive order, each federal agency is responsible for issuing regulations concerning standards of ethics and other conduct for agency employees.[320] For example, the standards promulgated by the Department of Justice state that "Department employees *shall* report to their U.S. Attorney or Assistant Attorney General, or other appropriate supervisor, any evidence or nonfrivolous allegation of misconduct that may be in violation of any law, rule, regulation, order, or applicable professional standards."[321] Federal agency lawyers would seem to have an implied duty under 28 U.S.C. section 535 (b) to report any information, allegations, or complaints of criminal misconduct received within their departments or agencies involving government officers and employees to the agency head or, if the agency head is involved, to the attorney general.[322] Public policy, as reflected in federal whistleblower protection statutes, also strongly encourages agency lawyers to come forward with information concerning violations of law, rule, regulation, or gross mismanagement, gross waste of funds, abuse of authority, or a substantial and specific danger to public health or safety.[323]

These reporting requirements can place federal lawyers in a dilemma due to their professional responsibilities concerning confidentiality, loyalty, and conflict of interest. Confidentiality, however, appears to be the preeminent issue that arises when a government lawyer learns of wrongdoing by other government employees. Model Rule 1.6 states that a "lawyer shall not reveal information relating to representation of a client unless the client gives informed consent," and Model Rule 1.13(a) makes it clear that the confidentiality duty is owed to the governmental entity. But in reality the government lawyer is dealing with people—the agents of the government—and it is to those people with whom the lawyer works that the lawyer's duty and loyalty normally flow, unless and until the lawyer learns of illegality or other wrongdoing. It is at this point where ethical problems may arise because "obligations to report wrongdoing within and without the agency may override normal duties of confidentiality owed to the agency and its responsible official."[324]

Upon encountering information concerning wrongdoing by another federal employee, what factors should a government lawyer consider before proceeding? Given the complex regulatory environment within government and the typical adverse reaction to whistleblowing by supervisors and coworkers, it may be advisable to proceed with caution. First, the lawyer should examine the nature of the wrongdoing that is involved. Distinctions must be drawn between significant violations of law, rules, and regulations and mere technical violations. While forms of corruption such as bribery or misappropriation of funds that rise to the level of a violation of law will merit disclosure, a coworker's habit of taking home pencils, or a lobbyist's buying a drink for the agency head, may better be ignored. There are "a maze of demeaning and nitpicking restrictions" that have been imposed "to prevent malingering and misappropriation of government property,"[325] the violation of which in the usual course of business does not merit the government lawyer's serious attention as a whistleblower. The whistleblower protection statutes were drafted to encourage reporting, but only the reporting of acts of gross mismanagement, waste, or abuse of authority, not trivial transgressions.

Another potential area of ethical concern arises when a lawyer confronts changes in policy within the larger administration or within his or her agency. A government lawyer may totally disagree with a change of policy, rule, or position for a number of perfectly sound reasons. Even though the lawyer may believe that a new policy is wrong or wrongheaded, the boundary is not based on agreement or consensus. If the proposed action is clearly illegal, or the lawyer is placed in the position of bringing a frivolous claim or defense without good faith basis for a modification or extension of existing law, there is discretion. Otherwise, unless violating another rule the lawyer must follow an order of his supervisors to proceed.[326] Lawyers who substitute their "individual moral judgment for that of a political process which is generally accepted as legitimate" should be viewed as acting unethically.[327]

A lawyer who strongly opposes a policy change may face both conflict of interest and confidentiality problems. If the lawyer so vehemently objects to the client's lawful objectives that he or she cannot advance them, then withdrawal from the representation may be appropriate. For a government employee this may entail requesting a transfer, attempting to withdraw from the matter and requesting reassignment to another project, or ultimately resigning. Confidentiality becomes an issue if the lawyer is so opposed to a lawful change in policy or position that he or she seeks to go public with sensitive information in an effort to sway public opinion against the change. Leaking of such information to the press or public interest groups would appear to be a violation of the agency's expectation of confidentiality under Model Rule 1.6 because the rule applies to all information relating to the representation, no matter what its source. Also, if the policy change is clearly illegal it would be appropriate for the agency lawyer to report first to authorities within the government.[328]

The Whistleblower Protection Enhancement Act gave the attorney another option. While not covering policy dissent, the law now protects disclosures about adverse consequences such as illegality or public health and safety threats from policy choices.[329]

A second factor to consider before proceeding to divulge information relates to the basis of the lawyer's knowledge concerning the wrongdoing. Is the knowledge based on rumor or innuendo or on documents or credible witnesses? The federal whistleblower statute requires a "reasonable belief" that evidences wrongdoing.[330] Considering the potential consequences of a false charge, one would be well advised to base accusations on a solid factual and legal foundation. Federal agencies have ethics officers with whom a lawyer could consult, and lawyers can always seek ethics opinions from bar associations, including the Federal Bar Association. Model Rule 1.13(b), which was discussed relating to in-house counsel, provides some guidance for resolving issues internally within an organization, and agency rules also may provide for informal methods of dealing with ethical concerns.

As was seen, a government lawyer who reasonably believes that another government officer or employee has violated the criminal law, or other rule, law, regulation, or ethics code may be required by statute or agency rule to report the wrongdoing to the appropriate authorities, unless such disclosure would be unlawful. Some information is made confidential by law or may have been ordered to be kept secret by executive order in the interest of national defense or in the conduct of foreign affairs.[331]

Government lawyers can learn of illegal activities in a number of ways, some of which do not raise issues of confidentiality, but when an employee of the agency personally provides self-incriminating information to the lawyer concerning an illegal act, that employee may have an unjustified expectation of confidentiality.[332] As in the corporate setting, employees who incriminate themselves to a government lawyer have no personal claim to confidentiality. The privilege is held by the entity. But unlike the duty of in-house counsel in the corporate setting, the government lawyer cannot remain silent and allow the illegal act to be ignored. The lawyer must report the act to the appropriate authorities within the agency, who are then required to inform the attorney general.[333] If the head of the agency is involved in the illegal activities, the lawyer would have to directly inform the attorney general.[334] It has been noted that "[t]he duty of disclosure inside the organization does not stop at the boundaries of the agency."[335]

As was noted earlier in the discussion of the federal Civil Service Reform Act, all federal employees are protected from retaliation for disclosing information that the employee "reasonably believes evidences a violation of any law, rule, or regulation or gross mismanagement, a gross waste of funds, an abuse of authority, or a substantial and specific danger to the public health or safety," if reported to the special counsel, or to the inspector general of an agency or other appropriately designated agency employees.[336] Federal employees can report this same information to anyone inside or outside government, including the media, Congress, or advocacy groups, unless the disclosure is specifically prohibited by law or required to be kept secret in the interests of national defense or in the conduct of foreign affairs.[337]

Federal government lawyers who are covered by these provisions may have a conflict between the statutory encouragement to disclose wrongdoing and their professional duty to maintain confidentiality. Confidentiality may not necessarily be an obstacle to a government lawyer's disclosure of a clear violation of law, but knowledge of other types of wrongdoing is more problematic. Reasonable people can disagree over what constitutes gross waste, gross mismanagement, abuse of authority, or a threat to public safety in particular circumstances. Personal opinion and political orientation can color one's perception of what constitutes gross behavior or a "reasonable belief." An agency lawyer can be placed in numerous situations where the line between appropriate whistleblowing and inappropriate revelation of confidential agency information is murky at best.[338] Any time an agency takes a position based on "questionable" legal authority, or plans a novel expansion of regulatory authority, or fails to act in the public safety area, and an agency lawyer who disagrees goes public, what are the consequences?[339]

Agency officials are likely to view disclosure of confidential positions, plans, and strategies as a disloyal act, one that breaches the lawyer's duty of confidentiality to the agency. The lawyer could then be disciplined by the agency for violation of an agency ethics rule or by the jurisdiction in which the lawyer was admitted for violation of that jurisdiction's ethical standards. The agency lawyer would, on the other hand, view such discipline as retaliation for legitimate whistleblowing and thus contrary to the statute.

Assuming that the lawyer's disclosures are based on a reasonable belief of wrongdoing and are not in and of themselves unlawful disclosures, it appears that agency regulations or state ethics rules requiring confidentiality do not override the whistleblower protection provisions.[340] The public policies reflected in the whistleblower protection statutes would override any federal agency regulations and preclude state disciplinary action.[341] "The supremacy clause assures that the federal policy of disclosure prevails over the inconsistent state policy of confidentiality."[342] Thus, although seemingly at odds with the legal profession's traditional view that confidentiality is fundamental to the lawyer–client relationship, the whistleblower protection provisions encourage whistleblowing by government lawyers at the expense of the traditional role of confidentiality. As one commentator has suggested, perhaps the American Bar Association, which generally supported enactment of the whistleblower protection provisions, "never considered the possibility that a lawyer might act as a whistleblower and that such conduct would be inconsistent with normal professional duties of confidentiality."[343]

SUMMARY OF KEY POINTS

- Public policies that seek to protect whistleblowers directly clash with the long-standing doctrine of employment at will, which remains in force in 49 states despite being eroded significantly via statute.
- Whistleblower protections also clash with traditional notions concerning the lawyer–client relationship, especially in situations involving lawyer employees of corporate and governmental entities.
- Animosity toward whistleblowers by supervisors and coworkers remains a problem. Employees are still hesitant to come forward, but financial incentives in false claims acts seem to be successful at overcoming this reticence.

NOTES

1. This is a revision of a chapter originally prepared by Robert Begg.
2. 20 OXFORD ENGLISH DICTIONARY, 258–59 (2d ed. 1989).
3. BLACK'S LAW DICTIONARY, 1596 (6th ed. 1990). For a detailed discussion of the definition of whistleblowing, see MARCIA P. MICELI & JANET P. NEAR, BLOWING THE WHISTLE: THE ORGANIZATIONAL AND LEGAL IMPLICATIONS FOR COMPANIES AND EMPLOYEES 15–21 (Lexington Books 1992).
4. See, e.g., The Government Accountability Project, http://www.whistleblower.org; U.S. DEP'T OF LABOR, OFFICE OF ADMINISTRATIVE LAW JUDGES, Law Library Whistleblower Collection, http://www.oalj.dol.gov/libwhist.htm.
5. The False Claims Act, 31 U.S.C. §§ 3729–3733, was originally enacted in 1863 (R.S. 3492) to deal with profiteering during the Civil War.
6. INTERNATIONAL BAR ASSOCIATION AND GOVERNMENT ACCOUNTABILITY PROJECT, Are Whistleblowing Laws Working? A Global Study of Whistleblower Protection Litigation (Jan. 2021), https://www.ibanet.org/MediaHandler?id=49c9b08d-4328-4797-a2f7-1e0a71d0da55; United Nations Secretariat: Secretary General's Bulletin No. ST/SGB/2005/21 (Dec. 19, 2005), http://www.un.org/en/ga/search/view_doc.asp?symbol=ST/SGB/2005/21; THE WORLD BANK, Staff Rule 8.02: Protections

and Procedures for Reporting Misconduct (Whistleblowing), http://siteresources.worldbank.org/NEWS/Resources/StaffRule8_02.pdf.

7. *See* DANIEL P. WESTMAN, WHISTLEBLOWING: THE LAW OF RETALIATORY DISCHARGE, 19–20 (BNA Books 1991).

8. *See* Tom Devine, *Government Accountability Project, A Whistleblower's Checklist,* http://web.archive.org/web/19990302054549/www.whistleblower.org/www/checklist.htm (also on file with editor).

9. MICELI & NEAR, *supra* note 3, at 180, 232. Organizational responses to whistleblowing range from doing nothing, to retaliation, to reward.

10. *See* H.R. Rep. No. 99-859, at 17 (1986) (stating that "[s]ince the establishment of the [Office of Special Counsel], one Special Counsel has taught a course for Federal managers on how to fire whistleblowers. Another has expressed disdain for whistleblowers by referring to them as 'malcontents and informants' and likening them to bag ladies and mental health patients. One Special Counsel even warned would-be whistleblowers to keep quiet or they would get their heads blown off"). *See also* David Culp, *Whistleblowers: Corporate Anarchists or Heroes? Towards a Judicial Perspective,* 13 HOFSTRA LAB. L.J. 109, 113 (1995) (noting that "[a] recent study of eighty-four whistleblowers revealed that 82% experienced harassment after blowing the whistle, 60% were fired, 17% lost their homes, and 10% admitted to attempted suicide"). *See generally* C. FRED ALFORD, WHISTLEBLOWERS: BROKEN LIVES AND ORGANIZATIONAL POWER (Cornell University Press 2001).

11. Admiral Hyman Rickover is quoted as saying: "If you are going to sin, sin against God, but not against the bureaucracy—God will forgive you, the bureaucracy never will." Bruce D. Fisher, *The Whistleblower Protection Act of 1989: A False Hope for Whistleblowers,* 43 RUTGERS L. REV. 355, 355 (1991). *See* MICELI & NEAR, *supra* note 3, at 224–30 (discussing the long-term consequences for the whistleblower and the organization).

12. For an examination of the personal variables that may affect whistleblowing, *see* Devine, *supra* note 8, and MICELI & NEAR, *supra* note 3, at 103–38.

13. *See* Lois A. Lofgren, *Whistleblower Protection: Should Legislatures and the Courts Provide a Shelter to Public and Private Sector Employees Who Disclose the Wrongdoing of Employers?,* 38 S.D. L. REV. 316 (1993); WESTMAN, *supra* note 7, at 24–27, 105. Examples of exceptions to the rule are health care workers, who may be required by law to report certain types of abuse and certain government employees required by law to report illegal acts.

14. *See* WESTMAN, *supra* note 7, at 23–24. An argument can be made that "the concept of loyalty to a corporation is a red herring because loyalty requires a mutual bond tying people to each other—reciprocity which a corporation is incapable of giving. Nevertheless, the concept of loyalty to employer is deeply rooted in American industrial relations." Martin H. Malin, *Protecting the Whistleblower from Retaliatory Discharge,* 16 U. MICH. J. L. REFORM 277, 307 (1983).

15. *See* WESTMAN, *supra* note 7, at 22.

16. John L. Howard, *Current Developments in Whistleblower Protection,* 39 LAB. L.J. 67, 71 (1988).

17. *See* Devine, *supra* note 8.

18. For example, in *Balla v. Gambro, Inc.*, 145 Ill. 2d 492 (1991), an in-house counsel was not protected from the consequences of whistleblowing even though he was required under the Illinois Rules of Professional Conduct to report his employer's intention to sell defective dialysis equipment. The precedent has been widely criticized, however, in subsequent decisions. *See, e.g.,* Burkhart v. Semitool, Inc., 5 P.3d 1031 (Mt. 2000), in which disclosure of confidential information did not bar an attorney's statutory unemployment compensation claim.

19. *See* Howard, *supra* note 16, at 71; ALAN F. WESTIN, WHISTLE BLOWING: LOYALTY AND DISSENT IN THE CORPORATION 134 (McGraw-Hill 1981).

20. *See* Howard, *supra* note 16, at 71.

21. DEVINE & MAASSARANI, THE CORPORATE WHISTLEBLOWER'S SURVIVAL GUIDE: A HANDBOOK FOR COMMITTING THE TRUTH 149–97 (Barrett Koehler 2011).

22. Note, *Protecting At-Will Employees against Wrongful Discharge: The Duty to Terminate Only in Good Faith,* 93 Harv. L. Rev. 1816, 1818 (1980) [hereinafter *Protecting At-Will Employees*]; 1 Henry H. Perritt, Jr., Employee Dismissal Law and Practice § 1.65, at 66 (4th ed. 1998).

23. Andrew D. Hill, "Wrongful Discharge" and the Derogation of the At-Will Employment Doctrine 5 (University of Pennsylvania Press 1987).

24. *Id.* at 4.

25. H.G. Wood, A Treatise on the Law of Master and Servant § 134, at 272–273 (2d ed. 1886); see Stuart H. Bompey et al., Wrongful Termination Claims: A Preventive Approach 2–4 (Practicing Law Institute, 2d ed. 1991).

26. See Jay M. Feinman, *The Development of the Employment at Will Rule,* 20 Am. J. Legal Hist. 118, 119–22 (1976); Hill, *supra* note 23, at 1; 1 William Blackstone, Commentaries, *425.

27. See Hill *supra* note 23, at 11–12; Committee on Labor and Employment Law of the Assn. of the Bar of City of N.Y., *At-Will Employment and the Problem of Unjust Dismissal,* 36 Rec. A.B. City of N.Y. 170, 175–80 (1981).

28. The first federal civil service statute was the Pendleton Act, ch. 27, 22 Stat. 403 (1883), which was enacted to eliminate abuses arising out of the patronage system. *See* Bush v. Lucas, 462 U.S. 367, 381–84 (1983), for a brief history of federal civil service reform.

29. *See, e.g.,* Pickering v. Board of Educ., 391 U.S. 563 (1968); Connick v. Myers, 461 U.S. 138 (1983); Waters v. Churchill, 511 U.S. 661 (1994).

30. National Labor Relations Act, ch. 372, 49 Stat. 449, § 7 at 452 (1935).

31. *See, e.g.,* Title VII of the Civil Rights Act of 1964, 42 U.S.C. §§ 2000e *et seq.* (2000); Age Discrimination in Employment Act of 1967, 29 U.S.C. §§ 621 *et seq.* (2000); Rehabilitation Act of 1973, 29 U.S.C. §§ 701 *et seq.* (2000); Americans with Disabilities Act, 42 U.S.C. §§ 12101 *et seq.* (2000). The Notification and Federal Employee Antidiscrimination and Retaliation Act of 2002, P.L. 107–174, also protects employees who report civil rights violations or bring civil rights suits from retaliation in the workplace.

32. *See* Cass R. Sunstein, *Interpreting Statutes in the Regulatory State,* 103 Harv. L. Rev. 405, 409 (1989); *Protecting At-Will Employees, supra* note 19, at 1827.

33. *See* Perritt, *supra* note 22, at 138–44.

34. Many of the federal statutes with such provisions are listed in the chart of federal statutes *infra*.

35. Wrongful Discharge From Employment Act, Mont. Code Ann. §§ 39-2-901 to 39-2-915.

36. The 2002 Census of Governments reported more than 21,000,000 government employees, of which 2,690,000 were federal civilian employees, 5,072,000 were state employees, and 13,277,000 were employed by local governments. United States Census Bureau, Compendium of Government Employment: 2002, 1, http://www.census.gov/prod/2004pubs/gc023x2.pdf.

37. James B. Helmer, Jr., et al., False Claims Act: Whistleblower Litigation xxi (3d ed. 2002).

38. Government Ethics Reform for the 1990s: The Collected Reports of the New York State Commission on Government Integrity 688 (Bruce A. Green ed., Fordham University Press 1991) [hereinafter Commission on Government Integrity].

39. John D. Feerick, *Toward a Model Whistleblowing Law,* 19 Fordham Urb. L.J. 585, 587 (1992).

40. Commission on Government Integrity, *supra* note 38, at 688; Feerick, *supra* note 39, at 587.

41. *See* Commission on Government Integrity, *supra* note 38, at 688.

42. "We have found that despite the existence of the whistleblowers statute, many public employees continue to have a deeply held fear of reprisals." *Id.* at 689. *See also* Roger C. Cramton, *The Lawyer as Whistleblower: Confidentiality and the Government Lawyer,* 5 Geo. J. Legal Ethics 291, 315 (1991).

43. Commission on Government Integrity, *supra* note 38, at 693.

44. 18 U.S.C. § 1001 (2000).

45. Garcetti v. Ceballos, 547 US 410 (2006).

46. *See, e.g.,* New York, N.Y., Admin. Code, § 12-113, http://public.leginfo.state.ny.us/frm load.cgi?MENU-43707233 (follow "Laws of New York" hyperlink; then follow "New York City Administrative Code" hyperlink).

47. 5 U.S.C. § 2302(b)(8) (2000).
48. *Id.* § 1103.
49. *Id.* § 1204.
50. *Id.* § 1212.
51. *Id.* § 1213. *See also* U.S. Office of Special Counsel, *Whistleblower Disclosures*, http://www.osc.gov/wbdisc.htm.
52. S. Rep. No. 103-358, at 2 (1994), reprinted in 1994 U.S.C.C.A.N. 3550 (noting that "[a]t that time, OSC had not brought a single corrective action case since 1979 to the Merit Systems Protection Board on behalf of a whistleblower").
53. *See id.* (stating that "[w]histleblowers told the Governmental Affairs Committee that they thought of the OSC as an adversary, rather than an ally, and urged the Committee to abolish the office altogether").
54. Whistleblower Protection Act of 1989, Pub. L. No. 101-12, 103 Stat. 16.
55. 5 U.S.C. § 2302(b)(2)(A) (2000). *See* the note following 5 U.S.C. § 1201 (2000) for the congressional purpose of the act. *See also* Thomas Devine, *The Whistleblower Protection Act of 1989: Foundation for the Modern Law of Dissent*, 51 ADMIN. L.R. 531 (Spring 1999).
56. 5 U.S.C. § 2302(b)(8) (2000). *Compare with* 5 U.S.C. § 2302(b)(8) (1980).
57. 429 U.S. 274 (1977).
58. 5 U.S.C. § 1221(e)(1) (2000).
59. 135 CONG. REC. 4509, 4518, 4522, 5033 (statements of Senators Grassley, Pryor, Explanatory Statement on S. 33, Rep. Schroeder, and letter from Attorney General Thornburgh) (1989).
60. 5 U.S.C. § 1221(e)(1) (2000).
61. *See* Thomas Devine, *The Whistleblower Protection Act Burdens of Proof: Ground Rules for Credible Free Speech Rights*, 2 E-J. INT'L & COMPARATIVE L. 137 (Oct. 2013).
62. S. Rep. No. 103-358, at 2 (1994), reprinted in 1994 U.S.C.C.A.N. 3550.
63. *Id.* at 2–3, and 3551.
64. Pub. L. 103-424, 108 Stat. 4361 (1994).
65. U.S. Senate, S.R. 12-155. The Whistleblower Protection Enhancement Act of 2012, 1, 4–8 (2012).
66. *Id.* at 9–11; Lachance v. White, 174 F.3d 1378, 1381 (Fed. Cir. 1999).
67. THE NEW WEBSTER'S COMPREHENSIVE DICTIONARY OF THE ENGLISH LANGUAGE, at 510 (De. Ed. American International Press 1985).
68. P.L. 112-99 (Nov. 27, 2012).
69. *Id.* §§ 101, 102; 5 USC §§ 2302(a)(2)(D) and 2302(f).
70. *Id.* §§ 109 (protection for Transportation Security Administration personnel) and 110 (scientific freedom); 5 U.S.C. 2302 note and 5 U.S.C. 2302 note.
71. *Id.* §§ 104 and 115; 5 U.S.C. §§ 2302(a)(2)(xi), 2302(b)(13) and 2302 note.
72. *Id.* § 106l 5 U.S.C. § 1215(a)(3).
73. Merit system principles are enumerated at 5 U.S.C. § 2301 (2000). Subsection (9) provides protection from reprisal for whistleblowers' disclosures.
74. 5 U.S.C. § 2302(b)(8) (2000).
75. *Id.* § 2302(b)(8)(B).
76. *Id.* § 2302(b)(8)(A). In *MacLean v. Department of Homeland Security*, 135 S. Ct. 913 (2015), by a 7-2 majority the Supreme Court held that "specifically by law" requires a statutory prohibition of public disclosure. WPA rights doe public freedom of expression override any agency restrictions. Nor may Congress delegate the specificity requirement to agencies for implementation through regulations.
77. *Id.* § 1213(b).
78. *Id.* § 1213(c)–(f).
79. 5 U.S.C. § 1213 (g)(1).
80. *Id.* § 1213(g)(2)(3).
81. *Id.* § 1213(h).
82. *Id.* § 7512(2).

83. *Id.* § 1221(a).
84. *Id.* § 1214(f).
85. *Id.* § 1214(b)(1)(A)(1). For practices and procedures for appeals and stay requests of personnel actions allegedly based on whistleblowing, see 5 C.F.R. §§ 1209.1 to 1209.12 (2007).
86. 5 U.S.C. § 1214(b)(2)(C) (2000).
87. *Id.* § 1221(h)(1).
88. 5 U.S.C. §§ 7703(b)(1)(B) and 7703(d)(2).
89. Federal Civil Service Law and Procedures: A Basic Guide, 126–127 (Ellen M. Bussey, ed., 2d ed., BNA Books 1990) (setting forth the four elements of the prima facie case but not including changes resulting from the 1994 amendments as the preceding text does).
90. *Id.* at 126, n. 41. *See also* Ellison v. Merit Sys. Protection Bd., 7 F.3d 1031, 1034–35 (Fed. Cir. 1993).
91. 5 U.S.C. § 1221(e)(1)(A)(B) (2000); *see* S. Rep. No. 103-358, at 8 (1994), reprinted in 1994 U.S.C.C.A.N. 3556.
92. *See* S. Rep. No. 103-358, at 9–10 (1994), *reprinted in* 1994 U.S.C.C.A.N. 3557–3558.
93. 5 U.S.C. § 1221(e)(1) (2000).
94. *Id.* §§ 1214(b)(4)(B)(ii), 1221(e)(2).
95. *Id.* § 1214(b)(4)(B)(i).
96. *Id.* § 1214(g)(1).
97. *Id.* § 3352(a).
98. *Id.* § 1214(g)(2).
99. *Id.* §§1214(g)(2) and 1221(g)(1)(A)(ii).
100. Unfortunately, due to failure to confirm a replacement for retiring members, since January 2017 the board has not been able to render final decisions and currently has a backlog of more than 3,200 cases. https://federalnewsnetwork.com/workforce-rightsgovernance/2021/01/historic-absences-at-mspb-hit-4-year-mark-creating-potentially-costly-backlog/.
101. Rivera v. United States, 924 F.2d 948, 951 (9th Cir.1991).
102. Premachandra v. United States, 739 F.2d 392 (8th Cir.1984); Rivera v. United States, 924 F.2d 948 (9th Cir.1991).
103. Bush v. Lucas, 462 U.S. 367, 388 (1983) (holding that the CSRA precluded a First Amendment Bivens claim and describing the CSRA as "an elaborate remedial system that has been constructed step by step with careful attention to conflicting policy considerations").
104. United States v. Fausto, 484 U.S. 439 (1988). The Tucker Act is codified at 28 U.S.C. §§ 1491 *et seq.* (2000).
105. Rivera v. United States, 924 F.2d 948, 951–52 (9th Cir. 1991).
106. 135 Cong. Rec. H750 (daily ed. Mar. 21, 1989), cited in Massimino v. Dep't of Veterans Affairs, 58 M.S.P.R. 318, 324 (1993).
107. *See, e.g.,* Gergick v. Austin, 997 F.2d 1237, 1239 (8th Cir. 1993); Rivera v. United States, 924 F.2d 948 (9th Cir. 1991).
108. *See* Massimino v. Dep't of Veterans Affairs, 58 M.S.P.R. 318, 324 (1993).
109. https://statelaws.findlaw.com/employment-laws/whistleblower-laws.html;https://www.peer.org/wp-content/uploads/attachments/overview.pdf.
110. Lofgren, *supra* note 13, at 326.
111. Westman, *supra* note 7, at 113 (noting that "[v]irtually any mismanagement in government affects the public interest because public monies may be squandered").
112. https://www.taf.org/state-laws.
113. *See, e.g.,* Neb. Rev. Stat. § 81-2703; N.Y. Civ. Serv. Law § 75-b; N.D. Cent. Code § 34-11.1-01; S.C. Code Ann. §§ 8-27-10, 8-17-370; Wis. Stat. Ann. § 230.80.
114. Westman, *supra* note 7, at 59, notes that civil service protections are much less satisfactory than specific whistleblower laws because (1) they may not provide an affirmative right of action including damages, but merely a defense to retaliation; and (2) the "just cause" standard gives civil service commissioners great latitude in specific whistleblower situations.

115. Lofgren, *supra* note 13, at 322; ALFRED G. FELIU, PRIMER ON INDIVIDUAL EMPLOYEE RIGHTS, 188 (BNA Books 1992).

116. Compare, for example, the difference in coverage between public- and private-sector employees in Florida. *See* https://www.wenzelfenton.com/blog/2018/02/19/protected-retaliation-florida-whistleblower-act/.

117. *See, e.g.*, D.C. CODE § 1-615.53; IDAHO CODE § 6-2104(3); ME. REV. STAT. tit. 26, § 833(1)(D); MASS. GEN. LAWS ANN. ch. 149, § 185(b)(3); NEB. REV. STAT. § 48-1114; N.H. REV. STAT. ANN. § 275-E:3; N.J. STAT. § 34:19-3(c); N.Y. LABOR § 740(2)(c); N.D. CENT. CODE § 34-01-20(1)(c); TENN. CODE ANN. § 50-1-304; UTAH CODE ANN. § 67-21-3(3); WYO. STAT. § 9-11-103(a)(v).

118. *See, e.g.*, CONN. GEN. STAT. § 31-40t; 820 ILL. COMP. STAT. ANN. § 255/14; OHIO REV. CODE ANN. 4113.52; 35 PA. STAT. § 6020.1112 (hazardous sites cleanup).

119. *See, e.g.*, DEL. CODE ANN. tit. 16, § 1154; IND. CODE ANN. § 16-28-9-3; MICH. COMP. LAWS § 333.20180; OR. REV. STAT. § 430.755 (drug and alcohol treatment); R.I. GEN. LAWS § 42-66.7-8 (long-term care); VA. CODE ANN. §§ 32.1-138.4, 32.1-138.5 (nursing facilities); WASH. REV. CODE ANN. § 43.70.075; WYO. STAT. ANN. § 35-2-910(b).

120. *See, e.g.*, ALA. CODE § 25-8-57 (child labor laws); N.D. CENT. CODE § 50-25.1-09.1; TENN. CODE ANN. § 37-1-410.

121. *See, e.g.*, CONN. GEN. STAT. § 16-8a; ME. REV. STAT. ANN. tit. 35-A, § 1316; 66 PA. CONS. STAT. § 3316.

122. *See, e.g.*, LA. REV. STAT. ANN. § 30:2027; MASS. GEN. LAWS ANN. ch. 149, § 185(b)(1); N.J. STAT. § 34:19-3(c)(3).

123. *See* Valerie P. Kirk & Ann Clarke Snell, *The Texas Whistleblower Act: Time for a Change*, 26 TEXAS TECH L. REV. 75, 102 (1994); Howard, *supra* note 16, at 71.

124. Kirk & Snell, *supra* note 123, at 103; Lofgren, *supra* note 13, at 326, 334.

125. Kirk & Snell, *supra* note 123, at 102–103; Howard, *supra* note 16, at 71.

126. For states that require internal reporting prior to outside disclosure, *see, e.g.*, COLO. REV. STAT. 24-50.5-103(2); FLA. STAT. § 448.102(1); ME. REV. STAT. ANN. tit. 26, §§ 833(2); N.H. REV. STAT. ANN. § 275-E:2(II); N.J. STAT. § 34:19-4; N.Y. CIV. SERV. LAW § 75-b(2)(b). Alaska allows employers to adopt internal reporting requirements in their personnel policies. ALASKA STAT. § 39.90.110(c). Several states, on the other hand, expressly prohibit employers from requiring whistleblowers to exhaust internal procedures before external disclosure. *See, e.g.*, KAN. STAT. ANN. § 75-2973(d)(2); MO. ANN. STAT. § 105.055(2)(2).

127. Malin, *supra* note 14, at 308.

128. *Id.* at 310.

129. *Id.* at 313.

130. *Id.* at 313; Kirk & Snell, *supra* note 123, at 90–91.

131. *See, e.g.*, ME. REV. STAT. ANN. tit. 5, §§ 21–33 (testimony by state employees to legislative committees); NEV. REV. STAT. ANN. § 218.5343 (testimony before legislature or committees).

132. WESTMAN, *supra* note 7, at 53–54.

133. *See, e.g.*, FLA. STAT. § 112.3187(6).

134. *See, e.g.*, CAL. GOV'T CODE § 8547.4; REV. CODE WASH. § 42.40.040.

135. WESTMAN, *supra* note 7, at 55.

136. *See, e.g.*, HAW. REV. STAT. § 378-62(2); ME. REV. STAT. ANN. tit. 5, §§ 21 to 33; N.H. REV. STAT. ANN. § 275-E:2(I)(b); R.I. GEN. LAWS § 28-50-3(2); UTAH CODE ANN. § 67-21-3(2).

137. *See, e.g.*, HAW. REV. STAT. § 378-68; IOWA CODE § 70A.28(8); ME. REV. STAT. tit. 26, § 839; MICH. COMP. LAWS § 15.368; MINN. STAT. § 181.934; N.H. REV. STAT. ANN. § 275-E:7; N.J. STAT. § 34:19-7; 43 PA. STAT. § 1428; R.I. GEN. LAWS § 28-50-8; TENN. CODE ANN. § 49-50-1411; TEX. GOV'T CODE § 554.009; REV. CODE WASH. § 42.40.070; W. VA. CODE § 6C-1-8.

138. *See, e.g.*, CAL. LAB. CODE § 1102.7; FLA. STAT. § 112.3189. *See also* Florida Department of State, Whistleblower Hotline, http://oss.dos.state.fl.us/inspector-general/hotlines.cfm. The federal government has a whistleblower hotline also: D.C.: (202) 254-3640; Continental U.S.: (800) 572-2249. The U.S. Office of Special Counsel home page has an online whistleblower disclosure form at http://www.osc.gov/documents/forms/osc12.htm.

139. *See, e.g.*, Fla. Stat. § 112.3188; Ga. Code Ann. § 45-1-4(c).
140. Westin, *supra* note 19, at 34.
141. *See, e.g.*, Okla. Stat. Ann. tit. 74, § 840-2.5; Fla. Stat. Ann. §§ 112.3187.
142. Kirk & Snell, *supra* note 123, at 85.
143. *Id.*
144. *See* Westin, *supra* note 19, at 40, 50 (telling the story of a General Electric engineer who was blackballed from corporate employment after his disclosures concerning the risks of a nuclear accident).
145. *See., e.g.*, 5 U.S.C. § 2302(b)(8) for federal civil service job applicants.
146. *See* Westin, *supra* note 19, at 48. Federal civil service law views a decision to order psychiatric testing or examination as a personnel action. 5 U.S.C. § 2302(a)(2)(A)(x) (2000).
147. Isidor Silver, 1 Public Employee Discharge and Discipline 8 (2d ed. 1995); Mourad v. Automobile Club Ins. Ass'n, 186 Mich. App. 715, 721 (1991) (explaining that "[a] constructive discharge occurs when an employer deliberately makes an employee's working conditions so intolerable that the employee is forced into an involuntary resignation or, stated differently, when working conditions become so difficult or unpleasant that a reasonable person in the employee's shoes would feel compelled to resign").
148. This is prohibited in Alaska. Alaska Stat. § 39.90.100(b).
149. This practice is prohibited in Indiana, Michigan, Tennessee, Virginia, Washington, Wisconsin, and Wyoming. Ind. Code Ann. § 16-28-9-3; Mich. Comp. Laws § 333.20180; Tenn. Code Ann. § 71-6-105; Va. Code Ann. §§ 32.1-138.4 to 32.1-138.5; Wash. Rev. Code Ann. § 43.70.075; Wis. Stat. Ann. § 51.61(5)(b), (d); Wyo. Stat. Ann. § 35-2-910(b).
150. *See, e.g.*, Alaska Stat. § 39.90.120(a); Cal. Gov't Code § 8547.8(b)–(c); Ky. Rev. Stat. § 61.103(2); Mont. Code Anno. § 39-2-905(2); N.J. Stat. § 34:19-5; N.C. Gen. Stat. § 126-87.
151. *See, e.g.*, Mass. Gen. Laws Ann. ch. 149, § 185(d); N.C. Gen. Stat. § 126-87.
152. *See, e.g.*, S.C. Code Ann. § 8-27-30; Tex. Gov't Code § 554.008(a).
153. Elletta Sangrey Callahan & Terry Morehead Dworkin, *Do Good and Get Rich: Financial Incentives for Whistleblowing and the False Claims Act*, 37 Villanova L. Rev. 273, 336 (1992).
154. *Id.* at 273, 278–83. In addition to the False Claims Acts, discussed *infra,* the federal government provides rewards to tax informers, 26 U.S.C. § 7623 (2000), and also for customs informers, 19 U.S.C. § 1619 (2000). *See also* Major Fraud Act, 18 U.S.C. § 1031(g) (2000) (authorizing the Attorney General to make discretionary awards to informants).
155. 31 U.S.C. §§ 3729–3733 (2000).
156. Black's Law Dictionary defines the qui tam action as "an action brought by an informer, under a statute which establishes a penalty for the commission or omission of a certain act, and provides that the same shall be recoverable in a civil action, part of the penalty to go to any person who will bring such action and the remainder to the state or some other institution." Black's Law Dictionary, 1251 (6th ed. 1990).
157. *See generally* Dr. Carl Pacini & Michael Bret Hood, *The Role of Qui Tam Actions Under the Federal False Claims Act in Preventing and Deterring Fraud Against the Government,* 15 U. Miami Bus. L. Rev. 273 (2007); ABA Section of Public Contract Law, Qui Tam Litigation Under the False Claims Act (1994).
158. 31 U.S.C. § 3729 (2000). The act generally applies to two classes of misconduct. "The first is the presentation of a claim knowing it to be false. The second is the use of false documentation in support of a claim." John Cosgrove McBride & Thomas J. Touhey, 2 Government Contracts § 14.30 at 14–13 (Lexis Nexis 2007).
159. 31 U.S.C. § 3730(b) (2000).
160. *Id.* § 3730(b)(2).
161. *Id.* § 3730(d)(1). If the government proceeds with the action, and the person bringing the action is the primary source of information rather than governmental sources or the media, the qui tam plaintiff will receive at least 15 percent but not more than 25 percent of the proceeds of the action or settlement of the claim, depending on the contribution to the prosecution of the action, plus expenses, lawyer's fees and costs.

162. *Id.* § 3730(d)(2). If the government does not proceed with a qui tam action, the person bringing the complaint or settling the claim shall receive an amount that the court believes to be reasonable, but in no case will it be less than 25 percent nor more than 30 percent of the proceeds plus expenses, lawyer's fees and costs.

163. *Id.* § 3730(d)(1) (stating that "[w]here the action is one which the court finds to be based primarily on disclosures of specific information (other than information provided by the person bringing the action) relating to allegations or transactions in a criminal, civil, or administrative hearing, in a congressional, administrative, or Government Accounting Office report, hearing, audit or investigation, or from the news media, the court may award such sum as it considers appropriate, but in no case more than 10% of the proceeds").

164. *See* Callahan & Dworkin, *supra* note 153, at 323–24 (discussing how large rewards may be a way to offset the significant personal and financial risks faced by whistleblowers). *See also* Devine, *supra* note 8, at 6 (describing how some firms are encouraged by the prospect of "pot of gold" victories in whistleblower cases, especially where punitive damages are available). There is also the Qui Tam Information Center on the Internet at http://www.quitam.com/, which helps potential whistleblowers with lawyer selection. The Taxpayers against Fraud organization also maintains an informative home page relating to the False Claims Act at http://www.taf.org/.

165. *See* Priscilla R. Budeiri, *The Return of Qui Tam*, 11 Wash. Law. 24, 27 (Sept./Oct. 1996). *See also* Dan McGuire & Mac Scheider, *Health Care Fraud*, 44 Am. Crim. L. Rev. 633, 674–79 (2007).

166. Devine & Maassarani, *supra* note 21, at 101.

167. U.S. Dep't of Justice Release, *Justice Department Recovers over $3 Billion from False Claims Act Cases in Fiscal Year 2019* (Jan. 9, 2020), https://www.justice.gov/opa/pr/justice-department-recovers-over-3-billion-false-claims-act-cases-fiscal-year-2019; U.S. Dep't of Justice Release, *Justice Department Recovers Nearly $6 Billion from False Claims Act Cases in Fiscal Year 2014* (Nov. 20, 2014), http://www.justice.gov/opa/pr/justice-department-recovers-nearly-6-billion-false-claims-act-cases-fiscal-year-2014.

168. Callahan & Dworkin, *supra* note 153, at 334–35.

169. Ethics Resource Center, *Reporting: Who's Telling You What You Need to Know, Who Isn't, and What You Can Do About It*, at 15 (2013), http://www.ethics.org/page/nbes-supplemental-research-briefs#sup6.

170. 31 U.S.C. § 3730(h) (2000); *see also* Timothy P. Olson, *Taking the Fear out of Being a Tattletale: Whistle Blower Protection under the False Claims Act and Neal v. Honeywell, Inc.*, 44 DePaul L. Rev. 1363 (1995).

171. 26 U.S.C. § 7623 (2014).

172. 15 U.S.C. § 78u-6 (2014).

173. 7 U.S.C. § 26 (2014).

174. U.S. Sec. & Exch. Comm'n, *2019 Annual Report to Congress on the Dodd Frank Whistleblower Program*, https://www.sec.gov/files/sec-2019-annual%20report-whistleblower%20program.pdf.

175. 17 C.F.R. 240 21-F-4 § (b)(4)(iii–v), (c)(3).

176. California False Claims Act, Cal. Gov't Code §§ 12650 *et seq.* (2007); Florida False Claims Act, Fla. Stat. Ann. §§ 68.081–68.092 (2007); Illinois Whistleblower Reward and Protection Act, 740 Ill. Comp. Stat. Ann. §§ 175/1 *et seq.* (2007). All three statutes provide anti-retaliation provisions: Cal. Gov't Code § 12653; Fla. Stat. Ann. § 68.088; 740 Ill. Comp. Stat. Ann. § 175/4(g).

177. *See, e.g.*, Arkansas Medicaid Fraud False Claims Act, Ark. Code Ann. §§ 20-77-901 *et seq.* (2005); Connecticut Health Insurance Fraud Act, Conn. Gen. Stat. Ann. §§ 53-440 *et seq.* (2007); Tennessee Medicaid False Claims Act, Tenn. Code Ann. §§ 71-5-181 *et seq.* (2007). Utah has a "False Claims Act" relating to medical benefits that does not provide for a qui tam action, Utah Code Ann. §§ 26-20-1 *et seq.* (2007).

178. S.C. Code Ann. § 8-27-20(B) (2006).

179. *See, e.g.*, 43 PA. CONS. STAT. §§ 1422 *et seq.* (2007); W. VA. CODE §§ 6C-1-2 *et seq.* (2007); *see also* Callahan & Dworkin, *supra* note 153, at 279.

180. WISC. STAT. ANN. § 230.83(2) (2007).

181. *See* LIONEL J. POSTIC, WRONGFUL TERMINATION: A STATE-BY-STATE SURVEY (BNA Books 1994) (providing a compilation of information on wrongful termination for each state plus very useful charts); Deborah A. Ballam, *Employment-at-Will: The Impending Death of a Doctrine*, 37 AM. BUS. L.J. 653 (2000); Richard A. Lord, *The At-Will Relationship in the 21st Century: A Consideration of Consideration*, 58 BAYLOR L. REV. 707 (2006).

182. *See, e.g.*, Bompey et al., *supra* note 25, at 19–21; JAMES N. DERTOUZOS ET AL., THE LEGAL AND ECONOMIC CONSEQUENCES OF WRONGFUL TERMINATION 5–7 (The Institute for Civil Justice—Rand 1988); Kenneth G. Dau-Schmidt & Timothy A. Haley, *Governance of the Workplace: The Contemporary Regime of Individual Contract*, 28 COMP. LAB. L. & POL'Y J. 313, 344–45 (2007).

183. *See* Rachel Leiser Levy, *Judicial Interpretation of Employee Handbooks: The Creation of a Common Law Information-Eliciting Penalty Default Rule*, 72 U. CHI. L. REV. 695 (2005).

184. LEX K. LARSON, 1 UNJUST DISMISSAL § 3.04[3](a–d) (Lexis Nexis 2007).

185. *See* RESTATEMENT (SECOND) OF THE LAW OF CONTRACTS § 90; Bompey et al., *supra* note 25, at 35–36; LARSON, *supra* note 184, at § 304[1].

186. *See* POSTIC, *supra* note 181; PERRITT, *supra* note 22, at § 6.29, at 388–89; RESTATEMENT (SECOND) OF THE LAW OF CONTRACTS § 205.

187. *See* SILVER, *supra* note 147, at 390–91; PERRITT, *supra* note 22, at § 6.61, at 469–72.

188. 174 Cal. App. 2d 184, 344 P.2d 25 (1959).

189. *Id.* at 188, 344 P.2d at 27.

190. *Id.*

191. *Id.*

192. *Id.* at 188–89, 344 P.2d at 27–28.

193. John Deguiseppe, Jr., *The Recognition of Public Policy Exceptions to the Employment-at-Will Rule: A Legislative Function?* 11 FORDHAM L. REV. 722 (1982).

194. *See* LARSON, *supra* note 184, at § 6.02.

195. New York is a prime example. *See* Horn v. N.Y. Times, 100 N.Y.2d 85, 90–94 (2003) (describing the development of New York's view that substantial changes to the nature of the employment relationship are to be made by the legislature).

196. LARSON, *supra* note 184, at § 6.02; STEPHEN M. KOHN & MICHAEL D. KOHN, THE LABOR LAWYER'S GUIDE TO THE RIGHTS AND RESPONSIBILITIES OF EMPLOYEE WHISTLEBLOWERS 40 (Greenwood Press 1988).

197. *See, e.g.*, LARSON, *supra* note 184, at § 6.02; Green v. Ralee Engineering Co., 19 Cal. 4th 66, 76 (1998).

198. WESTMAN, *supra* note 7, at 81.

199. *Id.* at 102.

200. *Id.* at 113.

201. *Id.* at 108.

202. *See, e.g.*, Harney v. Meadowbrook Nursing Ctr., 784 S.W.2d 921, 922 (Tenn. 1990); Green v. Ralee Eng'g Co., 19 Cal. 4th 66, 71 (1998).

203. *See, e.g.*, Palmateer v. Int'l Harvester Co., 85 Ill. 2d 124, 132; 421 N.E.2d 876, 879 (1981).

204. *Id.* at 132, 421 N.E.2d at 880.

205. *See, e.g.*, Geary v. U.S. Steel Corp., 456 Pa. 171, 319 A.2d 174 (1974); Campbell v. Eli Lilly & Co., 413 N.E.2d 1054 (Ind. App. 1980); Ryan v. Underwriters Labs., Inc., 2007 U.S. Dist. LEXIS 58452, 17–18, 2007 WL 2316474 (S.D. Ind. 2007).

206. *See, e.g.*, WESTMAN, *supra* note 7, at 112; Wagner v. City of Globe, 150 Ariz. 82, 89; 722 P.2d 250, 257 (1986).

207. WESTMAN, *supra* note 7, at 105–07, 113–55.

208. PERRITT, *supra* note 22, § 2.40 at 175.

209. *See* SILVER, *supra* note 147, at 428; PERRITT, *supra* note 22, at § 2.40.

210. U.S. CONST. art. VI.

211. PERRITT, *supra* note 22, at §§ 2.39–2.43, at 168–82; SILVER, *supra* note 147, at § 20.18.

212. *See, e.g.*, 43 Pa. Stat. § 1422; S.C. Code Ann. § 8-27-10(5); W. Va. Code § 6C-1-2(h).
213. *See, e.g.*, Conn. Gen. Stat. § 31-51m.
214. *See* Silver, *supra* note 147, § 20.5 at 403; Seymour Moskovitz, *Employment-At-Will & Codes of Ethics: The Professional's Dilemma*, 23 Val. U.L. Rev. 33, 56–66 (1988).
215. *See, e.g.*, Rocky Mount. Hosp. & Med. Serv. v. Mariam, 916 P.2d 519, 526 (Colo. 1996) (examining the legislative endorsement of the Colorado State Board of Accountancy rules).
216. For example, the New York Lawyer's Code of Professional Responsibility Disciplinary Rules have been adopted as court rules. 22 N.Y.C.R.R. §§ 1200 *et seq.*
217. *See, e.g.*, Wright v. Shriners Hosp., 412 Mass. 469, 589 N.E.2d 1241, 1244 (1992); Schodolski v. Michigan Consolidated Gas Co., 412 Mich. 692, 316 N.W.2d 710, 712 (1982); Sullivan v. Mass. Mutual Life Ins., 802 F. Supp. 716, 727 (D. Conn. 1992); McGrane v. Reader's Digest Ass'n, Inc., 863 F. Supp. 183, 185 (S.D.N.Y. 1994).
218. *See* Rocky Mount. Hosp. & Med. Serv. v. Mariani, 916 P.2d 519, 524–25 (Colo. 1996).
219. Gantt v. Sentry Ins., 1 Cal. 4th 1083, 4 Cal. Rptr. 2d 874, 881, 824 P.2d 680, 687 (1992); Firestone Textile Co. Div. v. Meadows, 666 S.W.2d 730, 733 (Ky. 1983); Brockmeyer v. Dunn & Bradstreet, 113 Wisc. 2d 561, 335 N.W.2d 834, 840 (1983); Horn v. N.Y. Times, 100 N.Y.2d 85 (2003). The boundary is not inflexible. In *Green v. Ralee Engineerring Co.*, 78 Cal. Rptr. 2d 16 (1998), disclosing violations of federal safety regulations was held sufficient for the public policy exception. Some minority precedent does not require a legislative base. *See, e.g.*, Payne v. Rozendaal, 520 A.2d 586 (Vt. 1986).
220. Rocky Mount. Hosp. & Med. Serv. v. Mariani, 916 P.2d 519, 524–25 (Colo. 1996).
221. *See, e.g., id.* at 528 (holding the Colorado State Board of Accountancy Rules of Professional Conduct to be a source of public policy for purposes of a claim of wrongful discharge).
222. *See, e.g.*, Pierce v. Ortho Pharmaceutical Corp., 84 N.J. 58, 417 A.2d 505, 512 (1980) (stating that "[i]n certain instances a professional code of ethics may contain an expression of public policy," but holding that under the circumstances of the case the Hippocratic oath did not contain a clear mandate of public policy that prevented the doctor's research).
223. *See, e.g.*, Kalman v. Grand Union Co., 183 N.J. Super. 153, 443 A.2d 728 (1982).
224. *See, e.g.*, Sullivan v. Mass. Mutual Life Ins. Co., 802 F. Supp. 716, 727 (D. Conn. 1992) (stating that because ethical codes in the securities industry are promulgated by private groups they do not have the force of law and cannot establish public policy).
225. *See, e.g.*, Wieder v. Skala, 80 N.Y.2d 628, 593 N.Y.S.2d 752, 609 N.E.2d 105 (1992) (limiting its holding to a specific "core" disciplinary rule); McGonagle v. Union Fidelity Corp., 383 Pa. Super. 223, 556 A.2d 878, 885 (1989); General Dynamics v. Super. Ct., 7 Cal. 4th 1164, 876 P.2d 487, 32 Cal. Rptr. 2d 1 (1994).
226. *See* Westman, *supra* note 7, at 91.
227. Model Rules of Pro. Conduct r. 1.6(a). *But see* Model Rules of Pro. Conduct r. 1.6(b)(3) (permitting a lawyer to reveal past criminal conduct if doing so would "prevent, mitigate or rectify substantial injury to the financial interests or property of another that is reasonably certain to result or has resulted from the client's commission of a crime or fraud in furtherance of which the client has used the lawyer's services").
228. Model Rules of Pro. Conduct r. 1.6(b)(1)–(3).
229. Model Rules of Pro. Conduct r. 3.3(a)(3), (b), (c).
230. Even though a lawyer's knowledge of a client's past criminal act gained in the course of the representation is normally privileged, there is an uncodified exception known as the crime-fraud exception. Courts have held that the privilege can be overridden if a client has used the lawyer's services to further the client's criminal or fraudulent acts. *See, e.g.*, United States v. Zolin, 491 U.S. 554 (1989); *In re* Grand Jury Investigation, 445 F.3d 266, 274 (3d Cir. 2006).
231. Model Rules of Pro. Conduct r. 8.4(a), (b), (c).
232. Model Rules of Pro. Conduct r. 1.16.
233. *See, e.g.*, Fracasse v. Brent, 6 Cal. 3d 784, 100 Cal. Rptr. 385, 494 P.2d 9 (1972).
234. *See* Model Rules of Pro. Conduct r. 1.16(a)(3) and cmt. 4.

235. MODEL RULES OF PRO. CONDUCT r. 1.16(b).
236. MODEL RULES OF PRO. CONDUCT r. 1.13(a).
237. *Id.* at r. 1.13(a) cmts. 1 and 2.
238. *Id.* at r. 1.13.
239. *See* MODEL RULES OF PRO. CONDUCT r. 1.13(b) and cmt. 4;
240. MODEL RULES OF PRO. CONDUCT r. 1.13(b).
241. *See* Stephen Gillers, *Model Rule 1.13(c) Gives the Wrong Answer to the Question of Corporate Counsel Disclosure*, 1 GEO. J. LEGAL ETHICS 289, 299 (1987).
242. AMERICAN BAR ASSOCIATION, REPORT OF THE TASK FORCE ON CORPORATE RESPONSIBILITY, 1 (2003), http://www.abanet.org/leadership/2003/journal/119b.pdf. The amendments to Model Rule 1.13 were intended to complement the Sarbanes-Oxley Act of 2002, P.L. 107–204, and rules adopted by the Securities and Exchange Commission (SEC) regulating the conduct of lawyers "appearing and practicing" before it. Those rules, promulgated under Section 307 of the Sarbanes-Oxley Act and codified at 17 C.F.R. Part 205, require lawyers to report material violations of the securities laws and other violations to the highest corporate authority, and they also permit lawyers to disclose such violations to outside authorities in order to prevent substantial injury to the corporation. AMERICAN BAR ASSOCIATION, REPORT OF THE TASK FORCE ON CORPORATE RESPONSIBILITY 2 (2003). For a good examination of whistleblowing under the Sarbanes-Oxley Act, *see* STEPHEN M. KOHN, MICHAEL D. KOHN, & DAVID K. COLAPINTO, WHISTLEBLOWER LAW: A GUIDE TO LEGAL PROTECTIONS FOR CORPORATE EMPLOYEES (Praeger 2004). *See also* MICHAEL DELIKAT, UNDERSTANDING DEVELOPMENTS IN WHISTLEBLOWER LAW 3 YEARS AFTER SARBANES-OXLEY (Practicing Law Institute 2006).
243. MODEL RULES OF PRO. CONDUCT r. 1.13(c).
244. *Id.* at (c)(2).
245. GEOFFREY C. HAZARD, JR., & W. WILLIAM HODES, 1 THE LAW OF LAWYERING §§ 17.2 to 17-8 (3d ed. 2006).
246. *See* Paula Schaefer, *Overcoming Noneconomic Barriers to Loyal Disclosure*, 44 AM. BUS. L.J. 417 (2007).
247. MODEL RULES OF PRO. CONDUCT r. 1.16(b). Subsections (2), (3), (4), and (7) may be particularly relevant to an in-house counsel wishing to resign rather than disclose corporate wrongdoing. Those sections provide for permissive withdrawal when the client "persists in a course of action involving the lawyer's services that the lawyer reasonably believes [to be] criminal or fraudulent"; "has used the lawyer's services to perpetrate a crime or fraud"; "insists upon taking action that the lawyer considers repugnant or with which the lawyer has a fundamental disagreement;" or for other good cause.
248. Schaefer, *supra* note 246.
249. AMERICAN BAR ASSOCIATION, REPORT OF THE TASK FORCE ON CORPORATE RESPONSIBILITY 9 (2003), http://www.abanet.org/leadership/2003/journal/119b.pdf.
250. AMERICAN BAR ASSOCIATION, REPORT OF THE TASK FORCE ON CORPORATE RESPONSIBILITY 10 (2003), http://www.abanet.org/leadership/2003/journal/119b.pdf.
251. MODEL RULES OF PRO. CONDUCT r. 1.16(d).
252. *See* AMERICAN BAR ASSOCIATION, REPORT OF THE TASK FORCE ON CORPORATE RESPONSIBILITY 4 (2003), http://www.abanet.org/leadership/2003/journal/119b.pdf (noting that "our system of corporate governance has long relied upon the active oversight and advice of the key participants in the corporate governance process, including the counsel to the corporation. Corporate responsibility and sound corporate governance thus depend upon the active and informed participation of independent advisers who act vigorously in the best interest of the corporation and are empowered to exercise their responsibilities effectively").
253. *See* CHARLES W. WOLFRAM, MODERN LEGAL ETHICS §§ 6.5.1–6.5.4 (1986).
254. MODEL RULES OF PRO. CONDUCT r. 1.16(b).
255. *See* LARSON, *supra* note 184, § 7.29, at 7-87 to 7-91.
256. MODEL RULES OF PRO. CONDUCT r. 1.16(b), for cases recognizing professional ethics rules as a source for the public policy exception to the at-will doctrine.

257. Balla v. Gambro, Inc., 145 Ill. 2d 492, 584 N.E.2d 104 (1991). The court relied heavily on the earlier Illinois case of Herbster v. North American Co. for Life & Health Ins., 150 Ill. App. 3d 21, 501 N.E.2d 343 (1986).
258. Balla v. Gambro, Inc., 584 N.E.2d at 107.
259. *Id.* at 107–08.
260. In 1991, the Illinois version of Rule 1.6(b) stated that a lawyer "shall reveal" as compared to the Model Rules' version of Rule 1.6(b), which states that a lawyer "may" reveal such information. Today this mandate appears in Illinois Rule 1.6(c).
261. Balla v. Gambro, Inc., 584 N.E.2d at 109.
262. *Id.*
263. *See* Damian Edward Okasinski, Annotation, *In House Counsel's Right to Maintain Action for Wrongful Discharge*, 16 A.L.R. 5th 239 (1993); Restatement (Third), The Law Governing Lawyers, § 32, Reporter's Notes, cmt. b (2000) (citing cases on the availability of retaliatory discharge claims for lawyer employees).
264. *See, e.g.*, Mourad v. Automobile Club Ins. Assn., 186 Mich. App. 715, 465 N.W.2d 395 (1991); General Dynamics v. Super. Ct., 7 Cal. 4th 1164, 876 P.2d 487, 32 Cal. Rptr. 2d 1 (1994).
265. Nordling v. Northern States Power Co., 478 N.W.2d 498, 502 (Minn. 1991).
266. General Dynamics v. Super. Ct., 7 Cal. 4th 1164, 876 P.2d 487, 32 Cal. Rptr. 2d 1 (1994).
267. *Id.* at 1170–71, 876 P.2d at 490.
268. *Id.* at 1171, 876 P.2d at 491.
269. *Id.* at 1177, 876 P.2d at 495.
270. *Id.*
271. *Id.* at 1179, 876 P.2d at 496.
272. *Id.* at 1180, 876 P.2d at 497.
273. *Id.* at 1181–82, 876 P.2d at 498.
274. *Id.* at 1187, 876 P.2d at 501 (emphasis in original).
275. *Id.* at 1188–89, 876 P.2d at 501–02.
276. *Id.* at 1189, 876 P.2d at 502–03 (emphasis in original).
277. *Id.* at 1189, 876 P.2d at 503.
278. *Id.* at 1190–91, 876 P.2d at 503–04.
279. *Id.* at 1190–91, 876 P.2d at 504.
280. *Id.*
281. *See* Rodd B. Lape, *General Dynamics Corp. v. Superior Court: Striking a Blow for Corporate Counsel*, 56 Ohio St. L.J. 1303, 1320 (1995).
282. *See, e.g.*, Heckman v. Zurich Holding Co. of America, 242 F.R.D. 606 (D. Kan. 2007); Hoffman v. Baltimore Police Dep't, 379 F. Supp. 2d 778 (D. Md. 2005); Meadows v. Kindercare Learning Centers, 2004 U.S. Dist. LEXIS 20450, 2004 WL 2203299 (D. Or. 2004); O'Brien v. Stolt-Nielson Transp. Grp., 838 A.2d 1076, 48 Conn. Supp. 200 (Conn. Super. 2003); Crews v. Buckman Labs Int'l, Inc., 78 S.W.3d 852 (Tenn. 2002); Burkhart v. Semitool, Inc., 5 P.3d 1031, 300 Mont. 480 (2000).
283. *See* Brett Lane, *Blowing the Whistle on Balla v. Gambro: The Emergence of an In-House Counsel's Cause of Action in Tort for Retaliatory Discharge*, 29 J. Legal Prof. 235 (2004–2005).
284. Model Rules of Pro. Conduct r. 8.3(a) and (c).
285. *See* Model Rules of Pro. Conduct r. 5.1.
286. *See* Model Rules of Pro. Conduct r. 5.2; ABA Inf. Op. 1203 (1972); ABA Inf. Op. 1203 (1972).
287. Andrew Seger, *Marching Orders: When To Tell Your Boss 'No'*, 87 Fla. Bar J. 37 (Feb. 2013).
288. *Id.*
289. *Id.*; ABA Inf. Op. 1203 (1972).
290. Russell Yerk, *When Does Another Lawyer's Unethical Conduct Become Your Problem?* For The Defense 37 (Oct. 2013).

291. Law firm partners can also become involved in whistleblower incidents. *See* Amy Boardman, *Whistleblower Seeks One More Hearing*, Legal Times 2 (Sept. 16, 1996).

292. *See* Parker v. M&T Chemicals, Inc., 236 N.J. Super. 451, 566 A.2d 215 (1989) (providing an example of a state whistleblower protection statute being applied to allow damages for wrongful discharge of in-house counsel).

293. Weider v. Skala, 80 N.Y.2d 628, 609 N.E.2d 105, 593 N.Y.S.2d 752 (1992).

294. *Weider*, 80 N.Y.2d at 633, 639. *See also* Horn v. N.Y. Times, 100 N.Y.2d 85 (2003); Sabetay v. Sterling Drug, 69 N.Y.2d 329, 506 N.E.2d 919, 514 N.Y.S.2d 209 (1987); Murphy v. American Home Products Corp., 58 N.Y.2d 293, 301, 448 N.E.2d 86, 461 N.Y.S.2d 232 (1983); Robert LaBerge et al., *Employment Law*, 44 Syracuse L. Rev. 243, 262–69 (1993).

295. Wieder v. Skala, 80 N.Y.2d at 633.

296. In *Weiner v. McGraw-Hill Inc.*, 57 N.Y.2d 458, 443 N.E.2d 441, 457 N.Y.S.2d 193 (1982), the court had provided for an exception to the at-will rule premised on an express limitation found in the language of the employer's personnel handbook.

297. Wieder v. Skala, 80 N.Y.2d at 635–36.

298. *Id.* at 636.

299. *Id.* at 636–37.

300. *Id.* at 637.

301. *Id.* at 638–39.

302. *See* Sandra J. Mullings, *Wieder v. Skala: A Chink in the Armor of the At-Will Doctrine or a Lance for Law Firm Associates?*, 45 Syracuse L. Rev. 963, 964 (1995). *See also* Rojas v. Debevoise & Plimpton, 167 Misc. 2d 451, 634 N.Y.S.2d 358 (N.Y. Sup. Ct. 1995) (providing an example of when a lawyer did not have an implied-in-fact contract action because she was not required to subvert the core purpose of the employment).

303. McGrane v. Reader's Digest Ass'n., Inc., 822 F. Supp. 1044, 1049 (S.D.N.Y. 1993).

304. *Id.* at 1049; *see* Mullings, *supra* note 302, at 994.

305. 17 C.F.R. § 240.21F-4 (b)(4)(1, 11) (2014).

306. Van Arsdale v. Int'l Game Tech., 577 F.3d 989, 994–96 (9th Cir. 2009).

307. 15 U.S.C. § 7245.

308. Stephen Gillers, *Model Rule 1.13(c) Gives the Wrong Answer to the Question of Corporate Counsel Disclosure*, 1 Geo. J. Legal Ethics 289, 294 (1987).

309. *See id.* at 294–95.

310. Wolfram, *supra* note 253, at § 13.9.2 at 757.

311. *See* Chapters 2 and 12 of this text for detailed discussions of the issue of who is the client for the government lawyer. *See also* Model Rules of Pro. Conduct r. 1.13, cmt. 9.

312. *See* Kathleen Clark, *Do We Have Enough Ethics in Government Yet? An Answer from Fiduciary Theory*, 1996 U. Ill. L. Rev. 57, 66 (1996). A number of federal agencies have adopted the American Bar Association's Model Rules or Model Code of Professional Responsibility by regulation. ABA Committee on Government Standards (Cynthia Farina, reporter), *Keeping Faith: Government Ethics & Government Ethics Regulation*, 45 Admin. L. Rev. 287, 290, 334 (1993) [hereinafter *Keeping Faith*].

313. *Conflicts of Interest in the Legal Profession*, 94 Harv. L. Rev. 1244, 1414 (1981).

314. *See* Geoffrey P. Miller, *Government Lawyers' Ethics in a System of Checks and Balances*, 54 U. Chi. L. Rev. 1293 (1987).

315. Cramton, *supra* note 42, at 294.

316. 5 U.S.C. § 552 (2000); *see* Wolfram, *supra* note 253, at § 6.5.6.

317. Cramton, *supra* note 42, at 295.

318. 18 U.S.C. § 1905 (2000) (providing for fines, imprisonment, and removal from office for improper disclosure of confidential information).

319. "The 'civil service' consists of all appointive positions in the executive, judicial, and legislative branches of the Government of the United States, except positions in the uniformed services." 5 U.S.C. § 2101 (2000).

320. Exec. Order No. 11222.

321. The Department of Justice Manual, vol. 1 at Title 1-37 (2d ed. 2007) (emphasis added).

322. *See* Cramton, *supra* note 42, at 303.
323. 5 U.S.C. § 2302(b)(8) (2000).
324. Cramton, *supra* note 42, at 301; *see* Wolfram, *supra* note 253, at § 13.9.2.
325. *Keeping Faith*, *supra* note 312, at 334.
326. *See* Cramton, *supra* note 42, at 303–04; Model Rules of Pro. Conduct r. 3.1.
327. *See* Miller, *supra* note 314, at 1294.
328. Cramton, *supra* note 42, at 305–06.
329. 5 U.S.C. § 2302(a)(2)(D).
330. *Id.* § 2302(b)(8) (2000).
331. *Id.*
332. *See* Model Rules of Pro. Conduct r. 1.13, cmt. 10 (discussing the situation where the organization's interests become adverse to interests of its constituents).
333. Cramton, *supra* note 42, at 303.
334. *Id.*
335. *Id.*
336. 5 U.S.C. § 2302(b)(8)(B) (2000).
337. *Id.* § 2302(b)(8)(A); *see also* Cramton, *supra* note 42, at 308.
338. *See* Cramton, *supra* note 42, at 309.
339. *Id.*
340. *Id.* at 312.
341. *Id.*
342. *Id.*
343. *Id.* at 314.

# CHAPTER 12

Lobbying Ethics
Heather Holt

> This chapter surveys federal, state, and local lobbying laws in regard to registration, disclosure, prohibited conduct, and enforcement.

BACKGROUND

There is a well-loved American legend that traces the concept of "lobbyist" to President Ulysses S. Grant. It claims that President Grant invented the moniker to refer to the people who would corner him in the lobby of the Willard Hotel in Washington D.C. (while he tried to enjoy a brandy, a cigar, and a respite from formal duties) to petition him for favors.[1] While President Grant may certainly have used the term, he also certainly did not invent it. The Oxford English Dictionary notes that the word "lobby" dates to at least 1640, when it was used to describe a place where members of the House of Commons and members of the public could meet to discuss matters.[2] And even the American use of "lobby" as a verb significantly predates President Grant's 1869 inauguration.[3]

Regardless of how the term originated, it is a concept as old as government itself. The founders of American democracy—tired of being ignored by King George III—protected the right "to petition government for the redress of grievances" in the First Amendment of the United States Constitution, right alongside freedom of speech.[4] The concept of a governed person's right to petition the government for assistance is much older than that, however, and the right to redress is even included in the Magna Carta of 1215.[5]

Protecting the right to petition government is a powerful way to help ensure that every person who is taxed by government may be heard by government. It also helps to ensure that public officials make fair and informed decisions.

> One of the risks of representative democracy is that elected officials may favor the narrow partisan interests of their most powerful supporters, or choose to advance their own personal interests instead of viewing themselves as faithful agents of their constituents. A robust right to petition is designed to minimize such risks. By being forced to acknowledge and respond to petitions from ordinary persons,

officials become better informed and must openly defend their positions, enabling voters to pass a more informed judgment.[6]

This petitioning of government is premised on an individual's right to make her own personal interests known. Lobbying as we know it is related but different, in that it refers to individuals who are paid to make other people's interests known. One of the earliest American lobbyists was William Hull, a former military officer who was hired in 1792 by Revolutionary War veterans to seek additional pay for their war service.[7]

Lobbyists can and do help individuals and organizations effectively communicate their views to government decision makers. They can thereby help to improve outcomes for a community as a whole.

> [L]obbying . . . plays an important role in our democracy. It is a way for citizens (including those who run businesses as well as those who lead citizen groups) to get their opinions heard by government officials; it is a way to educate government officials and the public; and it is a way to provide specialized expertise to government.[8]

What's more, lobbying is here to stay. According to OpenSecrets.org, there have been more than 10,000 registered lobbyists in Washington D.C. every year since 1999.[9] In addition, lobbying is big business. The health industry has spent more than $10 billion on federal lobbying efforts since 1998.[10] That tops the list, but even the industry coming in at 11th place (construction) has spent more than $1 billion.[11] And that's just federal lobbying. Billions more are spent on lobbying conducted at state and local levels.

But lobbying poses complicated ethical issues. As noted, it is a vital and protected part of our democratic form of government and can be used for great good. It is also, however, easily susceptible to corruption and, perhaps more importantly, the public's perception of corruption. Whether any particular lobbyist is engaging in unethical behavior or not, the general consensus leans toward an assumption that special interests with enough funding to hire lobbyists have special access to decision makers and are unfairly pulling strings to the detriment of the average voter. The concern, as Governor Andrew Cuomo of New York has been quoted as saying, is that "[t]oo often, government responds to the whispers of lobbyists before the cries of the people."[12] And it is a worldwide concern. Jacob Rees-Mogg, British Member of Parliament who serves as Leader of the House of Commons and Lord President of the Council, is said to have made the following statement:

> Lobbying has become a term of reproach, as if it were improper to push for a particular belief. This has happened because of paid lobbyists whose opinions are for hire and the fear that decision-makers, whether politicians or officials, are susceptible to their charms and wiles. This has tarred entirely proper lobbying with the same brush.[13]

To balance the right to petition government with the public's grievances regarding actual or perceived lobbying abuses, the federal government, all 50 states, and many local jurisdictions have adopted laws to regulate lobbying and lobbyists. The laws are not intended to eliminate or even limit lobbying activity but, instead, to shed light on the methods employed and the money infused into efforts to sway government decisions. They acknowledge that both lobbying and the regulation of lobbying are good for public policy. In a series of speeches to the Senate regarding its powers and functions, Senator Robert C. Byrd (D–West Virginia) stated the following:

> Congress has always had, and always will have, lobbyists and lobbying. We could not adequately consider our work load without them. . . . At the same time, the history of the institution demonstrates the need for eternal vigilance to ensure that lobbyists do not abuse their role, that lobbying is carried on publicly with full publicity, and that the interests of all citizens are heard without giving special ear to the best organized and most lavishly funded.[14]

The federal government's first comprehensive set of lobbying laws was the Federal Regulation of Lobbying Act of 1946, which was replaced by the Lobbying Disclosure Act of 1995.[15] The act states that "responsible representative Government requires public awareness of the efforts of paid lobbyists to influence the public decision making process . . . [and] the effective disclosure of the identity and extent of the efforts of paid lobbyists to influence Federal officials in the conduct of Government actions will increase public confidence in the integrity of Government."[16] While each jurisdiction's lobbying law is unique, these statements of purpose form the general basis for the regulation of lobbying at all levels of government.

Texas addresses the competing interests at play in the regulation of lobbying head-on by stating the following:

> The operation of responsible democratic government requires that the people be afforded the fullest opportunity to petition their government for the redress of grievances and to express freely their opinions on legislation, pending executive actions, and current issues to individual members of the legislature, legislative committees, state agencies, and members of the executive branch. To preserve and maintain the integrity of the legislative and administrative processes, it is necessary to disclose publicly and regularly the identity, expenditures, and activities of certain persons who, by direct communication with government officers, engage in efforts to persuade members of the legislative or executive branch to take specific actions.[17]

The Maine legislature has elegantly stated the purpose of its lobbying regulations. It "reaffirms its obligation to hear the requests and opinions of all the people, and to preserve and maintain the integrity and accessibility of the legislative process."[18] The legislature goes on to state, "Legislative decisions can fully reflect the will of all the people only if the opinions expressed by any citizen are known to all and debated by all, and if the representatives of groups of citizens are identified and their expenditures and activities are regularly disclosed."[19]

DEFINITIONS

As with most laws, foundational definitions in the regulation of lobbying are critical. There are two fundamental questions in the lobbying arena. The first is "What is lobbying?" and the second is "Who is a lobbyist?"

Lobbying

The concept of what constitutes "lobbying" is probably the most homogenous among all lobbying laws. While every jurisdiction defines it slightly differently, lobbying is essentially engaging in activity that is designed to influence government action, whether legislative or administrative.[20]

Illinois succinctly defines lobbying as "any communication with an official of the executive or legislative branch of State government for the ultimate purpose of influencing any executive, legislative, or administrative action."[21] Florida takes a slightly more expansive view by including attempts to influence both action and "nonaction," as well as attempts to "obtain the goodwill of a member or employee of the Legislature."[22] Oregon and Vermont also include attempts to obtain goodwill in their definitions.[23]

Some jurisdictions include public outreach in their concept of lobbying. The thinking is that, while a person may not be directly communicating with a public official to influence government action, the person may be spending money to encourage third parties to communicate; and the public is entitled to know about efforts to influence the government through others. At least six jurisdictions define "lobbying" to include "soliciting others to communicate" with public officials.[24] West Virginia refers to it as grass-roots lobbying, and San Francisco refers to it as "expenditure" lobbying.[25] It is not considered lobbying in Los Angeles, but a person who spends at least $5,000 in a quarter on public outreach in an attempt to influence city action is required to disclose that activity.[26]

Lobbyist

The second foundational question is "Who is a lobbyist?" More precisely, this asks who has met the qualification threshold in a particular jurisdiction and must, therefore, register as a lobbyist and publicly disclose lobbying activity.

At the most fundamental level, a lobbyist is an individual who communicates with a public official in an attempt to influence government action. In California, for example, lobbyists are those who "communicate directly or through his or her agents with any elective state official, agency official, or legislative official for the purpose of influencing legislative or administrative action."[27] Maine eliminates reference to communications through agents and requires an individual to communicate directly with a public official before regulation is triggered.[28] New York state addresses communication through social media.[29] And North Carolina treats candidates for office as public officials who may be lobbied.[30]

However, not every act of attempting to influence a government action will trigger registration or reporting requirements. Typically, an individual must be entitled to receive compensation for an attempt to influence action on behalf of another person in order to qualify as a lobbyist.[31] This means that individuals who petition government as volunteers (for a favorite charity, for example) or on their own behalf (such as for a zoning variance for a personal residence) are not generally regulated as lobbyists.[32] This hearkens back to and protects the First Amendment right to petition government.[33]

At least 14 jurisdictions specify compensation thresholds that must be met before registration is required.[34] The thresholds vary widely, depending on each jurisdiction's determination of what rises to the level of disclosable lobbying activity. For example, the threshold is $250 per quarter in Idaho and ten times higher than that in Pennsylvania.[35]

Some jurisdictions have registration thresholds that are not dollar values. In San Francisco, the threshold is the number of contacts with public officials. Their threshold is five contacts in a month for in-house lobbyists and one contact in a month for all other lobbyists.[36] Still other jurisdictions count the number of hours a person engages in lobbying activity. In Hawaii, the threshold is more than five hours in a month or more than ten hours in a year.[37] The threshold is more than eight hours in a month in Maine and more than ten hours in a 30-day period in Alaska.[38] In Los Angeles, the threshold is 30 hours and at least one lobbying communication with a public official in a consecutive three-month period.[39]

Although "lobbyist" is typically the term used to refer to an individual who has met the jurisdiction's qualification criteria, other terms are also used. In New Jersey, this individual is referred to as a "governmental affairs agent."[40] A lobbyist in Massachusetts may be either a "legislative agent" or an "executive agent."[41] And Michigan and Ohio call these individuals "lobbyist agents."[42]

There are often stated exceptions to the general definitions. The city of Los Angeles, for example, exempts government employees acting in their official capacities, media outlets that publish editorials, persons whose only activity is participating in a competitive bid process (unless they attempt to influence the Mayor, a City Council member, or their staffs), persons engaged in collective bargaining between the city and a recognized city employee organization (unless they attempt to influence the Mayor, a City Council member, or their staffs), and 501(c)(3) organizations that receive government funding and whose primary purpose is to represent indigent clients free of charge.[43] Seattle exempts lobbyists who engage in lobbying on no more than four days in a calendar quarter.[44] Other common exemptions include parties to quasi-judicial or enforcement actions (and their attorneys), individuals communicating on the public record, educational and religious institutions, union members acting on behalf of the union, political committees and their employees or contractors, and individuals serving on advisory bodies.[45]

It is important to highlight that the law is not based on a professional title—a lobbyist may have a business card that reads "CEO" or "Executive Director" or "Industrial Specialist" or "Government Affairs Consultant." Instead, the law is based on conduct. If you engage in activity that is regulated and meets your jurisdiction's qualification threshold, you are a lobbyist for purposes of that jurisdiction's requirements, regardless of your title. However, because of the negative connotations that may attach to lobbying (and the federal government's limitation on such activity for nonprofit organizations), there may be some reluctance to be classified as a lobbyist.

It is also important to note that the legal requirements are different in every jurisdiction. For some, this is good news. A nonprofit organization may qualify as a lobbying entity under a city law, for example, without necessarily endangering its tax-exempt status. For others, this is less good news. A company that is urging regional transportation reform could be required to navigate city, county, state, and federal laws—all of them unique and possibly complex.

Client

A third term used in lobbying laws is one that identifies the person on whose behalf lobbying is undertaken—or who pays for lobbying. That person is often referred to as a "client," including in this chapter.[46] However, other labels may be used. In at least 18 jurisdictions, the client is called a "principal."[47] And in at least 11 others, the client is referred to as a "lobbyist employer."[48] In Connecticut and Michigan, the client is, interestingly, called a "lobbyist."[49]

REGISTRATION

Once a qualification threshold is met, registration is required. Lobbyists and lobbying firms must identify themselves to the jurisdiction and the public. In some jurisdictions, clients must also register.[50]

Content

The content of registration statements varies, but—in keeping with the goal of informing the public about who is lobbying—registrants must universally disclose their names, contact information, and clients. Registrants are also typically required to disclose the government agencies that they will be lobbying and the issues regarding which they will be lobbying.[51] The general purpose or industry of a client that is a business or organization may also need to be identified.[52]

Some jurisdictions require additional registration information. For example, at least 13 jurisdictions require lobbyists to provide a written statement from each client that the lobbyist is authorized to represent, confirming the representation.[53] In Alaska, Indiana, and Tennessee, a lobbyist must disclose a spouse, domestic partner, or other relative who is a public official in the jurisdiction.[54] In Wisconsin and Indiana, lobbyists must provide their social security numbers.[55]

Timing

The date by which registration is required also varies from jurisdiction to jurisdiction. Registration is often required before any lobbying activity is undertaken. For example, prior registration is required in Virginia, unless all of the individual's lobbying activity occurs entirely outside the capital city. In that case, registration is required within 15 days after first engaging in lobbying.[56] Geography does not matter in at least 17 other jurisdictions, which prohibit an individual from engaging in any activity as a lobbyist before registering.[57]

In other jurisdictions, registration is required within a certain length of time. Typically, the deadline ranges from 3 days to 15 days after lobbying activity first begins or an individual qualifies as a lobbyist.[58] Los Angeles has an unusually long deadline of ten days after the end of the calendar month in which qualification occurs.[59]

Identification

The registration process may also include requirements designed to make it clear to public officials and others who is being paid to advocate. For example, at least ten jurisdictions, including Alaska, California, Illinois, Louisiana, Massachusetts, Pennsylvania, San Francisco, Tennessee, Vermont, and Washington, require lobbyists to provide recent photographs of themselves.[60] Lobbyist photos and biographical descriptions must be published on the website of Washington's public disclosure commission.[61]

Other jurisdictions impose name tag or badge requirements. Connecticut, for one, requires lobbyists to wear a "distinguishing badge" that identifies them as lobbyists.[62] Those who lobby the Maine or South Dakota legislatures must wear name tags that clearly display the individual's name and either the name of the individual's client or the term "lobbyist."[63] New Jersey and North Dakota also impose general badge or name tag requirements.[64]

Other jurisdictions are more precise about their requirements. For example, Kansas requires a name tag that is at least two inches by three inches, with identifying information readable at a distance of three feet.[65] New Hampshire's name tag is slightly smaller, at one and a half inches by two and a half inches, and its information must be in white letters on a "hunter orange" background.[66]

The secretary of state in Rhode Island is required to issue an identification badge for every lobbyist. The badge must include the lobbyist's name and registration number, as well as the word "lobbyist" in bold print, and the lobbyist is required to conspicuously display the badge while lobbying in a state government building.[67] In New Jersey and South Dakota, lobbyists must wear a name tag whenever engaged in lobbying.[68] In Utah, the name tag must be worn when lobbying in the capitol complex.[69]

Fees

In addition to disclosing information about themselves and possibly wearing identification badges, lobbying registrants are usually required to pay a registration fee. This helps the jurisdiction cover the costs of regulation. In most jurisdictions, registration terminates at the end of the calendar year and fees are, therefore, imposed annually.[70] Registration is annual in North Dakota, but it follows a fiscal year and runs from July 1 to June 30.[71]

In other jurisdictions, a lobbying registration is good for two years. In Kentucky and Oregon, for example, registration ends on December 31 of odd-numbered years.[72] And in Montana, New York state, Pennsylvania, and Utah, registration ends on December 31 of even-numbered years.[73]

Among jurisdictions that impose a flat fee by statute, the fee ranges from $10 per lobbyist in Idaho to $1,000 per lobbyist in Massachusetts.[74] Perhaps in recognition of the constitutional right to petition government, at least 20 states impose flat statutory fees of $100 or less, with Georgia and Oregon charging no fee at all.[75]

In other jurisdictions, such as Los Angeles, Nebraska, North Dakota, San Diego, Vermont, West Virginia, and Wisconsin, the registration fee increases with each client.[76] Still others set fees non-legislatively, such as through rulemaking or action by an ethics commission.[77]

Occasionally, the registration fee is reduced for organizations that are tax-exempt under section 501(c)(3) of the Internal Revenue Code and their employees. This is true in the District of Columbia, Indiana, and Texas, which specify their reduced fees by statute.[78] In Massachusetts, it is permissive—the organization may request a wavier and a wavier may be granted.[79] A waiver is mandatory in San Francisco for an organization with an annual operating budget of no more than $500,000.[80]

DISCLOSURE

In the spirit of transparency and accountability that undergirds lobbying laws, registered lobbyists and other lobbying entities are required to periodically disclose their lobbying activity. As with registration requirements, the content of a disclosure report is tailored to each jurisdiction. The frequency of reporting also varies.

Content

A jurisdiction must first determine what information must be disclosed. A key purpose of disclosure is to inform the public of how money is used to advance lobbying efforts. Every state requires disclosure of expenses related to lobbying, and some even refer to their disclosure reports as "expenditure" reports or statements.[81] All but a handful of states require filers to disclose all lobbying expenditures incurred during the reporting period. The handful that don't require global expense reporting do require the reporting of gifts, meals, or entertainment provided to public officials.[82] In at least 12 jurisdictions, filers must also disclose their campaign contributions—money that is tied to lobbying but infused into the election system.[83]

Another key purpose of disclosure is to inform the public of what issues are being lobbied. Filers in at least 29 jurisdictions are required to identify the issues for which lobbying took place or for which lobbying expenses were incurred.[84] Six jurisdictions, including the District of Columbia, Georgia, New York state, Rhode Island, San Diego, and San Francisco, also require filers to identify the public officials they lobbied.[85]

Wisconsin requires disclosure of the amount of time spent on lobbying, which must include a daily itemization of time for all compensated individuals, except for clerical staff and non-lobbyist staff who spend fewer than ten hours engaged in lobbying during the reporting period.[86]

In Maryland, lobbyists must disclose five days in advance a meal or reception that they put on for all the members of the legislature. They must then report the total cost of the event and each sponsor who contributed toward the cost.[87]

Frequency

In addition to determining the content of lobbying disclosure, jurisdictions must also determine the frequency. The more frequent the reporting, the better equipped the public is to make connections between money spent on lobbying efforts and government decisions—and to decide whether they want to communicate their own views to decision makers. Reporting is done in arrears, which means that lobbying activity that must be reported on a quarterly basis may not be disclosed for more than three months after it occurred. An issue can certainly be decided within that amount of time and, if it were, the general public would not know that lobbying had taken place until after it was too late to offer other viewpoints.

On the other hand, more frequent reporting may feel burdensome to those who must report. A lobbying firm with multiple lobbyists working on behalf of multiple clients, for example, could be required to submit many pages of information with each disclosure statement. Such a firm can probably employ one or more people to handle the paperwork, but that is an additional expense. And while sole practitioners may have less to report in absolute terms, it may not be less reporting proportionally. In addition, they may not be able to afford an employee who handles the reporting for them. They may wish or need to spend their regular work hours engaged on behalf of their clients, in which case they must work off hours to comply with a reporting requirement.

Most commonly, reporting is required on a quarterly basis.[88] However, there are a number of other reporting schedules, including annually,[89] semi-annually,[90] monthly,[91] and even semi-monthly.[92]

In some states, the clients who hire lobbyists are required to file reports—sometimes instead of their lobbyists and sometimes in addition to them.[93] Client reporting that is required in addition to lobbyist reporting can be a very effective enforcement tool that provides either corroboration of or questions about the accuracy of information disclosed about lobbying activity. The most common reporting schedule for clients is annual or semi-annual.[94] However, quarterly client reporting is required in six states.[95] And Rhode Island requires clients to report eight times per year.[96]

Identification

Some disclosure requirements apply in real time, rather than to after-the-fact written reports. The name tags and badges discussed in the previous section are one form of real-time disclosure. Some jurisdictions also impose an affirmative duty to identify oneself. For example, a lobbyist in North Carolina, Oklahoma, or Utah must inform a public official of the client's identity at the beginning of a lobbying communication.[97] Similarly, the client's name must be provided in testimony before the legislatures in Maine and North Dakota.[98] In other jurisdictions, the disclosure requirement is more passive, such as in Pennsylvania, where a lobbyist cannot refuse to identify the client when a public official asks who it is.[99]

PROHIBITIONS

Although the regulation of lobbyists and lobbying entities is not designed to limit their ability to engage in lobbying, it often does limit their ability to engage in other activities. As with disclosure requirements, these restrictions are designed to help guard against actual or perceived abuse and are often tied to money.

Generally

Many jurisdictions prohibit activity that can be viewed as underhanded, such as deceiving a public official regarding a material fact related to a government decision, attempting to create a false appearance of public sentiment regarding a proposed action, influencing the introduction of legislation for the purpose of being employed to secure the legislation's passage or defeat, and exerting undue influence over a public official.[100] Montana generally prohibits "any unprofessional conduct" on the part of both lobbyists and clients.[101] Pennsylvania prohibits lobbyists and clients from engaging in "conduct which brings the practice of lobbying or the legislative or executive branches of State government into disrepute."[102]

Other jurisdictions incorporate more precise prohibitions, perhaps borne out of the jurisdiction's specific history. The Colorado legislature has adopted a rule that prohibits lobbyists from, among other things, filing frivolous complaints against other lobbyists, misappropriating state office supplies, using copying machines without paying, entering a public official's office without permission, and removing a document from a public office without permission.[103] Illinois prohibits sexual harassment and, as part of the registration process, requires lobbying entities to confirm that they have sexual harassment policies.[104] In Tennessee, neither a lobbyist nor a client may permit a candidate for elected office or a public official to use a credit card controlled by the lobbyist or client.[105]

Several states prohibit lobbyists from being on the floor of a legislative body while the body is in session.[106] In a few states, appearing on the floor is acceptable when the lobbyist has received an invitation to do so.[107]

Some jurisdictions also impose prohibitions on clients. In Florida and Arkansas, no one may compensate anyone other than a lobbying firm for lobbying activity.[108] In Washington and West Virginia, the prohibition is against paying or *agreeing to pay* consideration for lobbying to a person who is not registered.[109]

Contingency Fees

Another frequently prohibited activity is providing representation or hiring someone under a contingency fee arrangement. At least 41 jurisdictions prohibit contingency fees.[110] When a contingency or "success" fee is employed, a lobbyist is paid only when a government decision is made in the client's favor. These types of payments are prohibited in order to eliminate the pressure for a lobbyist to succeed. If there is no financial reward unless you obtain a winning result, it may be very tempting to use any means necessary to reach a client's goal.

By prohibiting contingency fees, jurisdictions communicate to their constituents that they are accessible and impartial—not subject to embellishment from or undue influence by a lobbyist who is under pressure. And there may be serious repercussions for entering into contingency fee arrangements. In Kentucky, for example, a client who pays a contingency fee regarding a government contract is barred from doing business with the commonwealth for five years.[111]

North Carolina requires the forfeiture of payments made to lobbyists under a contingency arrangement.[112] Florida also requires the forfeiture of contingency fees but goes further by imposing criminal misdemeanor liability.[113]

Minnesota and Pennsylvania have made it a misdemeanor to accept a contingency fee.[114] In Michigan, it is a felony subject to imprisonment for up to three years and a monetary penalty of up to $10,000 (or $25,000 if the violator is not an individual).[115]

Governmental Ethics

Regulation in the lobbying world intersects with governmental ethics issues. For example, some jurisdictions address conflicts of interests by prohibiting lobbyists from representing a position adverse to a client's position without notifying or obtaining permission from the client.[116] Other jurisdictions address conflicts by prohibiting lobbyists from serving as employees or other decision makers within the jurisdiction.[117] Typically, the ban lasts for one year, but it's as short as 120 days in North Carolina and as long as two years in Kentucky.[118] The ban applies to both lobbyists and their immediate family members in West Virginia, which prohibits their participation in any decision that could result in a direct, personal economic or pecuniary benefit.[119]

Jurisdictions also commonly prohibit or limit gifts that are offered or made by lobbying entities. This is designed to help avoid the perception that government decisions are not made on the merits. Even a good decision can be tainted if a gift was exchanged and it appears that the decision was influenced by special favors.

To that end, Los Angeles, Michigan, and New York City ban gifts from lobbyists.[120] Lobbyists and clients are prohibited from providing a gift to a public official or the public official's family member in Connecticut, Nevada, and Tennessee.[121] In Oklahoma, lobbyists and clients are prohibited from making gifts, unless the gift is specifically permitted, such as a single item valued at $10 or less, "modest" items of food and non-alcoholic beverages, or a gift of up to $100 for an infrequent special occasion.[122]

Lobbyists and clients in New York state are prohibited from offering or making a gift to a public official or the official's spouse or unemancipated child.[123] In addition, the spouse or unemancipated child of a lobbyist or client may not offer or make a gift to a public official if it is reasonable to infer that the gift was intended to influence the official.[124]

Jurisdictions that permit gifts typically limit their value, and the limits take on a myriad of forms. Utah limits gifts to no more than $10 per day, California and San Diego limit them to no more than $10 per month, and Arizona limits them to $10 per year.[125]

Lobbyists in Nebraska may not give gifts totaling more than $50 per month to a public official or a member of the public official's family.[126] Oregon prohibits gifts totaling more than $50 in a calendar year to either a public official, a relative of the public official, or a member of the public official's household.[127] And Indiana prohibits individual gifts valued at $50 or more to a member of the legislature unless, prior to making the gift, the lobbyist informs the member of the cost of the gift and receives the member's consent to make the gift.[128]

New Jersey prohibits gifts totaling more than $250 per year to a public official or a member of a legislator's immediate family who lives in the legislator's household.[129] Gifts cannot exceed $500 per year in Texas.[130] In some jurisdictions, the gift limit extends also to clients, such as in Minnesota, Nebraska, New York, and North Carolina.[131]

There are typically exceptions to the definition of "gift," so it may be possible for a lobbyist to give a public official something of value without violating a law. California, for example, has a lengthy list of exceptions, which includes items received from immediate family members or from a person with whom the recipient is in a bona fide dating relationship, an inheritance, a bereavement offering for the passing of an immediate family member, benefits received as a guest at a wedding or civil union, two tickets from a nonprofit organization for its own fundraising event, and acts of neighborliness or human compassion.[132] Food or beverage valued at $15 or less per occasion is not a gift in New York state,[133] and neither are promotional items, plaques or awards that are presented publicly, or honorary degrees.[134] Items given in an exhibitor hall of a conference sponsored by a recognized organization of public officials is not a gift in Tennessee.[135] Another common exception exists for items of value that are not used and are either returned to the giver or donated to a charitable organization (without claiming a tax deduction).[136]

Campaign Finance

Lobbying regulations can also intersect with campaign finance laws, in that a number of jurisdictions prohibit campaign contributions from lobbying entities.[137] In Colorado, Kentucky, Minnesota, Nevada, New Mexico, Texas, and Vermont, contributions from lobbyists and clients are prohibited when the general assembly is in regular session.[138] And when a contribution is permitted in Minnesota, the lobbyist's unique registration number must be included with any campaign contribution the lobbyist makes.[139]

In New Mexico, contributions are prohibited from January 1 prior to a regular session of the legislature until up to 20 days after the close of the session.[140] In addition, New Mexico lobbyists are prohibited at all times from serving as a chairman, treasurer, or fundraising chair for a candidate.[141] A similar prohibition against serving as a treasurer or other office of a candidate committee applies to lobbyists in Kentucky, Maryland, New Mexico, South Carolina, and Pennsylvania.[142] In Maryland, a lobbyist cannot engage in fundraising for candidates, including soliciting contributions, delivering contributions, and serving on a fundraising committee.[143]

In Tennessee, lobbyists are prohibited from making campaign contributions to any candidate for elective office at any time.[144] Their clients are prohibited from making campaign contributions to legislative or gubernatorial candidates when the general assembly is in session.[145]

PUBLIC OFFICIALS

In addition to the individuals and entities trying to persuade public officials to take certain actions, the public officials, themselves, are often subject to regulation in the lobbying arena. San Francisco's Sunshine Ordinance, for example, requires the mayor, the city attorney, and each department head to keep a public calendar of all meetings related to city business and to identify the meeting's time and location and the issues discussed.[146] This is a broad requirement but certainly applies to meetings with lobbyists.

Public officials in some jurisdictions are explicitly prohibited from being lobbyists at the same time that they hold a public office.[147] It is also common for jurisdictions to impose cooling off periods, during which individuals who leave public service cannot lobby the jurisdiction. The typical cooling off period is one year,[148] but Montana and South Dakota impose a two-year cooling off period.[149] South Carolina applies its one-year cooling off period not just to its former public officials but also to their immediate family members.[150]

Public officials can also be prohibited from soliciting or accepting gifts from lobbyists.[151] Members of the U.S. House of Representatives and their staffs may not accept a gift of any value from a lobbyist.[152] In Nevada, the prohibition applies to legislators and members of their families.[153] Wisconsin applies the prohibition to both public officials and candidates for elected office.[154] Rather than a ban, Nebraska limit its public officials to no more than $50 per month in gifts from a lobbyist.[155]

Similar to a ban on soliciting gifts, members of the Vermont legislature may not solicit campaign contributions from lobbyists when in session.[156] Minnesota candidates cannot accept more than 20 percent of their campaign contributions from lobbyists.[157]

Requirements imposed on regulating agencies are also common. The requirements revolve around disclosure and helping to ensure that constituents and public officials know who is engaging in lobbying. For example, a jurisdiction's ethics commission or secretary of state may be required to post or publish the jurisdiction's lobbyists and clients.[158] A regulatory agency may also be required to report on lobbying activity. The ethics commission in Pennsylvania is required to post all lobbying filings online within seven days and to publish an annual report on lobbying activities.[159] Reports on the financial activities of lobbyists are required of the Maryland Ethics Commission and Mississippi's secretary of state.[160]

When the General Assembly is in session, Virginia's secretary of the commonwealth must provide a complete list of the information in each lobbyist registration statement to each member of the General Assembly every two weeks.[161] The secretary must also prepare a list of all public officials, by position and name, semi-annually and make that list available to lobbyists.[162]

In Tennessee, the ethics commission must post lobbyists and clients and also all subject matters lobbied.[163] The Tennessee commission is also required to audit up to 4 percent of lobbyist registration and disclosure statements each year.[164] In Pennsylvania, the secretary of the commonwealth must hire a CPA every two years to audit three percent of the registration statements and disclosure reports and determine whether they are materially correct.[165]

ENFORCEMENT

Governmental ethics laws, in general, codify aspirations. They describe the world as a particular community believes it should be. However, if they are to be truly effective, the laws cannot be simply aspirational. There must be consequences for those who fail to comply with the law. Violations must be enforced against, not only to hold violators accountable but also to assure the public that government is seriously pursuing the world as we believe it should be and to dissuade others from becoming violators, themselves.

This is as true for lobbying as it is for any other governmental ethics issue. To that end, jurisdictions that regulate lobbying have enforcement provisions for those who violate those regulations. In most jurisdictions, enforcement is administrative or civil. For example, the Texas Ethics Commission, the Los Angeles City Ethics Commission, and the San Francisco Ethics Commission may impose monetary penalties up to the greater of $5,000 or three times the amount of money at issue.[166] In Washington, administrative penalties of up to $10,000 may be imposed for violating a lobbying law.[167]

However, enforcement may also enter the criminal arena. In Ohio, failing to register, file a disclosure statement, or maintain expenditure receipts is a fourth-degree misdemeanor, subject to a penalty of up to 30 days' incarceration and a $250 fine.[168] Filing a false registration or disclosure report is a first-degree misdemeanor, subject to a penalty of up to 180 days' incarceration and a $1,000 fine.[169]

An intentional or knowing violation of the lobbying laws in Texas is generally a Class A violation of the state's prohibition against contingency fee arrangements is a third-degree felony, which may be punished by imprisonment for two to ten years and a fine of up to $10,000.[170]

The attorney general is responsible for enforcing the lobbying laws in Vermont and may seek civil penalties in superior court, up to $10,000 plus $1,000 per day for a continuing violation.[171] The attorney general is also required to post online each complaint and its resolution.[172]

Violating the lobbying laws in Colorado is a misdemeanor that can result in imprisonment for up to 12 months and a fine of up to $5,000.[173] In addition, the secretary of state may file for an injunction in district court when it appears that a person is *about* to violate the lobbying laws.[174]

Debarment

In some jurisdictions, there are repercussions for violations that extend beyond financial penalties or jail time and may prevent an individual from engaging in lobbying at all. For example, the Texas Ethics Commission may rescind or deny the lobbying registration of a person who is convicted of a criminal violation of the lobbying laws regarding conflicts.[175] In Pennsylvania, an individual may not register as a lobbyist for up to five years for violating the lobbying laws.[176] In Utah, a one-year debarment is imposed for violating the lobbying laws or criminally threatening legislators or disrupting meetings, and a five-year debarment is imposed for convictions related to bribery and altering legislation.[177]

Similarly, an individual who is convicted of criminally violating a lobbying law in Los Angeles may not act as a lobbyist for one year, and a civil court may prohibit an individual who intentionally violated a lobbying law from acting as a lobbyist for one year.[178] In addition, a person may not act as a lobbyist or lobbying firm in Los Angeles for four years if the ethics commission determines that the person engaged in political money laundering.[179]

In Oklahoma, a person who violates the lobbying laws three or more times is barred from engaging in lobbying activity for five years. Furthermore, engaging in lobbying activity while debarred is a felony.[180]

In Ohio, an individual cannot register as a lobbyist if the individual has committed felony bribery, intimidation, retaliation, theft, or corruption in Ohio—or an equivalent law in *any* local, state, or federal jurisdiction.[181] This prohibition is a lifetime ban.[182]

Other conduct may also preclude lobbying activity. In Wisconsin, an individual may not be licensed as a lobbyist if the person is delinquent on taxes, child support, or unemployment insurance contributions.[183] And a lobbying registration in Tennessee will be denied or revoked if the registrant has defaulted on a student loan.[184]

Late Fees

Late fees can be imposed, in addition to administrative and criminal penalties, for failing to file registration or disclosure statements in a timely way. In Illinois, the late fee is $50 for a report that is up to 15 days late and $150 for a report that is more than 15 days late.[185] Indiana imposes late fees of $100 per day up to $4,500.[186]

The late fee in Louisiana is $50 per day. In Massachusetts, the $50-per-day fee applies to the first 20 days past the filing deadline, and an additional $100 per day is imposed for every day beyond 20.[187] There is no cap on the amount of late fees in either jurisdiction.

Georgia takes late filings very seriously and imposes a fee of $10,000 for reports that are not filed within 21 days of the deadline when the General Assembly is in session.[188] A similarly serious approach exists in Seattle, where late fees in the 30 days prior to an election are $250 to $1,000 per day, with no cap.[189]

New York state extends leniency to first-time filers and reduces their late fees by 50 percent.[190]

Training

In light of the potentially significant penalties that can be imposed for violating a lobbying law, it is essential that those who are regulated understand that they are subject to the laws, how to comply with the laws, and why complying is important. This is particularly true because of the fact that individuals who qualify as lobbyists might have very different professional titles and not see themselves as such. To that end, it can be very beneficial to impose a training requirement.

Training is mandatory for lobbyists in California, Illinois, Los Angeles, Massachusetts, New York state, and New York City.[191] In Alaska, lobbyists must complete the training *prior* to registration, and both lobbyists and clients must take a training course annually.[192] In Tennessee and Utah, lobbyists must complete an ethics course annually.[193] In West Virginia, lobbyists must complete a training course prior to engaging in lobbying and every two years thereafter.[194] In Maryland and Los Angeles, training is required within six months of registering and every two years thereafter.[195]

Rhode Island requires the secretary of state to "[p]repare and publish educational materials."[196] Interestingly, the North Carolina Ethics Commission must create an educational program, but there is no corresponding requirement that lobbyists participate in the program. North Carolina's public officials, however, must complete the training within six months of being hired and every two years thereafter.[197]

Roberta Baskin, an award-winning journalist who is the former executive director of the Center for Public Integrity and the current executive director for AIM2Flourish, has been quoted as saying, "Lobbying is like the fourth branch of government. It's a very powerful part of our government and our democracy."[198] Lobbying can also be viewed as an *essential* part of our participatory form of government. But, as Senator Byrd noted, guarding against undue influence by special interests is also essential.[199] Balancing these important public interests is a critical function of legislative bodies, and regulatory schemes that both preserve the right to lobby and curb conduct by those involved in lobbying abound in a myriad of forms across the country.

SUMMARY OF KEY POINTS

- Lobbying poses complicated ethical issues. It is a vital and protected part of our democratic form of government, but it is susceptible to actual and perceived corruption. To protect public interests and promote transparency, the federal government, every state, and many local jurisdictions regulate lobbying.
- Regulators must define what constitutes lobbying and who qualifies as a lobbyist. Typically, a minimum threshold of compensation or contacts triggers a requirement to register with the jurisdiction and publicly disclose activity.
- Registration and reporting requirements vary by jurisdiction; but all require lobbyists to identify themselves and their clients, and most require the payment of registration fees. Periodic disclosure of lobbying activity, such as the money spent and the matters lobbied, is also typically required.
- Those who must register and report are often held to high ethical standards and may be subject to limits on activities such as giving gifts to public officials or making campaign contributions to candidates for elected office.

- Lobbying laws may impose late filing penalties and may include civil or administrative enforcement provisions.
- Training is key to helping the public and regulated parties understand who is subject to the lobbying laws, how to comply with them, and why complying is important.

NOTES

1. *Pittsburgh Post-Gazette* (Pittsburgh, PA), May 3, 1998; *see also* washington.intercontinental.com/history/.
2. *The Origins of "Lobbyist"*, Merriam-Webster Word History (merriam-webster.com/words-at-play/the-origins-of-lobbyist).
3. *See, e.g., The Evening Post* (New York, NY), Feb. 6, 1826 ("While this one lobby member from Dutchess was electioneering for this bill, three or four Albanians were lobbying in favor of a tow boat incorporation for this city.").
4. U.S. Const., amend. I; *see also* John Inazu & Bret Neuborne, *Right to Assemble and Petition*, Constitution Center, constitutioncenter.org/blog/interactive-constitution-right-to-assemble-and-petition.
5. *Magna Carta*, Chapter III, clause 61; *see* nationalarchives.gov.uk/education/medieval/magna-carta/index.php?page=source/3/9; *see also* Inazu & Neuborne, *supra* note 4.
6. Inazu & Neuborne, *supra* note 4.
7. Peter Grier, *The Lobbyist through History: Villainy and Virtue*, Christian Science Monitor, Sept. 28, 2009; Senator Robert C. Byrd (D, WV), speech to Congress September 28, 1987.
8. Robert Wechsler, *The Regulation of Local Lobbying* 2 (Feb 21, 2016).
9. *See* www.opensecrets.org/lobby/ (last visited May 10, 2022).
10. *See* www.opensecrets.org/lobby/top.php?showYear=a&indexType=i (last visited May 10, 2022).
11. *Id.*
12. brainyquote.com/authors/andrew-cuomo-quotes.
13. brainyquote.com/authors/jacob-rees-mogg-quotes.
14. Speech to Congress, Sept. 28, 1987.
15. 2 U.S.C. ch. 26.
16. 2 U.S.C. § 1601.
17. Tex. Gov. Code § 305.001.
18. Me. Rev. St. tit. 3 § 311.
19. *Id.*
20. *See, e.g.*, Ala. Code § 26-25-1(20); Ariz. Rev. Stats. § 41-1231(11)(a); Colo. Rev. Stat. § 24-6-301(3.5)(a); Iowa Code § 68B.2(13)(a); L.A. Muni. Code § 48.02; Kan. Stat. § 46-225(a); Ky. Rev. Stat. § 6.611(26)(a); La. Stat. § 24:51(4)(a); Mich. Comp. Laws § 4.415(2); Mont. Code § 5-7-102(11); Neb. Rev. Stat. § 49-1433; N.Y.C. Admin. Code § 3-211(c); N.Y. Legis. Law § 1-c(c); Seattle Muni. Code § 2.06.010(J); Tenn. Code § 3-6-301(15)(A); Utah Code § 36-11-102(13); W.Va. Code § 6B-3-1(6).
21. 25 Ill. Comp. Stat. § 170/2.
22. Fla. Stat. Ann. § 11.045.
23. Or. Rev. Stat. Ann. § 171.725; Vt. Stat. § 2-261(9)(c).
24. Ark. Code § 21-8-402; Conn. Gen. Stat. § 1091(11); Haw. Rev. Stat. § 97-1; R.I. Gen. Laws § 42-139.1-3(3); Vt. Stat. § 2-261(9)(B); Va. Code § 2.2-419.
25. S.F. Camp. and Gov. Cond. Code § 2.105; W. Va. Code § 6B-3-5.
26. L.A. Muni. Code §§ 48.02, 48.08(E).
27. Cal. Gov. Code § 82039(a)(1).
28. Me. Rev. Stat. tit. 3, § 312-A.

29. 19 N.Y. Code Rules and Regs. § 943.6(c).
30. N.C. Gen. Stat. § 120C-104.
31. *See, e.g.*, Ala. Code § 36-25-1(21)(b)(4); Conn. Gen. Stat. § 1-91(12); Fla. Stat. § 11.045(1)(g); L.A. Muni. Code § 48.02; Miss. Code § 5-8-3(I)(i); N.H. Rev. Stat. tit. I, § 15:1(I); N.M. Stat. § 2-11-2(E); N.C. Gen. Stat. § 163A-250(a)(19); Or. Rev. Stat. § 171-725; 65 Pa. Stat. and Cons. Stat. § 13A03; Seattle Muni. Code § 2.06.010(L); Va. Code § 2.2-419; Wis. Stat. § 13.62(11).
32. *See, e.g.*, N.D. Cent. Code § 54-05.1-02(2)(b); Wis. Stat. § 13.621(6)(a); *cf.* Colo. Rev. Stat. § 24-6-301(7).
33. *See* Wyo. Stat. § 28-7-101.
34. Ark. Code § 21-8-402; Cal. Gov. Code § 82039(a)(1); Conn. Gen. Stat. § 1-91; Ga. Code § 21-5-70(5); Haw. Rev. Stat. § 97-1; Ind. Code § 2-7-1-9; Md. Gen. Provis. § 5-702(a); Minn. Stat. § 10A.01(21)(a)(1); Mich. Comp. Laws 4.415; Mont. Code § 5-7-112; N.Y. Legis. Law § 1-e(a)(4); Or. Rev. Stat. § 171.725(9)(a); Tex. Gov. Code § 305.003; Wyo. Stat. § 28-7-101.
35. Idaho Code § 67-6618(c); 65 Pa. Stat. and Cons. Stat. 13A06(4).
36. S.F. Camp. and Gov. Cond. Code § 2.105.
37. Haw. Rev. Stat. § 97-1.
38. Alaska Stat. § 24.45.171(11)(A); Me. Rev. Stat. tit. 3, § 312-A.
39. L.A. Muni. Code § 48.02.
40. N.J. Stat. § 52:13C-20(g).
41. Mass. Gen. Laws tit. I, ch. 3 § 39; *see also* Ky. Rev. Stat. § 6.611(23)(a).
42. Mich. Comp. Laws § 4.415(5); OH § 101-70(F).
43. L.A. Muni. Code §§ 48.02, 48.03.
44. Seattle Muni. Code § 2.06.060(A0(2).
45. *See, e.g.*, Ariz. Rev. Stat. § 41-1232.04; Cal. Gov. Code § 86300(c); D.C. Code § 1-1161.01; 25 Ill. Comp. Stat. § 170/3(a); Ind. Code § 2-7-2-6; Md. Gen. Provis. § 5-702(b); Mo. Stat. § 105.475(2); N.C. Gen. Stat. § 120C-700(8); 65 Pa. Stat. and Cons. Stat. § 13A06; San Diego Muni. Code § 27.4004; S.F. Camp. and Gov. Cond. Code § 2.106(b); Tex. Gov. Code §§ 305.004, 305.0041.
46. *See* Colo. Rev. Stat. § 24-6-301(1); 25 ILCS § 170/2(m); L.A. Muni. Code § 48.02; Mass. Gen. Laws tit. I, ch. 3 § 39; Miss. Code § 5-8-3(m); Nev. Rev. Stat. § 218H.033; N.Y.C. Admin. Code § 3-211(b); N.Y. Legis. Law § 1-c(b); San Diego Muni. Code § 27-4002; Tex. Gov Code § 305.002(12).
47. Ala. Code § 36-25-19(24); Ariz. Rev. Stat. § 41-1231(16); Fla. Stat. § 11.045(i); La. Rev. Stat. § 24:51(E)(2)(a); Minn. Stat. § 10A.01(33); Mo. Stat. § 105.470(7); Mont. Code § 5-7-102(15); Neb. Rev. Stat. § 49-1434(1); N.C. Gen. Stat. § 120C-100(a)(21); Okla. Stat. § 74E-5.2(9); 65 Pa. Stat. and Cons. Stat. § 13A03; S.C. Code § 2-17-10(17); S.D. Codified Laws § 2-12-15(3); Tenn. Code § 3-6-301(7); Utah Code § 36-11-102(18); Vt. Stat. tit. 2 § 261(4); Va. Code § 2.2-419; Wis. Stat. § 13.62(12).
48. Cal. Gov. Code § 82039.5; Del. Code § 29-5831(a)(3); Ky. Rev. Stat. § 6.611(12); Me. Rev. Stat. tit. 3, § 312-A(5); Mont. Code § 5-7-203; N.M. Stat. § 2-11-2(F); Ohio Rev. Code §§ 101.70(G), 121.60(C); Seattle Muni. Code § 2.06.010(M); Tenn. Code § 3-6-301(8); Vt. Stat. tit. 2, § 261(4); Wash. Rev. Code § 42.17A.005(35); W.Va. Code § 6B-3-1(2).
49. Conn. Gen. Stat. § 1-91(12); Mich. Comp. Laws § 4.415(4).
50. Ariz. Rev. Stat. § 41-1232; Cal. Gov. Code § 86105; Miss. Code Ann. § 5-8-5; Ohio Rev. Code §§ 101.72(A), 121.62(A); 65 Pa. Stat. and Const. Stat. § 13A04; R.I. Gen. Laws § 42-139.1-5; S.C. Code § 2-17-25; Tenn. Code § 3-6-302; Vt. Stat. tit. 2, Ch. 11, § 263(b).
51. *See, e.g.*, Ala. Code § 36-25-18(b)(4); Alaska Stat. § 24.45.041(b)(5); Ariz. Rev. Stat. § 41.1232(A)(8); Chi. Muni. Code § 2-156-230(b)(iii); Conn. Gen. Stat. § 1-95(5); Del. Code § 29-5832(b)(5); D.C. Code § 1-1162.29(b)(1)(D); Idaho Code § 67-6617(e); 25 Ill. Comp. Stat. §§ 170/5(c)-(c.5); Ind. Code § 2-7-2-4(3); Kan. Stat. § 46-265(a); Ky. Rev. Stat. § 6.807(1)(c); Me. Rev. Stat. tit. 3, §§ 316(4-A)-(4-B); Md. Gen. Provis. § 5-704(b)(4); Minn. Stat. § 10A.03(5); Miss. Code § 5-8-5(2)(f); Mont. Code § 5-7-201; Nev. Rev. Stat. § 218H.210(5); N.H. Rev. Stat. § 15:3(I)(e); N.Y. Legis. Law §§ 1-e(c)(5)-(6); N.C. Gen. Stat. § 120C-200(b); Ohio Rev. Code § 101.72(A)(3); Or. Rev. Stat. § 171.740(1)(e); R.I. Gen. Laws §§ 42-139.1-4(b)(2)-(3); S.C. Code § 2-17-20(B)(2); S.D. Codified Laws § 2-12-2; Tenn. Code § 3060392(b)(2)(C); Tex. Gov. Code § 305.005(f)(4); Vt. Stat. Ann. § 2-263(c)(3); Va. Code § 2.2-423(A)(8); W.Va. Code § 6B-3-2(a)(5).

52. *See, e.g.*, Ariz. Rev. Stat. § 41-1232(A)(5); Chi. Muni. Code § 2-156-230(b)(i); D.C. Code § 1-112.29; Ga. Code § 21-5-71(b)(3); Idaho Code 67-6617(b); Ind. Code § 2-7-2-3(2); Ky. Rev. Stat. § 6.807(1)(b); Md. Gen. Provis. § 5-704(b)(3); Mich. Comp. Laws § 4.417(1)(c); Miss. Code § 5-8-5(2)(c); Neb. Rev. Stat. § 49-1480(3); Or. Rev. Stat. § 171.740(1)(c); Utah Code § 36-11-103(1)(c)(ii)(D); Va. Code § 2.2-423(a)(4); Wash. Rev. Code § 41.17A.600(1)(c); W.Va. Code § 6B-3-2(a)(2); Wis. Stat. § 13.64(1).

53. *See* Ala. Code § 36-25-18; CA § 86104(d)(2); Del. Code § 29-5833; Ga. Code § 21-5-71; N.C. Gen. Stat. § 120C-206; N.D. Cent. Code § 54-05.1-03(1)(d); N.Y.C. Admin. Code § 3-213(c)(4); N.Y. Legis. Law § 1-3; Or. Rev. Stat. § 171.740(2); Seattle Muni. Code § 2.06.020(A)(3); S.D. Codified Laws § 2-12-4; Wash. Rev. Code Ann. § 42.17A.600; Wis. Stats. § 13.65.

54. *See* Alaska Stat. Ann. § 24.45.041; Ind. Code Ann. § 2-7-2-4; Tenn. Code Ann. § 2-6-302.

55. Wis. Stats. § 13.63(1)(b); Ind. Code § 2-7-2-3(1).

56. Vir. Code § 22-411(A).

57. Colo. Rev. Stat. § 24-6-303(1); Del. Code § 29-5832(a); Ga. Code § 21-5-71(a)(1); Idaho Code §§ 67-6617(a), 67-6620; Iowa Code § 68B.36(1); Neb. Rev. Stat. § 49-1480; N.H. Rev. Stat. § 15:1(I); N.M. Stat. § 2-11-3; N.D. Cent. Code § 54-05.1-03(a)(a); Nev. Rev. Stat. § 218H.930(5); N.J. Stat. § 52:13C-21.1; Seattle Muni. Code § 2.06.110(A); S.D. Codified Laws § 2-12-5; Tex. Gov. Code § 36-11-103(1)(a); Utah Code § 36-11-103(1)(a); Wash. Rev. Code § 42.17A.655(2)(a); W. Va. Code § 6B-3-7(2)(A).

58. *See, e.g.*, Ala. Code § 36-25-18(a); Cal. Gov. Code § 86101; Chi. Muni. Code § 2-156-230; Haw. Rev. Stat. § 97-2(a); La. Rev. Stat. § 24:53(A); Ky. Rev. Stat. § 6807(a); Me. Rev. Stat. tit. 3; § 313; Mich. Comp. Laws § 4.417(1); Md. Gen. Provis. § 5-704(d)(1); Mo. Stat. § 105.473; Miss. Code § 5-8-5(1); Ohio Rev. Code § 101.72(A); Okla. Stat. § 74-4250(A); Or. Rev. Stat. § 171.740(1); 65 Pa. Stat. and Const. Stat. § 13A04(a); San Diego Muni. Code § 27.0407(a); S.F. Camp. and Gov. Cond. Code § 2.110(a); R.I. Gen. Laws § 42-139.1-4(b); S.C. Code § 2-17-20(A).

59. L.A. Muni. Code § 48.07(A).

60. *See* Alaska Stat. Ann. § 24.45.041; Cal. Gov. Code § 86103; 25 Ill. Comp. Stat. § 170/5; La. Rev. Stat. § 24:53(A)(6); Mass. Gen. Laws tit. I, Ch. 3, § 41; 65 Pa. Stat. and Const. Stat. § 13A04; S.F. Ethics Comm'n Reg. § 2.110-8; Tenn. Code § 3-6-302(a)(3); Vt. Stat. tit. 2, § 263; Wash. Rev. Code § 42.17A.605.

61. Wash. Rev. Code § 42.17A.605.

62. Conn. Gen. Stat. Ch. 10, § 1-101.

63. Me. Rev. Stat. tit. 3 § 327; S.D. Codified Laws § 2-12-8.1.

64. N.J. Stat. § 52:13C-28; N.D. Cent. Code § 54-05.1-03(1)(a).

65. Kan. Stat. § 46-270.

66. N.H. Rev. Stat. § 15:2(I).

67. R.I. Gen. Laws § 42-139.1-4(f).

68. N.J. Stat. § 52:13C-28; S.D. Codified Laws § 2-12-8.1.

69. Utah Code § 36-11-305.5.

70. *See, e.g.*, Ala. Code 36-25-1(a); Ark. Code § 21-8-601; Ga. Code § 21-5-71(d); Idaho Code § 67-6617(4); Ind. Code § 2-7-2-1(a); Kan. Stat. § 46-265(b); L.A. Muni. Code § 48.07(B); Me. Rev. Stat. tit. 3, § 314; Mass. Gen. Laws tit. I, ch. 3, § 41; Miss Code § 5-8-5(3); Mo. Stat. § 105.473(1); Neb. Rev. Stat. § 49-1486; N.J. Stat. § 52:13C-23a; N.M. Stat. § 2-11-3(E); N.Y.C. Admin. Code § 3-213(a)(1); Okla. Stat. § 74-4250; S.F. Camp. and Gov. Cond. Code § 2.110(f); Tex. Gov. Code § 305.005(b); Wyo. Stat. § 28-7-101(b).

71. N.D. Cent. Code § 54-05.1-03(1)(c).

72. Ky. Rev. Stat. § 6.807(2); Or. Rev. Stat. § 171.740(5).

73. Mont. Code § 5-7-103(1); N.Y. Legis. Law § 1-d(a)(3); 65 Pa. Stat. and Cons. Stat. § 13A04(a); Utah Code § 36-11-103(3)(b).

74. *See* Idaho Code § 67-6617; Mass. Gen. Laws Ch. 3, § 41.

75. Ala. Code § 36-25-1(a); Ariz. Rev. Stats. § 41-1232(E); Cal. Gov. Code § 86102(a); Ga. Code § 21-5-71(f)(2)(A); Idaho Code § 67-6617(1); La. Rev. Stat. § 24:53(I); Md. Gen. Provis. § 5-704(e)(1); Miss. Code § 5-8-5(1); Mo. Stat. § 105.473(1); N.H. Rev. Stat. tit. I, § 15:4; N.J. Stat. § 52:13C-23a; N.M. Stat. § 2-11-3(A); N.Y. Legis. Law § 1-e(e); Ohio Rev. Code § 101.72(E);

OKLA. STAT. § 74-4250(A); Or. Rev. Stat. § 171-740; 65 Pa. Stat. and Cons. Stat. § 13A10(a); S.C. CODE § 2-17-20(a); S.D. CODIFIED LAWS § 2-12-3; VA. CODE § 2.2-424; WYO. STAT. § 28-7-101(b).

76. *See, e.g.*, L.A. MUNI. CODE § 48.07(C); NEB. REV. STAT. § 218H.200; N.D. CENT. CODE § 54-05.1-03; SAN DIEGO MUNI. CODE § 27.4010(a); VT. STAT. tit. 2, § 263; W.VA. CODE § 6B-3-3a; WIS. STAT. § 13.75.

77. *See, e.g.*, FLA. STAT. § 11.045; NEV. REV. STAT. § 218H.500; N.J. STAT. § 52:13C-23; S.D. CODIFIED LAWS § 2-12-3; TENN. CODE § 3-6-301.

78. D.C. CODE § 1-1162.27(b)(2); IND. CODE § 2-7-2-1(c)(1); TEX. GOV. CODE § 305.005(c)(1).

79. MASS. GEN. LAWS tit. I, ch. 3, § 41.

80. S.F. ETHICS COMMISSION REG. § 2.110-11.

81. *See, e.g.*, KAN STAT. § 46-268(a); KY. REV. STAT. § 6.821; MISS. CODE § 5-8-9; N.M. STAT. § 2-11-6; N.D. CENT. CODE § 54-05.1-03(2); OHIO REV. CODE § 101.73; OR. REV. STAT. §§ 171-745, 171-750; 65 PA. STAT. AND CONS. STAT. § 13A-5(a); S.D. CODIFIED LAWS § 2-12-11.

82. *See, e.g.*, ALA. CODE § 36-25-19; DEL. CODE § 29-5835(b); N.D. CENT. CODE § 54-05.1-03(2); OKLA. REV. STAT. §§ 74E-5.21, 74E-5.22.

83. *See, e.g.*, CAL. GOV. CODE §§ 86113(a)(2), 86114(a)(7), 86116(g); COLO. REV. STAT. § 24-6-301(1.9)(c); D.C. CODE § 1-1162.30(a)(3); L.A. MUNI. CODE §§ 48.08(B)(6), (C)(8), (D)(9); MD. GEN. PROVIS. § 5-708; MASS. GEN. LAWS tit. I, ch. 3, § 43; N.H. REV. STAT. tit. I, § 15:6(V)(f); N.M. STAT. § 2-11-6(A)(2); R.I. GEN. LAWS § 42-139.1-6(a)(5); S.F. CAMP. AND GOV. COND. CODE § 2.110(c)(1)(H); S.C. CODE § 2-17-35(A)(8); WASH. REV. CODE § 42.17A.615(2)(c).

84. *See, e.g.*, COLO. REV. STAT. §24-6-301(1.9)(a)(X); DEL. CODE § 29-5836(a); D.C. CODE § 1-1162(a)(5a); GA. CODE §§ 21-5-73(3)(1)(D)-(E); HAW. REV. STAT. § 97-3(c)(5); IDAHO CODE § 67-6619(2)(d); 25 ILL. COMP. STAT. § 170/6(b-1); IND. CODE § 2-7-3-3(a)(4); LA. REV. STAT. § 24:55(D)(1)(a); ME. REV. STAT. tit. 3, § 317(1)(H); MD. GEN. PROVIS. §§ 5-704(b)(4), 705(b)(1); MASS. GEN. LAWS tit. I, ch. 3, § 43; MICH. COMP. LAWS § 4.418(1)(d); MO. STAT. § 105.473(12); MONT. CODE § 5-7-208(5)(d); NEB. REV. STAT. § 49-1488; N.J. STAT. § 52:13C-22(c)(1); N.Y. LEGIS. LAW § 1-h(b)(3); OHIO REV. CODE § 101.73(B)(2)(e); 65 PA. STAT. AND CONS. STAT. § 13A05(b)(1); R.I. GEN. LAWS § 42-139.1-6(a)(6); SAN DIEGO MUNI. CODE §§ 27.4017(a)(2)(B), (b)(2)(A), (c)(3); S.F. CAMP. AND GOV. COND. CODE § 2.110(c)(1)(D); SEATTLE MUNI. CODE 2.06.030(B)(4); S.C. CODE §§ 2-17-30(A)(3), 2-17-35(A)(3); TEX. GOV. CODE § 305.006(d); UTAH CODE §§ 36-11-201(g)-(h); WASH. REV. CODE § 42.17A.615(2)(d); W.VA. CODE § 6B-3-4(e).

85. D.C. CODE § 1-1162.30(a)(5); GA. CODE § 21-5-73(e)(1)(A); N.Y. LEGIS. LAWS §§ 1-h(b)(4); R.I. GEN. LAWS § 42-139.1-6(a)(7); SAN DIEGO MUNI. CODE §§ 27.4017(a)(2)(C), (b)(2)(B); S.F. CAMP. AND GOV. COND. CODE § 2.110(c)(1)(B).

86. WIS. STAT. § 13.68(1)(c).

87. MD. GEN. PROVIS. § 5-709.

88. *See, e.g.*, CHI. MUNI. CODE § 2-156-250; DEL. CODE § 29-5835; HAW. REV. STAT. § 97-3; L.A. MUNI. CODE § 48.08(A); N.J. STAT. § 52:13C-22; SAN DIEGO MUNI. CODE; § 27.4015; UTAH CODE § 36-11-201.

89. *See, e.g.*, N.D. CENT. CODE § 54-05.1-03; VA. CODE § 2.2-426.

90. *See, e.g.*, IND. CODE § 2-7-3-1; S.C. CODE § 2-17-30.

91. *See, e.g.*, MO. STAT. § 105.473; NEV. REV. STAT. § 218H.400; N.Y.C. ADMIN. CODE § 3-217; S.F. CAMP. AND GOV. COND. CODE § 2.110(c); WASH. REV. CODE § 42.17A.615.

92. *See, e.g.*, CAL. GOV. CODE § 86116; GA. CODE § 21-5-73; MISS. CODE § 5-8-9; N.Y. LEGIS. LAW § 1-h.

93. *See, e.g.*, MONT. CODE § 5-7-208, NEB. STAT. § 49-1483; N.Y. LEGIS. LAW § 1-j; OHIO REV. CODE §§ 101.72(B), 121.62(B); 65 PA. STAT. AND CONST. STAT. § 13A05; R.I. GEN. LAWS § 42-139.1-7; TENN. CODE § 3-6-303; VT. STAT. tit. 2, § 264; WASH. REV. CODE § 42.17A.630; WIS. STATS. §§ 13.67, 13.68.

94. *See, e.g.*, IOWA CODE § 68B.38; N.Y. LEGIS. LAW § 1-j; S.C. CODE § 2-17-35.

95. *See* ALASKA STAT. § 24.45.061; CAL. GOV. CODE § 86115; HAW. REV. STAT. § 97-3; N.C. GEN. STAT. § 120C-403(a); 65 PA. STAT. AND CONS. STAT. § 13A05; OR. REV. STAT. § 171.75.

96. 42 R.I. GEN. LAWS § 42-139.1-7.

97. N.C. GEN. STAT. § 120C-200(3); OKLA. STAT. § 74E-5.27; UTAH CODE § 36-11-305.5(3).

98. ME. REV. STAT. tit. 3 § 319-A; N.D. CENT. CODE § 54-05.1-06(3).

99. 65 Pa. Stat. and Cons. Stat. § 13A07(f)(1)(v).
100. *See, e.g.*, L.A. Muni. Code § 48.04; Cal. Gov. Code § 86205; Colo. Rev. Stat. § 24-6-308; Or. Rev. Stat. §§ 171.756, 171.764; Tex. Gov. Code § 305.021; Wash. Rev. Code § 42.17A.655.
101. Mont. Code § 5-7-302.
102. 65 Pa. Stat. and Const. Stat. § 13A07(f)(1)(x).
103. Joint Rule 136 §§ (b)(5.5)–(9) (Colorado General Assembly 2018).
104. 25 Ill. Comp. Stat. 170/4.7, 170/5.
105. Tenn. Code § 3-6-304.
106. *See, e.g.*, Ga. Code §§ 21-5-76(b), 28-7-4; Ky. Rev. Stat. § 6.811(10); S.C. Code § 217-110(E).
107. *See, e.g.*, S.D. Codified Laws § 2-12-8; Okla. Stat. § 74-4252; Tex. Gov. Code § 305.023.
108. Ark. Code § 21-8-607(a); Fla. Stat. § 11.045(4)(b).
109. Wash. Rev. Code § 42.17A.650; W.Va. Code § 6B-3-6 (exception: on condition that the person register as a lobbyist as soon as possible).
110. *See, e.g.*, Ark. Code § 21-8-607(b)(4); Chi. Muni. Code § 2-156-300; Conn. Gen. Stat. § 1-97(b); Cal. Gov. Code 86205(f); Colo. Rev. Stat. § 24-6-308(1)(a); Del. Code § 29-5834; Fla. Stat. § 112.3217; Fla. Stat. § 11.047; Ga. Code §§ 21-5-76(a), 28-7-3; Haw. Rev. Stat. § 97-5; Idaho Code § 67-6621(2)(f); 25 Ill. Comp. Stat. 170/8; Ind. Code § 2-7-5-5; Kan. Stat. § 46-267; Ky. Rev. Stat. § 6.811(9); Me. Rev. Stat. tit. 3 § 318(I); Md. Gen. Provis. § 5-714(1); Mass. Gen. Laws tit. I, ch. 3, § 42; Mich. Comp. Laws § 4.421(1); Minn. Stat. § 10A.06; Miss. Code § 5-8-13(1); Neb. Rev. Stat. § 49-1492(1); Nev. Rev. Stat. § 218H.930(4); N.J. Stat. § 1-K; N.M. Stat. § 2-11-8; N.C. Gen. Stat. § 120C-300; N.D. Cent. Code § 54-05.1-06(2); N.Y. Legis. Law § 1-k; Ohio Rev. Code §§ 101.77, 121.67; Or. Rev. Stat. § 171.756(3); 65 Pa. Stat. and Cons. Stat. § 13A07(e); R.I. Gen. Laws § 42-139.1-8; S.C. Code § 2-17-110(A); S.D. Codified Laws § 2-12-6; Tex. Gov. Code § 305.022; Tenn. Code § 3-6-304(k); Utah Code § 36-11-301; Vt. Stat. tit. 2, § 266(a)(1); Va. Code § 2.2-432; Wash. Rev. Code § 42.17A.655(f); Wis. Stat. § 13.625(1)(d).
111. Ky. Rev. Stat. §§ 11A.236.
112. N.C. Gen. Stat. § 120C-300(c).
113. Fla. Stat. § 11.047.
114. Minn. Stat. § 10A.06; 18 Pa. Stat. and Cons. Stat. § 7515.
115. Mich. Comp. Laws § 4.421(1).
116. *See, e.g.*, Idaho Code § 67-6621(2)(d); Tex. Gov. Code § 305.028; Colo. Rev. Stat. § 24-6-308(1)(e); 65 Pa. Stat. and Cons. Stat. § 13A07(d); Utah Code § 36-11-306; Wash. Rev. Code § 42.17A.655(2)(d).
117. *See, e.g.*, Colo. Rev. Stat. § 24-6-308(1)(k); 25 Ill. Comp. Stat. 170/3.1; L.A. City Charter § 501(d)(2); Md. Code § 5-704(f)(3)(i), Miss. Code § 5-8-13(4); Okla. Stat. § 74E-5.28; Or. Rev. Stat. § 171.756(4); Tenn. Code § 3-6-304(m).
118. Ky. Rev. Stat. § 6.811; N.C. Gen. Stat. § 120C-304(3).
119. W. Va. Code § 6B-3-3b.
120. L.A. Muni. Code § 49.5.8(C)(4)(a); Mich. Comp. Laws § 4.421(2); N.Y.C. Admin. Code § 3-225.
121. Conn. Gen. Stat. § 1-7(a); Nev. Rev. Stat. § 218H.930(2); Tenn. Code § 3-6-305(a)(1).
122. Okla. Stat. §§ 74E-5.6, 74E-5.8, 74E-5.12, 74E-5.13.
123. N.Y. Legis. Law § 1-m.
124. *Id.*
125. Ariz. Rev. Stat. § 41-1232.02(J)(1); Cal. Gov. Code § 86203; San Diego Muni. Code § 27.4030; Utah Code § 36-11-304.
126. Neb. Rev. Stat. § 49-1490.
127. Or. Rev. Stat. § 244.025.
128. Ind. Code § 2-7-5-8.
129. N.J. Stat. § 52:13C-21b.
130. N.J. Stat. § 52:13C-21b(3); Tex. Gov. Code § 305.024(a)(2)(B).
131. *See, e.g.*, Minn. Stat. § 10A.071(); N.C. Gen. Stat. § 120C-303(a); Neb. Stat. § 49-1490, N.Y. Legis Law § 1-m.

132. Cal. Gov. Code § 82028(b); 2 Cal. Code Regs. §§ 18942, 18946.4.
133. 19 N.Y. Code of Rules and Regs. § 934.4(a)(2).
134. N.Y. Legis. Law §§ 1-c(j)(iii)-(v).
135. Tenn. Code § 3-6-305(b)(7)(B).
136. *See, e.g.*, Cal. Gov. Code § 82028(b)(2); Ky. Rev. Stat. § 6.611(2)(b)(10).
137. *See, e.g.*, Cal. Gov. Code § 85702; Ky. Rev. Stat. § 6.811(6); L.A. City Charter § 470(c)(11); S.F. Camp. and Gov. Cond. Code § 2.115(e); S.C. Code § 2-17-80(A)(5); Tenn. Code §§ 3-6-304(i)-(j); Wis. Stat. §§ 13.625(1m)(a)(1)-(3).
138. Colo. Rev. Stat. § 1-45-105.5; Ky. Rev. Stat. § 6.811(7); Minn. Stat. § 10A.273; Nev. Rev. Stat. § 218H.30(9); N.M. Stat. § 2-11-8.1(B); Tex. Gov. Code § 36-11-305; Utah Code § 36-11-305; Vt. Stat. tit. 2, §§ 266(a)(3)(A)–(B).
139. Minn. Stat. § 10A.15(5).
140. N.M. Stat. § 2-11-8.1.
141. *Id.*
142. Ky. Rev. Stat. § 6.811(5); Md. Gen. Provis. § 5-715(d)(iii); N.M. Stat. § 2-11-8.1(A); S.C. Code § 2-17110(C); 65 Pa. Stat. and Cons. Stat. § 13A07(a).
143. Md. Gen. Provis. § 5-715(d).
144. Tenn. Code § 3-6-304(j).
145. *Id.* § 3-6-304(i).
146. S.F. Admin. Code § 67.29-5.
147. *See, e.g.*, Kan. Stat. § 46-232; L.A. City Charter § 501(d)(2); L.A. Muni. Code § 49.5.13; Miss. Code § 5-8-13(4).
148. *See, e.g.*, Del. Code § 29-5837; Ga. Code § 21-5-75(a); Ind. Code § 2-7-5-7; Me. Rev. Stat. tit. 3, § 318-A; Tenn. Code § 3-6-304(1); Vt. Stat. tit. 2 § 266(b)(1).
149. Mont. Code § 5-7-310(1); S.D. Codified Laws § 2-12-8.2.
150. S.C. Code § 2-17-15.
151. *See, e.g.*, L.A. Muni. Code §§ 49.5.8(C)(1), (C)(4)(a); Tenn. Code § 3-6-305(a)(2); Vt. Stat. tit. 2, § 266(a)(2) (behests for 501(c)(3)s excepted).
152. House Rule XXV, clause 5(a)(1)(A)(ii), 116th Congress (Jan. 11, 2019).
153. Nev. Rev. Stat. § 218H.930(3).
154. Wis. Stats. § 13.625(3).
155. Neb. Rev. Stat. § 49-1490(2).
156. Vt. Stat. tit. 2 § 266(a)(3)(4).
157. Minn. Stat. § 10A.27(11).
158. *See, e.g.*, Cal. Gov. Code § 86109.5; Ga. Code § 21-5-71(h); Kan. Stat. § 46-266; R.I. Gen. Laws § 42-139.1-4(a); S.D. Codified Laws § 2-12-2; Va. Code § 2.2-428(B).
159. 65 Pa. Stat. and Cons. Stat. §§ 13A08(d), 13A10(c).
160. Md. Gen. Provis. § 5-713; Miss. Code § 5-8-19(d).
161. Va. Code § 2.2-425(A).
162. *Id.* § 2.2-425(B).
163. Tenn. Code § 3-6-308(a)(8).
164. *Id.* § 3-6-308(a)(7).
165. 65 Pa. Stat. and Cons. Stat. § 13A08(f).
166. L.A. Muni. Code § 48.09(E); S.F. Camp. and Gov. Cond. Code § 2.145(b); S.F. Charter § C3.699-13; Tex. Gov. Code § 305.032.
167. Wash. Rev. Code § 42.17A.755(3)(b).
168. Ohio Rev. Code § 101.99(A).
169. *Id.* § 101.99(B).
170. Tex. Gov. Code § 305.031(b).
171. Vt. Stat. tit. 2 § 268(b)(4).
172. *Id.* tit. 2 § 267a.
173. Colo. Rev. Stat. § 24-6-309(1).
174. *Id.* § 24-6-309(2).
175. Tex. Gov. Code § 305.028(g).

176. 65 Pa. Stat. and Cons. Stat. § 13A09(e)(4).
177. Utah Code §§ 36-11-401(4)-(5).
178. L.A. Muni. Code §§ 48.09(B)(3), 48.09(C)(1).
179. *Id.* § 48.09(G)(1).
180. Okla. Stat. § 74-4255(B).
181. Ohio Rev. Code § 101.721(A)(3).
182. *Id.* § 101.721(C).
183. Wis. Stat. § 13.63(1)(b).
184. Tenn. Code § 3-6-309(b).
185. 25 Ill. Comp. Stat. § 170/3.
186. Ind. Code § 2-7-2-2.
187. Mass. Gen. Laws tit. l, Ch. 3, § 47.
188. Ga. Code §§ 21-5-71(f)(2)(B)-(C).
189. Seattle Muni. Code § 2.06.130.
190. 19 N.Y. Code Rules and Regs. §§ 943.10(g), 943.11(d), 943.12(b).
191. Cal. Gov. Code § 86103(d); 25 Ill. Comp. Stat. 170/4.5; L.A. Muni. Code § 48.07(H); Mass. Gen. Laws tit. I, ch. 3, § 41; N.Y.C. Admin. Code § 3-219(h); N.Y. Legis. Law § 1-d(h).
192. Alaska Stat. § 24.45.041(b)(8).
193. Tenn. Code § 3-6-114(b); Utah Code § 36-11-307(5).
194. W. Va. Code § 6B-3-3c.
195. Md. Gen. Provis. § 5-704.1; L.A. Muni. Code § 48.07(H).
196. R.I. Gen. Laws § 42-139.1-11.
197. N.C. Gen. Stat. § 120C-103(a).
198. Phillip Thiebert & Elizabeth Thiebert, Potato Chip Economics: Everything you need to know about business clearly and concisely explained (Washington: Business Books 2013).
199. *See* n.14.

CHAPTER 13

Conflicts of Interest
Rose Gill

> This chapter provides an overview of the various contexts in which conflicts can arise and the importance of conflicts of interest regulation to objective public decision making and freedom from the kind of self-interest that can even rise to the level of criminal activity.

It was my observation during my 12-year tenure as Investigations Commissioner for the City of New York[1] that the vast majority of municipal employees performed their work honestly and well. As I have now had the opportunity to work with many other city government administrations around the country, I continue to encounter honest and talented public servants who are simply interested in doing their jobs, serving their cities, and supporting themselves and their families.

Conflicts of interest are also part of the reality in government. I refer not only to cases in New York City but, much more broadly, to cases reported in the media involving officials in jurisdictions around the country. The power, leverage, access to things people need and want that are embedded in the jobs and roles city employees possess, give rise to conflict vulnerabilities. Conflict risks can often materialize when, inter alia, employees use city property for a personal purpose, misuse their city position to help gain something for themselves, a family member, or friend. Conflict risks arise with elected officials when, inter alia, they use staff for personal or non-city business purposes; misuse their office to benefit themselves, friends, family members; or to award political contributors. In the case of some city employees and elected officials, serving the public as well as themselves has gone hand in hand. It is also not uncommon for some municipal employees to feel that their public sector salaries (relative to the private sector) served as a justification for the behavior.

New York City has an independent agency, the Conflict of Interest Board (COIB),[2] that very effectively trains, adjudicates, and enforces the city's conflict of interest rules and regulations. I think the COIB is a best practice model for education, prevention, and compliance with NYC's comprehensive ethics code.[3] The COIB enjoys a reputation for independence and professionalism. Conflict of interest matters that could easily be politicized or swept under the rug are handled thoroughly in NYC by the COIB staff and board members. The COIB helps elevate the standard across the board of what is expected in NYC government. The Department of Investigation (DOI), where I served for 12 years, is the investigatory arm of the COIB. To that end, DOI collects facts and evidence that may substantiate conflict violations. Anyone who has studied this topic over time knows that, unfortunately, the same types of violations reoccur time and time again.

One common conflict scenario involves the revolving door: government officials in decision-making positions of management/power who go to work for a private sector company (or join a board) that did business with the official's agency. This draws questions about whether city-related decisions made by an official regarding procurements, hires, and so on, are, in actuality, being rewarded after the fact. Recent examples of this featured in the media foment public doubt as to whether city-related decisions were made objectively, when an official departs government through the revolving door and heads to a lucrative position at a company that did business with the official's former city agency. Some jurisdictions like New York have postemployment conflict rules that seek to construct temporal guard rails and other prohibitions to curb the deleterious impact of such arrangements.[4]

Other serious potential conflict questions generated by revolving-door circumstances include when the official began negotiating for a job with the new private sector employer; was it when the official had dealings with, and/or was making decisions about, or was engaged in transactions or procurements with the company. Then once the city official has moved to the private sector company, conflict regulations prohibit the disclosure of confidential information from the official's former government agency. While these regulations to avoid conflicts are in place, many people believe they are, in reality, hard to patrol and enforce.

Conversely, talented individuals with steep skills and experience from the private sector get tapped to serve in government, which can be a benefit to government agencies and the public. It can sometimes create appearances or actual conflict issues. If the new government post the official holds involves a prior employer in any way, alarms can go off with the media and the public. Claims of divided loyalty arise, which can be compounded if stock, 401k, pension, and other benefits are held by the incoming government official. Strict conflict rules requiring checks and balances on this type of situation range from divestiture, to transferring assets to blind trusts, to recusal on matters pertaining to the prior employer. Having said that, it can be hard to convince people in the court of public opinion that the official's prior affiliation isn't a conflict that may influence government action. The public sector benefits from having fresh ideas, and opportunities to recruit the best professionals in any given field. Navigating the transition to the public sector can be done to a significant degree with the right safeguards. Writing books about experiences in life, leadership, and governing is a frequent practice undertaken by government officials who garner notoriety and popularity, often by carrying out their duties in government. The separation between authors' official duties and their use of government personnel and resources to assist with such publications, can be porous. There are new and older cases that involve this identical type of conduct.[5]

Conflict investigations can and should ensue when an official's duties overlap with a company in which the official (or the official's spouse) is also an investor, owns stock, or other financial interest. In one recent case, companies were promoted by an official during the pandemic, under circumstances where the official had significant holdings in those companies.[6] The same conflict rules just discussed, seek to address this type of conduct and range from the government employee's immediate disclosure of the potential conflict, followed by other steps, that is, divestiture, blind trusts, recusal.

Federal employees may not use their public office for endorsements of products or services. Yet, in a recent case, federal officials posed with and posted photos of themselves with a product. Posing with products could constitute a conflict of interest, and in this particular case, why the officials posed with the product was the subject of various theories, including, it was speculated, they choose to endorse the product as a strategy to generate political votes and support from a particular demographic.[7]

Conflicts of interest can also rise to the level of criminal activity. Media reports are replete with examples, and at DOI we investigated hundreds of such cases each year. For example, city employees who took kickbacks from someone who is receiving city business. An official who has things of value paid for by parties doing, or seeking to do, business with the city. An inspector who uses his position and leverage to request a quid pro quo—a bribe—for doing something the inspector is supposed to do as part of the job. These types of cases are referred to prosecutors' offices for criminal action.

In New York, we saw that a rash of conflicts can also fester when there is abuse of the process by which public money is doled out on the say-so of elected representatives, to nonprofits that are supposed to use the funding for community/public purposes (i.e., the "member item" process and similar iterations). Repeatedly, the process was turned into schemes to funnel money to "friends and family," meaning to nonprofits that employed one or more family members of the elected official, or to friends who were then willing to use part of the funding to pay for personal items for the elected official. Often rising to the level of criminal activity, these arrangements were not only bright-line conflicts of interest, they were also a misuse of public money intended for programs like meals for senior citizens, after-school activities for kids, and supports for the disabled.

In one such case, a long-time elected official was convicted on federal conspiracy charges for a scheme to funnel government funding to friends and family, using nonprofits that he controlled. Just one example, he had the nonprofit appoint his girlfriend as executive director, where she received more than $300,000, even though the case showed he knew she was unqualified.[8] In another case, an elected official was convicted on fraud charges for taking more than $35,000 from a government-funded nonprofit that he founded and served on the board of. He wielded his position in government and at the nonprofit to direct the nonprofit to use its program funds to pay credit card bills and other invoices that were, in fact, for his personal expenses. The expenses paid for included payments toward his apartment, purchases of jewelry and sports tickets, and payments toward college tuition for a family member.

The abuse of power in these and other like cases, intertwined with the conflict of interests, ended in convictions. As a result of the vulnerabilities exposed by these cases in the member-item process, corrective measures were put in place in New York City some years ago to create better screening for conflicts in connection with the use of member-item funding, for example, vetting procedures, certifications under oath, and ethics training.

When government employees moonlight at second jobs, it can cause potential conflicts of interest (and operational) issues for a government agency. The outside employment can lead to the government employee misusing government property/resources/time, or to speak for or represent the employee's government agency in an unauthorized manner. Given those risks, many government agencies have strict secondary employment rules and proscriptions. One particularly serious abuse by an employee who was moonlighting involved a language translator in a city school system, who was simultaneously employed doing language and translation services at a private institution. The employee received a stiff fine from the conflicts board for billing the city for hundreds of hours of work that he actually spent at his private job. He improperly billed the city to the tune of hundreds of hours, representing thousands of dollars he was not owed. Other moonlighting conflict cases have involved attorneys in city positions who have outside law practices, where blurred lines result in private tasks being performed on government time, on government phones, computers, and so on. These cases highlight the problems posed by moonlighting, particularly when the government job and outside job are in the same field.

Questions about potential conflicts of interest are not confined to the public sector. In New York, self-dealing by public officials through nonprofit corporations was a significant factor leading to the adoption of legislation requiring such corporations to adopt codes of ethics addressing conflicts of interest, following strict procedures for effective recusal, and limiting transactions with parties related to board members and key employees. And just as a public official transgresses conflict-based rules by trading on confidential nonpublic information gained in the official's public service, misuse of that information can create criminal liability for corporate officials. A company that received a sizable federal loan for manufacturing saw a corresponding uptick in the value of its stock. When it was revealed that company insiders made additional valuable stock purchases in advance of the official public announcement about the government action, federal and internal company investigations were opened. Even absent substantiated findings of a conflict or other wrongdoing, investigations and allegations can derail projects and cause other negative impacts.

In conclusion, the public tends to feel strongly that government is not a private till. While conflicts rules are not entirely foolproof in ensuring public confidence in government, enforcing conflicts laws is still important. Constant reminders and annual conflicts training for the workforce can tend to be very helpful in reducing the violations.

NOTES

1. https://www1.nyc.gov/site/doi/about/legal-executive-authority.page.
2. https://www1.nyc.gov/site/coib/the-law/chapter-68-of-the-new-york-city-charter.page.
3. https://www1.nyc.gov/site/coib/the-law/the-law.page.
4. https://www1.nyc.gov/assets/coib/downloads/pdf2/mono/mono_postemployment.pdf.
5. https://apnews.com/article/385c518da6753c8bd5610ac3f35a7d4c.
6. https://www.nytimes.com/2020/05/26/us/politics/senators-stock-trades-investigation.html.
7. https://abcnews.go.com/Politics/ivanka-trumps-social-media-posts-goya-beans-provoke/story?id=71795732.
8. https://www.nytimes.com/2013/01/09/nyregion/seabrook-sentenced-to-5-years-for-corruption.html.

Index

A

agency
  former, defining, 134–136
  as term, 95n3
agency ban, 131–138
Alabama
  executive disclosure requirements in, 72
  financial disclosure law in, 82–83
  gifts in, 119
Alaska
  executive disclosure requirements in, 72, 76
  financial disclosure law in, 82–83
  honoraria in, 124
Albuquerque, 183
Anne Arundel County (MD), 154–155, 157–159, 183, 191
applicant disclosure, in local government ethics, 167–168
Aristotle, 10
Arizona
  executive disclosure requirements in, 72
  financial disclosure law in, 82–83
Arkansas
  executive disclosure requirements in, 72, 76
  financial disclosure law in, 82–83
  gifts in, 118
Athenian Oath, 10
attorney–client privilege, government clients and, 101–102
  confidentiality and, 98–99
  in criminal cases, 103
  determination of client, 108–109
  in District of Columbia Circuit, 105
  in Eighth Circuit, 104–105
  federal, 101–103
  Freedom of Information Act and, 102–103
  implementation concerns, 106–108
  independent legal counsel for criminal matters *vs.*, 109
  practical considerations with, 108–109
  professional conduct and, 98–99
  purpose prong in, 107–108
  in Second Circuit, 103–104
  in Seventh Circuit, 105–106
  statutes on, 99–101
  uncertainty about, 97, 108
at-will employment doctrine, 220–221, 239–240
audits, inspectors general and, 200–201
Austin, 186

B

Baltimore, 183
BCRA. *See* Bipartisan Campaign Reform Act (BCRA)
Bipartisan Campaign Reform Act (BCRA), 14–15
Blue Book, 201–202
Boston, 187
Branstad, Terry, 22
bribery, risk of, 4

C

California
  ethics reform efforts in, 20–21
  executive disclosure requirements in, 72, 76
  financial disclosure law in, 82–83
  honoraria in, 124
  lobbying ethics in, 286–287
  lobbyist defined in, 278
  postemployment restrictions in, 133
  transparency laws in, 39–40

campaign finance, lobbying ethics and, 287
campaign finance reform, 14–15
candor, 5
Charlotte, 188
Chicago, 183, 191
Citizens United, 15
Civil Service Reform Act (CSRA), 223, 225, 228–229, 232, 259
Clay, Henry, 9
Cleveland, 188
client(s). *See also* attorney–client privilege, government
   allegiance to, in government practice, 90–93
   allegiance to, in private practice, 90
   determination of, 108–109
   government attorney–client privilege and, 101–102
   officials as, 107
   "public interest" or "public" as, 93–95
client disclosure, 50, 53–54, 72–76
Clinton, Hillary, 15
codes of ethics
   conflicts of interest in, 164
   definitions with, 154
   exclusions, 155
   gifts and, 159
   inducement in, 164
   interests *vs.* conduct in, 154
   local government and, 154–165
   moonlighting and, 158
   paying to obtain municipal position, 162–163
   political activities and, 161
   pre-employment restrictions in, 162
   private entity compensation for municipal work, 160
   prohibited interest in, 156
   public office for private gain, 156–158
   superior–subordinate relationships and, 162
   waivers, 155–156
   whistleblower protection and, 164–165, 242–243
Colorado
   executive disclosure requirements in, 72, 76
   financial disclosure law in, 82–83
   lobbying ethics in, 289
   lobbying prohibitions in, 284–285
Columbus, 188
common law, local government ethics and, 153
Computer Matching and Privacy Protection Act, 207
confidence, public, 4
confidentiality
   codes of ethics and, 160
   government attorney–client privilege and, 98–99
   local government and, 160, 174–175
   postemployment restrictions and, 141
   role and, 2–3
   whistleblower protection and, 243–244, 258–259
conflicts of interest
   appearance of, 6
   in Constitution, 9–10
   as inevitable, 299
   local government and, 164
   moonlighting and, 302
   New York Bar Association and, 11–13
   revolving door and, 300–301
   role and, 2
Connecticut
   executive disclosure requirements in, 72, 76
   financial disclosure law in, 82–83
   gifts in, 116
   government attorney–client privilege in, 99
   honoraria in, 124
   lobbyist registration in, 281
Constitution
   conflicts of interest and, 9–10
   financial disclosure and, 48–50
contingent compensation, 158–159
Cook County, 183, 191
copy fees, 76
criminal cases
   government attorney–client privilege in, 103
   independent legal counsel for, 109

CSRA. *See* Civil Service Reform Act (CSRA)
Cuomo, Mario, 18, 25

D

Dallas, 187
DATA. *See* Digital Accountability and Transparency Act (DATA Act)
debarment, in lobbying ethics, 289–290
Delaware
    executive disclosure requirements in, 72, 76
    financial disclosure law in, 82–83
Denver, 186
dependents, 76
Detroit, 183
Digital Accountability and Transparency Act (DATA Act), 39, 42–43, 200
diligence, 5
director information, 72–75
disclosure, proactive, 42
District of Columbia, 186, 191
District of Columbia Circuit, government attorney–client privilege in, 105
duty speech, 223

E

El Paso, 187
electronic filing, 76
Emoluments Clauses, 15–17
employment information, in financial disclosure, by state, 72–75
enforcement
    in lobbying ethics, 289
    in local government ethics, 169–171, 183–190
ethical rules
    in early history, 10–11
    as first line of defense, 5–6
    future of, 25–26
    greater citizenry interest in, 24–25
    nature of public service and, 3–4
    public confidence and, 4
    purpose of, 1–7
    as risk management, 6–7
    role of regulated persons and, 1–3
ethics boards, 169–171, 183–193
Ethics in Government Act of 1978, 13–14
executive disclosure requirements, state, 72–79
extortion, risk of, 4

F

FACA. *See* Federal Advisory Committee Act (FACA)
False Claims Act, 232–233, 237–239
family, gifts to, 118–119
Federal Advisory Committee Act (FACA), 38–39
Federalist Papers, 10
financial disclosure(s)
    annual filing requirement, by state, 72–75
    annual filing requirement, in local government, 168–169
    auditing powers and, 54
    clients in, 50, 72–75
    complete, requirements by state, 72–75
    constitutionality of, 48–50
    criticisms of, 47–48
    employment of legislators and, 51
    history of, 47
    outside interests and, 51
    privacy and, 48–49
    public access to, 54–55
    purposes of, 47
    requirements by state, 72–75
    specific issues, 52–54
    in states, 50–56
financial disclosure statutes, state, 82–87
Florida
    ethics reform efforts in, 23
    executive disclosure requirements in, 72, 76
    financial disclosure law in, 82–83
    gifts in, 116, 120–121
    honoraria in, 125
    postemployment restrictions in, 133–134, 141
FOIL. *See* Freedom of Information Law (FOIL) (New York)
Foreign Corrupt Practices Act, 4
Fort Worth, 186
Freedom of Information Act (FOIA), 35–38, 102–103

Freedom of Information Law (FOIL) (New York), 40–41
Fresno, 188

G

Georgia
  executive disclosure requirements in, 72, 76
  financial disclosure law in, 82–83
gift(s). *See also* honoraria
  circumstances in which given, 117–118
  codes of ethics and, 159
  defined, 116–117
  exceptions, 117–122
  to family members, 118–119
  in lobbying ethics, 286–287
  local government and, 159
  nature of, 117–118
  recipient identity and, 118–119

H

Hatch Act, 161
HAVA. *See* Help America Vote Act of 2002 (HAVA)
Hawaii
  executive disclosure requirements in, 72, 76
  financial disclosure law in, 82–83
Help America Vote Act of 2002 (HAVA), 15
Honolulu, 184, 192
honoraria, 122–125
Houston, 186
Hughes, Charles Evans, 18

I

Idaho
  executive disclosure requirements in, 72, 76
  financial disclosure law in, 82–83
  gifts in, 118
  postemployment restrictions in, 142
IG. *See* inspectors general (IG)
IGEA. *See* Inspector General Empowerment Act (IGEA)
Illinois
  executive disclosure requirements in, 72, 76
  financial disclosure law in, 82–83
  honoraria in, 123
  lobbying prohibitions in, 285
impeachment, of Trump, 16–17
income amount, in state requirements, 72–75
Indiana
  executive disclosure requirements in, 73, 77
  financial disclosure law in, 82–83
Indianapolis, 184
inducement, local government and, 164–166
in-house counsel, whistleblower protection and, 244–252
in-person appearance, 76
Inspector General Empowerment Act (IGEA), 206–208
inspectors general (IG)
  audits and, 200–201
  community, overview of, 196–198
  dual reporting with, 198–200
  evaluations by, 201
  examples, 203–205
  impact of, 195
  independence of, 198–200
  inspections by, 201
  law enforcement authority of, 206
  legal framework and structure, 196–198
  overview of, 196–198
  powers, 200–206
  removal of, 197–198
  responsibilities of, 200–206
  special, 196–197
investment information, 72–75
Iowa
  ethics reform efforts in, 22
  executive disclosure requirements in, 73, 77
  financial disclosure law in, 82–83

J

Jacksonville, 184, 192
Jaffer, Jameel, 43
job title, 72–75

K

Kansas
    executive disclosure requirements in, 73, 77
    financial disclosure law in, 82–83
    lobbyist registration in, 281
Kansas City, 186
Kentucky
    executive disclosure requirements in, 73, 77
    financial disclosure law in, 82–83
    gifts in, 120
King County (WA), 192

L

Landemore, Hélène, 56n3
Las Vegas, 188
late filing penalties, 76
law firms, whistleblowing and, 252–255
law practice, disclosure of clients in, 53–54
Lobbying Disclosure Act, 277
lobbying ethics
    background to, 275–277
    campaign finance and, 287
    client defined in, 280
    complexity of, 276
    contingency fees in, 285
    debarment in, 289–290
    disclosure and, 282–284
    enforcement, 288–291
    fees in, 282, 285
    governmental ethics and, 285–287
    history of, 277
    lobbying defined, 278
    lobbyist defined, 278–279
    prohibitions in, 284–287
    public officials and, 287–288
    registration and, 280–282
    training, 290–291
local government ethics
    administration and, 169–175
    agency regulations and, 153
    annual disclosure in, 168–169
    appearances and, 158–159
    appearances by outside employers and, 166
    applicant disclosure in, 167–168
    codes of ethics and, 154–165
    common law and, 153
    confidentiality and, 160, 174–175
    conflicts of interest and, 164
    contingent compensation and, 158–159
    disclosure in, 166–169
    elements of, 150–151
    enforcement and, 169–171, 183–190
    ethics boards, 169–171, 183–193
    gifts and, 159
    inducement and, 164–166
    moonlighting and, 158
    paying to obtain position in, 162–163
    penalties in, 173
    political activities and, 161
    postemployment restrictions and, 163–164
    pre-employment restrictions, 162
    private citizen and company restrictions, 165–166
    process and, 153
    purpose of, 149
    reforms, 23–24
    representation and, 158–159
    sources of laws, 151–153
    state constitutions and, 152
    state statutes and, 152
    state *vs.*, 150
    superior–subordinate relationships and, 162
    transactional disclosure in, 167
Long Beach, 188
Los Angeles, 184, 192
Louisiana
    executive disclosure requirements in, 73, 77
    financial disclosure law in, 82–83
loyalty, 5

M

Madison, James, 10
Maine
    executive disclosure requirements in, 73, 77
    financial disclosure law in, 82–83

Maine, *continued*
  lobbying ethics in, 277
  lobbyist defined in, 278
  lobbyist registration in, 281
Maryland
  executive disclosure requirements in, 73, 77
  financial disclosure law in, 82–83
  honoraria in, 122
Massachusetts
  executive disclosure requirements in, 73, 77
  financial disclosure law in, 82–83
  gifts in, 117
  government attorney–client privilege in, 100–101
  lobbyist defined in, 279
matter ban, 131–132, 138–141
Maui County, 184, 192
McCain-Feingold law, 14–15
McDonnell, Bob, 22
Memphis, 187
Merit System Protection Board (MSPB), 224, 227–228
Mesa, 189
Miami, 189
Miami-Dade County, 184, 192
Michigan
  ethics reform efforts in, 23
  executive disclosure requirements in, 73, 77
  financial disclosure law in, 84–85
Milwaukee, 184
Minneapolis, 187
Minnesota
  executive disclosure requirements in, 73, 77
  financial disclosure law in, 84–85
Mississippi
  executive disclosure requirements in, 73, 77
  financial disclosure law in, 84–85
Missouri
  executive disclosure requirements in, 73, 77
  financial disclosure law in, 84–85

Model Rules of Professional Conduct, 143, 245–248, 252–253
Montana
  employment law in, 221
  executive disclosure requirements in, 73, 77
  financial disclosure law in, 84–85
Montgomery County (MD), 185
moonlighting, 158, 302
Moreland Act, 18
municipal ethics. *See* local government ethics

N

Nashville, 187
National Labor Relations Act, 221
Nebraska
  executive disclosure requirements in, 74, 78
  financial disclosure law in, 84–85
  lobbying ethics in, 286
Nevada
  executive disclosure requirements in, 74, 78
  financial disclosure law in, 84–85
  lobbying ethics in, 288
New Hampshire
  executive disclosure requirements in, 74, 78
  financial disclosure law in, 84–85
New Jersey
  executive disclosure requirements in, 74, 78
  financial disclosure law in, 84–85
  gifts in, 116
  lobbying ethics in, 286
  lobbyist registration in, 281–282
New Mexico
  executive disclosure requirements in, 74, 78
  financial disclosure law in, 84–85
  gifts in, 119–120
  lobbying ethics in, 287
New Orleans, 185
New York
  ethics reform efforts in, 18–20

executive disclosure requirements in, 74, 78
financial disclosure law in, 84–85
government attorney–client privilege in, 99–100
lobbying ethics in, 286–287
lobbyist defined in, 278
postemployment restrictions in, 133, 135–136, 138–140, 145n25, 146n63, 147n114
public access to disclosures in, 55
transparency laws in, 40–41
New York City
Conflicts of Interest Board, 299–300
ethics board in, 185, 192
ethics reform efforts in, 23–24
postemployment restrictions in, 134, 137–140, 144n1
New York City Bar Association, 11–13
Nixon, Richard, 57n14
non-elected officials, 76
North Carolina
executive disclosure requirements in, 74, 78
financial disclosure law in, 84–85
lobbyist defined in, 278
North Dakota
ethics reform efforts in, 21–23
executive disclosure requirements in, 74, 78
financial disclosure law in, 84–85

O

Oakland, 185
Obama, Barack, 16
Office of Government Ethics (OGE), 14
Office of Personnel Management (OPM), 224
Office of Special Counsel (OSC), 224, 226–227, 261n10
officer information, 72–75
OGE. *See* Office of Government Ethics (OGE)
Ohio
executive disclosure requirements in, 74, 78
financial disclosure law in, 84–85
government attorney–client privilege in, 100
lobbying ethics in, 290
postemployment restrictions in, 132, 136, 138, 140, 142–143, 147n101
Oklahoma
executive disclosure requirements in, 74, 78
financial disclosure law in, 84–85
lobbying ethics in, 290
Oklahoma City, 189
Omaha, 189
OML. *See* Open Meetings Law (OML) (New York)
Open Meeting Laws, 35, 38–39
Open Meetings Law (OML) (New York), 41
Oregon
executive disclosure requirements in, 74, 78
financial disclosure law in, 84–85
gifts in, 119–120

P

Pataki, George, 20
penalties, in local government ethics, 173
Pennsylvania
ethics reform efforts in, 23
executive disclosure requirements in, 74, 78
financial disclosure law in, 84–85
gifts in, 121
lobbying ethics in, 288
Perkins, Roswell B., 11
PFCRA. *See* Program Fraud Civil Remedies Act (PFCRA)
Philadelphia, 185, 193
Phoenix, 189
political activities, local government codes of ethics and, 161
Portland, 189
postemployment restrictions
activities covered by, 139–140
agency ban, 131–138
confidentiality and, 141
contracts and, 141
former agency defined for, 134–136

postemployment restrictions, *continued*
- level of involvement in matter and, 139
- local government and, 163–164
- matter ban, 131–132, 138–141
- in Model Rules of Professional Conduct, 143
- obtaining private employment with public position, 142–143
- partners and associates in, applicability to, 136
- representation of and further employment with government in, 137–138
- services prohibited by, 133–134

PRA. *See* Public Records Act (PRA) (California)

privacy, financial disclosure and, 48–49

privilege. *See* attorney–client privilege, government

professional conduct, government attorney–client privilege and, 98–99

Program Fraud Civil Remedies Act (PFCRA), 202

public access, to financial disclosures, 54–55

public confidence, 4

public interest, as client, 93–95

public policy exception, whistleblower protection and, 239–242

Public Records Act (PRA) (California), 39–40

public service, nature of, 3–4

public trust, 4–5

R

Reagan, Ronald, 16

real property information, 76

registration, lobbyist, 280–282

retaliation, whistleblowing and, 218, 235–236, 242

Rhode Island
- executive disclosure requirements in, 75, 79
- financial disclosure law in, 84–85
- lobbying ethics in, 291
- lobbyist registration in, 281

risk management, ethical rules as, 6–7

Roosevelt, Theodore, 9

Root, Elihu, 26

S

Sacramento, 189

St. Louis, 190

St. Paul, 187

San Antonio, 185

San Francisco, 185, 193

San Jose, 190

Sarbanes-Oxley Act, 20, 232, 270n242

Seattle, 186, 193

Second Circuit, government attorney–client privilege in, 103–104

self-dealing, 6

Seventh Circuit, government attorney–client privilege in, 105–106

Sharp, Frank, 21

South Carolina
- executive disclosure requirements in, 75, 79
- financial disclosure law in, 84–85
- postemployment restrictions in, 138, 141–142
- whistleblower protection in, 239

South Dakota
- executive disclosure requirements in, 75
- financial disclosure law in, 84–85
- lobbyist registration in, 281–282

spouse client information, 76

spouse employment information, 72–75

spouse investment information, 72–75

spouse real property information, 76

state constitutions, local ethics laws and, 152

state ethics reform efforts, 17–23

state executive disclosure requirements, 72–79

state financial disclosure statutes, 82–87

Stevenson, Adlai, 115

supremacy clause, 260

swing states, 23

T

Tampa, 186

Tennessee
- executive disclosure requirements in, 75, 79
- financial disclosure law in, 84–85

honoraria in, 124
lobbying ethics in, 287–288
Texas
　ethics reform efforts in, 21
　executive disclosure requirements in, 75
　financial disclosure law in, 84–85
　lobbying ethics in, 277, 289
　postemployment restrictions in, 133
transactional disclosure, in local government ethics, 167
transparency
　accessibility and, 42–43
　in California, 39–40
　candor and, 5
　defining, 36
　Freedom of Information Act and, 35–38
　importance of, 36
　improving, 41–43
　laws, 36–41
　meaningfulness and, 42–43
　in New York, 40–41
　Open Meeting Laws and, 35, 38–39
　proactive disclosure and, 42
　in state laws, 35
Trump, Donald, 15–17, 55
trust, public, 4–5
Tucson, 190
Tulsa, 187
Twain, Mark, 115

U

unitary executive theory, 95n6
Utah
　executive disclosure requirements in, 75, 79
　financial disclosure law in, 86–87
　lobbying ethics in, 286

V

Vermont
　executive disclosure requirements in, 75, 79
　financial disclosure law in, 86–87
Virginia
　ethics reform efforts in, 22–23
　executive disclosure requirements in, 75, 79
　financial disclosure law in, 86–87
　lobbying ethics in, 288
Virginia Beach, 190

W

waivers, codes of ethics and, 155–156
Washington
　executive disclosure requirements in, 75, 79
　financial disclosure law in, 86–87
Washington, D.C., 186, 191
Watergate, 13–14, 57n14
West Virginia
　executive disclosure requirements in, 75, 79
　financial disclosure law in, 86–87
Westchester County (NY), 193
whistleblower, defined, 217
whistleblower protection
　Civil Service Reform Act and, 223, 225, 228, 232, 259
　common law, 239–242
　communications and, 234–235
　conduct protected in, 233–234
　confidentiality and, 243–244, 258–259
　consumer protection, 231
　environmental, 230
　False Claims Act and, 232–233, 237–239
　federal, 223–228
　financial institutions, 231
　hazardous industries, 231
　in-house counsel and, 244–252
　intergovernmental communications, 231
　labor and workplace safety, 230–231
　law firms and, 252–255
　in local government ethics, 164–165
　Merit System Protection Board in, 224, 227–228
　military, 229
　need for public sector, 222–223
　Office of Personnel Management in, 224
　Office of Special Counsel in, 224, 226–227, 261n10
　outside merit system, 228–232

whistleblower protection, *continued*
  public policy exception and, 239–242
  special issues for lawyers, 243–260
  state level, 232–237
  statutes, 229–232
  transportation, 231
Whistleblower Protection Act (WPA), 224–226, 228–229
Whistleblower Protection Enhancement Act (WPEA), 225–226, 258
whistleblowing
  abuse of, 219
  at-will employment doctrine and, 220–221, 239–240
  as breach of employment expectations, 218–219
  as controversial, 218–220
  corporate, 254–255
  as duty, 219
  duty speech in, 223
  federal government lawyers and, 255–260
  financial incentives for, 237–239
  Model Rules of Professional Conduct and, 245–248, 252–253
  passive, 223
  retaliation and, 218, 235–236, 242
Wichita, 190
Wisconsin
  executive disclosure requirements in, 75, 79
  financial disclosure law in, 86–87
WPA. *See* Whistleblower Protection Act (WPA)
WPEA. *See* Whistleblower Protection Enhancement Act (WPEA)
Wyoming
  executive disclosure requirements in, 75, 79
  financial disclosure law in, 86–87

Y

Yellow Book, 200–201